ANNE THACKERAY
RITCHIE

WINIFRED GÉRIN

ANNE THACKERAY RITCHIE

A BIOGRAPHY

0211800542552 3

Oxford New York Toronto Melbourne
OXFORD UNIVERSITY PRESS
1981

Oxford University Press, Walton Street, Oxford OX2 6DP
London Glasgow New York Toronto
Delhi Bombay Calcutta Madras Karachi
Kuala Lumpur Singapore Hong Kong Tokyo
Nairobi Dar es Salaam Cape Town
Melbourne Wellington
and associate companies in
Beirut Berlin Ibadan Mexico City

British Library Cataloguing in Publication Data
Gerin, Winifred
Anne Thackeray Ritchie.
1. Ritchie, Anne Isabella Thackeray, Lady –
Biography
2. Novelists, English – 19th century – Biography
823'.8 PR5227.R7 80-49704
ISBN 0-19-812664-6

Set by King's English Typesetters Ltd
Printed in Great Britain
at the University Press, Oxford
by Eric Buckley
Printer to the University

FOR
BELINDA NORMAN-BUTLER
IN GRATEFUL TRIBUTE

No one ever had such a life as mine, or such love in it, each after its own kind.

ANNE THACKERAY RITCHIE

She will be the un-acknowledged source of much that remains in men's minds about the Victorian age. She will be the transparent medium through which we behold the dead. We shall see them lit up by her tender and radiant glow. Above all and for ever she will be the companion and interpreter of her father, whose spirit she has made to walk among us not only because she wrote of him but because even more wonderfully she lived in him.

VIRGINIA WOOLF

PREFACE

ANNE THACKERAY RITCHIE was born in the last days of William IV and lived to the end of the First World War. She was taken as a little girl in the 1840s in Paris to visit Chopin, and lived to see the publications of her niece by marriage, Virginia Woolf, in whose early novel *Night and Day* she figured as Mrs Hilbery.

Her life thus spanned nearly two-thirds of the nineteenth century and the first two decades of the twentieth. As the daughter of an Eminent Victorian, and great novelist, Thackeray, she was born into a circle that included in its range and variety every aspect of an age rich in great men. The companion and confidante of her father from her early teens, she inherited at his death not only his illustrious name – and some considerable talents of her own – but the whole circle of his friends, which included Tennyson, the Carlyles, the Brownings, Barry Cornwall, Edward FitzGerald, Richard Monckton Milnes, in whose company she may be said to have grown up and whose distinction she took for granted from earliest childhood.

She was as much at home in the studios of the fashionable painters, Watts, Burne-Jones, Millais, Holman Hunt, Leighton, as in those of her father's illustrators, Richard Doyle, Charles Collins (the husband of her great friend Kate Dickens), and the Bohemian fringe whom her father liked to help with every rise in his own fortunes. The entire Dickens family were her playmates. She was taken about Rome and Paris as an adolescent by the great singer Adelaide Sartoris, the sister of Fanny Kemble the actress, who, in turn, like Mrs Cameron the pioneer photographer, became one of her closest friends. At the Browning and Carlyle firesides she was a petted guest from girlhood.

Deprived of a feminine upbringing by the tragic lunacy of her mother, she had the compensating advantage of a liberal education, almost a boy's education, at her father's hands. It was part of the good fortune of this informal education that she spent her formative years in Paris, with her grandparents, and thus imbibed a dual culture that saved her from being insular, either socially or religiously, as were so many of her contemporaries. The keynote of her resultant character was its unconventionality.

Inevitably, in such surroundings, she was directed towards the pursuit of letters and early showed herself to be a novelist of sensibility and humour. She never mastered the art of plot-construction; the charm of her novels lies in their atmosphere, the fleeting images of her fancy, the intensity of her feeling. The world she conjures up is very much the world of Boudin's paintings, with a high wind blowing bright clouds and women's veils.

She wrote some eight novels, all successful in their day, but her real gift as a writer was as a memorialist and critic of the literary scene at whose centre she lived for over eighty years. Her most valuable contributions to literature are the Biographical Introductions she wrote to the complete works of her father, published in 1898, and her own delightful memoirs – *Chapters from Some Memoirs* – in which she related, with wit and relish, the colourful incidents of her girlhood. Her most stylish work is *The Life of Madame de Sévigné*.

Through the marriage of her sister, Minny Thackeray, to Leslie Stephen, Anny, who shared their home, came into contact with the new generation of writers then being published under Leslie Stephen's editorship in the literary periodicals of the day – amongst them Swinburne, Hardy, Meredith, Henry James, the young Robert Louis Stevenson, all of whom became friends. The gap between her father's generation that had formed her tastes and the new writing was thus bridged. Her own mercurial temperament and darting imagination were far more attuned to the 'impressionist' writing of her niece Virginia Woolf than to the reasoned static style of her own contemporaries. In the lambent quality of her wit, her closest affinity among the Victorians was with Mrs Gaskell.

Her records of Tennyson, the Carlyles, George Eliot are precious, not only for their vivid pictorial freshness, but for their personal angle of vision, uninfluenced by the accepted criteria of the times. She brought to the portraits of the well-known faces a new expression that her kindling enthusiasm could alone call up. She had what Desmond MacCarthy described as an 'amazing emotional memory'. Leslie Stephen said of her that her greatest gift was sympathy; and this was apparent in all she was and did. Marriage to her cousin Richmond Ritchie, a highly cultured man who ended up as Permanent Under-Secretary of State for India, brought her children and the sort of family life for which she was, unlike some literary ladies, most admirably fitted. She was an inspired home-maker.

Her sympathies reached far beyond the wide human circle of her affections to include animals, nature in all its moods, old places, old houses, gardens; and she had a genuine genius for describing them. This is what made her so brilliant a letter-writer. Her letters to an enormous circle of friends are the quintessence of her zestful spirit, and a delight to read.

It is to her letters and journals that the biographer has to look to capture her likeness. They supply not only the facts of her richly varied life, but reveal the idiosyncrasies of her complex character. Considerable as were her literary achievements, it was *herself*, as Leslie Stephen said, that was the best of all.

Virginia Woolf has left some deeply perceptive descriptions of her, but so far no full-length biography has been attempted. It struck me, therefore, as more than time that this highly original, lovable woman, should be better known.

Finally, if further reason were needed for writing this book, it lies for me in the fact that to know Anne Ritchie is to rediscover Thackeray, to see him in an entirely fresh light: in the role of father, for which nature so pre-eminently designed him. To see him in relation to his daughters, enlightened and loving, is a wholesome corrective to the hackneyed portrait of him as cynic and snob, and adds inches even to his towering stature.

WINIFRED GÉRIN

ACKNOWLEDGEMENTS

It is no empty compliment to say that this book could not have been written but for the generous loan of Anne Thackeray Ritchie's unpublished letters, journals, memoranda, and notebooks made to me by her granddaughter, Mrs Belinda Norman-Butler. Since only a meagre selection of them had been previously published, in a long-since out-of-print edition, no first-hand record of her life was available for the prospective biographer. It is, therefore, with a very special sense of gratitude that I pay tribute here to Mrs Norman-Butler's co-operation; in token whereof I beg her to accept the dedication of this book, which is so pre-eminently hers.

All writers on Thackeray and Thackeray's connections must primarily delve into the vast storehouse of material collected by Professor Gordon Ray for his monumental works: *The Letters and Private Papers of W. M. Thackeray* in four volumes, and his unsurpassed and unsurpassable biography of Thackeray: *The Uses of Adversity* and *The Age of Wisdom*. These are the corner-stone to any edifice to be reared by subsequent writers. To him, therefore, I express my grateful thanks for permission to quote from his volumes, and for his personal encouragement to me in my task.

I gratefully acknowledge permissions from the following to quote from their copyright material: Mr John R. Murray to quote from the letters of Anne Thackeray Ritchie to George Smith, in his possession; Mr Alexander R. James for permission to quote from the 'Letters of Henry James to Anne Thackeray Ritchie' preserved in the Houghton Library, Harvard; to whom I likewise extend my thanks for allowing me photocopies of the originals; Alan Bell for permission to quote from his *Leslie Stephen's Mausoleum Book*; and the Executors of Virginia Woolf to quote from her works.

Every book owes much to its editor, but I feel that this one owes a special debt to my friend and editor Peter Sutcliffe of the Oxford University Press, for his devoted labours. No less am I grateful to Irene Kurtz for so gallantly retyping the truly labyrinthine script.

In addition, I am most grateful to the following for their help in supplying information, for permissions to use copyright material, or family portraits: Lord Tennyson, Professor R. A. Colby, Alan

Bell, the Executors of the Estate of Leonard Woolf, A. R. James, the National Trust, and the National Portrait Gallery, London.

My thanks would be very incomplete if I omitted to mention the exceptional, expert, and unfailingly kind help of Mr Douglas Matthews of the London Library, who has been available at all times to answer my queries and to supply my needs. It gives me great pleasure to thank him cordially here.

W.G.

CONTENTS

LIST OF ILLUSTRATIONS

REFERENCES AND ABBREVIATIONS

Chapters   *Chapters from Some Memoirs* by Anne Thac-
                        keray Ritchie, 1894

Fuller   *Thackeray's Daughter: Some Recollections of
                        Anne Thackeray*, 1951, by Hester Fuller and
                        Violet Hammersley.

Mausoleum Book   *Sir Leslie Stephen's Mausoleum Book*, ed.
                        Alan Bell.

MS Letters   The unpublished letters of Anne Thackeray
  N–B Collection   Ritchie, in the possession of her grand-
                        daughter, Mrs Norman-Butler.

MS Journals   ibid.

MS Reminiscences, 1864–5 ibid.

Memoir for Laura,   MS by Anne Thackeray Ritchie, written for
  1877   her niece, Laura Stephen.

Ray   *The Letters and Private Papers of W. M.
                        Thackeray*, 4 volumes, 1945–6.

Ritchie Letters   *The Letters of Anne Thackeray Ritchie*, by
                        Hester Ritchie, 1924.

SBC   *The Brontës and their Circle*, by Clement K.
                        Shorter, 1914.

W & S   *The Brontës: Their Lives, Friendships and
                        Correspondence: In Four Volumes*, 1932, by
                        Thomas J. Wise and John A. Symington.

PART I

THACKERAY'S DAUGHTER

CHAPTER I

'A NOBLE LITTLE THING'

WILLIAM MAKEPEACE THACKERAY was married to Isabella Shawe at the British Embassy in Paris on 20 August 1836. He was twenty-five and she twenty. Both were ardently in love, neither had any money, except what he could earn with his pen and pencil. He was at the time employed as Paris correspondent to the *Constitutional* newspaper at a nominal salary of £400 a year. Within six months it had failed. They could have no expectations from their parents, who were themselves living on military pensions. The Shawe family's sole reason for living in Paris was economy.

No marriage could have been more imprudent, as Thackeray was himself the first to admit. He called it 'absurdly imprudent' in later life, but added that he always loved to hear of a young fellow testing his fortune bravely in that way.[1] He remained a strong advocate of early marriages, if love dictated them.

Isabella's father, Lieutenant-Colonel Matthew Shawe, had died in 1826. He had been a Peninsular veteran serving under Wellington. The courtship, however, was opposed at every turn by Isabella's mother, a virago with five children to bring up on an army pension of £80 a year, and the temper of Mrs Mackenzie in *The Newcomes*, as Thackeray was later to find. This should have prepared him for the tornadoes ahead, but it had only inflamed the lovers' passion more strongly, and helped to throw Isabella into Thackeray's arms. She adored him with all the force of her tender and highly vulnerable nature. Happily for her, the reception given to the news of the engagement by Thackeray's own mother and stepfather – the noble-hearted Major Carmichael-Smyth (the prototype of Colonel Newcome) – was as warmly welcoming as the imprudence of the step could warrant.

Thackeray's adoring mother wanted him married and settled before all things and was prepared to trust in his choice. Socially,

[1] Ray, iii. 210 n.

Thackeray and Isabella came from much the same Anglo-Indian background: Thackeray's father was Collector of Alipore for the East India Company – a highly successful administrator, like Jos Sedley. Isabella, an Indian Army officer's child, was born like Thackeray in India. Of Irish parentage, she had as good an education as most girls of her time, and was moreover genuinely musical, playing the piano with above-average talent and endowed with a charming voice. Her devotion to her numerous little brothers and sisters, towards whom she filled the role of tender parent so lamentably wanting in their real mother, promised well for the future. As for Thackeray himself, his mother had such faith in his powers that she did not even query his proposed domestic role; and in this she was, surprisingly, quite right.

No one was more surprised than Thackeray himself to discover the fund of feeling that his engagement aroused. Indolent by temperament, pleasure-seeking, vastly sociable, open-handed, a rebel to all routine, he threw himself into the duties of married life with zest and humour, and, what was harder for a man with his bohemian tastes, with regularity. Isabella's happiness was paramount; in providing for her he put up with some hitherto wholly alien disciplines.

He had been brought up to expect a fortune on his majority of some £20,000 from his late father; hence the easy swagger, the 'lordly' air that came naturally to him, and the lavish tipping that convinced postilions and inn porters on his travels that he was, indeed, a 'milord'. When this failed to materialize as a result of the Indian Bank collapse, the necessity to become niggling and mean was all the more hurtful to his pride. It was a lesson in illusion that he never forgot. From *The Rose and the Ring* to the bankruptcy of 'Colonel Newcome', the theme of ruin overtaking the gullible runs through his work. However alien to his nature, the need to write for a living became the driving force in his life. For the sake of his wife and later of his children, he drove himself to the limit – and eventually beyond the limit of his physical capacities. Born in the East, his was a slack physique, not braced for continual effort. He sustained it, however, out of devotion to those he was pleased to call his 'Little Women'.

At the time of his marriage, Thackeray's parents were still living in England, though shortly afterwards they were to settle in Paris for some twenty years. He was not without all connections there himself; his dreadful old grandmother, Mrs Butler, between whom and himself there was no love lost, lived in Paris, and he had occasionally lodged with her during his art-student days. His closest confidante on the spot was his Aunt Ritchie, his father's sister, the same who had received him as a child of five on his arrival from India and 'whose sweet face, always kind and tender', he recollected all his life. His Aunt and Uncle Ritchie had at that time been living in Chiswick, and in Thackeray's first letter home to India he told his mother how kind his aunt was to him and how much he liked going to Chiswick and playing with the Chiswick boys.[2] He was, fortunately, to become one of the Chiswick boys himself at Dr Turner's School at Walpole House (next door to Minerva Lodge, the young ladies' seminary). The contrast between his father's kindly kin and his mother's high-nosed, highly bred and tyrannous relatives, the Bechers of Fareham in Hampshire, to whom she originally committed him, could not have been sharper. The Bechers, while initiating him into eighteenth-century tastes and manners, and providing him with the models for the Miss Crawleys and the Martha Honeymans of his novels, sent him to a savage school at Southampton, from which the Ritchies rescued him for the happier regime of Chiswick. There was always an unspoken rivalry between the two families, the Ritchies being 'in trade', the Bechers in the King's Service with a long record of distinction behind them.

From his Aunt Ritchie and his cousins, Thackeray received the moral backing he constantly needed throughout his troubled courtship. (He later told his publisher George Smith that his situation was very exactly described in *The Adventures of Philip*[3].) To the cousins he was soon and lastingly attached. The girls, Charlotte and Jane, were like sisters to him (he always called them 'mes bonnes sœurs'), and with William in particular he remained very close; an affection that lasted into the second generation when a son of William's married a daughter of Thackeray, the subject of this biography.

It was to his aunt's home in the rue des Ternes that, after a lightning honeymoon at Versailles, he took his bride. His chances of getting to know Isabella had been few during the time of his

---

[2] Introduction to the Biographical Edition of Thackeray's Complete Works, Vol. viii, *The Newcomes*, p. vx.
[3] Gordon Ray, *Thackeray, Vol. i. The Uses of Adversity*, p. 186.

courtship, because of Mrs Shawe's violent changes of mood towards him. Clandestine meetings occurred before breakfast under the trees of the Champs Élysées where Isabella took an early airing with her little brothers and sisters (like Charlotte Baynes in *Philip*) and would find Thackeray hovering by the great fountains of the Rond Point where he also was taking his morning walk. Of an evening, if he dared to call at the *pension de famille* where the Shawes lived, he might see Isabella but only in the company of her mother and the other residents.[4]

A large colony of Anglo-Indians elected to live in Paris at this time for economy's sake. The boarding-houses and furnished apartments in and around the Champs Élysées were full of them; there they could keep up appearances on their meagre resources as they could never do in England. They could array themselves in their faded finery and attend the receptions at the British Embassy and the balls at the Tuileries given by the Citizen King, Louis-Philippe; and Thackeray himself, as he related in *Philip*, could appear in his shabby coat and with holes in his shoes with no loss of caste. The veneer of meretricious smartness imposed on public life after the *coup d'état* of 1851 by Louis-Napoleon had not yet obliterated the essentially homely, bourgeois aspect of Parisian society in the late 1830s and 1840s.

So, Thackeray and his little inexperienced wife, whose ignorance of domestic matters was complete (as soon appeared when they moved into a home of their own, in furnished rooms at 15a rue Neuve Saint-Augustin), could live bravely on his £7 a week and be deliriously happy, as perhaps neither of them had ever been before. The only threat to the marriage, that could have been so lastingly happy, came not from practical considerations, but from the continued interference of Mrs Shawe, who worked on the timid nature of her daughter to undermine the self-confidence and foster the sense of inadequacy which dependence on her husband's love created. Thackeray's delight when Isabella became pregnant was immense. To escape Mrs Shawe, and more especially to secure more remunerative work, he decided to return to England in the spring of 1837. His parents offered him a home with them pending better times, and in March he and Isabella arrived in London to live with the Carmichael-Smyths at 18 Albion Street, Hyde Park. It was

---

[4] Introduction, Biog. Ed., Vol. xi, *The Adventures of Philip*.

there that, on 9 June 1837, their first child Anne Isabella, named after Thackeray's mother and his wife, was born.

Nothing could have been kinder than the reception given by the elders to the pretty daughter-in-law Thackeray brought home. Despite her overwhelming presence – Mrs Carmichael-Smyth retained into old age the beauty and the grand manner that had suited her social status in India – Isabella took an instant liking to the older lady and accepted unquestioningly her superior wisdom in all things. This submission nearly cost her her life. When the child's birth was imminent, Mrs Carmichael-Smyth insisted that it be conducted on homœopathic principles, with herself in sole and supreme command. It was only Thackeray's last-minute rush to fetch the nearest doctor that averted a double catastrophe. The traumatic experience left its mark on mother and baby alike; but the near-tragedy altered nothing of Mrs Carmichael-Smyth's rooted scorn for regular medical practitioners and she remained an unrepentant homœopath throughout her long life. It was probably just as well for the young couple that by the time their second child was expected – she was born in July 1838 – the Carmichael-Smyths had decided to emigrate to France.

Isabella came through her second confinement well, with neither mother nor mother-in-law to heighten the tension. She seemed 'born for child-bearing', wrote Thackeray in his jubilation. His love for Isabella remained intense. 'Here we have been nearly two years married', he wrote to his friend Bedingfield, 'and not a single unhappy day.'[5] The poor man spoke too soon. The baby, Jane, died at the age of eight months, in March 1839. Years later Thackeray recalled that sorrow and left instructions to be buried by her side. The experience made him singularly responsive to other people's griefs.

Before the baby's birth, the departure of the Carmichael-Smyths for Paris had made a move into quarters of their own necessary for the Thackerays, and they had gone to live at 13 Great Coram Street, Bloomsbury. It was from there that Anne Thackeray's first precocious memories dated – happy memories of her young mother, little more than a child herself, singing, dancing, romping in and out of doors in the neighbouring Coram's Fields. She was always gay, in the child's memories. Isabella, who wrote charming letters to her

---

[5] Ray, i. 353–4.

own mother and to her mother-in-law in Paris, reported in July 1839 on 'Tottie's progress' (Anny went by many names at the time: she was 'Pussy' to her father, 'Great fat deedle-deedle', 'Miss Thackeray' in her naughty moments): 'Tottie and I were picking daisies and clover in the gardens of Brunswick Square when she got a handfull [sic] she said she must carry them home and put [them] in a glass of water' so there they are and the sweetest nosegay that has adorned our table this year.' Isabella, who had a true love of music, added: 'I went to the Foundling and heard the Messiah. I shall never be able to tell you what I felt. It seemed to give one an idea of what music in Heaven must be.'[6] The images associated with her in her daughter's mind were 'of pretty tunes played on the piano', prettier tunes even than those played by the organs in the street outside. The attractions of the street to Anny were compulsive. She remembered 'a fine morning, music sounding, escaping my nurse and finding myself dancing in the street to the music along with some other children. Someone walking by came and lifted me up bodily on to his shoulder and carried me away from the charming organ to my home, which was close by. As we went along this stranger, as usual, became my father, whom I had not recognised at first.'[7]

Anny, who would soon be telling her father 'What a funny fellow you are, Papa', saw in him, not only the stranger appearing as by magic in unpredictable places, the wizard who drew comic pictures and told her uproarious stories and swung her high in the air from the giddy altitude of his six foot three, but also a bowed and absorbed man sitting writing at a table. He was indeed tied to his writing, struggling to make a living. It was the time of greatest hardship in his career – despite the young love, and the babies and his wife's sweet confidence in him: a time of insecurity, certain only of the £10 or £12 per sheet (16 magazine pages) paid monthly by *Fraser's Magazine*, on to the staff of which he had been taken through the friendship of the editor, William Maginn. Looking back on the hack work he accepted in those years from sheer necessity, he said he had borne it because of his conviction that he would become a writer, and that this was the best training he could get towards that end. And the cares and the bills and the insecurity were all blown away for this fundamentally jovial man at the sight or sound of 'Missy' who took an ever-growing place in the home

---

[6] Ray, i, 389.
[7] Introduction, Biog. Ed., Vol. iii, *The Great Hoggarty Diamond*.

and in his heart. 'Little Pussy is delightful, and that's the fact,' he wrote to his mother in December 1839; 'her voice drives all cares out of one's head . . . Missy's little voice I can hear carolling in the parlor. . . . She is a noble little thing, and a perpetual source of pleasure to me, that's the fact: may God keep her to us, and we do our duty by her and ourselves.'[8]

Both parents had begun to notice that she had a tendency to squint. 'I fear the sight is weak and she will turn her head', wrote her father, 'in the manner of a canary bird . . . it is a thousand pities such a noble-looking child as it is.'[9] 'Here comes a certain little person', he wrote again to his mother in March 1840, 'who says, "Papa, breakfast's ready." The fact is my dear little Pussy has grown to be more delightful than ever. She is wonderfully well: and talks quite plainly and has a thousand charming ways.'[10]

On 27 May 1840 Isabella's third baby was born. It was another little girl, whom they called Harriet Marian, known as Minny all her life. During her mother's lying in, Anny made herself indispensable to her father. 'Missy is delightful,' he reported to his mother. 'She is very kind to me, and comes to see me in bed. The little baby is very like the dear little one we lost – strangely like in voice.'[11]

Their cup of contentment now seemed full, all the more so that Thackeray had at last made a success with his series of articles on Paris, published as *The Paris Sketch-Book* at this time, and well reviewed in the June and July periodicals. It brought in its wake offers from several other publishers for regular work. The worst seemed over, a measure of prosperity assured. There could be no question yet of 'making his name', since he wrote under pseudonyms, most often as 'Michael Angelo Titmarsh', but his mind was teeming with plots and plans that only needed peace and freedom from duns to clothe with life.

It was at this moment, a couple of months after the baby's birth, that the first intimations of disaster made themselves felt. Isabella was exceptionally slow in recovering her strength and, above all, her spirits; her post-natal depression was very marked. She found it difficult to describe her state. Reporting on the baby's christening in August 1840 to her mother-in-law, she wrote, 'I confess to you I feel excited – my strength is not great and my head flies away with

[8] Ray, i. 397.   [9] Ray, i. 416.
[10] Ray, i. 423.   [11] Ray, i. 447.

me as if it were a balloon. This is *mere* weakness and a walk will set me right.'[12] Thackeray described her as in 'an extraordinary state of langour and depression' and decided on taking her to the seaside. With the children's devoted nurse, Brodie, they went to Margate by boat, as was usual at that time. 'Miss Thackeray' was reported as saying to Brodie, 'I have come a long long way, but I wish to kiss Papa and Mamma before I go to bed.' 'God bless her,' Thackeray wrote to his mother, 'She is a noble little girl. Your big heart would have thumped to see her toddling about the deck, embracing in her fine innocent warmth every little child about her.'[13]

Margate did not, however, provide the cure for Isabella's condition that they had all reckoned on. Brodie had increasingly to take charge of the children and the domestic arrangements, as Isabella showed herself increasingly incapable of any responsibility. It was at Margate that Anny was given a sudden insight into terrifying forces in real life that she had only glimpsed as yet in the wicked wizards of fairy-tales. As she walked on the sands at Margate with her mother along the margin of the sea, to watch the great waves come in, she felt herself suddenly and fiercely caught up by her mother and thrown into the surf. Incapable of realizing the meaning of the action, she could only feel, and intensely feel, the terror and resentment roused by her mother's conduct. Whether she even spoke of it to her father at the time is not certain; the shock of it would be all the worse for being kept to herself.[14]

It was still two months before Thackeray himself had irrefutable proof of his wife's madness, but it was at Margate that the truth was made plain to Anny. At the age of three she suddenly found herself deprived of everything her mother stood for: the fountain head of all the gaiety, the games, the music and laughter, the love. Unconsciously, Anny, bereft of her mother and increasingly aware of her little sister, barely three months old at the time, transposed their roles. Towards Minny she would assume ever more completely the place of the mother they were losing, whom Minny would never know.

[12] Ray, i. 462.   [13] Ray, i. 463.   [14] Ms Reminiscences, 1864–5.

ISABELLA'S TRAGEDY

ISABELLA'S symptoms were deceptively variable. At one time she would be worse, at another almost normal. Thackeray's wavering hopes and despairs were exacerbated by the desire to believe his wife curable. He was assured by the doctors that her condition was purely due to post-natal depression and would respond to time and normal occupations. For the first time in his life he had more work to do than he could easily manage, and he tried on their return home to combine keeping commitments which he could not afford to break with watching over Isabella. It was desperate work at times, 'shutting the children in one room and his wife raving in another'.

He had an offer from Chapman & Hall for an 'Irish Sketch-Book', on the pattern of his Paris book, for which they offered him £350; it was too good to refuse. It seemed, moreover, like the solution to their immediate troubles. Isabella's mother and family were by then back in Ireland, living in Cork, and Thackeray, catching at any straw, suggested they go there, for Isabella to have the companionship of her sisters, especially of Jane her next and favourite sister, and the care of her mother, while he set about gathering material for his book. The suggestions delighted Isabella who, despite their grievances, remained fondly attached to her family.

On 12 September 1840 the family set off from the Port of London for Cork. It was a three-day crossing. Jessie Brodie, who gave up an immediate prospect of marriage so as not to desert the children in their great need, went with them. Thackeray, as his wife failed him, was ever more wrapped up in the children. Just before leaving home, he wrote to his mother: 'I wish you could see Missy in her bath; such a picture of health and beauty, and our dear, dear little Harriet, that I love more than the last even, the sweetest tempered little thing that God ever made, surely.'[1] But he was almost at the end of his tether. 'I think it would drive me mad to be much longer alone with it,' he also wrote to his mother, referring to Isabella's melancholy. He counted on the change of scene to restore her, and she was quite passive and apparently contented enough at the prospect of the journey. It proved to be the turning-point in her malady. She took the first opportunity that offered to attempt suicide. Thackeray described the event to his mother later: 'the poor thing flung herself into the water (from the water closet) and was twenty minutes floating in the sea, before the ship's boat even *saw* her. O my God what a dream it is! I hardly believe it now I write. She was found floating on her back, paddling with her hands . . . This it was that told me her condition. I see now she had been ill for weeks before, . . . and Powell and the surgeons must tell me that there was not the slightest reason to call a physician, that nothing was the matter with her, that change of air would cure her, and so on.'[2]

Even in spite of this he still hoped something might come of the visit to Cork, but it proved a total disaster. Mrs Shawe, who had expressed herself overjoyed at the prospect of seeing her beloved child, absolutely refused to receive her once she realized the gravity of Isabella's condition. She refused to allow them her large spare room and forced Thackeray to take lodgings in the town, which proved not only exorbitantly expensive but filthy and bug-ridden. He was distraught at the wreck of his hopes and at his total inability to work. He had counted on touring the country in search of material for his book while Isabella was in the care of her family, but Mrs Shawe's refusal to co-operate wrecked this plan. Money was still very tight and wholly contingent on his ability to work, a situation which Mrs Shawe soon made the subject for further recriminations. He was held responsible not only for his wife's illness, but for the family's 'pauperism'. Her lamentations were loud over her poor daughter's disastrous marriage. It was war to the death between Thackeray and his mother-in-law, but he had no defence against her insults which were so deeply wounding to his pride.

Once he realized that no improvement was to be hoped for in Isabella's condition and that she could only deteriorate in such an atmosphere, he determined on retreat. From Paris he had received

[1] Ray, i. 472.   [2] Ray, i. 483.

letters of sympathy and understanding and offers of help from his mother and stepfather; they urged him to bring Isabella and the children over to them. Despite the hazards of the journey, with Isabella distraught and two young children to manage, he made the double crossing, first to Liverpool and then from London to Boulogne, and reached Paris in November 1840.

The kindness of his mother's reception made him realize more than ever before in his life how close they were to each other. Despite the innumerable differences in their principles and opinions, they were deeply attached; and her goodness to Isabella and her doting fondness for the children affected him deeply at a time of near despair. Mrs Carmichael-Smyth was, happily, a young grandmother, only eighteen years older than her son, and therefore only forty-seven years old at this time. She was an exceptionally active and capable woman, both mentally and physically, and long accustomed to command. The situation had nothing in it to daunt her. She had living with her, moreover, young Mary Graham, her dead sister's child whom she had virtually brought up (like 'Mrs. Pendennis' and 'Laura' in Thackeray's novel). She was able to help in looking after the two little girls.

Fortunately for Isabella and Thackeray, Paris was medically well in advance of England in the treatment of madness at the time. What in comparison appear quite 'modern' methods of treating mental patients, with gentleness and considerable freedom of movement, were already in vogue. Thackeray consulted more than one specialist and was advised to place Isabella in a very enlightened 'maison de santé' at Ivry, in the Paris banlieu, for a trial period of six months. As she had become quite docile again, she was allowed much liberty of movement, given the freedom of the large garden, and, more important still, given a piano which she continued to play with all her former charm. She was allowed to see her husband on his frequent visits to Paris, when her innocent pleasure in seeing him and the sweetness of her singing would rend his heart.

Throughout his life, wherever he was settled, whether in France or later in England, he placed Isabella in the best available home for the mentally sick that existed at the time; mostly in private care. In 1841 he tried thermal treatment at Marienberg. Her sweet disposition made her loved wherever she was. At Chaillot, where her little girls were taken to visit her when they were old enough, she romped with them in the garden. On the return to England she was first at Epsom and finally at Leigh-on-Sea with a couple who became her devoted friends. She survived Thackeray by thirty-one years, dying on 11 January 1894 at the age of seventy-six.

Eight years after the disastrous crossing to Cork when she had attempted suicide, Thackeray wrote to her young sister Jane: 'I . . . look over often in my mind that gap of time since she has been dead to us all and see that dear artless sweet creature who charmed us both so. What a whirl of life I've seen since then, but never her better I think. "N'est ce pas mourir tous les jours" – don't you recollect her singing and her sweet sweet voice?'[3] Again years later, he wrote: 'And although my own marriage was a wreck as you know, I would do it once again, for behold Love is the crown and completion of all earthly good.'[4]

When he left Isabella in the doctor's care at Ivry, in the autumn of 1840, he was to be six years without a home. These were among the most unhappy years of his life.

[3] Ray, ii. 431.   [4] Ray, iii. 210 n.

CHAPTER 3

A PARISIAN CHILDHOOD

For the little girls it was the beginning of a long stay in France. Those six years with their grandparents in Paris inevitably shaped their education and coloured their outlook on life. Anny, already a very precocious child, was immediately receptive to the changed circumstances in her little world. While the colourful spectacle of Parisian life would deeply absorb her, the gaiety and games she had hitherto associated with her young mother were exchanged for the solemnity and decorum of her grandparents' home. Had it not been for the frequent visits of their father – frequent but always hurried as his ever-increasing burden of work dictated – the fantasy and brightness that had characterized their home would have disappeared altogether. Happily he always came in forced high spirits, with wonderful stories to tell and endless jokes, and comic drawings to show them. He had early been impressed with the need to feed their minds with fantasy: 'There is a grand power of imagination in these little creatures,' he had written to his mother the year before. 'I am determined that Annie shall have a very extensive . . . store of learning in Tom Thumbs, Jack-the-Giant-Killers. . . . What use is there in the paltry store of small facts that are stowed into these poor little creatures' brains?'[1] He had no use for the 'matter-of-fact' systems of education advocated by the Miss Edgeworths of his time, and was all for stimulating the imagination as being vital to the growth of the child's intelligence.

Not until much later, when the girls were in their teens, was there any active divergence in their views on education between Thackeray and his mother, and then it was purely on the subject of religion which, for Mrs Carmichael-Smyth, was paramount. She respected her son's highly unorthodox opinions while the children were little, and it was not until his absence in America ten years later that she made serious efforts to turn them into little Calvinists.

[1] Ray, i. 395.

They were then sufficiently matured, she reckoned, for the lessons to bear fruit. For the time being she gave them what they most needed, her immense love and a stable home.

The Carmichael-Smyths lived in an old street off the Champs Élysées, the Avenue Sainte-Marie, long since demolished, of which Anny left a very detailed description. 'The first house in which we lived at Paris', she wrote, 'was an old house in an old avenue enclosed by iron gates which were shut at night. It was called the Avenue Sainte-Marie, and led from the Faubourg du Roule to the Arc de Triomphe. The avenue was planted with shady trees; on one side of it there were houses, on the other convent walls. At the door of one of the houses an old·man sat in his chair, who used to tell us as we passed by that in a few months he would be a hundred years old and then they would put him into the papers. I used to play in the courtyard belonging to the house in which we lived. There was a pump, and there was a wall with a row of poplar trees beyond it. There was a faded fresco painted on the wall. . . . Frescoes must have been in fashion at the time when the Avenue Sainte-Marie was built, for there was also a dim painting on the convent wall opposite our porte cochère. . . . From beyond this wall we used to hear the bells and the litanies of the nuns.'[2]

The house and the street are recognizably the same as those Anny described in her first novel, *The Story of Elizabeth*, set in Paris. The Paris of the 1830s and 1840s that Anny first knew was still largely the Paris of Louis XVI, or even of Louis XIV – far more romantic in appearance than the widened, cleaned-up city that Baron Haussmann made of it in the 1860s under Louis-Napoleon. The old Paris still had cobbled narrow streets, and irregular angular houses with mansarded roofs, shuttered windows, dark *portes-cochères*, such as Anny described, leading into inner courtyards with water pumps, with steep stairways in the corners leading to the upper floors of the surrounding houses. The whole had an unpretentious, provincial look, with vines and fig trees growing in the courtyards and rustic gardens running behind the houses. There were few features apart from the river and the Tuileries and the Louvre that distinguished Paris from the big provincial towns, and half the working population came from the provinces and still wore their picturesque provincial dress. The street vendors, from the surrounding market gardens, supplied the essential domestic commodities, and filled the

[2] *Chapters*, p. 33.

1. William Makepeace Thackeray and his wife in early married
life

2. Anny with her Papa

3. Major and Mrs Carmichael-Smyth

air with their distinctive and often musical cries. Despite the dirt and the darkness of the old by-ways and the huddled houses with their peeling façades, it was an enchanting place for children, with a constant stream of pictorial life passing under their windows, and the blare of military music to quicken their eager steps as, in the charge of their grandparents' 'Bonne', Justine, they went for their daily walks.

At an early age Anny saw and recorded one of the great historical events of the time, very shortly after her arrival in Paris – the 'Retour des Cendres' as the second funeral of Napoleon was called, when his body was brought back from St. Helena and interred in the Invalides on 15 December 1840. Her memory of it was, as usual, sharply pictorial: 'I began life at four or five years old as a fervent Napoleonist. The great Emperor had not been dead a quarter of a century when I was a little child. He was certainly alive in the hearts of the French people . . . Influenced by the cook we adored his memory, and the *concierge* had a clock with a laurel wreath which for some reason kindled all our enthusiasm.

'As a baby holding my father's finger I had stared at the second funeral of Napoleon sweeping up the great roadway of the Champs Élysées. The ground was white with new-fallen snow, and I had never seen snow before; it seemed to me to be a part of the funeral; a mighty pall indeed, spread for the obsequies of so great a warrior. It was the snow I thought about, though I looked with awe at the black and glittering carriages which came up like ships sailing past us, noiselessly one by one. They frightened me, for I thought there was a dead emperor in each. This weird procession gave a strange importance to the memory of the great Emperor, and also to the little marble statuette of him on the nursery chimney-piece. It stood with folded arms contemplating the decadence of France, black and silent and reproachful.'[3]

While Minny was still a baby, Anny's only playmate was a little girl, the concierge's niece, who went to school at the convent opposite and was otherwise distinguished by wearing a locket with a medallion of the Virgin. Anny's first strong impression of life in Paris was of the streets, which not surprisingly she found more interesting and gay than her grandparents' home. She wrote in later years: 'Every day we children used to go out with our *bonne* to play round the Arc de Triomphe, near which we lived, and where,

[3] *Chapters* pp. 29–30.

alternating with ornamental rosettes, the long lists of Napoleon's battles and triumphs were carved upon the stone. The *bonne* sat at work upon one of the stone benches which surround the Arc, we made gravel pies on the step at her feet and searched for shells in the sand, or when we were not prevented by the guardian, swung on the iron chains which divide the inclosure from the road. We paid no attention whatever to the inscriptions, in fact we couldn't read very well in those days. . . . One day the guardian in his brass buttons, being in a good humour, allowed us all to climb up without paying, to the flat lead terrace on the roof. There were easy steps inside the walls . . . when we . . . came out upon the summit we saw the great view, the domes and the pinnacles and gilt weathercocks of the lovely city all spreading before us, and the winding river, and the people looking like grains of sand blown by the wind, and the carriages crawling like insects, and the palace of the Tuileries in its lovely old gardens shining with its pinnacles.'[4]

So, in childhood were laid the solid foundations of Anny's love of France, of French civilization, of French living, which permeates her adult writing. The Champs Élysées was a place of marvels to her childish mind: with its Guignols, its gingerbread woman's stall, and its rousing echoes of military music, with flags flying, penny trumpets ringing, strollers and spectators lining the way, and a long interminable procession of carriages in the centre rolling steadily towards the Bois de Boulogne.

The strongest influence came, quite naturally, not from her grandparents but from the *bonne* or cook. When Mrs Carmichael-Smyth changed the latter, and at the same time changed her apartment – they moved to 81 Champs Élysées, the Maison Vallin — Anny's politics suffered a radical change. 'I cannot clearly remember', she wrote later, 'when I became an Orleanist, but I think I must have been about six years old . . . and I had happened to hear my grandfather say that Napoleon was a rascal . . . Then came a day – shall I ever forget it? – when a yellow carriage jingled by with a beautiful little smiling boy at the window, a fair-haired, blue-eyed prince. It was the little Comte de Paris, who would be a king some day they told me, and who was smiling and looking so charming that then and there I deserted my colours and went over to the camp of Orleans.' Her heart was lost to the little prince, whose portrait she acquired in a print shop off the rue de Rivoli,

[4] Ibid., pp. 31-3.

and all her outings were in the hope of catching a glimpse of him. One joyful *mi-carême* she was taken to see the rejoicings and found herself squeezed in a court of the Tuileries with a crowd clamouring to see the King. 'I was hustled to the front of a crowd and stood between my two protectors looking up at a window. Then . . . a venerable, curly-headed old gentleman, Louis-Philippe himself, just like all his pictures, appears for an instant behind the glass, and then the people shout again and again, and the window opens and the King steps out on to the balcony handing out an old lady in a bonnet and frizzed white curls, and, yes, the little boy is there too. Hurrah! Hurrah! . . . I am now an Orleanist and ready to suffer tortures for the kind old grandpapa and the little boy.'[5]

It was only gradually that Anny began to take stock of the characters, prejudices, and peculiarities of her grandparents. It emerged, for one thing, that they were rabid republicans who, as one regime after another was swept away, did not hesitate to wear republican rosettes. They also lived very enclosed lives, never mixing with French nationals, but forming a little society of English expatriates, who had little money, were great sticklers for forms and observances, and very irritating to Thackeray on his various visits. In this society, as Anny observed, her grandmother 'seemed to reign from dignity and kindness of heart'. She was no exception to the general rule of grandmothers, as Anny put it: she was 'stately, old-fashioned, kindly and critical . . . She had been one of the most beautiful women of her time; she was very tall, with a queenly head and carriage; she always moved in a dignified way. She had an odd taste in dress. . . . She was a woman of strong feeling, somewhat imperious, with a passionate love for little children, and with extraordinary sympathy and enthusiasm, for any one in trouble or in disgrace. How benevolently she used to look round the room at her many *protégés* . . . Her friends . . . adopted her views upon politics, religion and homœopathy, or at all events did not venture to contradict them.'[6] With such a wife, it is not surprising that the Major was content to leave all decisions to her. Yet his rank did carry weight in this society. 'A Major is a Major,' wrote Anny. 'He used to sign their pension papers, administer globules for their colds, give point and support to their political opinions. I can see him still sitting in his arm-chair by the fire with a little semicircle round about the hearth. Ours was anything but a meek and

[5] Ibid., pp. 36–8.   [6] Ibid., pp. 15–16.

disappointed community. We may have had our reverses – and very important reverses they all seem to have been – but we had all had spirit enough to leave our native shores and settle in Paris, not without a certain implied disapproval of the other people who went on living in England regardless of expense.'⁷

The Major, in particular, was adamant in his refusal to return home. He had reason to be. A man of honour, he was deeply mortified by the fact that his 'reverses' had left him with debts unsettled. Though the sums involved were negligible, he could not, without the intervention of his stepson, return without risking arrest. This was an injustice and humiliation that he unhappily brooded over for many years. The fact that Thackeray needed and preferred to live in England, and, as time passed, made his name and fortune by doing so, carried little weight with his parents. Anny recalled how they used to ask, 'Why . . . did he remain in that nasty smoky climate, so bad for health and spirits? Why didn't he settle in Paris and write books upon the French?'⁸

The Major was devoted to his wife and lacked nothing so long as she was there. 'I don't think we ever came home from one of our walks', Anny wrote, 'that we did not find our grandfather sitting watching for our grandmother's return. We used to ask him if he didn't find it very dull doing nothing in the twilight, but he used to tell us it was his thinking-time.'⁹

Of the routine of that home in which the children's first years were spent, Anny had the clearest recollections: 'one day was just like another; my grandmother and my grandfather sat on either side of the hearth in their two accustomed places; there was a French cook in a white cap, who brought in the trays and the lamp at the appointed hour. . . . We lived in a sunny little flat on a fourth floor, with windows east and west and a wide horizon from each, and the sound of the cries from the streets below, and the confusing roll of the wheels when the windows were open in summer. In winter time we dined at five by lamplight at the round table in my grandfather's study. After dinner we used to go into the pretty blue drawing-room, where the peat fire would be burning brightly in the open grate, and the evening paper would come in with the tea. I can see it all still, hear it, smell the peat, and taste the odd herbaceous tea and the French bread and butter. . . . While my grandmother with much emphasis read the news (she was a fervent republican, and so

⁷ Ibid., pp. 20–1.   ⁸ Ibid.   ⁹ Ibid., p. 18.

was my grandfather) my sister and I would sit unconscious of politics and happy over our story-books, until the fatal inevitable moment when a ring was heard at the bell and evening callers were announced. Then we reluctantly shut our books, for we were told to get our needlework when the company came in, and we had to find chairs and hand tea-cups, and answer inquiries, and presently go to bed.'[10]

Jessie Brodie had returned to England and to another situation, and no compensating homely presence was found to enliven their lives. The great excitement in the children's monotonous days was the lightning visits of their father, never expected, seldom announced even an hour before, but happening suddenly, as work and wind and tide permitted. He brought so breathless, so miraculous an atmosphere with him that Anny remembered thinking him Jesus Christ. They watched his every movement, spellbound by the dexterity with which he shaved; and, while he dressed, he would 'tear out long pictures in paper with little pigs all trotting after one another'. He was true to his promise to feed their imaginations on fairy-tales. 'One of the nicest things that ever happened to us when we were children at Paris,' Anny recalled, 'was the arrival of a huge parcel, which my Grannie cut open and inside there were piles and piles of the most beautiful delightful wonderful fairy tale books all painted with pictures – I thought they would never come to an end but alas! in a week we had read them all. They were called the *Felix Summerly Series* and on the first page was written – To my three daughters, Laetitia, Henrietta and Mary – I dedicate these volumes. I used to think that they must be the happiest little girls in the world but I never thought we should know them.'[11]

'Felix Summerly', the pen-name of Henry Cole, was a friend of Thackeray's, and with his wife and daughters was to become one of the closest and kindest friends of the Thackeray girls after they had settled in England. Mrs Cole then invited them regularly once a week to her home.

Between the girls and their great-grandmother, Mrs Butler, who had spent all her life in India, and who now had her own modest establishment in Paris, there was always friction. She had 'a brown face and bright dark eyes' and was 'very, very unkind' to them, always scolding Anny. That Anny was rebellious and unamenable she herself frankly confessed. She was precocious and wilful (her

[10] Ibid., pp. 18–20.   [11] Memoir for Laura.

father said of her that 'she fought every inch of the way, even to putting on her stockings') and her natural high spirits rebelled against the claustrophobic environment in which so much of her time was spent. The list of her misdemeanours mounted; one notable day she was guilty of picking cherries off a tree, kicking a gentleman's legs, and running away three times. Being locked up in a cupboard did not prove to be the right treatment. On another occasion her refusal to say Grace coincided fortunately with the moment when little Minny was seen to be standing up on her own for the first time and beginning to walk. Everything was forgiven, so great was her grandmother's delight. Did Mrs Carmichael-Smyth but know it, in little Minny she would find her best ally; for from the moment Minny could walk and play and run with Anny, all Anny's strong maternal instincts were aroused, and she became absorbed in making Minny happy.

Every summer when the hot weather set in, the grandparents took the children to the country, to a little property they had near Creil (40 kilometres from Paris) called Mennecy, a former hunting lodge belonging to Henry IV. It was there that Anny absorbed so much of her knowledge of French provincial life of which she later made use in her novels. It was, as she recorded, 'a rural quiet spot among willow trees, a perfect retreat in hot summer weather. There was an old paved *place* in the centre of the village, leading to a fine old church . . . of which the Sunday bells clanged far across the country. We used to see the congregation assembling in cheerful companies, arriving from outlying farms . . . a congregation with more of talk and animation than with us, with blue smocks, and white linen *coiffes* and picturesque country cloaks and *sabots*.' Anny compared the dramatic interest of the Catholic service (which their 'cross maid-of-all-work Louise' attended), with 'its incense and organ rolling out its triumphant fugue', to the Protestant services they themselves attended, which lacked all excitement and mystery. Thus one of the differences between the two civilizations was early brought home to her. At Mennecy she observed too the rigid structure of French rural society: the respective status of the Chatelaines at the old château, of the Curé, of the Maire, of the peasantry. The little 'heretic' English girls could find no place in it.

Anny also remembered going to Montmorency in the summer of 1843 and to Chaudefontaine in Belgium the next. Chiefly she recalled how naughty she was considered and the punishments she brought down upon herself: 'shut up in her room a long while on one occasion, and whipped on another'. The summer holidays of 1845 began in Normandy at Calvados, where their father joined them before bringing them all to England. As a sort of experiment, to please his mother, he took them to stay with the Bechers, her old relatives at Fareham, near Southampton, where he himself had been so wretched as a child. The weather was disastrous and it rained most of the time. Leaving the grandparents at Fareham, he had the little girls to stay with him in London where he gave them a succession of treats which he considered suitable for their age. Those were enchanted days: 'Our father was living in chambers opposite St. James's Palace', Anny wrote, 'and he came to meet us at the station and immediately gave us each 2 wax dolls, and at breakfast he gave us bigger helps of jam than we had ever had in our lives and after breakfast he took us to feed the ducks in St. James Park.' Then he bought them picture-books, the *Arabian Nights* and Grimms' Fairy-Tales, and took them to the 'Diorama' and the Colosseum. Anny's comment on the day's extravagant delights was: 'I thought he would spend all the money he had in the world when I saw how much he had to pay for us.'[12] On the following day, he took them to call on Mrs Brookfield, who was to him at that time only the kind and pretty wife of an old college friend, the Revd William Brookfield. Anny recalled that 'Aunt Job', as she was known to them from her initials (Jane Octavia Brookfield), 'was quite a young lady with curls . . . who gave us a book'.[13]

This too brief reunion with his children made Thackeray more than ever determined to have them for good; their return to Paris at the end of the holiday left him feeling more bereft than ever. In October 1845 he took a first step towards fulfilling his purpose. He brought Isabella over to England and placed her in the care of 'an excellent woman', Mrs Bakewell, at Camberwell, and started house-hunting. He was entering the busiest period of his life. In addition to his regular commitments to *Punch* and *Fraser's*, and his reviewing for *The Morning Chronicle*, he had accepted a commission from Bradbury & Evans, *Punch*'s publishers, to give them a full-length novel in twenty parts in the manner of Dickens, which was to appear monthly at 1s. an issue and for a monthly fee of £60 – big money in his then circumstances. After many initial delays, he began work on the new book simultaneously with the acquisition of

[12] MS Reminiscences, 1864–5.   [13] Ibid.

a new house, in the autumn of 1846. The book was advertised on 28 November in *Punch* as 'Vanity Fair, A Novel without a Hero' by W. M. Thackeray. It was the first time that he had discarded his pseudonyms and written under his own name. He had an early premonition that it would soon become famous. Writing to his mother at Christmas, he said, 'My prospects are much improved and *Vanity Fair* may make me.'

In June 1846 Anny was nine. She was three years older than her little sister, and twice as advanced intellectually. 'She is now of an age', wrote Major Carmichael-Smyth to his wife, 'when she can receive a great deal of useful information with much advantage, and she has a mind thirsting for knowledge.'[14] Towards this important objective Thackeray had taken the first step by renting a Queen Anne period house at 13 Young Street in Kensington – bow-fronted, solid yet graceful, and congenial to him in every way. It was large enough to accommodate the whole family, if his parents would consent to join him. 'There are 2 capital bed-rooms and a little sitting room for you and GP', he wrote to his mother after taking possession, 'a famous bedroom for G.M. on the first floor – 2 rooms for the children on second very airy and comfortable; a couple of rooms big enough for Servants, and 2 little ones quite large enough for me – There's a good study for me down stairs and a dining room and drawing room, and a little court yard or garden and a little green house: and Kensington Gardens at the gate, and omnibuses every 2 minutes. What can mortal want more?'[15]

It was neither for himself nor for the children that he so warmly made the offer; and, in all probability, though he was too kind to say so, he was much relieved when they declined it. No persuasion would bring the Major to London. On suitable occasions and in fine weather, Mrs Carmichael-Smyth would be happy to visit her son, especially if he had need of her.

Thackeray took the house on a seven-year lease and these were the most formative years of Anny's life. Entering the house as an ignorant child of nine, she left it a highly perceptive, romantic young woman of sixteen, educated less through the curriculum of the schoolroom than by the wisdom of an exceptional father, in whose intimacy she grew up like a healthy plant constantly exposed to the sun. Barely able to write when she reached London, she left Young Street as her father's reliable amanuensis, and the first reader

[14] Ray, ii. 250.   [15] Ray, ii. 238.

of works whose critical acumen were to form her own strong critical judgements.

Her Parisian childhood was not, however, without its lasting and enriching effect. Its positive gain was to preserve her from insularity, and to lay the foundations of the cosmopolitan outlook that distinguished her through life.

CHAPTER 4

YOUNG STREET

IT was late in the afternoon of a dark November day in 1846 when the children arrived at their new home. Their time of arrival had been miscalculated and their father was not there to receive them. He had, however, engaged an efficient staff: Mrs Gray, cook and housekeeper; Eliza, the housemaid; and a handyman. Anny noted how the fires were all lighted and how kind Eliza was waiting to show them to their rooms. 'What family would be complete without its Eliza?' she reflected in later life.

They were shown the drawing-room, with its bow window at the front, and their father's empty study behind it; peeped through the uncurtained windows at the dark gardens behind, and into his bedroom upstairs. Their own rooms were on the upper floor and consisted of a big double nursery–bedroom and an adjoining schoolroom. There they found the evidence of their father's thoughtful preparations. The pictures which he had hung on the nursery walls included Thorwaldsen's prints, 'Hunt's delightful sleepy boy yawning at us over the chimney-piece', and a picture of Thackeray as a child which Eliza told them he had hung up himself. Knowing his children's love of animals, there was even a little black cat to welcome them. As Anny recorded, 'Once more after his first married years, my father had a home and a family – if a house, two young children, three servants, and a little black cat can be called a family.'[1]

A conviction on the part of the Carmichael-Smyths that the experiment could not work, Thackeray being so busy, the children so young, and there being no mistress to control the servants, may explain the arrival shortly afterwards from Paris of their great-grandmother, Mrs Butler – 'an old lady wrapped in India shawls', as Anny remembered. Fortunately for the children they saw very little of her; she rarely spoke and was almost always in her room.

[1] Fuller, p. 45.

Thackeray described her as being fairly content with her lot: 'orders the dinners: seems very fond of me: bullies Anny . . . pleased with her little household occupations, fidgetting the servants quite unrestrained and ringing the bells with unbounded liberty'.[2] She read the numbers of *Vanity Fair* as they came out, and derived satisfaction from her grandson's growing reputation, even over-looking his portrayal of her as 'Miss Crawley'. For a time Thack-eray handed over the housekeeping money to her, until he noticed the condition of his children's clothes.

Her major, unspecified, role was to play propriety in Thackeray's bachelor establishment against the advent of a resident governess for the children. His mother had been vehemently opposed to this plan from the outset, pointing out its glaring impropriety. In vain Thackeray had undertaken to choose only the plainest of candi-dates; Mrs Carmichael-Smyth was not appeased. Bending at last to the necessity of a governess, she wrote to say she would herself select the lady. She and the Major knew several young women who might suitably fill the bill. Thus, in the late autumn they announced the arrival from Paris of a Bessy Hamerton, an unimpeachable young woman from their circle of acquaintances who, though neither experienced nor precisely qualified, was anxious to get to London. With her began the ten-year saga of Thackeray's governes-ses, who caused him more annoyance, insomnia, and loss of appetite than whole chapters of his books in arrears for the printer. In the space of the next four years the children disposed of as many governesses – with long interregnums – each one proving more unsatisfactory than the last. Not until the advent of Miss Truelock in 1850 , who remained several years with them, was everybody satisfied.

The great rambling house in Young Street with its sloping floors, attics and basement, steep winding stairs, and views from the attic windows over the old Kensington roofs, was a liberation for the children after the confinement of their Parisian homes. And living with Thackeray was a liberal education in itself. They watched him, rather awestruck, writing his books. One thing Anny early noticed was his love of drawing. It was a quite different thing with him from his writing, a passion rather than a preoccupation. Often, when his day's writing was done, and nearly always on Sunday mornings, and invariably on holidays, he would fetch out his drawing-board

[2] Ray, ii. 289, 292.

and begin sketching. Inevitably, encouraged by him, the children early picked up the habit and drew for pleasure as naturally as they read their story-books. There were times when, as illustrator of his own *Punch* articles, his work as draughtsman was as serious a commitment as his writing. The children, as Anny recalled, were often summoned from their schoolroom then to pose for him. 'We were to be trusted', she wrote, 'to stand upon chairs, to hold draperies and cast a shadow, to take the part of supers on our father's stage. There were also wood-blocks ready to fascinate us; and it was often our business to rub out the failures, and to wash the chalk off the blocks. I still remember a dreadful day when I washed away a finished drawing, for which the messenger was at that moment waiting in the hall.' Anny's memory was, like her father's, a pictorial one, and the events of those early years in Young Street were fixed in her mind in a succession of images. 'My father's silver-grey head is bending over his drawing-board as he sits at his work, serious, preoccupied, with the water-colour box open on the table beside him, and the tray full of well-remembered implements. . . . My father used to write in his study at the back of the house in Young Street. The vine shaded his two windows, which looked out upon the bit of garden, and the medlar tree, and the Spanish jessamine of which the yellow flowers scented our old brick walls. I can remember the tortoise belonging to the boys next door crawling along the top of the wall, where they had set it, and making its way between the Jessamine sprigs. . . . Our garden was not tidy . . . but it was full of sweet things. There were verbenas – red, blue and scented; and there were lovely stacks of flags . . . and bunches of London Pride . . . and there were some bush roses at the end of the garden.'[3]

The house still stands today, but the old garden now serves only to garage delivery vans.

Anny liked the large schoolroom at the top of the house best of all: 'the sky was in it', she wrote, 'and the evening bells used to ring into it across the garden, and seemed to come in dancing and clanging with the sunset; and the floor sloped so that if you put down a ball it would roll in a leisurely way right across the room of its own accord. And then there was a mystery – a small trap door between the windows which we could never open. Where did that trap-door lead to! It was the gateway of paradise, of many paradises to us.'[4]

³ Fuller, pp. 53 and 45–6.   ⁴ *Chapters*, p. 75.

Young Street was named after the architect who built the adjoining Kensington Square the year before James II threw the Great Seal of England into the Thames. The houses in the Square had first been built for the court officials of King William III and the Maids of Honour of Queen Anne. They had lovely fanlights over the doors, wrought-iron balustrades, torch-extinguishers, horse-posts and ornate foot-scrapers for the miry top-boots of the messengers hurrying to and from the court. By this time the Square was chiefly occupied by professional men – lawyers, bishops, and doctors – and by flourishing seminaries for young ladies. Just round the corner from their home at 44 Kensington Square lived Dr John Merriman, physician in ordinary to the Duchess of Kent at the Palace, and shortly to become Thackeray's doctor and friend. Across the turnpike road at the top of Young Street were Kensington Gardens, laid out by William and Queen Anne, where the children walked in the care of Eliza or of Miss Hamerton. Queen Anne seemed to live again in the Thackeray household; out of fashion as Victorian taste had decreed her style to be, whether in houses or furniture, for Thackeray it was the supreme expression of English culture, as his life's work would testify.

Busy as their father was, he insisted that they have breakfast with him every day; and if in the evening he had not to go out and dined at home they joined him again, sitting on little stools at his feet while he told them stories. Before a month was out, he reported to his mother with some frankness the perfect success of the arrangment: 'My dearest Mammy,' he wrote on 4 December 1846, 'Now that the children are with me I am getting so fond of them that I can understand the pangs of the dear old mother who loses them. . . . But it is best that they should be away from you: – at least that they should be away either from you or me. There can't be two first principles in a house. We should be secretly jealous of one another; or I should resign the parental place altogether to you, and be a batchelor still. Whereas now God Almighty grant I may be a father to my children. . . . Continual thoughts of them chase I don't know how many wickednesses out of my mind: Their society makes many of my old amusements seem trivial and shameful. What bounties are there of Providence in the very instincts which God gives us . . . Only I write . . . to give my dearest old Mother a consolation in her bereavement. Remember the children are in their natural place: with their nearest friend working their natural influence; getting and giving the good let us hope which the Divine

Benevolence appointed to result from the union between parents and children.'⁵ So far, he could assure his mother that the arrangement with Bess Hamerton was working, at least on the domestic front, if not the educational. He wrote at Christmas, 'Bess is great in the household affairs and the best and briskest of all managers. She manages the children admirably: she gives me too good dinners that is her only fault.'⁶

Thackeray's close friends, the Procters, the Coles, the Crowes at Hampstead, who had stood by him in his adversity and given him some semblance of home life when first he lost Isabella, now rallied again to welcome his little girls, especially in those homes where there were children. Sooner than Anny could dare hope, they were invited to the Coles who lived near them in Kensington. The envied Laetitia, Henrietta, and Mary, whose father 'Felix Summerly' wrote such engrossing story-books for the young, now became special friends. Anny and Laetitia, slightly her senior, founded a Society for 'The stoppation of starvation' the world over, with Anny as its first secretary, her function being to solicit funds from the famous in all walks of life to further that excellent purpose. But having acquainted her grandmother with the project, she did not receive the encouragement she had counted on. 'Mrs. Carmichael-Smyth, having been informed of the favor to-day conferred upon me,' she wrote to Laetitia, 'started an objection, which though *I* am perfectly sure of its voidness, yet I cannot in any sincerity refrain from mentioning it, namely that she was not quite sure whether my honoured father would entirely approve of my writing begging letters to my friends.' Pending receipt of approval from her father who was away at the time, Anny had a fruitful counter-suggestion to make: 'If I was you,' she wrote to Laetitia, 'I'd post a prospectus to the Prince of Wales, he might send us £50 and as his father is the patron of the great one, why should he not be patron of the little one?' Modelling herself in all things on her father, Anny signed her communication 'Your obdt Servant. A Thanakins Titmarsh.'⁷

For their first Christmas in London, the children were invited with their father to the Crowes at Hampstead, and at New Year to the Procters. B. W. Procter, who wrote under the name of 'Barry Cornwall', his wife, and their daughter Adelaide, who was twelve years older than Anny, lived in Harley Street. Thanking them for their kindness to the children on the occasion, Thackeray wrote on

⁵ Ray, ii. 255.   ⁶ Ray, ii. 258.   ⁷ *Ritchie Letters*, pp. 25–6.

15 January 1847: 'The sashes are the prettiest of ribbons – an appy and grateful father wears them round his art. I can't help thinking how extraordinarily good and kind every one was to my little girls at your house. My views of human nature are beginning to change entirely, and I find myself getting fond of new good and kind people every day.'[8]

Outside the circle of his Cambridge friends who had gravitated to London – Tennyson, Edward FitzGerald, Monckton Milnes, Brookfield, who were all young and busy striving to make their way in the world – Thackeray's closest friends were the Procters and the Carlyles. The girls never forgot their first walk from Kensington through the lanes of hawthorn to the famous house in Cheyne Row nor the kindly welcome they received from Mrs Carlyle. It was in frosty weather with snow on the ground, and when they arrived, 'numb and chilled and tired we found in the dining-room below, standing before the fire, two delicious hot cups of chocolate all ready prepared for us, with saucers placed upon the top. "I thought ye would be frozen," said she; and the hot chocolate became a sort of institution. Again and again she has sat by, benevolent and spirited, superintending our wintry feasts, inviting our confidences, confiding in us to a certain degree.'[9] With time, Thomas Carlyle became as good a friend to the girls as was his wife.

Meanwhile, unfashionably dressed as they might be, lacking a mother, the girls were happy and busy in their new home, aware of their father's wonderful assortment of visitors, but quite unconscious of their privilege in meeting them; entering freely and unsnubbed into the general talk. Tennyson was first remarked 'through a cloud of smoke' from his pipe, and remembered for his grave kindness to them. He was lonely and unknown as yet, seeking relaxation with his friend, their father. He himself remembered years later, and reminded Anny of the time Minny looked up from the book she was reading and broke into the conversation with: 'Papa, why don't you write books like Nicholas Nickleby?'[10]

Minny was chiefly absorbed in animals and loved them all of no matter what species; 'and so was my father,' commented Anny, 'at least, he always liked *our* animals. Now, looking back, I am full of wonder at the number of cats we were allowed to keep. . . . The

[8] Ray, ii. 269.   [9] *Chapters*, pp. 135–6.
[10] *Records of Tennyson, Ruskin and Robert and Elizabeth Browning*, p. 39.

cats used to come to us from the garden . . . My sister used to adopt
and christen them all in turn by the names of her favourite heroes;
she had Nicholas Nickleby, a huge grey tabby, and Martin Chuz-
zlewit, and a poor little half-starved Barnaby Rudge, and many
others . . . . Their saucers used to be placed in a row on the little
terrace at the back of my father's study, under the vine where the
sour green grapes grew.'[11] Anny noted that Dickens's books were as
much a part of their home as those of their own father.

There was always the day towards the end of the month when
Thackeray had finishing his stint of writing on the current book (it
was still *Vanity Fair* during the first year at Young Street) and
wanted to celebrate his hard-won freedom by a day's outing. He
early communicated to the children his love of the theatre, though
when he took Anny and Miss Hamerton to see *King Lear* it was not
a happy occasion: Anny was so distressed by the King's curses on
his wicked daughters that she stopped her ears and wept aloud. As
the spring advanced, the outings were into the country, by hackney
cab, or even hansom cab, when he took the children to his favourite
haunts – Hampstead, Richmond, Greenwich – and treated them to
a meal, regarding gastronomy as part of their education.

But by the spring of 1847 it had become evident that Miss
Hamerton was not the ideal person to bring up Thackeray's
children. Determined to be master in his own house on the subject
of their education, he sat down and wrote two letters on the same
day, one to Bess Hamerton herself and the other to his mother. To
the latter, despite her known views, he was the more outspoken,
impressed as he keenly was by the exceptional intelligence of his
elder daughter who, not yet ten, already commanded his respect as
well as his paternal affections. To Bessy he wrote on 16 March:
'After all your care and kindness it seems very ungrateful to say to
you "Don't stay with us any more," but it would be worse not to
speak openly. . . . You have not got the affection of the children.
They are afraid of you . . . I think the little girls won't give you
their confidence . . . My Gmother [Mrs Butler] knows nothing of
my feelings . . . I have checked Anny twice or thrice when about to
make complaints.'[12] To his mother he wrote on the same day: 'My
dearest Mammy will be thunderstruck at this manifesto but it is
quite necessary. Anny and Bess do not go on well together. The
child is the woman's superior in every respect: and subject to a

[11] MS Reminiscences, 1864–5.   [12] Ray, ii. 284.

vulgar worrying discipline which makes her unhappy. . . . She's not an English lady – that's the fact . . . this is not the woman to rule such a delicate soul as my dearest Nanny's. What a noble creature she is thank God. May I love her and be her friend more and more. As for Minny who can help loving her? . . I am in treaty for a Paragon-Governess to all accounts – a Miss Drury – clergyman's daughter . . . not pretty and 27.'[13]

By 6 April the 'Paragon' had arrived, and as Thackeray frankly admitted to his mother she was 'not such a paragon as I expected – but lady-like. . . . They have begun their lessons to-day in the school room. They dine at 3. GM likes her dinner then . . . Anny is employed in taking Miss Drury's measure. . . . She will be the Governess's mistress I expect.'[14] The comment anticipates the description of Ethel Newcome, another clever girl, who did 'battle with the governesses, and overcame them one after another'.[15]

Thackeray had, as expected, been reproached for dismissing Bess. He told his mother with growing anger that she had 'made his gorge rise at her coarseness', and finally he exploded '*She* tell my little princesses they were vulgar! . . . Peace go with her; but I want a lady for my children.' Being the man he was, when he heard some years later that Bess had been ill in Paris and was in need of various small comforts, he sent her through his mother money to provide them.

To begin with, Miss Drury seemed 'just the thing', as Thackeray reported on 15 April, whilst assuring his mother that he was confident that he would not fall in love with her.[16] In the event she lasted six months. Thackeray found her tolerable initially because she seemed to understand and appreciate 'our dear Anny's great noble heart and genius'. But the demands upon her were to be too great.

By September the situation was complicated by the return to Paris of Mrs Butler. Without dramatic illness, the old lady had been visibly failing for some time, and, restored to the care of the Carmichael-Smyths, she died quietly on 1 November 1847. The children had gone to Paris with her, leaving Thackeray 'alone in this dismal Kensington', wrestling with the latest number of *Vanity Fair*. It was little Minny who distinguished herself by kindness towards the dying woman – as Anny insisted when Thackeray was

[13] Ray, ii, 285–6. [14] Ray, ii. 289.
[15] *The Newcomes*, p. 135 (Oxford Edition). [16] Ray, ii. 289.

inclined to give her the credit. Between the two girls there was no sort of rivalry, their different natures perfectly complementing each other. To the surprise of the family, Mrs Butler left no ready money. It was Thackeray who sent over the £50 for her funeral expenses.

One event, never forgotten by Anny, occurred during this visit to Paris. She was taken to visit Chopin and heard him play. His devoted Scots admirers, Jane Sterling and her sister Mrs Erskine, hosts on his previous tours of Scotland, were friends of the Carmichael-Smyths and Miss Sterling was passing through Paris at this time. Knowing him already to be cricitally ill she had prepared a hamper of delicacies for him and was about to drive to his lodgings when Anny happened to call bearing a note from her grandmother. As she recorded later:

I had not the presence of mind to run away as I longed to do, and somehow in a few minutes found myself sitting in a little open carriage with the Scotch lady, and the basket on the opposite seat. I thought her, if possible, more terrible than ever – she seemed grave, preoccupied . . . We drove along the Champs Élysées towards the Arc, and then turned into a side street, and presently came to a house . . . at which the carriage stopped. The lady got out . . . and told me to follow, and we began to climb the shiny stairs . . . two flights I think; then we rang at a bell and the door was almost instantly opened. It was opened by a slight, delicate-looking man with long hair, bright eyes, and a thin, hooked nose. When Miss X. saw him she hastily put down her basket . . . caught both his hands in hers, began to shake them gently, and to scold him in an affectionate reproving way for having come to the door. He laughed, said he had guessed who it was, and motioned to her to enter, and I followed at her sign with the basket – followed into a narrow little room, with no furniture in it whatever but an upright piano against the wall and a few straw chairs . . . He made us sit down with some courtesy, and in reply to her questions said he was pretty well. Had he slept? He shook his head. Had he eaten? He shrugged his shoulders and then pointed to the piano. He had been composing something – I remember that he spoke in an abrupt, light sort of way – would Miss X. like to hear it? 'She would like to hear it', she answered, 'of course, she would dearly like to hear it, but it would tire him to play; it could not be good for him.' He smiled again, shook back his long hair, and sat down immediately; and then the music began, and the room was filled with continuous sound, he looking over his shoulder now and then to see if we were liking it. The lady sat absorbed and listening, and as I looked at her I saw tears in her eyes – . . . I can't, alas, recall that music! I would give anything to remember it now: but the truth is, I was so interested in the people that I scarcely listened. When he stopped at last and looked round, the lady started up. 'You mustn't play any more,' she said; 'no more, no more, it's too beautiful.' – and she praised him and thanked him in a tender, motherly pitying sort of way, and then hurriedly said we must go; but as we took leave she added almost in a whisper with a humble apologising look, – 'I have brought you some of that jelly, and my sister sent some of the wine you fancied the other day; pray, pray, try to take a little.' He again shook his head at her. . . . 'It is very wrong; you shouldn't bring me these things,' he said in French. 'I won't play to you if you do,' – but she put him back softly, and hurriedly closed the door upon him . . . and hastened away. . . . She looked hard at me as we drove away. 'Never forget that you have heard Chopin play,' she said with emotion, 'for soon no one will ever hear him play any more.'[17]

The children's departure for Paris with Mrs Butler in September had made the termination of Miss Drury's engagement the easier for Thackeray, without recrimination on either side, but the search for the ideal governess had to be resumed. On 2 November, the day after his grandmother's death, he wrote to his mother to say he had found somebody suitable: 'I have just engaged with a nice plain kind-looking governess – about 28, with 6 or 7 brothers and sisters living at Richmond with their Pa and Ma – an ex-captain in the army . . . Miss Alexander is to come as soon as I like. . . . Shall I send her over to you to bring the children back? – She has friends at Paris who would receive her.'[18]

By Christmas the children were back in Young Street. Despite his joy in their return, their father was so late with his month's work as to be 'almost out of his mind', and held up for want of some special information about Madras, about which he didn't want 'to make blunders'.

Miss Alexander was duly installed, and fairly soon found to be far from ideal. On 7 January Thackeray reported to his mother: 'The governess is very good very honest very eager to do her duty . . . not by any means wise, or fit to guide Anny's mind. But she can teach her geography and music and what they call history and hemming – and my dear old Nan goes on thinking for herself, and no small beer of herself – I am obliged to snub her continually, with delight at what she says all the time. They are noble children. Thank God. And the governess – a nuisance.'[19]

[17] *Chapters*, pp. 23–7.   [18] Ray, ii. 321–2.   [19] Ray, ii. 334–5.

The problem of fathering a too-clever child – whose sharp perceptions delighted him, even while needing correction – was becoming as permanent a feature of Thackeray's life as the problem of his creative work. Like the fictional characters taking shape in his mind, Anny seemed to have a way of slipping out of his control and leading a life of her own. The picture of the author of *Vanity Fair*, reputedly the most cynical novelist of the Victorian Age, plagued and perplexed by his children's schoolroom problems, would be hard to credit but for the repeated evidence of his letters. The rivals and literary enemies, who liked to represent him as the most selfish and self-indulgent of men, would find it hard to explain why, if there were a problem over his daughters' education at home, he did not solve it by sending them to a boarding-school. The simple explanation that he delighted in their company would probably have escaped them.

Writing to FitzGerald, perhaps his oldest and certainly his closest friend in March 1848, he said: 'My little women are delightful. They are drawing at my work table at this minute: and they act upon me after the world like soda water. God bless em. I have a governess for them an excellent woman but a great ass . . . But I dont like to part with her she is so kind and thoroughly good.'[20] So much for Miss Alexander. To his mother he had to admit the same thing: 'Alexander is another bore: but admirable in many points keeping the children to their work unceasingly always kind and good-humoured with all their factiousness and bent on doing her duty – only she is no more a fit match for Anny's brains, than John [his servant] is for mine.'[21] Anny, who had had lessons at times from her grandmother herself, was reported by Thackeray again as 'always wishing for you. Alexander has not brains enough to get a strong hold upon her heart and she must have a good deal of solitude. Not that this is harmful for her with her particular bent and strong critical faculty; she will learn for herself more than most people can teach. Pray God she may always continue to be, as she is now, generous and loving and just'.[22] By 5 June Thackeray had decided that Miss Alexander must go. 'She is not clever enough for Anny', he wrote. 'My dear old girl. She is as wise as an old man. In 3 years she will be a charming companion to me – and fill up a part of a great vacuum which exists inside me.'[23] That was the crux of the

---

[20] Ray, ii. 367.   [21] Ray, ii. 373.
[22] Ray, ii. 379.   [23] Ray, ii. 382.

matter – Thackeray's loneliness and the eternal dilemma of his enforced bachelorhood.

On 28 June 1848 he finished *Vanity Fair* after a week in which, as he wrote to his friend Mrs Procter, 'I have been like a raving maniac, trying to be done on time.' To Mrs Brookfield, reckoned a kind friend also, but the more dangerous because she was beautiful and a neglected wife and a clinging character, he wrote not only about his real life but about his imaginary characters: 'You know you are only a piece of Amelia – My mother is another half: my poor little wife y est pour beaucoup': revealing words from the creator of Emmy, the first of the exacting, jealous women in whose portrayal he was to excel.

For the time being, relief at the lifting of the burden of work was so immense that, to celebrate his liberty, he 'took the children to the Play', as he told Mrs Procter. Presumably it was to see Macready, as the very next night, he and the children were invited to Mrs Macready's. 'My father was very fond of going to the play', Anny remembered, 'and he used to take us when we were children, one on each side of him, in a hansom. He used to take us to the opera too, which was less of a treat. Magnificent envelopes, with unicorns and heraldic emblazonments, used to come very constantly, containing tickets and boxes for the opera. In those days we thought everybody had boxes for the opera as a matter of course. We used to be installed in the front places with our chins resting on the velvet ledges of the box . . . Alas! I never possessed a note of music of my own, though I have cared for it in a patient, unrequited way all my life long. My father always loved music and understood it too; he knew his opera tunes by heart.'[24]

On finishing *Vanity Fair*, Thackeray took a holiday by himself at Spa, between 26 July and 21 August, leaving the children to be looked after by Miss Alexander in her house at Twickenham. Minny was in fact 'very much attached to her' and even Anny 'suffered her very dutifully'. By a curious coincidence, the Alexanders' home, Chapel House, was bought by Tennyson on his marriage in 1850. It was there that Hallam, his first son, was born. Anny described it later as 'a beautiful old house with an oak staircase, and panelled rooms. On the staircase there was a statue of a Bishop, carved in oak, with his hands out.'[25]

Thackeray himself was almost immediately busy again with the

[24] *Chapters*, pp. 69–70, 73.   [25] Memoir For Laura.

opening chapters of *Pendennis*, but he planned on his return to take the children on holiday to Brighton. He hoped to persuade his parents to join them, and even to consider settling there, since the Major so much disliked London. Houses, large enough to accommodate them all, were to be had for £60 a year. The parents, as usual, proved intractable, and would not tie themselves to any permanent arrangement; but longing to see the children, they came over on 17 October on what proved to be a visit that lasted well over a year. The reunion between grandparents and children touched Thackeray deeply: 'It was quite a sight to see the old mother with the children,' he wrote to Mrs Brookfield.

For the time being, the governess problem solved itself, with his mother supervising the girls' lessons, and visiting teachers taking them for music and drawing. His own privacy, however, was so often invaded by the visitors that he found working at home impossible. He had to slink away, as he put it, to work on 'Pen' at the Reform Club, where the printer's devil had to pursue him. The first monthly part of *Pendennis* appeared on 1 November 1848.

The domestic pattern thus established received few changes during the following year. Thackeray was still thankful to report in the spring of 1849 that 'I have my mother with me now who is my comfort my housekeeper and governess in chief'; and of Anny that she was so 'deeply engaged with masters and examinations' that he did not wish to accept invitations for her that took her from her studies.[26]

To his brother-in-law, Captain Shawe, he wrote in May 1849 of the children: Minny was now turned nine, and Anny nearly twelve – 'a great sensible clever girl with a very homely face, and a very good heart and a very good head and an uncommonly good opinion of herself . . . and both have a great deal of spoiling and fondness from my mother, who supplies to them the place of their own – now nearly nine years removed from them. She is at Epsom very well . . . I got a letter yesterday from Mrs Bakewell to say that she was quite happy and very much pleased at seeing the folks pass by to the Derby.'[27]

In July 1849 the grandparents took the children for a holiday to Wales, while Thackeray found refuge in Brighton to work in peace on 'Pen'. During a short business trip to Paris in early September, he wrote to Mrs Brookfield enclosing a letter to be forwarded to

[26] Ray, ii. 528–9.   [27] Ray, ii. 545.

Anny: 'I think about my dear honest old Fatty', he wrote, 'with the greatest regard and confidence – I hope please God that she'll be kept to be a companion and friend to me.' It was not a morbid fear of her early death but of marriage which he quite selfishly dreaded and yet was ashamed to confess to. 'Will poor Anny have to nurse an old Imbecile of a father some day?' he reflected.[28]

Mrs Brookfield, as his correspondence shows, was gradually taking the place of his closest confidante and friend, to whom he unburdened not only his tormented feelings for her but all the other problems of his life. She was twenty-seven at the time, gifted, capable of judging his work, and her critical reactions were valuable to him. She was also kind to his little girls. On the other hand she was a married woman, and her husband was an old friend. But a kind of solemn bond had been made between them, in the previous October, on the occasion of his first visit to Clevedon, her girlhood home in Somerset, the property of her brother Sir Arthur Elton. It was then, while yet blind to the sexual element in their attraction, that they entered into their 'pact of brotherly/sisterly love' to fill the great emotional void in their lives. What had begun, as far back as 1842, as a simple acquaintance between the lonely Thackeray and one of many hospitable young couples who befriended him, had gradually become an obsession. Jane Brookfield, who like so many unoccupied and childless Victorian wives suffered from nerves and poor health, was ordered to keep to her couch, and in the absences on business of her husband[29] she turned to Thackeray for relief from boredom. While he was falling in love he remained for her the 'brother', the soul mate who filled the gap left by Brookfield's absences. As his growing fame made him a 'literary lion', the more she was flattered by his attentions. Her married status made her 'moral' position unassailable, in her own estimation at least. But the daily companionship of a beautiful and appealing woman was straining Thackeray's endurance to breaking-point. Repeatedly, he sought to sever the connection while there was yet time; repeatedly, even pettishly, she recalled him. For her, there was no risk in their friendship; as Thackeray all too clearly perceived, she did not love him – he had to be thankful for what he got.

Towards her husband, his former friend, one of the inner Cambridge 'set' which included Monckton Milnes (later Lord

[28] Ray, ii. 581, 583.
[29] He was appointed Inspector of Schools early in 1848.

Houghton), Tennyson, and Hallam, Thackeray's feelings inevitably changed. The handsome and witty Brookfield, whose social graces made him one of the most sought-after diners-out in town, had once captivated him too; till jealousy and his penetrating vision perceived the 'whited sepulchre within the beautiful outside'. Then he drew his scarifying likeness in the Revd Charles Honeyman of *The Newcomes*.

If Brookfield was as yet purblind to the situation between his wife and Thackeray, her 'moral' security was jealously guarded by her uncle, Henry Hallam the historian, a near neighbour of the Brookfields at Wilton Place, who called on her almost as often as Thackeray, and did not hesitate to express his disapproval of the intimacy; and when the breach came, it was largely at his instigation.

During 1849 and through most of 1850, Mrs Brookfield remained the trusted friend and chief adviser whose influence Thackeray did not hide even from his mother, although she greatly feared the connection. In September 1849, while the grandparents were away with the children in Wales, he was suddenly taken gravely ill. The symptoms were not immediately recognized, but he had cholera. Nursed by his household and his friends, by Mrs Procter and Mrs Brookfield in particular, he absolutely forbade them to alert the family till he was reckoned out of danger. Nevertheless the alarm and the precipitate return of the travellers from Wales was something never forgotten by Anny. As they hurried from post–town to post-town from the remote region where they were staying – Lake Arne in Caernarvonshire – their terror mounted as they became aware that the sickness that had struck down their father was epidemic: as they passed through Monmouth and Gloucester the church bells ringing for services of intercession sounded a sinister note.

They returned home to find their father still in bed and looking ghastly, 'so thin and changed' they hardly knew him. He was a long time recovering, and chose to go to Brighton with his servant John, who pushed him in a Bath chair along the chain-pier. He wrote from there to Anny, still very weak: 'My dearest Fat. The sea air does me all the good in the world and I know that you and Minny will be glad to have so much news from your loving Father.' His illness caused a three-month interruption in the serialization of *Pendennis*. As he revived, he used what strength he had to write not

Pendennis but a 'Christmas Book', at the instance of his publishers – *Rebecca and Rowena*, which proved a considerable popular success. 'My dearest little Misses,' he wrote to the children later in October, 'I've done a good days work yesterday and after that I'm always better. . . . I've had a famous days work again today: and been to church too.'[30]

He remained very low for weeks after returning home. No sooner was he better than his mother, who had seen him through his convalescence, was struck down with acute rheumatism, aggravated no doubt by the many stairs of the old house, the damp of London in autumn, and the English climate in general. To his Aunt Ritchie in Paris Thackeray wrote on 19 November 1849 that his mother was crippled and without rest night or day, the Major devotedly waiting on her. The illness was a deciding factor in their return to Paris as soon as Mrs Carmichael-Smyth could travel. They had been over a year in England and as usual it had not suited them.

Their departure left Thackeray once again with a governess problem on his hands. As it happened, this time he was lucky. The new candidate for the post, Miss Truelock, was the best the girls ever had and stayed with them, with the exception of holidays, over the next four years. They were the years that coincided with their father's most resounding successes; the years of *Esmond* and *The Newcomes*, for which Anny was already fit to act as his amanuensis; of his triumphant lecture tours; of his foreign travel and widening contacts; the years that saw them out of childhood into young girlhood.

[30] Ray, ii. 604–5.

CHAPTER 5

A LIBERAL EDUCATION

In the Autumn of 1849, when the subject of governesses happened to be a peculiarly sore one with Thackeray, Charlotte Brontë's dedication of the second edition of *Jane Eyre* to him released a flood of libellous rumours, that involved both him and the unknown 'governess' author, Currer Bell. No innocent gesture of genuine admiration of one author for another ever precipitated a more damaging result. In the literary coteries it was openly reported that Currer Bell was a dismissed governess of the Thackeray household who had revenged herself by portraying him as the 'seducer' Rochester whose wife, like Thackeray's, was mad.

The mischief had been done so simply. On the publication of *Jane Eyre* on 16 October 1847, the publishers, Smith, Elder, had sent a complimentary copy to Thackeray. Greatly struck by it, he had written to them on 23 October: 'I wish you had not sent me Jane Eyre. It interested me so much that I have lost (or won if you like) a whole day in reading it at the busiest period with the printers . . . Who the author can be I can't guess . . . I have been exceedingly moved and pleased by Jane Eyre. It is a woman's writing, but whose? Give my respects and thanks to the author.'[1] The message was passed on to Currer Bell, whose pleasure in Thackeray's commendation was immense, since he was by far her favourite among living authors. When the runaway success of *Jane Eyre* called for a second edition in January 1848, she dedicated it to him, entirely innocent of his domestic circumstances. While Thackeray felt the dedication to be an 'enormous compliment', he already anticipated the backlash of the association of his name with Currer Bell's; for he was in a position to hear, as she in her remote village could not, the current gossip.

Thackeray felt that it was only honest to tell 'Currer Bell' of his private life, lest the rumours should reach her, and he wrote to her

[1] Ray, ii. 318–19.

under cover of her publishers. She was deeply moved by his letter. 'The very fact of his not complaining at all and addressing me with such kindness, notwithstanding the pain and annoyance I must have caused him, increase my chagrin,' she wrote to them in reply. 'I am very, *very* sorry that my inadvertent blunder should have made his name and affairs subject for common gossip.'[2] Telling her about his mad wife, Thackeray had also revealed to her that reports that *Jane Eyre* had been written by a governess in his family were current, 'and that the dedication coming now' had confirmed everybody in their surmise. What hurt Thackeray most in this ludicrous affair was the credence some friends gave to the slander. Even his mother, who had always predicted disaster from his engaging a resident governess, blamed him for his want of caution. Writing to the great singer, Mrs Sartoris, in 1856 he said: 'My relations some 7 or 8 years ago accused me too (no didn't accuse, only insinuated) that I had cast unlawful eyes on a Governess – the story of Jane Eyre, seduction, surreptitious family in Regents Park, etc., which you may or mayn't have heard, all grew out of this confounded tradition – and as I never spoke 3 words to the lady and had no more love for my Governess than for my grandmother, and as the calumny has been the cause of a never-quite-mended quarrel and of the cruellest torture and annoyance to me, whenever I hear of poor gentlemen and poor governesses accused of this easy charge, I become wild and speak more no doubt from a sense of my own wrongs than theirs.'[3]

The attack on Charlotte Brontë's reputation when it came was no less damaging. In a belated review of *Jane Eyre* in the *Quarterly Review* for December 1848 the whole tone of the novel ('rebellious', 'irreligious'), as well as the doubtful morality of its unknown author, were castigated by the reviewer, Lady Eastlake, who expressed the opinion that if the unknown 'Currer Bell' were a woman 'she was one who had forfeited the society of her sex'. This appeared just at the time of Emily's death, and struck at a heart already grievously wounded. It was touch and go whether the world would ever hear of Currer Bell again.

But on 26 October 1849 *Shirley* was published and greeted with a chorus of praise. Not only did sales of the book shoot overnight to record figures but interest in the unknown author was keenly revived, not by malicious gossips only, but by her fellow authors,

[2] *SBC*, p. 383.   [3] Ray, *The Age of Wisdom*, p. 11.

Harriet Martineau, Elizabeth Gaskell, and Thackeray. Her publisher George Smith felt that the time had come when he must try to make Currer Bell a part of the literary scene. He was a shrewd business man, young, unmarried, and his firm's reputation had yet to be made. In Currer Bell he had spotted a winner; and it is a curious fact that his first great success, and the least known of his authors, was instrumental in the end in bringing to Smith, Elder the best-selling novelists of the time: Thackeray, Elizabeth Gaskell, and Trollope amongst them. He invited Currer Bell to come to London and make his mother's home in Westbourne Place her headquarters.

She came, on 29 November, and stayed a fortnight. During that time she met the leading critics and writers of the day, including Thackeray. Smith invited him to dinner, exacting from him a promise to respect her incognito since she was painfully shy and dreaded of all things to be 'lionized'. Thackeray had only just recovered from his severe attack of cholera that autumn, and recalled that meeting in later years: 'I saw her first as I rose out of an illness from which I never thought to recover. I remember the trembling little frame, the little hand, the great honest eyes. An impetuous honesty seemed to me to characterize the woman . . . I fancied an austere little Joan of Arc marching in upon us, and rebuking our easy lives, our easy morals. She gave me the impression of being a very pure, and lofty, and high-minded person.'[4]

Charlotte Brontë wrote home the next day to her father: 'Yesterday I saw Mr. Thackeray. He dined here with some other gentlemen. He is a very tall man – above six feet high, with a peculiar face – not handsome, very ugly indeed, generally somewhat stern and satirical in expression, but capable also of a kind look. He was not told who I was, he was not introduced to me, but I soon saw him looking at me through his spectacles; and when we all rose to go down to dinner he just stepped quietly up and said, "Shake hands"; so I shook hands. He spoke very few words to me, but when he went away he shook hands again in a very kind way . . . I listened to him as he conversed with the other gentlemen. All he says is most simple, but often cynical, harsh, and contradictory. . . . Most people know me, I think, but they are far too well bred to show that they know me, so that there is none of that bustle or that sense of publicity I dislike.'[5] She would have been appalled if she had heard Thackeray later that evening, as he burst in on his cronies of the

---

[4] *Cornhill*, April 1860: 'The Last Sketch'.   [5] *W & S* iii. 54.

Garrick Club smoking-room with the exultant shout: 'Boys! I have been dining with Jane Eyre!'[6]

The paths of the two so profoundly dissimilar authors were to cross several times again in the next few years. Self-conscious as both were, ill at ease in each other's company, nothing was to bring them closer than their reading of each other's works had already done. Both were genuine in their admiration and understanding of the other's genius. Forbidden reading for many young persons at the time, *Jane Eyre* was also devoured by the Miss Thackerays, though Anny admitted that a great deal of it was 'absolutely unintelligible' to them. They knew, however, all about the secret of its unknown author, and their father's high opinion of her writing, by the time 'Currer Bell' was entertained at Young Street in the following June.

The reading of novels, like their father's friendships with the men and women who wrote them, was all a part of the girls' liberal education. Dickens's novels, as Anny recorded, were the staple diet of their childhood: 'it is curious to remember', she said, 'considering how rarely we met and what a long way off we lived from one another, the important part the Dickens household seemed to play in our early life. The little girls were just about our own age; K.M.[7] and my sister were the same age; Mary Dickens . . . paired off with me. The Dickens books were no less a part of our home than our father's own books. Mr. Pickwick, Little Nell, Nicholas Nickleby and the glorious company in which they all belonged, lived with us no less than did Becky and Dobbin and Major Pendennis and the beloved inhabitants of Fairoaks.'[8] Thackeray himself, in one of his American lectures, on '*Charity and Humour*' revealed a domestic detail when he said, thinking of Minny, 'All children ought to love Dickens; I know two that do, and read his books ten times for once they peruse the dismal preachments of their father. . . I know one who when she is happy, reads Nicholas Nickleby; when she is tired reads N.N. when she is in bed reads N.N. when she has nothing to do reads N.N. and when she has finished the book reads N.N. again.'

The friendship with the Dickens girls, which was to be one of the closest and longest-lasting of Anny's life, began when the children

[6] L. Huxley, *The House of Smith, Elder*, pp. 67–8.
[7] Kate Macready Dickens, later their close friend.
[8] *From the Porch*, 'Charles Dickens as I remember Him', pp. 32–3.

were yet very young, motherless, and still unaccustomed to Christmas parties. 'The Dickens children's parties were shining facts in our early London days – nothing came in the least near them,' Anny later recalled.

There were other parties, and they were very nice, but nothing to compare to these; not nearly so light, not nearly so shining, not nearly so going round and round. Perhaps it was not all as brilliantly wonderful as I imagined it, but most assuredly the spirit of mirth and kindly jollity was a reality to every one present, and the master of the house had that wondrous fairy gift of leadership. . . . One special party I remember, which seemed to me to go on for years with its kind, gay hospitality, its music, its streams of children passing and re-passing. We were a little shy coming in alone in all the consciousness of new shoes and ribbons but Mrs. Dickens called us to sit beside her till the long sweeping dance was over, and talked to us as if we were grown up, which is always flattering to little girls. Then Miss Hogarth found us partners. . . . I remember watching the white satin shoes and long flowing white sashes of the little Dickens girls, who were just about our own age, but how much more graceful and beautifully dressed. Our sashes were bright plaids of red and blue, a tribute from one of our father's Scotch admirers (is it ungrateful to confess now after all these years that we could not bear them?) our shoes were only bronze . . . after the music we all floated into a long supper room, and I found myself sitting near the head of the table by Mr. Dickens, with another little girl . . . and then all the *jeunesse dorée*, consisting of the little Dickens boys and their friends, ranged along the supper table, clapped and clapped, and Mr. Dickens clapped too. . . . And then he made a little speech, with one hand on the table . . . this much I do remember very clearly, that we had danced and supped and danced again; and that we were all standing in a hall lighted and hung with bunches of Christmas green, and . . . everything seemed altogether magnificent and important, more magnificent and important as the evening went on, and more and more people kept arriving. The hall was crowded, and the broad staircase was lined with little boys . . . they were making a great noise . . . presently their noise became a cheer, and then another, and we looked up and saw that our own father had come to fetch us, and that his white head was there above the others; . . . and some one went up to him – it was Mr. Dickens himself – who laughed and said quickly, 'That is for you!' and my father looked up surprised, pleased, touched, settled his spectacles and nodded gravely to the little boys.'[9]

Thanks to their father's position in society, and in consideration of their motherless state, the girls were early included in invitations

[9] *Chapters*, pp. 79–82.

to which, in that very formal Victorian society, their age did not entitle them. Looking back on that time, Anny remembered how lucky they were. 'My father liked to take us about with him, and I am surprised, as I think of it, at the great good-nature of his friends, who used so constantly to include two inconvenient little girls in the various invitations they sent him. We used to be asked early and to arrive at all sorts of unusual times. We used to lunch with our hosts and spend long afternoons, and then about dinner-time our father would come in, and sit smoking after dinner, while we waited with patient ladies upstairs.'[10]

To Mrs Brookfield, who lived in Portman Street in those days, they went frequently. The intimacy with her, so far as the children were concerned, received a fresh impetus with the birth of her first baby, a girl to be called Magdalene, laconically introduced to Thackeray by the father as 'a wench'. During the period of Mrs Brookfield's lying in, her friend Mrs Fanshawe stayed with her and brought up to London her own little girl, Tottie, who lodged at the Thackerays' and, to Anny's great delight, was allowed to share her bed. Thackeray was profoundly jealous of the new baby. He resented his exclusion from Portman Street apparently on its account, or on the plea of the mother's delicate state of health. But his exclusion was in fact by order of William Brookfield himself. Thackeray showered her with gifts of flowers, notes, and enquiries, and eventually finding the situation unbearable he went to Paris, from where he wrote: 'Don't fancy that I am come here to forget you, quite the reverse – the chain pulls tighter the farther I am away from you.'[11] His children's contacts with the Brookfield nursery were his only comfort at the time, and he was happy to receive Anny's reports on how well they all got on together.

The hospitality towards Tottie Fanshawe was returned in May when the Thackeray girls were invited to Southampton by Mrs Fanshawe. He sent them without their governess, trusting in Anny's good sense: announcing their arrival by train from Waterloo, he said: 'they will bring no-body with them, nor no maid nor nothink. And there's no use in meeting them for Anny will be instructed to call a coach and say to the Driver "Driver drive to 3 West Marlands." ' It was their first excursion into the world without their grandmother or father or governess to shield them. They behaved perfectly and were very happy. Thackeray as usual

[10] Ibid., p. 94.   [11] Ray, ii. 650.

was overwhelmed with work, trying to take advantage of the quiet at home to make headway with *Pendennis*.

Just as he was expecting their return, he was horrified to hear from Miss Truelock, who was on holiday, that she had received so good an offer for another post that she felt she ought to accept it. In utter despondency, Thackeray wrote to the girls, dreading the prospect of 'all the business to do over again'. 'Why don't you get a little older', he groaned, 'and do without a governess.' He did not know what was to become of them that summer while he still had three to four months' work to do on *Pendennis*. 'If Miss Truelock is going away, what the deuce are we to do?' he wrote to them again. 'A plague upon such misadventures.' He was so rattled by the setback that he seriously thought of sending them away to school after the midsummer holidays if no governess could be found. 'And then you'd learn something,' he wrote grumpily. But with immense relief he was able to write again on 3 June and tell them that Miss Truelock was not going away after all. She had agreed to remain with them. Within the week the children were home and Miss Truelock was back again.[12]

Charlotte Brontë was again staying with George Smith, and Thackeray's conscience prompted him to give a dinner in her honour. It was fixed for 12 June, and on the morning of that day he paid her a formal visit, which lasted two hours. George Smith, who joined them after some time, found what he later described as 'a queer scene'. Charlotte was lecturing Thackeray on his levity, telling him of the duty towards his readers that his great genius imposed. She had been particularly angered by the tone of *Rebecca and Rowena* which was written, she said, as though Mephistopheles stood on his right hand and Raphael on his left.[13] He was not doing justice to himself by his flippancy. Well might George Smith be amazed, knowing better than most Charlotte's admiration for the man she had described as 'a Titan, so strong that he can afford to perform, with calm the most herculean tasks'.[14] Now this shy woman spoke out, finding herself face to face with him. 'The giant sat before me,' she wrote home later the same day. 'I was moved to speak to him of his short-comings (literary of course) one by one the faults came into my mind, and one by one I brought them out. . . . He did defend himself like a great Turk and heathen – that is to say, the

4. Thackeray's house at No. 18 Albion Street, Hyde
Park

5. No. 13 Young Street, Kensington

excuses were often worse than the crime itself. The matter ended in decent amity.'[15]

'Decent amity' perhaps, but hardly a propitious opening for the evening's party. He had invited only ladies (Carlyle, as it happened, came with his wife), but at the last minute, in some panic, he invited Richard Monckton Milnes: 'Miss Brontë dines here to-morrow at 7. If you are by any wonder disengaged, do come too.' He did not. The selected guests were: Mrs Procter and her daughter Adelaide; the Carlyles; Mrs Brookfield of course; and Kate Perry and her sister, Mrs Elliot. These last, who lived together in Chesham Place at the Elliots' home, were among Thackeray's closest and most trusted friends, his 'bonnes sœurs' as he liked to call them, to whom he confided his most secret despairs and sufferings over Jane Brookfield. Kate Perry had described the spontaneous growth of their friendship when they first met at Brighton in 1846[16] as something quite different from the usual growth of normal intimacy, 'going through no gradations, but more like Jack's bean stalk in a pantomime which rushed up sky high without culture and so remained'.

The party for Charlotte Brontë was best described by Anny Thackeray, for whom, just turned thirteen, it was a sensational experience. The girls were allowed to sit up for the dinner to meet the famous author. Anny wrote later:

One of the most notable persons who ever came to our old bow-windowed drawing-room in Young Street is a guest never to be forgotten by me, a tiny, delicate, little person, whose small hand nevertheless grasped a mighty lever which set all the literary world of that day vibrating. I can still see the scene quite plainly! – the hot summer evening, the open windows, the carriage driving to the door as we all sat silent and expectant; my father who rarely waited, waiting with us; our governess and my sister and I all in a row, and prepared for the great event. We saw the carriage stop, and out of it sprang the active, well-knit figure of young Mr. George Smith, who was bringing Miss Brontë to see our father. My father, who had been walking up and down the room, goes out into the hall to meet his guests, and then after a moment's delay the door opens wide, and the two gentlemen come in, leading a tiny delicate, serious, little lady, pale, with fair straight hair, and steady eyes. She may be a little over thirty; she is dressed in a little *barège* dress with a pattern of faint green moss. She enters in mittens, in silence, in seriousness; our hearts are beating with wild excitement . . . The

---

[15] *W & S* iii. 118.
[16] C. and E. Brookfield, *Mrs. Brookfield and Her Circle*, ii. 311–12.

moment is so breathless that dinner comes as a relief to the solemnity of the occasion, and we all smile as my father stoops to offer his arm; for, genius though she may be, Miss Brontë can barely reach his elbow. My own personal impressions are that she is somewhat grave and stern, specially to forward little girls who wish to chatter; Mr. George Smith has since told me how she afterwards remarked upon my father's wonderful forbearance and gentleness with our uncalled-for incursions into the conversation. She sat gazing at him with kindling eyes of interest; lighting up with a sort of illumination every now and then as she answered him. I can see her bending forward over the table, not eating, but listening to what he said as he carved the dish before him . . .[17]

But in later years, when Anny heard that Monckton Milnes had also been invited, she exclaimed:

Would that he had been present! – perhaps the party would have gone off better. It was a gloomy and a silent evening. Everyone waited for the brilliant conversation which never began at all. Miss Brontë retired to the sofa in the study, and murmured a low word now and then to our kind governess, Miss Truelock. The room looked very dark, the lamp began to smoke a little, the conversation grew dimmer and more dim, the ladies sat around still expectant, my father was too much perturbed by the gloom and silence to be able to cope with it at all. Mrs Brookfield, who was in the doorway by the study, near the corner in which Miss Brontë was sitting, leant forward with a little commonplace, since brilliance was not to be the order of the evening. 'Do you like London, Miss Brontë?' she said; another silence, a pause, then Miss Brontë answers, 'Yes and No' very gravely . . . My sister and I were much too young to be bored in those days; alarmed, impressed we might be, but not yet bored. A party was a party, a lioness was a lioness; and – shall I confess it? – at that time an extra dish of biscuits was enough to mark the evening. We felt all the importance of the occasion; tea spread in the dining-room, ladies in the drawing-room; we roamed about inconveniently, no doubt, and excitedly, and in one of my excursions crossing the hall after Miss Brontë had left I was surprised to see my father opening the front door with his hat on. He put his fingers to his lips, walked out into the darkness, and shut the door quietly behind him. When I went back to the drawing-room again, the ladies asked me where he was. I vaguely answered that I thought he was coming back. I was puzzled at the time, nor was it all made clear to me till long years afterwards, when Mrs Proctor asked me if I knew what had happened when my father had invited a party to meet Jane Eyre at his house. It was one of the dullest evenings she had ever spent in her life, she said. And then with a good deal of humour she described the situation – the ladies who had all come expecting so much

[17] *Chapters*, pp. 60–5.

delightful conversation, and the gloom and the constraint, and how finally, overwhelmed by the situation, my father had quietly left the room, left the house, and gone off to his club. The ladies waited, wondered, and finally departed also.[18]

Though unable to make small talk, Charlotte Brontë was of course very observant. She had noticed how pretty Adelaide Procter was, and how evidently George Smith admired her. 'During our drive home', Smith later recorded, admitting how greatly at the time he had been attracted to Miss Procter, 'I was seated opposite to Miss Brontë and I was startled by her leaning forward, putting her hands on my knees, and saying: "She would make you a very nice wife." "Whom do you mean?" I replied. "Oh! you known whom I mean" she said.'[19] George Smith, who got on very well with her despite the crippling shyness, and whose male gatherings in her honour were generally successful, may have reflected that the night's disaster was attributable to Thackeray's inviting only women. Mrs Brookfield certainly does not appear to have helped. One of the smartest women in London, her comments were confined to the guest's external appearance: her provincial dress, her ill-braided hair.[20] It was not, apparently, required of a 'well-bred' lady to put shy genius at ease.

The ice once broken between Thackeray and George Smith, the latter was not slow to secure an agreement with the fashionable author: he offered him a down payment of £1,000 for the rights of his next novel – which in the event was *Esmond*. Thackeray thought it a 'stunning' offer, as he hurried upstairs to tell the girls. Ever since reading Macaulay's *History of England* in 1848 he had planned a book about the reign of Queen Anne, and after his first visit to Clevedon, in October of the same year, had found the perfect setting for it. He was eager to begin, once *Pendennis* was dispatched. He accepted Smith's offer, not only for his next novel but also for his next Christmas Book, which had to be planned and written in the course of the summer. He had already had the idea for the *Kickleburys on the Rhine* as a suitable farcical subject, but had trouble with his usual publishers, Bradbury & Evans, over it. Smith's offer came opportunely and confirmed him in his plan to make a quick trip abroad for a Rhine holiday to gather 'atmosphere' for the book.

[18] *Chapters*, p. 65.   [19] *George Smith, A Memoir*, pp. 98–9.
[20] Brookfield, ii. 305.

What might have been a problem, the question of the girls' holidays, settled itself in the pleasantest way imaginable to him: they and their governess were to join Mrs Brookfield and her baby in furnished rooms at Southampton – still considered a 'seaside resort' in those days. Rooms were taken at Park Lodge, Carlton Crescent from 6 August for the party, Thackeray sending money for the girls' expenses to Miss Truelock. His own fugitive appearances, when he took a room at the Dolphin, could be represented to the absent Mr Brookfield as wholly outside the proposed plan. He came and went, delaying his departure for the Continent, for he was extremely happy. Anny and Minny too were enjoying their holiday, delighted to have the baby as a playfellow. At last he left them, and the day after his departure he wrote to Jane Brookfield: 'I wonder whether ever again I shall have such a happy peaceful fortnight as that last? How sunshiny the landscape remains in my mind, I hope for always; and the smiles of dear children and the aspect of the kindest and tenderest face in the world to me . . . . How it takes off the solitude and eases it! May it continue pray God till your head is as white as mine . . . . O Love and Duty – I hope you'll never leave us quite! Instead of being unhappy because that delightful holiday is over or all but over, I intend that the thoughts of it should serve to make me only the more cheerful and help me, please God, to do my duty better.'[21] How much of his most intimate feeling and experience went into the writing of *Esmond*, the product of the next crucial year, is best realized by reading such confessions of his faith to Mrs Brookfield.

Mrs Brookfield, like many of the ladies of her time and class, thought it incumbent on her to visit the local school. She did so one day, taking Anny with her. They arrived to a scene of pandemonium, the whole class of girls being in uproar, three of them in weeping hysterics and one near fainting. It appeared the clerical headmaster had just been beating them 'for inattention at church'. Mrs Brookfield reported somewhat humorously to her husband on the affair, in his capacity as Inspector of Schools, urgently prompted to do so by Anny who, she wrote, had 'quite burst into tears at his cruelty and has been urging me to tell you and get you to mention it in your Report of the school'.[22] As the grandmother of the girl who had fainted was taking up the affair, Mrs Brookfield seemed to think she was justified in troubling her husband; though

[21] Ray, iv. 426, Appendix xxvi.   [22] Brookfield, ii. 319.

she assured him that 'no stick' had been used on the girls, only the master's hand.

An autumn of intense pressure of work on Thackeray, with *Pendennis* to finish (it was in fact finished on 28 November), and *The Kickleburys* to write and produce before Christmas, meant in consequence a dull time for the girls. They were kept hard at their lessons, but enlivened by the prospect of Christmas in Paris, which Thackeray had promised them in compensation once his commitments were out of the way. In the event, their treat was postponed by a death in the Brookfield family. Mrs Brookfield's young cousin Arthur Hallam, the historian's son, died suddenly and was buried at Clevedon on 23 December. Thackeray did not hesitate to attend the funeral, to bring what consolation he could to the bereaved family of which he felt himself so much a part. To Anny he wrote on 24 December in regret and explanation for missing their Christmas treat and trusting to her good sense: 'My dearest Fat – This will be one more of those disappointments which are blighting your miserable existence.' He was much shaken by the funeral and from witnessing the father's grief; but it roused him to make one clear behest regarding his own, whenever it might be: 'But the ceremonial and the scarfs, and feathers and hatbands of the Funeral annoyed me. . . . When I am buried, you will have the goodness to remember that there are no hatbands scarfs or feathers.'[23] It was a command which, when the time came, his daughters adhered to strictly.

He wrote to his mother on 3 January to assure her that he was only waiting now for the Channel storms to abate to bring the girls over for a two- or three-week holiday; and promising her further their company during his long absence in America later in the year. It was the first mention of the dreaded separation that his projected lecture-tours would bring. His mother, he promised her, should attend their inaugural series in London in the coming May. The year 1851 promised from its very opening to be decisive for him; he little knew how decisive.

With the girls he crossed over on 8 January, deposited them with their grandparents, took expensive quarters for himself near by, worked all day, and tried to amuse himself at night. Bereft of Mrs Brookfield, he was wretched; and there was little in his surroundings to cheer him. He had briefly visited his parents in the summer,

[23] Ray, ii. 716–17.

but it was a full year since he had spent much time in their house, and what he found now shocked and pained him. While his own life-style was greatly enlarged by his success, it seemed to him that theirs had grown narrower and meaner in the interval. He wondered what his emancipated young women would make of the change. He wrote to Mrs Brookfield: 'My old folks seem happy in their quarters and good old GP bears the bore of the children constantly in his room with great good humour. But ah somehow its a dismal end to a career. A famous beauty and a soldier who has been in 20 battles and led a half dozen of storming parties to end in a garret – and its not the poverty I mean but the undignified dignity, the twopenny toadies, the twaddling mean society.' He doubted whether the girls would be happy for long in Paris: 'the simple habits of our old people will hardly suit the little women. Even in my absence in America I don't quite like having them altogether here. I wonder if an amiable family as is very kind to me will give them hospitality for a month?'[24] He was already looking to her to mitigate the misery of that prospect, for the girls as for himself. He still saw her as the one steady beacon in a shifting world.

It was in the course of this visit to Paris in January 1851 that Anny witnessed yet another turning-point in French history: the caracoling figure of the 'Brummagen Emperor', Napoleon III, 'in a cocked hat and on an arab steed' riding down the Champs Élysées, barely a month after the *coup d'état* that carried him to power. 'Shall I ever forget', she wrote, 'the sight of the enthusiastic crowds lining the way to see the President entering Paris in a cocked hat on a curveting Arabian steed . . . to be followed in a year or two by the still more splendid apparition of Napoleon III riding into Paris along the road the great Emperor's hearse had taken – a new Emperor, glittering and alive once more, on a horse so beautiful and majestic that to look upon it was a martial education.'[25] Every sight, every experience was in fact an 'education' to the impressionable Anny at this time.

By the first week in February they were back in Young Street, the girls hard at their lessons with Miss Truelock again. For Thackeray, the prospect of the American tour at the year's end continued to prey on his mind; all his spare time was spent preparing the series of lectures that were to crown his reputation and, if all went well, make his fortune. The plan was to give them first in London at the

[24] Ray, ii. 732–3.   [25] *Chapters*, pp. 40–1.

height of the fashionable season that summer – a season expected to
be more than usually brilliant with the Great Exhibition drawing
crowds from all over the country – followed by provincial tours to
Oxford, Cambridge, and Edinburgh; and finally, for a six-month
tour of the States. Thackeray loathed the idea of the separation from
all those he loved, but it was on their account, to make money for
his '3 little women', as he always spoke of his wife and the girls, that
he agreed to it. More than usual at this time he talked to the girls, on
their customary long walks, of the importance of the step he was
taking, of the need of their help in making it bearable for all. 'What
a comfort they are those little women,' he wrote to his mother,
'their goodness and kindness to me is quite touching; we have had
many walks and a good deal of time together and it's always a
pleasure to me to be with them and talk with them.'[26] Anny was
being very helpful. She was prepared to go to school in his absence.
Telling Mrs Brookfield of this unhoped-for solution to his worries,
he added: 'And when I'm away you'll have them on Sundays, won't
you, Aunt Jane? The school to which I am recommended is close by
you in Chester Square.'

He chose as the subject for his lectures 'The English Humourists
of the Eighteenth Century'. The ground was familiar to him, and
further study could provide background for the new novel commissioned by George Smith – the novel on the reign of Queen Anne
that he had been planning for some time – which was to appear
eventually as *Esmond*.

Each month, on those days of relaxation after the strain of
writing his monthly instalments for the press, Thackeray would go
on his excursions with the girls. 'Sometimes', as Anny remembered,
'we used to go to Sir Edwin Landseer's beautiful villa in St. John's
Wood, and enjoy his delightful company.' From Landseer's they
would go on to his neighbour, the artist Charles Leslie, where they
frequently found Dickens; and the day would be so filled with
excitement for the girls in the houses of their friends, that in Anny's
memory it seemed that there were 'fireworks perpetually going off
just outside their windows.' They returned home on one such day
'in a big blue fly, with a bony horse, – it was a bright blue fly, with a
drab inside to it, and an old white coachman on the box – my father,
after a few words of consultation with the coachman, drove off
again, and shortly afterwards returning on foot, told us that he had

[26] Ray, ii. 752.

just bought the whole concern, brougham and horse and harness, and that he had sent Jackson (our driver had now become Jackson) to be measured for a great-coat. So henceforward we came and went about in our own private carriage, which, however, never lost its original name of 'the fly,' although Jackson's buttons shone resplendent with the Thackeray crest, and the horse too seemed brushed up and promoted to be private.'[27]

The lectures were planned in a series of six; tickets for the whole course costing two guineas, and single tickets 7s. 6d. Willis's Assembly Rooms in King Street, St. James's were booked as suitably central for the fashionable audience Thackeray aimed at enticing, and the time was fixed at 3 p.m. They were extensively advertised in the preceding weeks, as opening on Thursday 22 May and continuing on successive Thursdays. Thackeray had chosen the following 'Humourists' for his subjects; Swift; Congreve and Addison; Steele; Prior, Gay and Pope; Hogarth, Smollett and Fielding; Sterne and Goldsmith. An obvious choice, but somewhat arbitrary in the space allotted to each.

In Young Street the event created an understandable ferment. Mrs Carmichael-Smyth arrived from Paris to hear her son, and the girls were given a holiday from lessons to accompany her. What was a holiday for them was nervous anguish to their father, who had never lectured before. Anny's memory of the opening day captures both the anguish and the excitement of the event. 'One day', she wrote, 'Jackson drove the blue fly up to the door, and my father, looking rather smart, with a packet of papers in his hand, and my grandmother who had come over from Paris, and my sister and I all got in, and we drove away, a nervous company, to Willis's Rooms to hear the first of the lectures upon the English Humorists. My father was of course very nervous, but as we drove along he made little jokes to reassure us all; then together we mounted the carpeted staircase leading to the long empty room, and after a time he left us. I have no very pleasant recollection of that particular half-hour of my life. I remember the unoccupied chairs, and people coming in rather subdued, as if into a church. Many of the windows were open, the sky looked very blue over the roof-tops, our hearts were thumping, the carriages outside came driving up . . . People kept coming in more and more quickly and filling up the places in front of us, behind us, all round us, settling down, unfastening their

[27] *Chapters*, pp. 89–91.

wraps, nodding to each other. I was gazing at a lady who had taken off her bonnet and sat in a little Quaker cap just in front of me, when suddenly, there stood my father facing this great roomful'.[28]

What Anny did not know was that in the interval between leaving the hall and appearing on the platform, a short half-hour after-wards, Thackeray had experienced about the worst accident that can befall a lecturer. His manuscript sheets had been dropped and scattered over the floor, and they were not numbered. The innocent cause of the disaster, his great friend the actress Fanny Kemble, left an eyewitness account of of the incident. Dining with her a few days previously, Thackeray had begged her to attend the lecture, to give him courage. She frequently gave readings from Shakespeare in those same rooms and, on arriving and finding Thackeray standing conspicuously and nervously in the hall, with the public pouring in, she led him out behind the platform into the 'retiring room'. He was terribly nervous. '"Oh Lord," he exclaimed, as he shook hands with me, "I'm sick at my stomach with fright! . . . if I could only get at that confounded thing to have a last look at it!"' He had left the manuscript in the hall on the reading-desk. Mrs Kemble offered to fetch it for him, and made a dash on to the platform, which she hoped would be unobserved, to secure it. When she gave readings, she did so sitting; consequently the desk was low, whereas as Thackeray intended standing the desk had been raised to its maximum height – so that, as she explained, 'when I came to get his manuscript it was almost above my head. Though rather discon-certed, I was determined not to go back without it, and so made a half jump and a clutch at the book, when every leaf of it . . . came fluttering separately down about me.' Gathering them as best she could, she returned to Thackeray, crying: 'Oh! look, look what a dreadful thing I have done.' With characteristic charity, he said, 'My dear soul, you couldn't have done better, for me. I have just a quarter of an hour to wait here and it will take me about that to page this again.'[29]

After a hesitant beginning, the lecture was a huge success. Among other things Anny noticed and remembered, was 'the proud and happy look of light and relief' in her grandmother's face, 'her beautiful grey eyes all shining when the people applauded'. The lecture was 'over just as unexpectedly as it had begun, and the lady in the Quaker cap tied her bonnet on again – somebody said she was

[28] Ibid., pp. 123–6.   [29] Ibid., pp. 124–5.

the Duchess of Sutherland – the people were all talking and crowding up and shaking hands with the lecturer. Then came the happy drive home; Jackson made the horse gallop, and my father laughed and made real jokes without any effort, and we laughed and enjoyed every jolt and turning on the way home.'[30]

George Smith, aware of the immense interest the lectures would afford Charlotte Brontë, invited her up to town to hear them. She managed to attend four and left an eyewitness account – a shrewd eyewitness acount – of the second. In writing to her father on 31 May, Charlotte described the scene with her usual passion for detail. The lecture was 'delivered in a large and splendid kind of saloon – that in which the great balls of Almack's are given. The walls were all painted and gilded, the benches were sofas stuffed and cushioned and covered with blue damask. The audience was composed of the *élite* of London society. Duchesses were there by the score, and amonst them the great and beautiful Duchess of Sutherland, the Queen's Mistress of the Robes. Amidst all this Thackeray just got up and spoke with as much simplicity and ease as if he had been speaking to a few friends by his own fireside. The lecture was truly good . . . It was finished without being in the least studied; a quiet humour and graphic force enlivened it throughout. He saw me as I entered the room, and came straight up and spoke very kindly. He then took me to his mother, a fine, handsome old lady, and introduced me to her.'[31] Charlotte was accompanied by Mrs Smith, her publisher's notable mother (the eventual prototype of Mrs Bretton in *Villette*), who long remembered the scene. In introducing his mother, Thackeray had committed the solecism of presenting her as 'Jane Eyre in ringing accents. All eyes were immediately turned upon her and, to her dismay, on her leaving the hall at the lecture's end, a path was made for her between rows of curious and eagerly admiring faces. Mrs Smith felt Miss Brontë's hand on her arm tremble to such a degree that she feared she might faint. It was the very sort of ordeal that this shyest of authors had most wished to avoid.

Unaware of the havoc he had wrought, Thackeray called on Miss Brontë the following morning, and was wholly taken aback by the battery of reproaches with which he was met. George Smith, who found them in the heat of the encounter, compared the scene to 'the dropping of shells into a fortress', Charlotte, very white, head

<hr/>

[30] Ibid., p. 125.   [31] W & S iii, 239.

thrown back standing before the 'giant', venting her outraged feelings. Poor Thackeray seemed destined never to 'hit it off' with Charlotte Brontë, the most genuine and percipient admirer of his works. His mother, however, smoothed things over by calling later on the susceptible little lady, bringing Anny with her. Charlotte wrote home that she understood Mrs Carmichael-Smyth was the original of Helen Pendennis and liked her 'better than she had expected'.

The lectures enormously enhanced Thackeray's reputation and his social prestige. The great London hostesses vied with each other that season to secure him for their parties. Unlike Charlotte Brontë he was perfectly at home in society; and the better the society the more at ease he was. He frankly admitted to having aristocratic tastes. It brought him enemies, as he was aware, and his critics did not hesitate to call him a snob. In so far as he hated the second-rate, he was a snob; and it grieved him to see, as he had recently written, his old parents contenting themselves with 'toadies' and 'twaddling mean society'. It was not the material poverty that disgusted him (he knew all about that) but the poverty of mind.

Among his severest critics in this respect was again Charlotte Brontë. Thackeray dined at George Smith's in her company on 13 June that season and, as she wrote home the next day, 'left very early in the evening in order that he might visit respectively the Duchess of Norfolk, the Marchioness of Londonderry, Ladies Chesterfield and Clanricarde, and see them all in their fancy costumes of the reign of Charles II before they set out for the Palace! His lectures, it appears, are a triumphant success. He says they will enable him to make a provision for his daughters; and Mr. Smith believes he will not get less than four thousand pounds by them. . . . Of course Mr. T. is a good deal spoiled by all this, and indeed it cannot be otherwise.'[32]

What roused the disapprobation of Miss Brontë delighted the Misses Thackeray, aged respectively fourteen and eleven: 'One wonderful and never-to-be-forgotten night', Anny remembered, 'my father took us to see some great ladies in their dresses going to the Queen's fancy-dress ball at Buckingham Palace . . . We drove to some big house . . . We were shown into a great empty room and almost immediately some doors were flung open, there came a blaze of light, a burst of laughing voices, and from a many-twinkling

[32] W & S iii. 247.

dinner-table rose a company that seemed, to our unaccustomed eyes, as if all the pictures in Hampton Court had come to life. The chairs scraped back, the ladies and gentlemen advanced together over the shining floors.

'I can remember their high heels clicking on the floor; they were in the dress of the court of King Charles II, the ladies beautiful, dignified and excited. There was one, lovely and animated in yellow; I remember her pearls shining. Another seemed to us even more beautiful, as she crossed the room, all dressed in black, but she, I think, was not going to the ball; and then somebody began to say Sir Edwin Landseer had promised to rouge them and then everybody to call out for him, and then there was an outcry about his moustaches that "really must be shaved off" for they were not in keeping with his dress.

'Then, as in a dream, we went off to some other great house, Bath House[33] perhaps, where one lady, more magnificently dressed than all the others, was sitting in a wax-lighted dressing-room and just behind her chair stood a smiling gentleman, also in court dress, whom my father knew, and he held up something in one hand and laughed, and said he must go back to the house from whence he had come and the lady thanked him and called him Sir Edwin. We could not understand who this Sir Edwin was, who seemed to be wherever we went, nor why he should put on the rouge. Then a fairy thundering chariot carried off this splendid lady and the nosegays of the hanging footmen seemed to scent the air as the equipage drove off, under the covered way . . . there was again a third house where we found more pictures, two beautiful alive young pictures and their mother, for whom a parcel was brought in post-haste, containing a jewel all dropping with pearls. That evening was always the nearest approach to a live fairy tale that we ever lived; and that ball more brilliant than any we ever beheld.'[34]

That summer was marked for Anny by two other memorable events. On 9 June, when she was just turned fourteen, her father first began to make use of her as his secretary, as she proudly recorded, and to dictate his books to her. It became a close partnership that ended only with his death. Her large sprawling writing first appears in the manuscript of *Esmond*, and gradually, as use refined it, figured neatly in all succeeding manuscripts.

<hr />

[33] The town house in Piccadilly of Lord and Lady Ashburton, who soon became friends of Thackeray.

[34] Ritchie *Letters*, pp. 35–7.

The other notable event of that summer was the girls' first Continental holiday outside France or Belgium, on which their father took them immediately at the close of the lecture series. The last lecture was given on 3 July and, exactly a week later, they sailed from St. Katharine's Docks for a six-weeks' tour up the Rhine, through Switzerland and into Italy. Every incident of that first contact with truly foreign towns and famous beauty spots made a deep impression on Anny's receptive mind, and she left a breathless summary of its highlights. In her estimation it was the 'Grand Tour of Europe', much grander than all the summers spent abroad with their grandparents during their Parisian childhood; this 'was to be something different from anything we had ever known before', and their 'young souls thrilled with expectation'.

They had started 'one sleety summer morning from London Bridge', from where the Antwerp packets sailed. Thackeray 'had bought a gray wide-awake hat for the journey, and he had a new sketch-book in his pocket, besides two smaller ones for us, which he produced as the steamer was starting.'[35] It was a night crossing. At that time in their youth they stayed on deck (though there was a general Ladies' Cabin below) and braved out the discomforts. The sea was rough, the decks were awash, and smuts from the funnel kept pouring down upon them, but bad as it was the crossing was the gateway to untold delights. The Kingsley family were on board, young Charles Kingsley and his parents, the Vicar of Chelsea and his wife, by whom the Thackeray girls were welcomed and under whose umbrella they took refuge. Remembering how young and inexperienced they were – 'scatter-brained little girls', Anny admitted – she was chiefly conscious in retrospect of their ill-judged packing, which included every unwanted article imaginable and lacked every necessity. The thought of one acquisition, however, consoled her: 'I felt, that whatever else might be deficient', she wrote, 'our *new bonnets* would bring us triumphantly out of every crisis. They were alike, but with a difference of blue and pink wreaths of acacia and brilliant in ribbons to match, at a time when people affected less dazzling colours than now. Of course these treasures were not for the Channel . . . they were carefully packed away. . . . When the happy moment came at last, and we had reached foreign parts and issued out of the hotel dressed and wreathed and triumphantly splendid, my father said: "My dear children, go back and put those bonnets in your box and don't ever

[35] *Chapters*, p. 104.

wear them any more! Why, you would be mobbed in these places if you walked out alone in such ribbons!"[36] She remembered the awfulness of the moment. Minny, being only eleven, did not care; 'but at thirteen and fourteen one's clothes begin to strike root. I felt disgraced . . . utterly crushed, and I turned away to hide my tears.'[37]

Their destination was the Italian Lakes. From every stop on the route, from Coblenz, and Heidelberg, from Baden, Strasbourg, and Basle, Thackeray sent letters home, reporting on their progress. It was all old ground to him, but it was the children's reactions that interested him most. 'The Journey has been very pleasant', he wrote to his mother from Heidelberg on 15 July, '. . . and my dearest Nanny enjoys it delightfully – not quite so much Minny who is scarce old enough – but she is very pleased in her way, and to see them makes me pleased, and we rush on very gaily together'.[38]

Five days later, from Baden, he wrote to Mrs Brookfield – more frankly than to his mother: he was worried sick at getting no letters from her, despite the minute posting instructions he had given. Minny also was causing him anxiety. Usually so sweet-tempered, she had proved refractory from the outset; she was too young to appreciate the sights and missed her pets and dolls. At eleven, she was as much younger for her age as Anny was advanced. Thackeray watched her, nonplussed at her tantrums, her 'beckified arts and ways', spiteful to Anny, sweet as syrup to him – 'so unlike her usual self.' He was never quite easy in his mind about her mental stability, remembering the warning the doctor had given him after Isabella's collapse. The girls had always been bound up in each other and any disharmony was unnatural between them. Great was his relief, therefore, when on returning from a long walk up the mountain side he found them happily absorbed. 'There was Anny with Minny on her knees and telling her a story, with a sweet maternal kindness and patience, God bless her – This touched me very much and I didn't leave them again till bed time.' Describing their subsequent journeys by train and by boat, he was charmed at the way Minny, restored to good humour and cheerfulness, 'laid out the table of the first class carriage (they are like little saloons and delightful to travel in) with all the contents of the travelling-bag, books, O de Cologne, ink, etc. . . . the sight of the young ones' happiness is an immense pleasure to me; and these calm sweet landscapes bring me calm and

[36] Ibid.   [37] Ibid, pp. 104–5.   [38] Ray, ii. 791.

delight too.' A few days later, on the route down into Italy, he continued his long letter to Mrs Brookfield: 'As for my dear young ones, I am as happy with them as possible. Anny is a fat lump of pure gold – the kindest dearest creature as well as a wag of the first order. It is an immense blessing that Heaven has given me such an artless affectionate companion . . . O may she never fall in love absurdly and marry an ass! Luckily as she has no money nor no beauty people won't be tempted: and if she will but make her Father her confidant, I think the donkey wont long keep his ground in her heart.'[39] He could as yet think as selfishly as this, Anny being a mere child, but as she grew older it became a very real fear that she would wreck her life by some misplaced love, and that he would lose her. His own misfortunes made him doubly apprehensive.

Thackeray himself was wretched for most of the journey because of the separation from Mrs Brookfield; and, as the days passed, the absence of letters from her. He was impatient to return home, but nothing would make him cut short the children's pleasure. At the end of the month he wrote to his mother: 'the Swiss week was a series of wonderful sights and golden days; and the best sight of all was the happiness of my dearest little women.'[40] On the return journey they visited Weimar where he had spent six months in his student days, and seen the aged Goethe and been presented at court. For Anny it was an entrancing experience, finding herself 'actually *alive* in past shadow, almost living it alongside with him'; meeting his former tutor, walking up the street where his old lodgings were, looking up at the shutters of the first-floor rooms where he had lived; seeing the sights, calling on the ladies of the Goethe family, visiting his house, hearing everywhere the name of Goethe mentioned. 'At the age that I was then', she recorded, 'impressions are so vivid that I have always all my life had a vague feeling of having been in Goethe's presence. We seemed to find something of it everywhere, most of all in the little garden-house, in the bare and simple room where he used to write . . . and my father's pleasure and happy emotion gave a value and importance to every tiny detail of that short but happy time.'[41]

[39] Ray, ii. 793.   [40] Ray, ii. 796.   [41] *Chapters*, p. 116.

CHAPTER 6

PAYING GLAD LIFE'S ARREARS

THEY were back home by 22 August. Thackeray, who had had no letters from Mrs Brookfield at any stage of the journey, hurried round to Cadogan Place at the earliest moment, dreading to hear that she was ill. The situation that greeted him was far more shattering. Jane met him with an incoherent edict. In the absence of the master of the house, it was left to the tearful Jane to convey his orders to Thackeray that they were to cease their relationship. It had become compromising to her and irksome to him, was the gist of her husband's message, and he must beg Thackeray to discontinue his visits.

Thackeray was at first incredulous, then furious. Jane knew better than anyone how 'innocent' had been their connection – how agonizingly innocent at times for him – and for her to submit meekly to her husband's sudden tyranny looked like an admission of guilt. Jane was without defence. Her weakness and total compliance were instigated, Thackeray had every reason to suspect, as much by the pressure brought to bear on her by her uncle, Henry Hallam – who had never approved the friendship with Thackeray – as under pressure from her husband. She was highly susceptible to her family's feelings, in comparison with which, Thackeray bitterly perceived, his own ranked low. He had served his purpose when she had need of him, during the long years of her husband's indifference, though she was not honest enough with herself to acknowledge as much. Brookfield's jealousy was now roused and he demanded her total subservience. She declared herself greatly alarmed on the score of his health, advancing that, rather than the plain fact of his jealousy, as the reason for her submission. Brookfield believed himself a sick man (so she reported), he had a cough (probably the result of overstraining his voice in the pulpit), and was unlikely to survive another winter in England. He had decided therefore to winter abroad, and her place was indisputably at his side. It was also a fact that he had been considerably piqued by Jane's remaining in London throughout the previous season to attend Thackeray's lectures, whilst he had gone to the seaside by himself. Even when she did join him on the coast, the continuous stream of Thackeray's letters from abroad only served to envenom the situation. He forbade her to answer them.

Her total lack of fight in defending a friendship that had been dear to her – Thackeray had fondly believed as dear to her as to him – was what shocked and wounded him. Though heard from her own lips, he could not believe she spoke of her own free will and he returned to the charge over and over again. At last Brookfield, having sheltered long enough behind her, returned to face his one-time friend and make the situation painfully clear to him. He would no longer tolerate his wife's intimacy with Thackeray. Thackeray's rage was commensurate with his passion. Conscious of all he had forgone in loyalty to his friend and the absolute 'virtue' of the friendship between him and Jane, he did not spare Brookfield in the fearful scene that ensued. Yet as he left the house – for ever – he knew that the injury he had sustained did not come from Brookfield but from Jane, who had allowed such a catastrophe to happen. Hers was the treachery, not Brookfield's.

Thackeray's mind was in such a turmoil that he could not bear to stay any longer in London. He packed his bags and, leaving the girls and the house in the care of Miss Truelock, hurried away without purpose or objective, as his restless itinerary shows. Possibly some idea of safeguarding his health – he might indeed fear a stroke – dictated his movements. He went to Matlock, then to Chatsworth, and Bakewell. From there, on 24 September, he wrote a laconic note to Anny: 'My dearest Fat – I write to tell the place is pretty and I'm quite well. Send letters tomorrow to The Rutland Arms, Bakewell, and God bless you.'[1]

The tone of his note to Anny would seem to indicate that he had taken her into his confidence and that she knew the cause of his sudden flight and of his misery. It is unlikely that he could hide it from anyone. Anny recorded later that it was from this year that she became her father's secretary and worked in closest contact with him. Mrs Brookfield's desertion would have to be explained, in part at least, to the girls, for they had been so accustomed to visiting her since the baby's birth.

[1] Ray, ii. 802.

Mercifully for Thackeray, he had a very full programme of work to keep him sane. By the end of October, before the Brookfields' departure for Madeira for the winter, Thackeray was persuaded by their mutual friends, Lord and Lady Ashburton, to meet them at a farewell house party at the Ashburtons' house in Hampshire, The Grange, from where he wrote to Anny on 10 November, showing that she was by then fully aware of the situation: 'My dearest Fat. Things went off very comfutably, and I'm very glad I came down to shake hands with poor Brookfield and poorer Mrs. B. She looks and is worse than he I think.'[2] To his mother, from whom he had never hidden his feelings for Jane, he wrote on 10 November: 'The Brookfield party is finally off for Madeira and we met at the Grange and parted not friends, but not enemies – and so there's an end of it.'[3] It was the end of the happiness, of the trust, of the confidence that her friendship had brought him, but it was not the end of his love or of his suffering. Both lasted to the end of his life.

The sense of betrayal and of outraged loss, together with his continued longing for her, coloured the novel on which he was engaged – under contract to George Smith to produce it by the following May before his American tour. *Esmond* was the book he had been so much looking forward to writing. Aware of the obsessive suffering under which he had been working, he told his mother in a letter of 17/18 November 1851: 'The novel is getting on pretty well and gaily I mean – What I wrote a month ago is frightfully glum. And I shall write it better now that the fierceness of a certain pain is over. The truth is I've had an awful time of it; and don't know how miserable I was until I look back at such and such days. But I'm easy now.'[3] Easily said but far from the truth, as the follow-up to his letter betrayed: 'I could fill pages with blue devils of what good would it be to anyone? and these are blue devils that I cannot show to my mamma; as you could not tell me about your secrets about GP[4] so the griefs of my elderly heart can't be talked about to you: and I must get them over as comfortably as I best may.'

With a clear insight into the root-cause of his wretchedness – not just the defection of Jane Brookfield but the want of a woman in his life – he wrote with amazing frankness to his mother: 'Very likely it's *a* woman I want more than any particular one: and some day may be investing a trull in the street with that priceless jewel my

² Ray, ii. 808.   ³ Ray, ii. 809.   ⁴ Her husband, the Major.

heart – It is written that a man should have a mate above all things. The want of this natural outlet plays the deuce with me.' Tied for life to an insane wife he saw only too clearly what his nature cried out for and what were the only outlets offered him. His was too fastidious a temperament to accept them. 'Why can't I fancy some honest woman', he continued, 'to be a titular Mrs. Tomkins? I think that's my grievance: and could I be suited I should get happy and easy presently – It isn't worth while writing letters of this grumbling sort is it? . . . for say I got my desire, I should despise a woman; and the very day of the sacrifice would be the end of the attachment.'

He saw too clearly ever to deceive himself. And here the strength and importance of his love for his daughters came to his rescue. In them lay the salvation and the objective of his ruined life. 'And my dear girls are sitting in the next room', he added, 'busy with their innocent work and cheerful, and artless and tender as heart can desire – what a brute a man is that he is always hankering after something unattainable!'[5]

In the warmth of his home affections and in his work he found, if not consolation, at least the outlet for his exceptionally strong feelings. He could express them in novels which would outlast the suffering and enlighten generations of readers. So in *Esmond*, written between August 1851 and August 1852, he wrote as never before or after in his work of the heart's betrayals, of the faith that outlives faithlessness, of the love that immeasurably transcends the pettiness of anger. The bitterness he felt, however, can be judged by his letter to his intimate friends, Kate Perry and her sister Mrs Elliot, who knew the whole story: 'I wish that I had never loved her. I have been played with by a woman, and flung over at a beck from the lord and master – that's what I feel. I treet her tenderly and like a gentleman: I will fetch, carry, write, stop, what she pleases – but I leave her. I was packing away yesterday the letters of years. These didn't make me cry. They made me laugh as I knew they would. It was for this I gave my heart away. It was "When are you coming dear Mr. Thackeray", and "William will be so happy," and "I thought after you had gone away how I had forgot, etc," and at a word from Brookfield afterwards it is – "I reverence and admire him and love him with not merely a dutiful but a genuine love" – Amen. The thought that I have been made a fool of is the bitterest

<hr>
[5] Ray, ii. 813.

of all, perhaps – and a lucky thing it is perhaps for all that it should be so.'[6]

How matured, softened, spiritualized through the medium of art these feelings became, can be seen in a passage in *Esmond* where he salutes them as from across the grave in a noble dirge, to give them their quietus. Thackeray, in the final reckoning of his loss, realizes only his lasting gain. 'Who', he writes, 'in the course of his life, hath not been so bewitched, and worshipped some idol or another? Years after this passion hath been dead and buried . . . he who felt it can recall it out of its grave, and admire, almost as fondly as he did in his youth, that lovely queenly creature. I invoke that beautiful spirit from the shades and love her still; or rather I should say such a past is always present to a man; such a passion once felt forms a part of his whole being, and cannot be separated from it; it becomes a portion of the man of to-day, just as any great faith or conviction . . . Parting and forgetting! What faithful heart can do these? Our great thoughts, our great affections, the Truths of our life, never leave us. Surely, they cannot separate from our consciousness; shall follow it whithersoever that shall go; and are of their nature divine and immortal.'[7]

Who, on reading such passages and remembering that Anny was her father's amanuensis in the writing of the greater part of *Esmond*, can wonder at her early maturity and breadth of mind, at her independence of judgement, formed in daily contact with his honest heart? She witnessed at close range the self-probing search for truth, the dismissal of hypocrisy and false sentiment. And who can wonder that in the approaching confrontation with her grandmother, she would reject the ancient moral code to which she and her Calvinist friends in Paris still so rigorously adhered? For Anny, unfortunately, this was a problem which had soon to be faced.

On the departure of her father in October 1852 on his American tour, which was expected to last six months, no more suitable solution had been found (Mrs Brookfield being now out of the reckoning) than that Anny and Minny should go to their grandparents in Paris. They were still very young; Anny fifteen and Minny twelve. It was too long to leave them solely to the care of Miss Truelock in the London house. They were still shockingly ignorant in conventional schooling and Thackeray asked of them, as a personal favour, to work hard at their French and their music, two subjects they could perfect themselves in better in Paris than elsewhere, and meet him on his return with notable improvement in both.

He embarked from Liverpool on 30 October 1852, having funked the parting from the girls by leaving them in mid-holiday with his parents at Frankfurt, on the understanding that he would shortly join them again in Paris before setting out for good. When it came to the wrench he could not face it. He pretended to be too occupied with the business of sub-letting the London house, paying off kind Miss Truelock (with whom they always remained friends), and generally preparing for his departure. *Esmond* was published on the very eve of his embarkation, and many of the complimentary copies personally inscribed by him bear the date '28th October 1852' – Charlotte Brontë's among them.

Thackeray undertook the tour to make money for the girls. He always set himself as a target for his final legacy to them the sum of £20,000, the inheritance he had lost, partially by his own extravagence as a young man, and partially by the loss of his father's fortune in the Indian bank collapse. In the event, the American tour brought him in £2,500 after all expenses had been covered. Added to the gratifying returns from his English lecture-tours in London and the principal provincial cities so far, he was satisfied that the lectures were a good 'investment' as supplementary sources of income to his earnings as a writer.

For the old people, the added responsibility of looking after two growing girls much accustomed to having their own way, was not without its problems. For the girls themselves, deprived of their father, of their home, friends, and their freedom all at one stroke, it proved the unhappiest period of their youth. They might indeed say with the poet that they were paying 'glad life's arrears'.

Even before Thackeray sailed, his mother, scrupulous in all her dealings, wrote to him from Mennecy, while still on holiday, to broach the subject of major contention that had always existed between them – the want of religion in the girls' upbringing: 'And now to come to the painful difference that alas! and alas is come between us', she wrote. 'If the children were not with me, I would shut it up and only refer to it in my prayers – but they are here, they are under my teaching and that teaching must be from what I believe it to be the "word of GOD" – I must dwell upon every passage that more particularly assures the believer of the promises made to him . . . . My conscience says I can do no other, but it also says you are condemning their Father, and it is an infinite pain to me . . . My honest purpose is to show you that I cannot have them with me, without teaching them.'[8]

She saw the differences in Thackeray's moral teaching of them and her own as symbolized by an image: 'You put them to sea', she wrote, 'without a compass and pointing to a star, tell them they are to keep it before them and that they will arrive at it' (no bad summary of his manner with them), and contrasted it with her own deeply felt conviction that they must be taught the scriptures as God's commands to be literally followed. Already, in her contacts with Anny over the years, she had recognized a decided hostility to such a hard-and-fast moral code and told Anny's father plainly: 'poor Nanny's is a stiff heart of unbelief, and it came upon me like a thunderbolt when I heard her declare that she "did not care for the old Testament and considered the New only historical."'[9]

Although Mrs Carmichael-Smyth did not send this letter until she had had several weeks' experience of her granddaughters' intractable views on religion, Thackeray knew his mother well enough to realize that she would take this opportunity to work her hardest to secure their 'Salvation' – as she had done for him in his youth. Before sailing, he wrote to Anny to warn her of what she might expect in that regard and, forgetting perhaps the full extent of his own youthful revolt under similar pressure, wrote placatingly: 'I should read all the books that Granny wishes, if I were you: and you must come to your own deductions about them as every honest man and woman must and does . . . To my mind Scripture only means a writing and Bible means a book. It contains Divine Truths: and the history of a Divine Character . . . And so God bless my darlings and teach us the Truth. Every one of us sees . . . a different meaning and moral and so it must be about religion. But we can all love each other and say Our Father.'[10] This was as much as he had ever judged it necessary to teach the children. He did not regard religion as a subject for agonizing self-scrutiny, but as a way of life, conveyed rather by example and, very rarely, by precept, if the occasion called for it. He saw the essential lesson of Christianity to be the practice of charity and mercy, but beyond that he judged it tyrannous. And it was ill-mannered to thrust one's own beliefs upon others. From time to time he had taken the children to church, but he had never allowed religion to be presented as something terrible, a threat to life's freedom and joy, inducing guilty thoughts and a tortured conscience. Now they were suddenly being offered a choice between salvation and damnation.

Thackeray had foreseen that his mother might make an attempt to influence the girls, but he was indignant and angry at the lengths to which she went. They were sent to the Confirmation classes given by the leading preacher of the Calvinist community in Paris, the Pasteur Adolphe Monod, a man of magnetic and commanding presence, adulated by his followers and famous for his powerful influence over the young. His weekly classes were attended by highly emotional teen-age girls, who sat in rows of cane-bottomed chairs in wrapt attention to his eloquent exhortations, easily moved to tears as the triviality of their lives was brought home to them in words of fire. Years later Anny remembered and commented: '"Ah! mes enfants, fuyez, fuyez ce monde! Fly the world!" If ever the world was delightful and full of interest, it was then . . . if ever our hearts were open to receive, not to reject it, it was then.'[11] The students were expected to produce a weekly essay on a special point of doctrine and to be submitted during the class to a close examination of their knowledge of and state of grace with regard to crucial tenets of the Protestant faith, quoting chapter and verse in illustration of their answers. Poor Anny and Minny showed themselves woefully deficient in these exercises. These were aspects of religion as alien to their upbringing as they were repulsive to their young hearts, and the effect was not to gain two more proselytes to the Church of Calvin but to make rebels of them. Anny in particular, as the more mature and the one far better able to express herself, entered into a continual conflict with her grandmother which was equally painful to both of them. Poor Mrs Carmichael-Smyth was experiencing again the old spirit of rebellion with which her son had first reacted against her narrow creed. To her deep chagrin she did indeed find in Anny 'a stiff heart of unbelief'. Towards Minny she felt the more thwarted as she was convinced that if left to her own undivided care she would prove tractable. In her were the seeds of repentance. But Minny was wholly dependent on Anny and looked to Anny to rescue her from every difficulty and disagreeable crisis in her life. There was no severing the bond between them. As the nature of her problem became fully evident to

[11] *Chapters*, p. 151.

her, Mrs Carmichael-Smyth sent her son the letter she had written some months before, to lay on him, perhaps, the full blame for his daughters' spiritual peril.

Answering his mother on 4 January 1853, he deplored their continued differences over religion and the influence she was trying to bring to bear on the girls. 'Of course I am unhappy,' he wrote, 'and you knew I would not like it that my children should be sitting under a French Calvinist – but his views being yours it was your duty to pursue them in spite of me.'[12] Writing again on 26 January he referred to 'that confounded Monod', and wished him at the 'bottom of the sea' because of his attempts to influence his daughters. 'If the girls were to be brought round to think with you,' he continued, '. . . they would be unhappy about their father: as you have been.' He repeated his regret that she had sent them to Monod. 'I had hoped for a neutrality: but what you have done is your duty. Amen. . . . I shall speak of it no more.'[13]

Mrs Carmichael-Smyth was obliged to concede defeat. 'You may find some assurance of the children's faith in you,' she wrote to her son, 'when I tell you that they would think it a crime to think otherwise than as you have told them – and so firmly am I convinced that I *can* do nothing, that I have ceased for some time to read the Scriptures with them, they taking them as the word of Man . . . I *firmly* believing them to be the word of GOD, read with so different a spirit that nothing good could arise from the communication. I have begged them to read the Bible daily.'[14]

Thackeray was fully aware how miserable such a submission would make his mother – having lived through it all before in his own youth – and pitied while resenting her persistent interference in the lives of others. Writing to such close friends as Kate Perry he voiced his own strong resistance to the old pressures, now directed against his defenceless daughters. As far as his mother was concerned, he claimed the right to express his own opinions on religious matters just as she had; he gave her *carte blanche* to hold her views on condition she gave him an equal right. The real issue between them was that her religion made her miserable, and he would not stand having his home life made miserable by divisions with his children. How miserable the Calvinist creed made her grandmother and threatened to make them all, Anny was only to experience to the full when she had lost her father for good.

[12] Ray, iii. 169.   [13] Ray, iii. 188.   [14] Ray, iii. 86–7.

Thackeray knew his mother so well, her tyrannous and her tender sides, that he could afford to forgive her much. It would not and could not be so with the girls. Thackeray could write to the friend of his boyhood, Mary Holmes, who had known it all years before, analysing the springs of his mother's emotions: 'It gives the keenest tortures of jealousy and disappointed yearning to my dearest old mother (who's as beautiful now as ever) that she can't be all in all to me, mother sister wife everything but it mayn't be – There's hardly a subject on which we don't differ. And she lives away at Paris with her husband a noble simple old gentleman who loves nothing but her in the world, and a jealousy after me tears and rends her. Eh! who is happy? When I was a boy at Larkbeare, I thought her an Angel and worshipped her. I see but a woman now, O so tender so loving so cruel. My daughter Anny says O how like Granny is to Mrs Pendennis Papa – and Granny is mighty angry that I should think no better of her than that.'[15]

Though Anny also wrote to her father, she wished to spare him the knowlege of her wretchedness, and did not reveal to the full the disharmony in which she lived with her grandmother. So she tempered her accounts of Monod's classes by attempts at sprightliness, and by reports on current events more likely to be of interest to him. 'To-day we have been to M. Monod's Cours and presented our "Analyses" tied with red ribbon, but next week we shall get purple for the Empire,' she wrote to him in November. 'There are about twenty girls and twenty mothers all round the room. There is Blanche Girot, the beauty, beautifully dressed, and Miss Stumff, the stupid one – isn't it a good name? – and Zélie de Marville (Oh, if I had been called Zélie de Marville) and Marie Petit, the tall one, and Lucie de Latouche, and a great many more.

'We were half as happy at your letter, as when you came back, dear Papa. It came just as I was reading out the most dreary passages of *Iphigénie*, and the maid came in with "Connaissez-vous cette éctriture-là, Mademoiselle?" Mrs. Collemache sent us the *Globe* with some verses of yours which Grannie said were like Lord Byron and which I thought were like you, as melancholy as Agamemnon in *Iphigénie*, and Grannie and I both burst out laughing at seeing ourselves both crying a little. I wonder what makes people cry when they are unhappy, and when they are happy too, and when they are neither the one nor the other?'[16]

'I am afraid Grannie is still miserable about me,' she admitted

[15] Ray, iii. 13.   [16] Ray, iii. 137–8.

more frankly in her next letter, 'but it bothers me when the clergymen say that everybody ought to think alike and follow the one true way, forgetting that it is they who want people to think alike, that is, as they do. Monsieur Monod tells us things about the Garden of Eden, which he proves by St. Paul's epistles. I don't understand how God can repent and destroy His own work, or how He can make coats as He did for Adam, or shut a door, as they say He shut Noah in, and it is things like these that they think one must go to hell for not respecting and believing. I am sure when Christ talks about "My words" He means His own, not the Bible, as Grannie says, but I don't know what it means when He says He did not come to destroy the law but to fulfil it, and so I suppose everybody is right and nobody knows anything. Minny and I can love you and Grannie with all our heart, and that is our business.'[17]

It was impossible for Anny to live in Paris, even under such circumstances, without absorbing the sound and colour and quality of life. The Carmichael-Smyths had moved since her last long stay with them and lived now in an old house, No. 19 rue d'Angoulême, Faubourg St. Honoré, off the Champs Élysées. It was in a very central position, affording them a front-row view of the spectacular happenings crowding those first eventful months of the new emperor's regime, during which he sought by alternate blandishments and threats to hold the people in proper subjection. Anny wrote to her father: 'To-day at church we had to pray for His Majesty the Emperor and all the Royal Family, and on Thursday we had a holiday to go and look at His Majesty riding into Paris. Minny prepared a purple cockade, which she put upon G.P., and you may guess how disgusted Grannie was. There were soldiers all down the Champs Élysées and splendid aides-de-camps with feathers galloping about. Generals with their staffs trotting off to St. Cloud, regiments dashing by, all in the drizzling rain, and opposite a whole regiment of Dragoons, there was sitting one of Mr. Doyle's little dogs looking up at them, and nothing would induce him to move. After waiting about four hours (we were in an entresol) there came more regiments and elegant aides-de-camps, and I determined that that is what I should like to have been born. And Jerome on horseback very unsteady and fat, and then all alone in front of a Regiment his Royal Highness, who was too far off for me to see plainly, on a prancing horse with a red velvet saddle and golden

[17] Ray, iii. 141.

bridles, and I forget what coat Louis Napoleon wore, but he had a fine red ribbon across his body. They cried "Vive l'Empereur!" a little, not very much. Grannie says she counted twelve, but I assure you there were more. The only way the Champs Élysées were adorned, was a piece of calico stretched across the Rond Point, which was not half long enough to reach from one side to the other.

'I think I am a Napoleonist, for he has done so many good-natured things; all the poor who have pawned their mattresses and any other things within four days may take them back for nothing, and all debtors under I don't know what, are let out of prison, – the warnings to the newspapers are taken away, and little crimes are forgiven, and the soldiers got an extra day's pay. Yesterday we saw him, but as I couldn't see his face I didn't know who it was till a little man rushed up to Grannie and said: "C'est l'Empereur!" "Phuiff!" says Grannie, and walks on.'[18]

Anny maintained her independence of thought as best she could. Her father had recommended her to read Macaulay's *History* during her time in Paris, and this she did – as some counterbalance to the daily scriptural reading on which her grandmother insisted; and confessed to having snatched up a copy of *Pendennis* on leaving home as the book in which she seemed to find her father more completely than in any of his others.

The perplexities of her inquiring mind and her all too vulnerable heart, left for the first time without her father's protective guidance, would form the subject of her first attempt at a novel, the very immature *Story of Elizabeth*, written less than ten years later. In it her experiences among the Calvinist community of Paris are narrated in a barely disguised fictional form. Far more explicitly than in her letters to her father at the time, she describes her revulsion at the lessons of the Calvinist preacher – Pasteur Tourneur in the novel. Elizabeth's mother, a worldy woman, is described as having fallen under the spell of the pasteur, accepting him as her husband and being transformed by the marriage. Her daughter perceived that the root cause of her new contentment was the acquisition of power – even of power over her husband – 'himself a man in authority'. 'Now she found that by dressing in black, by looking stiff, by attending endless charitable meetings, prayer-meetings, religious meetings . . . she could eat of the food her soul longed for.'[19]

[18] Ray, iii. 140–1.   [19] The Story of Elizabeth, Ch. III, p. 56. See p. 126.

Mrs Carmichael-Smyth was far too clever a woman, and knew her son's wishes too well, to neglect the girls' education even while attempting the salvation of their souls. She engaged a governess for them for three hours daily. She was so charming a young woman that Thackeray, on his return, groaned when he met her. He urgently needed a governess to take back to London, but he would never dare engage this one. As he wrote to his American friends, the Baxters, she was 'far too young and too pretty to come to a single man's house, and too proud to bear the subordinate position these ladies must take in London'.[20]

In addition to the daily morning lessons there were afternoon walks with young friends – approved of by Mrs Carmichael-Smyth – and piano practice with which each day's duties began before breakfast. As always when living in France, the girls made great friends with their grandparents' *bonne* and this winter they received much kindness, as Thackeray later reported, from Louise the maid, whose departure affected Minny in particular. Through such contacts they learnt more about the real France than in all their studies of the seventeenth-century classics.

In America Thackeray was also, in his way, 'paying glad life's arrears', with a gruelling programme to get through. The least of his fatigues were the lectures; they were enthusiastically received and he got through them with tolerable ease. It was the incessant, the daily, the almost hourly siege of visitors demanding admittance to his rooms, from breakfast-time to late at night; men with nothing to say and little understanding, but resolved, as of a right, to grasp his hand. Some real friends he made, the Baxter family of New York in particular, father, mother, and young girls (with Sally he fell not a little in love). But he had more social invitations than either his nerves or his stomach could digest, and by the end was profoundly weary of the way in which he was expected to live.

A letter to the girls' ex-governess, Miss Truelock, reveals his views on the young American girls he met everywhere, who tended to be admitted to full social status at a much earlier age than their English counterparts. 'How I *wouldn't* like the girls to live here!' he wrote. 'I never saw such luxury and extravagance such tearing polkas such stupendous suppers and fine clothes. I watched one young lady at 4 balls in as many new dresses and each dress of the most "stunning" description. Fancy Anny and Minny in yellow and silver – the Lord forbid! Anny writes me delightful letters from

[20] Ray, iii. 269.

Paris and Minny sends funny little scraps. She has grown very tall Nan writes and they seem as happy as affection can make them. . . . Have you found successors for them? I hope you have and that you will always remember how grateful their father is to you.'[21]

Wherever he was, the thought of the girls and of their well-being was always uppermost in his mind. On his return he would be quick to see the changes in them and was no doubt better able to detect the consequences of living in the rue d'Angoulême than the children were themselves. 'Anny', he wrote to the Baxters after he got back, 'is grown a complete young woman – not pretty a bit – but with a healthy fair complexion and proportions of the Miss Berryman order. . . . Minny is no beauty neither but quite pretty enough for me: and I would not change them for girls 10 times as handsome.' What was to strike him most was: 'the funny little world my old folks live in . . . I've not been well since I have been here. That has given the kind old step-father an opportunity to administer globules – He is 72 and the brave old soldier who mounted breaches and led storming parties is quite a quiet old man lean and slippered. My mother is as handsome and as good as ever: and all her little society worships her. . . . From a twaddling society what can you have but twaddling? It's hard that there should be something narrowing about narrow circumstances. The misdeeds of maids-of-all-work form no small part of the little conversations I hear.'[22]

In the rue d'Angoulême, he realized sadly, there were but two subjects of talk that could be classed as not trivial, politics and religion, and the bigotry that surrounded them was all too plain both to him and to the girls. Fortunately there was one way in which they had profited immeasurably from their six months' sojourn in Paris – in their piano playing. 'They have made immense progress,' he wrote to the Baxters, 'they will really play very well and all for love not of music but of their father – they know what tunes I like – solemn old fashioned airs of Haydn and Mozart and intend to treat me to these.'

At last 'the long summer and winter of their separation', as Anny remembered it, were over, and Thackeray's return, sooner than had been expected, was announced. 'I believe', Anny wrote years later, 'he saw a steamer starting for home and could stand it no longer, and then and there came off.'

On 12 May 1853 he arrived in Paris. 'I can still remember sitting

[21] Ray, iii. 255–6.   [22] Ray, iii. 268–9.

with my grandparents, expecting his return,' wrote Anny. 'My sister and I sat on the red sofa in the little study, and shortly before the time we had calculated that he might arrive came a little ring at the front-door bell. My grandmother broke down; my sister and I rushed to the front door, only we were so afraid that it might not be he that we did not dare to open it, and there we stood until a second and much louder ring brought us to our senses. "Why didn't you open the door?"" said my father, stepping in, looking well, broad, and upright, laughing. In a moment he had never been away at all.'[23]

[23] *Chapters*, pp. 171–2.

CHAPTER 7

THE NEWCOMES ABROAD

THACKERAY had got into the habit, prompted by the pace of life in America, of moving quickly, of plunging several irons into the fire at once. He could spare his family barely a fortnight in Paris, for he had several commitments awaiting him in London.

Firstly, there was the contract to sign with Bradbury & Evans for his new book (*The Newcomes*). They were offering him the biggest fee of his career, £3,500 for the English rights and £500 for the American and Tauchnitz rights. The new work was to be in twenty-four serial parts, and as Thackeray had already fashioned it in his imagination it was clearly going to call for a good deal of foreign travelling. The hero, Clive Newcome, was to be a painter, following in the well-worn footsteps of generations of art students – as had Thackeray himself in his youth – in the studios of Paris, across the Alps, to that ultimate source of inspiration for all artists and poets, Rome. In retracing these essential steps in his hero's progress, Thackeray had decided that his daughters should be his fellow-travellers – a prospect so intoxicating to those young persons that they could not wait to be gone. There were, however, several matters of lesser delight demanding their father's attention before the grand migration could take place.

There was the question of the house. The seven years' lease of Young Street was nearly up, and Thackeray was resolved on buying a new house in a more central position. He had been advised to look in the newly fashionable areas in South Kensington and Brompton, where houses were springing up in pleasant Squares, Crescents, and so-called 'Gardens'. In a hurry as ever, he settled on a house at 36 Onslow Square. It was the first house he had bought (as opposed to renting) and he paid £2,100 for it, payable over three years. He left instructions for its complete and rather sumptuous decoration during his absence. Meanwhile, to complete the lease of the Young Street house, he sublet it to a pleasant young couple called Synge whom he had met in the States. Synge was a young English diplomat with an American wife. They took over the house almost immediately.

On 24 June Thackeray hurried back to Paris, collected the girls, and within a week was on his way to Baden with them. He needed to find a place where he could write the opening sections of the book in peace, and as he intended that a central section of the novel was to take place in Baden, he decided to settle there for a start. He found it a beautiful and stimulating place, but he realized that it was not the ideal resort for his young daughters, even though their happiness depended more on release from grandparental bondage than on the beauty of their surroundings. Baden, or any lesser spot, would delight them equally. He wrote to his mother on 18 July: 'The children are famous: but they want something to do. When we are moving it is well enough: but when I am absorbed in my work, and thinking of it out of work-hours I am a bad companion for them or any one: and they pretend to read French and German for a couple of hours but I guess they dawdle: and I can't be on the look out – to see and keep their young noses to the grind-stone. If I find fault, it puts me in a flutter for a day before and after. O model Governess where are you and where can I find you? This place is as beautiful as heart can desire: so pretty that I wonder rather why I go – pleasant little society and so forth for me at least: but the girls are too old and too young – too old for the children, and too young for the out young ladies. Come quick O model Governess!'[1]

It seemed that the problems of the 'widower' father were not lessening but increasing as the girls grew up. Yet they brought him heart warming comfort more often than they worried him. He ended the same letter to his mother: 'The girls are singing as they pack in the next room. Isn't it pleasant to hear their kind voices? A Mrs. Hogg, Mr. Harness's niece, a London acquaintance has been very kind to them: and we have been very comfortable at the hotel; . . . and in a word Baden has been a *success*. May the next halting place answer as well – So we go on from stage to stage; until the Journey is over: and there's no more pleasure, no more pain, no more birthdays. God bless me dearest old Mother this and all other days in the year.'[2]

He often wondered why he rushed from place to place, and why life was a 'perpetuum mobile'; but he was always restless, especially

[1] Ray, iii. 287.   [2] Ray, iii. 288–9.

7. William Makepeace Thackeray, 1811–1863

8. Minny reading

9. Château de Bréquerècque, Boulogne-sur-Mer, 1854

when in the first stages of creation, and for the girls it was the best education he could offer. If left them ignorant of book learning (as was all too apparent to their later circle of friends, Leslie Stephen in particular) but it stimulated their already vivid imaginations and certainly broadened their outlook on life. They went via Vevey to Berne on 6 August. It was in a 'little wood near Berne', as Anny remembered, where Thackeray wandered off on his own, that the full story of the *Newcomes* was 'revealed ' to him. 'I can still remember that day', she wrote years afterwards, 'and the look of the fields in which we were walking, and the silence of the hour, and the faint, sultry summer mountains, with the open wood at the foot of the sloping stubble. My father had been silent and pre-occupied when we first started, and was walking thoughtfully apart. We waited till he came back to us, saying he now saw his way quite clearly, and he was cheerful and in good spirits as we returned to the inn.'[3]

Anny was his secretary and confidante on their journey. He called her in to write at his dictation and then grumbled at her great sprawling hand that ate up his supply of writing-paper. There were times when it was a release for him to dictate; the thoughts flowed more freely. To Sarah Baxter, writing a long straggling letter between 26 July and 7 August, he said: 'I called in Miss Anny at the above moment of writing, and we had a good time till dinner-time the story advancing very pleasantly.'[4]

By the beginning of September, he had to be back in London, to see his illustrator, Richard Doyle. It was as much to help Doyle, out of a job at the time, as to save him having to make the blocks for the plates himself, though frankly both he and the girls preferred his own drawings to Doyle's. He was still in search of a governess. The great design, to winter in Rome, was still uncertain, partly because of the threat of war in Italy. But Rome was essential for the book, since Clive must study art at Rome; and it was necessary also in order to keep his promise to the girls to fill in the time while the new house was being decorated. The prospect so far as they were concerned was intoxicating; all their time was spent preparing for the journey. 'We I and mine', wrote Thackeray to the Baxters, 'have just been into the City buying things for our trip to France and Italy – plated forks and spoons not liking to take our valuable and ancient

[3] Introduction, Biog. Ed., vol. viii, *The Newcomes*, p-xxii.
[4] Ray, iii. 297.

plate.'⁵ The intention was to rent a furnished apartment in Rome for the whole winter.

The sense of camping temporarily in the old house was heightened by the presence of the tenants, the Synges, excellent young people who unfortunately prevented Thackeray from working: 'my lodgers, the best of people possible, and very helpful in acting chaperones for the girls, put me out of the way, and I can't write for them.' He fled to his Club and stayed in town all day, checking proofs, arguing with his illustrator, with the printers, at Bradbury & Evans's offices. He kept a few social engagements, and among others he met the Brookfields – he had already met them once to break the ice after his return from the States. Evidently he took the girls with him, and he reported to his mother: 'We have seen the poor Brookfields and the moral I have come to is "Thou shalt not pity thy neighbour's wife". Keep out of his Harem; and it is the better for you and him.'⁶ Was this conclusion reached by the evidence of some smugness in Jane and evident satisfaction with the new state of affairs? No regrets were apparently expressed.

The first number of the *Newcomes* was due on 1 October, and having seen it out, Thackeray could consider himself free to get away at last on the first stage of his 'grand tour', to be spent in Paris, again chiefly on Clive Newcome's behalf. It was decided in advance that Thackeray and the girls would stay independently of the old people in lodgings of their own; close enough to them to cause no heart-burning and to allow of constant toing and froing between the households. They settled at No. 67 Champs Élysées. Paris, as he had expected, was not very conducive to work. There was always too much to do and to see, and too much hospitality. After a full month there he told Mrs Baxter on 3 November that 'Anny and I have been only able to compose one number of the Newcomes.'⁷

It was time to move on to Rome, 'to see the artists'. After a lightning business trip to London for Thackeray between 11 and 18 November, everything was at last ready for the grand departure. They left Paris on the first lap of the journey to Rome on 27 November 1853.

Thackeray had brought his manservant Charles Pearman with him, and a great comfort he proved. They went by train to Lyons, where they took the Rhône steamer for Avignon, and on from there by train for Marseilles. It was bitterly cold 'coming down the

⁵ Ray, iii. 308.   ⁶ Ray, iii. 306.   ⁷ Ray, iii. 313.

Rhone in the steamer', Anny wrote to her grandmother. 'The best
of all was getting into the steamer by torchlight at Lyons.' She said
they could not sleep, but already her enthusiasm was overflowing at
the sight of Lyons, which she thought the 'most beautiful of cities'.
They slept overnight at Marseilles. She was only at the beginning of
her raptures. Recalling that experience years later Anny wrote: 'We
laid our travelling plaids upon our beds to keep ourselves warm, but
though we shivered, our spirits rose to wildest pitch next morning
in the excitement of the golden moment. The wonderful sights of
the streets are before me still – the Jews, Turks, dwellers in
Mesopotamia, chattering in gorgeous colours and strange lan-
guages; the quays, the crowded shipping, the amethyst water. I can
still see . . . a barge piled with golden onions floating along the
quays guided by a lonely woman . . . . "There goes the Lady of
Shalot" said my father.'[8] They did not as yet know their Tennyson, did not even know the meaning of the word 'shalot', so the
joke had to be explained to them. It was one more proof for poor
Thackeray of how ignorant they were. The coming winter might
remedy some of that.

The crossing from Marseilles was scheduled to take twenty
hours. Anny recalled how, though it was cold, they were glad to
find that the portholes had been left open by the steward, as they
loved fresh air. 'We scrambled into our berths and fell asleep', she
recorded. 'I lay at the top, and my sister in the berth below.' They
awoke to the slop of water on the cabin floor. 'The ship was
sinking, we were all going to be drowned', was her instant thought,
and calling to Minny to follow, she rushed on deck, shrieking out
her 'fatal' announcement to all. The steward, much amused by her
alarm, led her down again, scolding her the while, screwed up the
portholes, and brought them some dry bedding. Next morning, she
had the 'inexpressible mortification' of hearing people tell the story
to each other, and she fled out of earshot of their laughter.[9]

There was a call at Genoa, where there was time for Thackeray to
buy them warm woollen shawls and to take a local train to Leghorn
and Pisa where, she recalled, it was the sudden hot sunshine and not
Shetland wool that warmed them deliciously. They were late in
getting back to Genoa in the evening and forced to hire a boat in
company with two more belated passengers, two young men, to get
back to the steamer in time for the departure. The 'great ship'

---

[8] *Chapters*, p. 174.   [9] Ibid.

looked bigger than ever, it seemed to Anny in the twilight, and they saw and heard the warning rockets sent up to hurry their return. Barely had the sailors rowed twenty strokes from the shore than they shipped their oars and demanded 50 francs over and above the bargained price. While the young men argued with them the ship sent up two more warning rockets and the boatmen did not budge. Thackeray suddenly stood up in the stern of the little boat, and looking huge, roared at them in English: 'Damn you, go on!' The effect was magical; it needed nothing more to make them grab their oars and get on their way. It was a well-known trick of Genoese watermen, the passengers were told on reaching the ship, which did not always pay off.

One more trick frequently practised on the unwary traveller was played on them as they were crossing the Campagna in their 'mouldy post-chaise', as darkness was falling on the December day. The carriage came to a halt, Charles Pearman got out to see what was amiss, and came back to report that one of the traces had broken. Within seconds, they were surrounded by what appeared to be a horde of 'satyrs, shepherds, bearded creatures with conical hats with pitchforks in their hands'. Fortunately the postilions, appeared to be on the side of their passengers and succeeded in dispersing their assailants.

It was 8 p.m. on 3 December when they reached their destination. Anny was asleep, but roused by her father she awoke to see the 'Dusky dome of St. Peter's, gray upon the dark-blue sky'. All the rest of her life, it seemed to Anny, would date from those 'old Roman days', such a revelation of the fullness of being did they bring. The very first morning, waking in their hotel bedroom (they had gone straight to Thackeray's old quarters at the Hotel Franz in the Via Condotti off the Piazza d'Espagna), the enchantment worked. 'It was Sunday morning,' she recorded, 'all the bells were flinging and ringing; and they seemed to be striking and vibrating against that wonderful blue sky overhead. How well I remember my first Roman contadina, as she walked majestically along the street below; black-haired, white-becapped, white besleeved, and covered with ornaments, on her way to mass. The Piazza d'Espagna, at the end of our street was one flood of sunshine.'[10] After a few days Thackeray rented a whole floor in an old house, the Palazzo Poniatowski, recommended by the Brownings, in the

[10] Ibid., p. 184.

Via della Croce. They moved in on 8 December and stayed a full two months. They were still in the same quarter, only a couple of streets away, bisecting the Spanish Steps, which had been the artists' favourite meeting-place ever since the time of Keats and indeed long before that.

'One can hardly imagine a more ideal spot for little girls,' Anny recorded years later. It was a large apartment over a pastry-cook's, up a great stone staircase with a 'handsome wrought-iron banister', to a first floor of palatial rooms leading one into another, the drawing-room with seven windows, the whole effect imposing and delightful, making them feel 'like enchanted princesses in a Palace', Anny said, as they flew from room to room.[11] To complete their domestic comfort Thackeray engaged an old cook called Octavia.

Thackeray had come away to work, and to work well he counted on steeping himself again in the life of Rome. The rush and turmoil of the city had to be experienced, and above all, that transfiguring light that made everything look ethereally, celestially lovely. He could not shut himself away at a desk while the pageant of life was passing under his windows. Therefore, as much for himself and his work as for the girls, he set out to show them the monuments of Rome, visiting every famous landmark demanded of the tourist, including of course St. Peter's, which he disliked. His reactions to it, seen with older eyes than before, are faithfully reflected in his fictional descriptions, although as a fashionable novelist with a duty to please his readers, he might have been expected to spare them the unpleasing truth as he saw it. Clive Newcome's reaction is much the same as that of Thackeray as described in a letter to his mother: 'We went to St. Peter's yesterday', he wrote on 5 December, 'and Miss Anny and I agreed Pisa is the best . . . and the founder of the religion utterly disappears under the enormous pile of fiction and ceremony that has been built round him, I'm not quite sure that I think St. Peter's handsome: yes as handsome as one of those splendid strumpets I saw at the ball at Paris. The front is positively ugly that's certain: but nevertheless the city is glorious – we had a famous walk on the Pincio, and the sun set for us with a splendor quite imperial.'[12]

For Clive Newcome, the first sight of the dome, seen at night driving in from Cività Vecchia, made his heart beat, just as it had Anny's, 'rising solemnly up into the grey night, and keeping us

[11] Ibid, pp. 188–9.   [12] Ray, iii. 326.

company . . . as if it had been an orb fallen out of heaven with its light put out'. But, seen by daylight, in Clive's view, the façade was 'ugly and obtrusive . . . As long as the dome overawes, that façade is supportable. You advance towards it . . . and the dome seems to disappear behind it. It is as if the throne was upset, and the king had toppled over.' But, once again echoing Thackeray's letter, Clive felt that, 'As you look at it from the Pincio, and the sun sets behind it, surely that aspect of earth and sky is one of the grandest in the world.'[13]

The Thackerays were soon to find other friends from home, and to make new ones who would contribute to their happiness and enjoyment that winter. The first of these was Mr Macbean, the English banker, to whose offices Thackeray hurried within hours of arrival. All expenses of the journey paid, he found he had something between 80 and 90 louis left in his pockets. Mr Macbean, as Anny recorded afterwards, 'was the kindest of bankers'; he not only made the necessary financial arrangements for Thackeray's stay in Rome and acted as the *poste restante* for his mail, but interested himself instantly in the girls, constituting himself their librarian. He lent them 'great piles of the most delightful books to read', wrote Anny. 'Lockhart's, Scott's and Bulwer's heroes and Disraeli's saint-like politicians all came to inhabit our palazzo . . . Zanoni and that cat-like spirit of the threshold are as vivid to me as any of the actual people who used to come and see us.'[14]

Thackeray, observant and amused by the beneficial effect of novel-reading on his young women (he sketched them at it on the sly), which created the silence essential for his work, would overhear some of their reactions to the latest spell-binder. Writing to the Baxters in New York, he broke off in the middle of a sentence to note: 'Here breaks in a controversy about "Zanoni" Anny all enthusiasm Minny as usual taking matters coolly.'[15] Minny's reported 'coolness' was towards books in general (no writer succeeded Dickens in her childish devotion), and did not extend to Rome. Not greatly impressed on the previous year's Rhine holiday, she was now catching up with Anny and relishing every excitement of the trip.

---

[13] *The Newcomes*, p. 465 (Oxford Edition).
[14] *Chapters*, p. 187.
[15] *Zanoni*, by Bulwer Lytton, just reissued in 1853: Ray, iii. 331.

Thackeray was fortunate in finding at Rome so many friends who proved invaluable in taking the girls off his hands during his working hours. First and foremost were the Brownings; then the Storys (William Wetmore Story the American sculptor and his wife); and Mrs Sartoris, the great singer, Fanny Kemble's sister. With all of them the contacts were not only highly stimulating and educational for young creatures like Anny and Minny, but they were the start of lifelong friendships lasting long after Thackeray was gone.

Of these new acquaintances Anny declared at once that she liked Mrs Browning best. She left this impression of her: 'I think Mrs. Browning the greatest woman I ever knew in my life.' (Anny's life had so far extended to sixteen years.) 'She is very very small, not more than four feet eight inches I should think. She is brown, with dark eyes and dead brown hair, and she has white teeth and a low harsh voice, her eyes are bright and full of life, she has a manner full of charm and kindness. She rarely laughs, but is always cheerful and smiling. She is great upon mysticism and listens with a solemn eager manner to any nonsense people like to tell her upon that subject.'[16] The Brownings were living at 43 Bocca del Leone, a neighbouring street to the Via della Croce where the Thackerays were now settled, on their recommendation. Mrs Browning seldom went out, except for drives to specific places of interest, and she welcomed the Thackeray girls all the more kindly on account of her small boy, the four-year-old 'Pen' (christened Robert Wiedeman). The Thackeray girls were at that maternal stage of adolescence that delights in small children and they soon had a circle of little friends in Rome.

The Brownings had decided to winter there very much at the instance of their American friends, the Storys. Their arrival coincided, sadly enough, with a tragedy in the Story family. They were a young couple, with two children: Edith, and a little boy, Joe. The very morning following their arrival, Edith was brought round by a servant to say Joe was taken ill and her parents begged the Brownings to keep Edith out of harm's way, in case of infection. It was found to be gastric fever and in the course of the night the little boy died. Overwhelmed by their friends' sorrow, the Brownings helped in every way they could. For Mrs Browning it was a harrowing experience: her first outing in Rome, so often dreamt about in anticipation, was not, so she said, to fall into a Catacomb but into a fresh-made grave.[17] She accompanied poor Mrs Story to the Protestant Cemetery to choose a resting-place for the child. They found a plot next to Shelley's grave, where he was laid.

Thackeray had also previously met the Storys on his Continental trips, and hurried round now to call on them, only to learn of the tragedy. The death of a young child was something to move him peculiarly (he always kept the anniversary of his own little Jane's death) and his kindness to the bereaved parents was something they never forgot. He visited them daily. Mrs Story wrote about his sympathy later. 'We often urged him to forget us, and not to be drawn into the depth of our sorrow, but rather disport himself in the cordial sunshine of appreciation, among his own people, to which he had so good a right. But he would not hear of this, and came again and again, listening to our tale of grief as if it had happened to himself, with a kindness and sympathy never to be forgotten. Once he surprised me when I had in my hand a little worn shoe which had for me an intense association; he shed tears over it with me and understood what it meant to me as few could have done.' Aware of the general opinion of Thackeray as a cynic and a snob, Mrs Story saw him without the protective mask he could assume in society. 'Under what people called his cynical exterior and manner, his was the kindest and truest heart that ever beat, large in its sympathies and gracious in its giving. I think he must have liked us – we liked *him* so much and took such pleasure in his society. When alone with us he talked abundantly but when people were numerous he seemed to have little to say.'[18]

It was sitting by Edith Story's bedside (for she too was ill for a time) that Thackeray invented *The Rose and The Ring*, a 'Christmas Pantomime' as he called it, which from an amusement intended for a sick little girl became and has remained one of his most popular stories. He would read her the chapters as they came from his pen, leaving her in delicious suspense until the next instalment. Henry James related how 'the tenderest recollection' of Edith Story was 'of Thackeray reading *The Rose and the Ring* (as yet unpublished, a book of plates, so to speak, before the letter) to the little convalescent girl who was always so happy to remember that . . . the immortal work had, in the old Roman days, – between daylight and

[17] Dorothy Hewlett, *Elizabeth Barrett Browning*, p. 273.
[18] H. James, *William Wetmore Story and his Friends*, i. 367–8.

dusk, as the great author sat on the edge of her bed – been tried on her. The first edition of the book has been known to contain . . . the image of an obsequious flunkey presenting a little rose and a little ring on a salver, with, in facsimile of the author's beautiful hand, his "most respectful compliments to Miss Edith Story".'

Anny recalled how *The Rose and the Ring* originated. By 6 January 1854, 'the Misses Thackeray' were so well launched on Roman society as to give a Twelfth Night party of their own to their young friends. 'We wanted Twelfth Night characters', Anny later recorded, 'and we asked my father to draw them. The pictures were to be shaken up in a lottery. . . . My father drew the King for us and the Queen, Prince Giglio, the Prime Minister, Countess Gruffanuff. The little painted figures were lying on the table after the children were gone, and as he came and looked at them, he began placing them in order and making a story to fit them.'[19] The readings to Edith Story followed in due course.

Through Mrs Browning the girls made the acquaintance of Mrs Sartoris. They were soon being admitted to her home-rehearsals of forthcoming concerts, and invited to her receptions. Anny's first 'definite picture' of Mrs Sartoris was when Thackeray called on her, taking the girls with him. 'We were standing in a big Roman drawing room with a great window to the west, and the colours of the room were not unlike sunset colours. There was a long piano with a bowl of flowers on it in the centre of the room . . . a beautiful little boy in a white dress, with yellow locks all a-shine from the light of the window, was perched upon a low chair looking at his mother, who with her arm round him stood by the chair, so that their two heads were on a level. She was dressed (I can see her still) in a sort of gray satin robe, and her beautiful proud head was turned towards the child. She seemed pleased to see my father who had brought us to be introduced to her, and she made us welcome, then, and all the winter at her home.'[20]

Mrs Kemble herself was in Rome that winter, staying with her sister. She intrigued and possibly slightly shocked the Thackeray girls by her peculiar ways. Her dress varied – red, or black, or white – according to her moods, and bore no relation to what might be deemed suitable for any particular occasion. Anny remembered young American friends amazed to see her in a delicate white silk

[19] Introduction, Biog. Ed., vol. ix, *The Rose and the Ring*, p. lv.
[20] Fuller, p. 79.

embroidered gown, sweeping indifferently over the anemones of the Pamphili Doria gardens. She used to take the girls out driving with her beyond the city gates into the Campagna, singing aloud as they drove along. In recollection, Anny wrote, 'I could box my own past ears for wondering what the passers-by would think of it, instead of enjoying that bygone song.'[21] On the other hand Mrs Kemble could at times appear to be quite a domestic character, sitting quietly sewing by Mrs Browning's fireside.

Writing to his mother on 25 January 1854, Thackeray reported the girls' activities: 'the girls, thank God, are as fresh and as gay as happy girls can be. Now, they're going to dress to go to Mrs. Sartoris; to hear the rehearsal of her weekly concert. I can't care for going to the concert or rehearsal – A man who has been a pleasuring for twenty years begins to settle down as a sort of domestic character. . . . And lucky it is that I have work to do. . . . There are only about 6 pictures and statues of all I have seen here that I care to see again. Eh! where are the joyful eyes and bright perceptions of youth? These are transferred to Anny and Minny.'[22]

Even the Italian lessons were a part of the human drama of Rome. Anny wrote of them years later: 'Our education was not neglected. We had a poetess to teach us Italian, a signora with a magnificent husband in plaid trousers, to whom I am sure she must have written many poems. Once she asked us to spend an evening in her apartment. It was high up in a house in a narrow street, bare and swept, and we found a company whose conversation (notwithstanding all Madame Eleonora Torti's instructions) was quite unintelligible to us. We all sat in a circle round the great brass brazier in the centre of the bare room. Every now and then our host took up an iron bar and stirred the caldron round, and the fumes arose. Two or three of the elder people sat in a corner playing cards – but here also we were at fault. The cards represented baskets of flowers, coins, nuts, unknown and mysterious devices; among which the familiar ace of diamonds was the only sign we could recognise.

'After these social evenings our servant[23] used to come to fetch us home, through moonlight streets, past little shrines with burning lamps, by fountains plashing in the darkness. We used to reach our own great staircase, hurry up half–frightened of ghosts and echoes, and too much alive ourselves to go quickly to sleep. Long after my

[21] Ibid., p. 80.   [22] Ray, iii, 336–9.   [23] Charles Pearman.

father had come home and shut his door we would sit up with Mr
Macbean's heroes and heroines, and read by the light of our flaring
candles till the bell of the Frate in the convent close by began to
toll.'[24]

The main object of the visit to Rome had been to get on with *The
Newcomes*. Before long it seemed to Thackeray that he might have
done his work just as well at Brompton as at Rome, as he confessed
to Mrs Procter. 'I haven't seen Rome, and don't know a single
Roman except the housemaid, and my landlord who speaks English.' He was growing 'glummer and glummer every day; or lazier
and lazier'.[25] Rome, he decided, after grudging renewal of acquaintance with the galleries and museums for the girls' sake, was best
seen in the streets. The winter had been benign, but even so the
climate did not suit him. His low spirits and general disenchantment
with Rome were not merely a consequence of the lost enthusiasms
of youth, but the effect of positive ill health. It was only after his
return home that he realized that his repeated bouts of fever had
been malaria, 'The confounded Italian Malaria' as he called it, from
which he suffered recurrent attacks for the rest of his life.[26] Within
the first ten days of their visit, he reported to Mrs Baxter that he had
had four days of illness and been treated with leaches, blisters, and
calomel. It was not just Rome that did not agree with him, he
concluded, but foreign life generally. Cold brisk weather suited him
best and he was always the better for it. He said there was a
'something in the air (or in the mind is it?) which causes a perpetual
languor'. Looking back on the whole Roman visit he was inclined
to see it as a fiasco for himself, though enthralling for the girls. 'My
health has been awful,' he wrote to his friend Percival Leigh. He
had not seen anything of the jolly artistic life he had specifically
gone to look for, and the only consolation was that the girls were
the 'very best in the world; the most cheerful: pleasant to be with:
affectionate – *they* have been happy this tour at any rate, however
wiceswursy their Father has been'.[27]

Despite illness and the glumness of his disposition he had in fact
got on very well with his work. Minny too was writing to his
dictation by then, and he had not only kept up with each month's
number but written several numbers in advance. Reports of the
book's reception were not wholly encouraging. The publishers

[24] *Chapters*, pp. 92–3.   [25] Ray, iii. 340.
[26] Ray, iii. 362.   [27] Ray, iii. 350.

gently intimated that the readers found it slow-going. Thackeray, who was well aware of this, was only further irritated by the reports, especially as he knew that the forthcoming numbers were livening up the pace. He wanted to avoid discussing the matter, and this at least was one of the benefits of being abroad. Anxious to keep out of reach for a while longer and advance his work in peace, he planned to go on to Naples after giving the girls their two months of Rome, and fixed on 6 February for their departure.

As they were about to leave, however, he received news from Paris of the death of his aunt, Mrs Ritchie, his father's sister, whose tender welcome of him as a five-year-old boy, freshly arrived from India, he had never forgotten. Mrs Ritchie, long since a widow, had lived in Paris with her daughters, Charlotte and Jane. The news of her death keenly affected Thackeray. He felt his cousins had need of him in their sorrow, and offered to return immediately to Paris. Mrs Ritchie's son William, a favourite cousin of Thackeray's, was in India and thus beyond reach in the emergency. In due course, William's children, two little girls, Augusta and Blanche, had been sent home from India to the care of their grandmother and aunts. They were a very kindly and united family, for whom Thackeray had far more affection than for his mother's kin, the Bechers. He felt an obligation towards William to take his place now in the family bereavement, and stand by his sisters. 'I sit at the paper and don't know what to write,' he wrote to Charlotte and Jane Ritchie on getting the news. 'I pray God to amend my life and purify it against the day when I shall be called to go whither my dearest Aunt has preceded us. . . . My dear old William whose children you watch over so fondly will bless and love his sisters for their care of them and his mother. You will keep your hearts up for those innocent little girls.'[28] Within a year or two, a considerable addition to their care was created by the arrival of three more of William's children: another little girl, Emily, and two boys, Gerald and Richmond, the youngest of them all. It was Richmond who would change the whole course of Anny's life.

But after a day and a night's debate on what could best be done, and realizing how much too late for his aunt's funeral he would be by the time he could reach Paris, Thackeray decided after all to keep to his original plan, and go on to Naples. He wrote hurriedly to his mother on 7 February: 'At night as I thought the matter over more

[28] Ray, iii. 344-5.

calmly, it seemed to me a pity now we are here not to continue our tour . . . instead of making the journey at this season through France – moving out of warmth into cold, and not quite strong though immensely improved in health myself . . . And my dear old Aunt in Heaven I think would best prefer that it should be so; and my cousins won't think I am ungrateful because I don't come to them for a while. Will you send this letter over to them I am pained about writing it.' Thackeray also knew that if he went to Paris he would go to London and see his publishers. 'If in London I should be listening to their petitions, and it's better to be as we are: profit by the beautiful season: and work in a calm.'[29]

They left Rome early in the morning on 8 February and reached Naples on the second day, 'driving in the moonlight through the unknown mysterious streets and reaching a comfortable place of a hotel, with hospitable rooms prepared, a meal spread at a round table, and a wood fire',[30] as Anny related. It was the Hotel Vittoria. 'For a happy unbelievable week', she wrote, 'we lived among supremely delightful things.' They visited Herculaneum and Pompeii and Posilipa and all the customary sites. Then, after a drive out to watch a beautiful sunset, Anny awoke one night with a high temperature. She had caught scarlatina. In the diary he was keeping of their journey, Thackeray noted on 1 March: 'Yesterday Anny fell ill for the first time since we have been together. A good deal of fever and restlessness to-day. Minny a dear little nurse.' Anny fully corroborated this tribute: 'Nobody was such a good nurse as Minny. Her little hands always seemed to send pain away – when her kitten was ill she stroked it quite well, and once she kept a little fly in a doll's teapot for two days with rose leaves. We told her it was dead, but she wouldn't hear of it, and the second day she took up the lid and put some sugar crumbs in, and out flew the little fly!'[31]

Inevitably, Minny caught scarlatina too and both girls remained sickly until 16 March when Thackeray noted in his diary: 'Min up and dressed for the first time. Laus Deo.' He could then resume work on *The Newcomes*. 'If it had not been for a nonsensical Xmas book I have been writing I don't know what I should have done in these last dreary weeks', he admitted to Mrs Baxter. The book, of course, was *The Rose and the Ring*.[32]

[29] Ray, iii. 346.   [30] Fuller, pp. 81–2.
[31] 'Memoir For Laura'.   [32] Ray, iii. 357.

The doctor insisted they stay at least two to three weeks more to complete their convalescence, so they were not able to leave Naples before 31 March, when they took the 'screw steamer' for Marseilles. They reached Paris a week later. Leaving the girls to convalesce with his parents and after a short stay with them himself, during which he visited the Ritchies, Thackeray returned to London. With one foot in Young Street and one in the new, as yet quite unfurnished, house in Onslow Square, he got through a great deal of business, with his publisher and illustrator first, and then by attending furniture sales – 'being desirous', as he told his mother, 'to have good handsome things this time: and the old traps looking very decrepit in the neat new house'.[33] The 'old traps' were the relics of his first homes in Albion Street and Great Coram Street, the only ones he had shared with his poor wife. They had seemed good enough at the time of the move to Young Street, but they were not good enough now. He had some intention of spoiling himself, and every intention of spoiling his daughters.

[33] Ray, iii. 364.

CHAPTER 8

ONSLOW SQUARE

THACKERAY moved into the new house on 18 May 1854, and brought the girls from Boulogne three days later. Though considerably smaller than the old Young Street house (and with far less character) it could be made more comfortable materially, and was within easier reach of town in the fashionable Brompton district, not yet merged into the up-and-coming South Kensington. Narrow, four-storeyed with windows overlooking the pleasant square, Thackeray described it as 'a neat pretty little house'. The girls were given a whole floor to themselves (over his rooms, which, in turn, were over the drawing-room) and a personal bathroom was installed for them. This innovation, Thackeray admitted to his American friends the Baxters, had been inspired by their New York house which he had often visited.[1]

Refurnishing the rooms entirely, one of his first purchases had been '2 nice new beds for his little women'. He grudged no expense to make the house attractive to the girls. 'What Comforts they are to me!' he wrote at the time. 'My dearest old Fat is the best girl I see anywhere: and I am brutally happy that she is not handsome enough to fall in love with: so that I hope she'll stay by me for many a year yet.'[2] The girls' first impression on arriving was of 'a pleasant bowery home with green curtains and carpets. Our windows look out upon the elm trees of Onslow Square.'[3]

In due course Anny made sketches of the rooms' interiors. They show the drawing-room's trellised wallpaper, glazed chintz curtains with a pattern of green leaves and red flowers, tied back with violet ribbons, wool-work bell-pulls on each side of the fireplace, with its mirrored overmantel. A round walnut table, with paraffin lamp, filled the window recess, and a 'sociable' filled the centre of the room. All the servants from Young Street followed them to Onslow Square: Mrs Gray, the cook, Eliza, the devoted maid (who had

[1] Ray, iii. 312.   [2] Ray, iii. 368.   [3] Fuller, p. 83.

guarded the empty Young Street house throughout Thackeray's absence in America the previous year); Charles Pearman, of course; and, shortly, a young additional footman.

But it was impossible to settle. After little more than a month, which was filled with social engagements, they were on the move again. Thackeray could not write in London and he decided to establish the girls in an old French château near Boulogne with their grandparents for the summer. It would allow him to come and go as he pleased or as his commitments dictated. He had already rented it and knew that it would be large enough for the whole party, with a good study on the ground floor for him. So by 26 June, Thackeray and the girls were on their way back to Boulogne where they joined up with the old people.

The holiday in the château de Bréquerècque at Boulogne was made enjoyable for the young people largely because of the presence of the Dickens family, also spending the summer there.[4] Thackeray reported the presence of the whole family, which by this time included nine children, seven of them boys. The two families dined together, and played 'forfeits' and the game of 'buzz'. For Anny and Minny Thackeray, meeting the Dickens girls again was great good fortune. Anny paired off with Kate and Minny with Maimie and they met almost every day. Lasting friendships were formed; in the case of Anny and Kate the friendship was to continue throughout adult life.

The rural French setting of many of Anny's subsequent novels – *The Village on the Cliff*, *The Story of Elizabeth* – that showed so intimate a knowledge of French peasant life, received new stimulus from the personal contacts of this summer at Boulogne. She was seeing things freshly, with adult eyes. Her quality as a writer was ultimately to lie in swift impressions, not in connected descriptions – in images received by flashes of observation. She was keenly sensitive to light and colour and scintillating movements of sky and water and blinding sunshine – as most frequently seen at the coast.

Thackeray, meantime, was still labouring to finish *The New-comes*, and reading hard for a new lecture series which he planned to take to the States, on the theme of *The Four Georges* – a logical sequel to his previous Queen Anne Series. He was also completing *The Rose and the Ring* for publication that Christmas. In the girls' absence he engaged a secretary. He missed them sorely but was too

[4] They stayed at the Villa du Camp de Droite close to Napoleon's column on the cliffs.

harassed to find a governess to take charge of them and the house. Then a happy solution presented itself, which proved a blessing to all. His old Hampstead friends the Crowes (whose artist son, Eyre, had accompanied him to America as secretary and companion) had two daughters, the younger of whom, Amy, was left disconsolate and unprovided for by the death of her mother. Thackeray suddenly realized how Amy could both be helped and help him: he wrote her an impetuous letter offering her a home with him as governess and companion to the girls. 'Your coming will be the greatest comfort and service to all of us. There is no family in all the country that wants such a person as we do.'[5] Amy not only accepted with joy, but was soon like a third daughter in the house. She was settled in by early November. The girls took to her instantly; she became their inseparable companion and, in a few subjects, their teacher. Being small and very gentle and called Amy, they soon named her 'Little Dorrit'. She lived with them for eight years, and when she left it was to marry a Thackeray cousin, with Thackeray acting as 'Father' to give her away. He was so cut up at her departure that he was barely able to get through the ceremony.

On the girls' return to Onslow Square in October they were again troubled by their father's ill health. He had been ill, on and off, during most of their absence and repeatedly interruped in his work. The recurrent 'spasms', as he called them, confined him to bed for days at a time. 'My book would have been written but for them, and the lectures begun, with which I hope to make a few thousand more dollars for those young ladies,' he wrote to his friend Bradford Reed on 8 November.[6] The question of money was again becoming a veritable 'hantise'. He had got little enjoyment from the considerable sums he had earned in the past year, which he had spent lavishly on the purchase and fitting-up of the house. He was driven by the constant dread that he might leave the girls – like the daughters of so many of his friends (Crowe's daughter, Amy, among them) – without adequate means. He was troubled and shaken too by Russell's dispatches from the Crimea to *The Times*. He felt that his fiction had little to offer the public in comparison with the awful truths sent back from the front, the stories of incapacity, mutiny, imbecility. 'Je frissonne en y pensant,' he wrote to his friend Lady Stanley.[7]

But the need to finish *The Newcomes* remained paramount, and

[5] Gordon Ray, *Thackeray, Vol. ii: The Age of Wisdom*, p. 234.
[6] Ray, iii. 401.   [7] Ray, iii. 403.

this meant once again disposing of the girls. He decided to send them to their grandparents for Christmas so as to avoid the interruptions that the festive season with them at home would inevitably bring. He refused all invitations for himself, lacking the courage to go anywhere in consequence of his 'hawful state of health',[8] and hid in Brighton in order to work without interruption.

He paid a hurried visit to Paris in January to see the girls and was there for Anny's very first ball, a treat which she owed to Mrs Story. The Storys were spending the winter in Paris, mercifully consoled for their previous year's loss by the advent of another little boy – a healthy and beautiful child who fascinated Mrs Gaskell on one of her visits to Rome some years later. Mrs Story recalled taking Anny to the ball at the Hôtel de Ville (presumably the New Year Ball) and was particularly struck by Thackeray's great interest in Anny's dress, appearance, and enjoyment which, she wrote, 'was delightful to see. He sat up for her, to have the details of the evening before she had lost her fresh impression, and enjoyed to the full her enthusiasm over the splendours she had seen.'[9]

Thackeray stayed part of January in Paris and on 1 February went over again to bring the girls home. They would now, he hoped, settle down to be very industrious for some months. Minny in particular, only fourteen as yet, needed a good deal more 'learning', and despite the happy arrangement with Amy Crowe he decided to engage a visiting German governess to help supply it. His answer to an advertisement from one has been preserved. It reads:

Mr. Thackeray who desires to find a German lady (as non-resident) instructress for his daughters will be glad of an interview with A.A.

Mr. T. will not be in town till Wednesday Mg. next between 12 and 2 the young ladies (aged 17 and 14) will not need a governess before the 1st Feb: perhaps A.A. will have the kindness to write previously to state, what her terms will be for mornings (from 10 till 1½) tuition.

The lady came, a Miss Liegel, and was engaged.[10]

Anny was now considered an 'out young lady' and, while still sharing Minny's morning lessons, began to take her part in the dreary and sometimes alarming social round of paying and receiving 'calls', and attending dinner parties. She made a good resolution of keeping a diary in which she would note 'those adventures which I

[8] Ray, iii. 408.   [9] Ray, iii. 615.   [10] Ray, iii. 412.

hope are going to happen to me'. If nothing much happened in the way of 'adventures', there were moments of mortification. Called on to act as her father's hostess, she became all too conscious of her inadequacy in the role. Intensely interested in people as she had always been, and happy to watch and listen to all that went on around her, she found entertaining a very different and much more onerous matter. The sense of failing her father was very painful to her.

She dutifully called on Mrs Brookfield among the rest – 'in a dreadful fright', as she confided to her journal. But she also began to meet several of the women who were to be her close friends: Mrs Cameron, the pioneer photographer; Mrs Prinsep; the Sterlings who had taken her as a child to visit Chopin; and their friendly neighbours in Onslow Square, Marochetti, the Italian sculptor, and his family. She enjoyed acting hostess to them. And her father's indulgence knew no limits. 'How kind they are to me!' he wrote to his mother. 'What daily increasing comforts and blessings many and many a night as I lie awake or when I walk off moping and melancholy, I think of them with the keenest pleasure and thank God for giving them to me. Why, perhaps it is better than the wife whose want has made me so uncomfortable these many years past. I have 2 little wives not jealous of each other; and am at last most comfortable in my *harem*.'[11]

Watching the skating on the Serpentine, walking out with Amy and Minny, were part of Anny's daily round that winter when she was evolving from a teenager into a thoughtful young woman, beginning to question not only the views of others but her own. World affairs, and in particular the war news, were beginning to make an impact. As she recorded in her journal later that year: 'how I can put down all this nonsense when such news has come in this week. The death of Nicholas, the battle of Eupatoria, and the birth of an arch-duchess. What a queer thing it is to think that I care more if my father's finger aches than if the whole Imperial family be extinguished. That to me everything happens only to make part of *my* existence. Kings die, armies are defeated, treaties signed, victories won – all are parts of this tremendous play. To myself it seems acted for me alone, and I suppose it does to every other human being. . . . Perhaps Minny sees the trees blue, not green, and Amy thinks them red. How is it that we do not all like the same persons?'[12]

[11] Ray, iii. 415.   [12] *Ritchie Letters*.

Another major test of endurance had to be faced by her and Minny that autumn and winter – their father's second visit to America. He planned to sail on 13 October and the thought of parting was as bitter for him as for them. As the time drew closer he was ever more loath to go.

He had finished *The Newcomes* in Paris on 28 June, 'at 7 o'clock in the evening . . . with a very sad heart . . . That finis at the end of a book is a solemn word. One need not be Mr. Gibbon of Lausanne to write it. There go 2 years more of my life spent over those pages: I was quite sorry to part with a number of kind people with whom I have been living and talking these 20 months past.'[13] Anny recalled how moved he was towards the end. 'I remember writing the last chapters of *The Newcomes* to my father's dictation. I wrote on as he dictated more and more slowly, until he stopped altogether, in the account of Colonel Newcome's last illness when he said he must now take the pen into his own hand, and he sent me away.'[14] The book finished, he was able to give himself and the girls a six-week holiday in Strasbourg, Hamburg, Baden, and Brussels, but Anny's enjoyment of the trip was marred by the approach of the 'fatal 13th October'.

It was on their return to London at the end of July that she discovered Fanny Burney's diaries in her father's room, and fell completely under their spell. Reading them set her a new incentive; she resolved on keeping her own journal, so sporadic up to then, regularly and fully, and deplored her wasted opportunities and lost time. 'I am very sorry I have not written down minutely all that I have seen and heard. Surely Mr. Carlyle is our Dr. Johnson and I don't think my father is unlike Goldsmith, I am sure that he has as tender a heart though perhaps a better head.' Noting the names of guests at a recent dinner party, she commented: 'As I had not read Madame D'Arblay then, I don't remember much of their conversation.'

Everything in her upbringing had conspired to make a writer of her, but she was still too immature to reach a definite choice, to bind herself apprentice to one stern taskmaster when there were so many other tempting trades. 'I have been drawing pictures for Aunt Shawe but I care for too many other things ever to do one perfectly. At one minute I'm mad to be an artist, the next I languish for an

[13] Ray, iii. 459.   [14] Fuller, p. 84.

author's fame, the third, I would be mistress of German, and the fourth practise five hours a day at the piano.'[15] Had Thackeray read this confession he would doubtless have recognized his young self in his daughter, with two great differences: whereas she had abundant enthusiasm and he was indolent by nature, he had the genius that compels a man in spite of himself, and she manifestly lacked direction.

The girls' wretchedness in their grandparents' home during Thackeray's previous absence in America was still too fresh in their memories for the arrangement to be repeated. They were considered old enough this time to travel under the wing of Mrs Sartoris, who was wintering in Paris, and to live on their own, with their maid, Eliza, in an adjoining apartment to their grandparents, in the same old house in the rue d'Angoulême. To avoid hurting the old people's feelings, Thackeray made 'GP' their banker, sending him £100 to cover their expenses; it was to him they were to apply for cash. They would naturally call on the old people frequently, living under the same roof, but be independent of each other. He wished the girls to go on with their German and music and was firm about their having French lessons from a man, not a woman, so as to be taught the grammar thoroughly, and recommended Dr Kalisch of the rue des Petites Écuries. Otherwise they were free to accept invitations from friends. Having arranged all things for the best Thackeray sailed from Liverpool on 13 October (1855), taking Charles Pearman with him. The Onslow Square house was left in the care of Amy's brother, Eyre Crowe, with the cook, Gray, to look after him.

Fortunately for the girls, several of their friends were in Paris that winter: firstly Mrs Sartoris, with whom they travelled; then the Storys and the Brownings; all of whom ensured that the girls spent both a profitable and an enjoyable winter. In addition, they had the permanent presence of their Ritchie relatives, their cousins Charlotte and Jane and the little Anglo-Indians, William's children who filled the old house in the rue Godot de Mauroy with cheerfulness and animation. Thanking his cousins afterwards for their kindness Thackeray revealed a particular concern for Minny whom he did not wish to be exposed again to the depressing guardianship of her grandparents. He wrote of 'the trouble and gloom prevailing in the

[15] *Ritchie Letters*, p. 72.

sad old house in the Rue D'Angoulême. . . . My poor wife's youngest daughter mustn't be subject too too much of it. I always tremble about my little Minny.'[16]

The happiest stroke of fortune for the girls was the presence of the Dickens family in Paris as well. Dickens rented a small house on the Champs Élysées – No. 49 – within easy reach of the Carmichael-Smyths in the rue d'Angoulême. In no time (Dickens did everything at lightning speed) it was arranged that the Dickens and Thackeray girls should share the same drawing lessons, and very happy the arrangement proved. Writing to Wills, his chief editor on *Household Words*, Dickens had described the unimaginable filth and chaos reigning in the house on the arrival of Georgina and himself in advance of his wife and children waiting at Boulogne and their frenzied efforts to scour and 'purify' every room on every floor, with the aid of an army of porters, upholsterers, cleaners, male and female, and not least, of himself and Georgina, in order to make it fit for human habitation. 'You must picture it as the smallest place you ever saw,' Dickens wrote, 'but as exquisitely cheerful and vivacious, clean as anything human can be, and with a moving panorama always outside which is Paris in itself.'[17]

Anny recalled their frequent visits to the little low house, so typical of the old romantic Paris, vine-trellised, sandwiched in between taller houses – probably dating from before Louis XIV – and the many interesting people she saw there, who seemed always to be either going up or coming down the stairs as she arrived. An art master was recommended to Dickens by Ary Scheffer himself, to whose studio they were occasionally admitted. Their master taught them, Anny recorded, 'to do gigantic ears and classic profiles; he was never tired of talking and of praising Mr. Ary Scheffer. . . . On one occasion we all adjourned to Ary Scheffer's actual studio to hear Mr. Dickens read: but I was too wool-gathering in those days; life was too brimful of everything; I looked about at the pictures, I watched the company, I admired chivalrous Ary Scheffer's military strides . . . but meanwhile, alas! I carried away little of the reading itself, so engrossed was I with the fact and the scene of it all.'[18] As her subsequent books would show, Anny was more concerned with the atmosphere of a scene than with the

[16] Ray, iii. 645.
[17] *From the Porch*, 'Charles Dickens as I Remember Him', pp. 36–8.
[18] Ibid.

substance of the scene itself. Thackeray was pleased when he heard of the presence of the Dickens family. 'I am very glad to think that his girls and mine are friends,' he wrote to Anny from Baltimore and added in reply to some mistaken comment of hers: 'I don't dislike your friend I liked the elder best but the pretty one may have the good qualities I liked in the elder, or qualities as good though different.'[19]

Anny's memories of Madame Sartoris were equally impressionistic: 'We used to go to tea,' she recalled, 'in a beautiful old house in the Rue Royale, she used to have music there and pink lamps, and beautiful ladies and grand looking gentlemen. Of an evening she used to sing most wonderfully, and the house seemed all full of light and music. One day I went to dine with Mrs. Sartoris, and after dinner she took me to the play – and while the play was acting she said: "Look!" and there in a box was a lady with coal black hair and a hard red face and a light black silk dress and a cameo brooch. "That is George Sand, my child," said Mrs. Sartoris. I was very glad to have seen her once tho' I did not think she looked very nice or at all like her beautiful thoughts.' An evening such as this would have been unthinkable two years before when Anny was subjected to the rule of her grandmother. As it turned out, this period in Paris was one of the most educative of her youth. The Thackeray girls were welcomed by all their father's illustrious friends. Anny visited Mrs Browning 'in a little warm, sunny, shabby, happy apartment, with a good fire always burning, and a big sofa, where she sat and wrote her books out of a tiny inkstand, in her beautiful delicate handwriting. Mr. Browning would come in and talk. Pen was a little boy with long curls, and some of the grand gentlemen from Mrs. Sartoris' used to come in and sit round the fire.'[20]

Anny was eighteen and a half that winter. From the tone of an unusually stern and warning letter from her father, it must be supposed that she had shown unmistakable signs of a budding attachment for a young friend of the family called Robert Creyke, a parson. Thackeray had just managed to avoid attending the marriage in New York of Sally Baxter, the girl to whom he had been not a little attracted on his previous visit. The extravagant display of luxury on such a New York occasion had turned his thoughts to his own girls' prospects, and made him more than usually glum. He

[19] Referring to Kate and Maimie Dickens: Ray, iii. 537.
[20] Fuller, pp. 85–6.

wrote to Anny on 18 December: 'My girls I suppose must undergo
the common lot; but I hope they wont Sallify – Indulge in *amours
de tête* I mean. Indeed I don't like to think of their entering into that
business at all unless upon good reasonable steady grounds – with a
Tomkins who is likely to make them happy and has enough to keep
them – and who above all falls in love with them first – for say he is
the best of young fellows but cannot keep himself – who is to do it?
– the old father to keep the family? . . . No, my dearest old Fat you
mustn't hanker after a penniless clergyman with one lung. It is as
much as I can do to scrape together enough to keep my 3 daughters
(your mother being one): and you must no more think about a
penniless husband, than I can think about striking work. . . .
Besides has he ever thought about you? Girls are romantic, vision-
ary, love beautiful whiskers and so forth – but every time a girl
permits herself to *think* an advance of this sort she hurts herself –
loses somewhat of her dignity, rubs off a little of her maiden-
bloom. Keep yours on your cheeks till 50 if necessary. Creyke has
nothing – an incurable illness – and all the habits of a rich man – his
illness prevents him from earning (I'm very fond of him you know
and think him a fine fellow) – but you might as well ask me to give
you a diamond necklace as to accomodate you with this luxury of a
husband, of little darlings, of bills to pay, house to keep, Etc. etc –
You must marry a man that can keep you – and you've just pitched
precisely on the gentleman that cannot. I dont say banish him from
your mind – perhaps it is a fatal pashn ravaging your young bussom
– perhaps only a fancy which has left already a head that has taken
in a deal of novels – but settle it in your mind that it would be just as
right for you to marry Charles Pearman (What do I say? Charles is
healthy and can make his £40 a year) as poor Creyke – and so
despair and peridge, or resume your victuals and be jolly –
determining that this thing never can be. . . . God bless my dearest
old Fat.'[21]

It was not until he got home that Thackeray's alarm was fully
dispelled. Then he learned that the 'romance' was chiefly of his
mother's imagining, and that Anny herself was so heart-whole that,
the young man happening to be in London, Thackeray could ask
him to dinner, after consulting the girls, who had both laughed at
his fears. Was he being humbugged? he asked himself. But he

[21] Ray, iii. 524.

decided that he was not: 'if there had been anything in it, I am sure my girl would have told me'.[22]

The American tour, even more trying to his health than the previous one, was a financial success and earned Thackeray £3,000. He sailed from Boston on 25 April 1856 and was home on 8 May. The girls were at King's Cross station to meet him, having come over from Paris with their grandmother. Anny, entering the event in her journal under a wrong date (a habit that would grow on her), wrote: 'We . . . waited half an hour in dimness and desolation, till ring a ring a ring, up go the lamps, a hundred people start out of the earth, in drubs the train with its two yellow eyes flurrying along the line, out pour the passagers and we were just getting frightened, when yes there he is. And so thank God for bringing him home again. Grannie had a better day than yesterday. Papa has done her good already.'[23]

[22] Ray, iii. 613.   [23] Journal, 3 Apr. 1856: *Ritchie Letters*, p. 90.

CHAPTER 9

IN SEARCH OF A WAY

WITH Thackeray's return to London in the spring of 1856 there was every prospect of a gay and carefree season for the girls. Minny was to 'come out' that summer, and Anny was invited everywhere. But it proved to be a trial for them all. There was the problem of Thackeray's constant ill health (in between his lecture-tours up and down England), of the illness of the old people in Paris, and for the girls there was disappointment upon disappointment. Thackeray was more than once impressed by the good humour and philosophy with which Anny took these repeated trials. 'What a bore for my poor Nanny!' he wrote in the June after his return. 'I have been able to take her to very few parties, and come away at one o'clock from the one or two balls we have been at just when the fun is at it's best. She comes off or doesn't go at all, quite good-naturedly and says, "You know I shouldn't like the balls near so much if I went oftener." She is very much liked and so is little Miss Min thank God – that is amongst my old fogeyfied set – the men (and women too as she is no beauty) praising her good humour and good manners.'[1]

America had provided the subject for his next book. He had been thinking about it ever since writing *Henry Esmond*, and especially after his first visit, but had been still too harassed by his lecture-tours to give it his full attention. Now, with a deeper insight into American life and problems, he was seized by the idea, and began work on the book soon after his return in 1856. He told his daughters that he had 'found a very pretty title for it; I am going to call it "The Virginians".' The first number did not appear, however, until 1 November 1857; and he did not finish it until October 1859. In 1856 there were just as many interruptions as in the previous year. His commitments to give the 'Four Georges' here, there, and everywhere, and particularly in the big northern and Scottish towns, continually broke his concentration. Like all its

[1] Ray, iii. 608.

predecessors, the plot demanded changes of scene – of which there were plenty – but what was wholly lacking was time and solitude.

In August he made a resolute bid for both by taking the girls abroad, hoping to find another Berne in which to see *The Virginians* 'revealed'. They went to Spa, to Aix, and to Dusseldorf, where they had news of a death in the Major's family. Believing themselves needed by the old people in Paris, they hurried there, only to find them absent. Awaiting them, and remaining with them on their eventual return, absorbed another month of precious holiday.

By then it was time to return to England and prepare for Thackeray's next visit to Edinburgh. He intended taking the girls, to compensate them for their broken Continental holiday, and to introduce them to some of his new Scottish friends – Dr John Brown in particular, with whom he had struck up a warm friendship. It was to be a joyful trip, especially for Minny who was included in several house-party invitations on the way, and was to make her official social début 'in a nice little frock and a nice little twopenny diamond cross that a certain Papa bought' – as he wrote to American friends in relating the mishap which upset all their plans. A telegram from Paris informing them that Mrs Carmichael-Smyth was seriously ill sent father and daughters hurrying across the Channel again. On arrival, they found that her case was not nearly so serious as the old Major, 'in a prodigious fright' as Thackeray called it, had imagined.

Tended as usual by homœopaths, even Mrs Carmichael-Smyth had become uneasy and had sent for 'the Regulars', under whom she rapidly improved. The poor girls had once again to miss their treat, and remain as nurses for their grandmother, while Thackeray kept his Edinburgh engagement, sick at heart for their disappointment. 'In all these botherations', he wrote, 'the girls are behaving like trumps – take their disappointments with the sweetest good-humour – and we try to do our best for keeping the commandment which promises us that our days shall be long in the land.'[2]

The situation with the old people was fast getting out of hand. Thackeray totted up the time spent travelling to and fro between London and Paris that year purely on account of them and their refusal to live in London within reach of his care. He reckoned at least three months had been wasted thus 'in dodging about' at their beck and call. He had repeatedly urged them, if they would insist

[2] Ray, iii. 628.

on staying in Paris, to take another maid (at his expense), or suitable companion, but to no effect.

He hoped, at least, to persuade them to come to London for Christmas, and planned the best accommodation for them: the girls were to give up their twin beds for Granny and her maid; Anny would make way for GP; he himself would give up his front room and sleep in the 'back drawing room and smoke howdaciously in the drawing room'.[3] But it was all to no avail. He could have guessed the answer. As he told his cousins, Charlotte and Jane Ritchie: 'what a perplexity it is about our sad old house in the R. d'Angouleme. If GP comes to me in London as I have begged him to do he will be ill – if he stays at home my mother will be worse. She has been worn down by years of gloom and watching and care over that dear good old man – has no amusement, wants it – he only wants his fire side and her by it to read the paper. I doubt whether her coming will do any good – She'll have the parting with us over again – I lay awake hours and hours last night trying to see a way out of this doubt and trouble and gloom.'[4] But again perhaps his deepest concern was not so much for the old people as for Minny, who had been subjected all too often to the 'gloom' of their house. Small wonder that at last he firmly ordered his daughters home; they had given three months to their not-so-sick grandmother. 'It pains me to call you away,' he wrote in exasperation, 'but you can't live always away from your father. The arrangement must be made now or later.'[5]

This proved to be the only Christmas they spent with their father in Onslow Square, and it was a thoroughly happy occasion. In their absence a personal invitation had come from Mrs Dickens for Anny to attend the family theatricals at Tavistock House. It was printed, Thackeray told her, on 'such a beautiful play bill in black and red ink', announcing the performance of Twelfth Night 'at a quarter before 8 o'clock precisely, of AN ENTIRELY NEW ROMANTIC DRAMA in Three Acts by Mr. Wilkie Collins called THE FROZEN DEEP – Under the Management of Mr. Charles Dickens'. In the kindest terms it expressed the hope that Anny and Mr Thackeray and Minny would be with them on the night, assuring them 'that it will give Mr. Dickens great pleasure to have you among the audience'.[6] The entire Dickens family was requisitioned to take part in the

---

3 Ray, iii. 638.   4 Ray, iii. 645.
5 Ray, iii. 643.   6 Ray, iii. 643 n.

performance. Forster was to speak the Prologue, Mrs Dickens acted as hostess, always kind and considerate as the Thackeray girls had known her from childhood, and Mr Dickens was in charge of the production, the cast, the machinery, and properties.

With the advent of 1857 and the acquisition of a new diary, Anny resumed her sporadic journal. She was at a priggish age and opened it with some sententious remarks. On 25 January she wrote: 'I can remember writing such an enormous quantity of melancholy these last two years in my journal, that it's quite a relief at last to say what fun we have been having. We came home yesterday at half past five in the morning, from Minny's first ball at Mount Felix.[7] I wore a white silk gown and lilac flowers in my hair. Minny had a green wreath and plenty of partners. I had only thirteen. Waltzing is Oh! so delightful and I danced with a cousin of Mr. Synge's who pleased me absurdly by a compliment as to my dancing. Minny looked very nice indeed just as a girl should look. I am so glad that this has been such a good beginning for her.' Seeing themselves as the little novices they were, out of their depth in their first immersion in Vanity Fair, she commented: 'It is much more wholesome to be undignified and happy than to know the world and be sullen. I have come home thinking twenty-one is not such a tremendous age after all.'

With Fanny Burney for her model, the will to write was beginning now to take firm hold of her. Thackeray, worrying over his daughters' future prospects in the event of his sudden death, had already forecast that Anny would keep herself by her pen; and then immediately, as was his wont, had doubted her ability to do so. He had taken a firm line with her in her teens when she had begun to scribble stories, 'several novels and a tragedy', and forbad her to continue until she had read the best authors.

Despite the happy relations with her father, who treated her as an intellectual equal, she appears to have had an unusually prolonged and painful adolescence. The depression, the sense of nothing achieved, the want of an overmastering object in life, typical of her age, appear from her diaries to have been acute. The way ahead was still undefined. In her 1856 Journal (25 June) she was beginning to realize this. Minny had been telling her how 'cross' she was getting sometimes, which made Anny look for the cause. 'Twenty isn't a great deal but things seem to pierce through and through my brain

[7] The country house of Russell Sturgis, Thackeray's banker friend.

somehow, to get inside my head and remain there jangling. I wonder if it is having nothing to do all day pottering about with no particular object?' She was experiencing other painful effects as well, nightmares that awoke her 'with a wretchedness impossible to describe'.

It was not a secure or stable life. There were sudden and uprooting departures, long separations when the whole settled structure of family life was lost, and their own sense of young-womanhood too, in narrow and nagging surroundings in which they became children again. Their sense of dependence, of subjection, of restriction, just because they were girls, began to rankle also. The intensity of Anny's feelings on the subject increased over the next two years. By March 1859, at one of her father's dinners, her partner at table, Mr Harcourt, so riled her by the aggravating things he said about women, that a young volcano was erupting inside her, as she listened to him talking to Mr Brookfield (dining with his old friend for the first time since the quarrel). 'O ye heavens!' noted Anny of the offending Mr Harcourt in her Journal for 8 March, 'look at him and then look at me! Why am I to be contemptible all my days long? – Why is he to be so much more worth in his own, in everybody else's estimation? Why has he got work and leisure and strength and height and a thousand more advantages which I can't get at, not if I try till I burst like the frog in the fable. Why am I so ridiculous when I spar at him with foolish little thrusts, I'm sure my brains are as good as his.'[8] That was the fact that needed establishing in her mind. Once the long struggle out of adolescence was past, and she could find not only herself but an object in life, she would achieve something. Her first book in fact appeared the following year.

There would still be the trying interludes with her grandmother, and the consequent self-doubt. (Had not Thackeray suffered from it all his life?) Thackeray was always torn between two major problems: to make enough money for the girls – which meant unremitting work – and to ensure their present happiness. He was never fully aware of his mother's destructive influence on the children, for they never revealed to him the full extent of their dread of her. They were anxious not to worry him, and they were sorry too for the old woman who had given them so much love in their childhood. Thus it was that in the spring of 1857 he persuaded his

[8] Journal, 1859; *Ritchie Letters*, p. 110.

mother to come to England to shake off the 'glooms' and the ill health of her Paris way of life and have a holiday from the over-loving and over-anxious Major. She came in April and stayed nearly three months. During that time Thackeray went lecturing in the West Country and foolishly allowed himself to be persuaded to stand for Parliament (as Independent candidate for Oxford), instead of making a start on *The Virginians*. Predictably he lost the seat at the polls on 21 July and £850 as well. 'It was a cowardly robbery of a poor, innocent, rightly-served man', he told his Scots friend Dr Brown,[9] and only then settled down to the opening chapters of his new book.

Mrs Carmichael-Smyth returned much refreshed to Paris and at the end of July Thackeray took the girls away for a month's holiday to Brighton, where they learnt to ride, and bathed, and, as Anny noted in her Journal, 'were really happy'. The active quality of this happiness – in contrast perhaps to the foregoing months – was such that she and her father fell to talking about it. 'That is what Papa and I were talking about just now, happiness I mean; and indeed when one comes to think of it apart from religion, life and happiness are utterly incomprehensible.'[10] She might talk freely to him, but it is doubtful whether she showed him her Journal, which was either too close an imitation of his style, or too naïve. 'If one were to die tomorrow', she wrote, 'how dreadfully idle and vain and selfish one's past life will have been. I don't steal or lie or get into passions, it would be too much trouble . . . . I say to myself I cannot understand religion therefore I leave it alone and read novels on a Sunday because I do not think it wrong, while Brother Tompkins at the Oratory is starving and thrashing himself because he thinks it right.'[11]

The first number of *The Virginians* (the first four chapters) appeared on 1 November 1857, and proceeded regularly from then on. Thackeray was in a sufficiently relaxed mood to accept and enjoy a Christmas house party to which his girls, including Amy, were invited by his rich friend, Russell Sturgis, the 'Merchant Banker' at his house in Walton. With his Christmas greetings to his parents he wrote an account of the festivities: 'I must send my dear old Mother and GP a line of Xmas greeting and tell them how well and happy the young ones are and poor little Amy whom I left a couple of hours ago at Walton, in the midst of such lavish

[9] Ray, iv. 64.   [10] Journal, 21 Aug. 1857.   [11] Ibid.

splendours and magnificence as I have never seen the like of in the finest houses here – all which splendors, Christmas trees loaded with presents fountains of Champagne and Hock drives in coaches and four and I don't know what more are lavished upon 8 or nine young girls and 2 or 3 gentlemen. One of them was busy all day writing a speech which he is to let off in an hour or two at the City of London Tavern in behalf of the Commercial Travellers School. Anny to whom I dictated the speech remembers all the points, and the very words deuce a one of which I can recall verbally. I should not be sorry to fail for then people won't ask me again and I shall be rid of a very severe tax which is laid on men in prominent positions – We are to have more holiday making at the Pollocks, and I can't resist for I can't bear that the girls should lose any pleasure, and meanwhile how is No. IV to be got out? Well, other folks have their drawbacks and their encumbrances. . . . O dear. I should like very much to stop at home for 3 days and get on with that No. IV! It was very kind of the Sturgis's to ask Amy and as much is made of her as of any one and very well she looks too and so does Miss Anny who has got thinner and is a comfort to look at especially to her father.'[12]

He needed all the comfort Anny could bring him that year. Harassed by work and flagging inspiration, by bad health, and the acutely disagreeable affair at the Garrick Club, it was a singularly trying year for him.

Leslie Stephen's account of the Garrick Club Affair, written years later for the *Dictionary of National Biography*, gives the basic facts. In June 1858 the journalist Edmund Yates published a 'personal portrait' of Thackeray in his gossip column in the paper *Town Talk*, which Thackeray considered to be 'slanderous and untrue'. The author himself conceded that it had been marked by 'silliness and bad taste'. But Thackeray was outraged not so much by the contents of the article as by the way in which Yates had acquired his information. It could only have been from conversations at the Garrick Club, of which both men were members. These, in Thackeray's view, were privileged: no man of honour would abuse the gentleman's code of confidentiality on such occasions. He laid the matter before the Committee of the Club, and at a general meeting in July a resolution was passed calling upon Yates to apologize under penalty of further action. Dickens warmly took his part, arguing that the Club had no right to interfere. In the

---

[12] Ray, iv. 62.

10. No. 36 Onslow Square, Brompton

11. Thackeray's last house at No. 2 Palace Green, Kensington

12. Alfred and Emily Tennyson walking in the garden at Farringford with their sons Hallam and Lionel, c. 1862

event Yates was expelled, but for Thackeray the most unhappy consequence of the affair was the prolonged estrangement between Dickens and himself.[13]

Whatever the vexations of public life, at home he found tranquillity of a sort. 'When I am lying upstairs in bed . . . dreadfully ill with those spasms, yet secretly quite contented and easy,' Thackeray wrote to his American friends, he could think of Anny and say, 'Good God what a good girl that is!'[14]

After the Yates Affair, he took the girls on a 'jolly little Swiss tourkin' for five weeks (12 July to 17 August) to Berne, Lucerne, and Heidelberg, where Thackeray worked away at the second instalment of *The Virginians*. 'It was lovely weather,' Anny remembered, 'and music was in the air; the students used to sing at night as they marched along the streets. Some of the students were the sons of certain good Scotch friends; they used to come and smoke with him and talk with him . . . all seemed to be enjoying the sunshine and the pleasant season.'[15]

After less than a month at home he was off again to Paris, on 13 September, unable to settle to his work. 'I don't know what is the matter with Brompton in September but its the most deadly place to me at that time and I think at all,' he told Lady Stanley, whereas he found Paris as always 'like perpetual Champagne'.[16] Leaving the girls with their grandparents he settled at the Hôtel Bristol and to a successful spell of work, finishing Part XII (the October number) of *The Virginians* without another hitch.

A hitch of a different and quite unexpected nature early in October marred any plans the girls might have made for the autumn: their grandmother was knocked down in the street (unintentionally) by some boys and received a fractured leg. Such a tribulation brought out all the old lady's latent heroism; it was only nervous illness that fretted her and lowered her spirits. But for the girls it meant yet again remaining behind to nurse her when their father had to return home, and yet another Christmas apart. Making the effort to get across the channel just to spend Christmas Day with them, he was taken ill and forced to spend the day in bed.

Not until mid-January 1859 could the girls safely leave their

[13] *DNB*, article on Thackeray by Leslie Stephen.
[14] Ray, iv. 109.
[15] Introduction, Biog. Ed., *The Virginians*, pp. xl–xli.
[16] Ray, iv. 111.

grandmother and return – 'all very cheerful and thankful to be at home and together again', Anny reported to Dr John Brown, to whom she wrote on her father's behalf. He was now often leaving his correspondence to her. 'You see I write just as if I know you,' she told him, 'but I haven't read your books and heard Papa talk of Edinburgh, without learning to count you as a friend. Please say how d'ye do to Mrs. Brown and Jock for us, and believe me very truly yours.'[17]

Anny was now twenty-one. There had been times, as she confided to her Journal, when she had acutely felt her 'hobble-dehoy' status, in the company of such grand ladies as Mrs Sartoris and Mrs Kemble, and other of her father's illustrious friends, sometimes finding herself speechless in their presence. But she was gaining confidence and more importantly that sympathy which allowed her to become absorbed in other people and forget her own inadequacies. From this came the urge to create character and not simply to tell tales, so that when she did come to write fiction it had the merit of being her own, based on first-hand observation, and not a replica of her father's.

[17] Ray, iv. 128. Brown was author of *Rab and His Friends*.

CHAPTER 10

ENTRY BY A SMALL SIDE DOOR

ON 19 February 1859 Thackeray received from George Smith, the publisher, the text of a proposed agreement relating to Smith's projected magazine which was to start the following year. Smith wished to secure Thackeray's forthcoming novels as monthly contributions and offered him a fee of £350 a month and half-profits on subsequent publication in book form. The size of the fee and the security it offered Thackeray, in place of the twenty-four monthly parts at 1s. a copy of his previous arrangements with Bradbury & Evans – subject as these were to the fluctuation of popularity and the public's caprice – left him with little doubt on the course to take. Smith wrote in his accompanying note: 'I wonder whether you will consider it, or will at once consign it to your waste paper-basket'; to which Thackeray replied, 'with a droll smile', as Smith remembered, 'I am not going to put such a document as this into my wastepaper-basket.' The agreement was soon made; 'with characteristic absence of guile', as Smith put it, Thackeray let him see that he regarded the terms as phenomenal. He had every reason to be jubilant: an assured payment for his next two novels with no dependence on their popularity or failure – which would amount to £8,400 in the next two years. 'Prodigious!' was how he summed up his good fortune, remembering as he all too often did the bad times when there had been no money for doctors when the babies were ill.[1]

While he had still several numbers of *The Virginians* to complete for Bradbury & Evans, Smith approached him again with a further offer of the post of Editor of his new magazine, at a salary of £1,000 a year – which he doubled when the magazine became an unprecedented success. Unable to decline this offer either, Thackeray made only one stipulation and that was that his own contributions to the magazine should at first be confined to short pieces (*Lovel the Widower* and *The Four Georges*), as he settled into the editorial

[1] Ray, iv. 130.

chair before embarking on his new full-length novel. He would also, as editorial space required, contribute the occasional essay – a genre in which he was as much at home as his admired Augustans. These were eventually to become so popular as to demand publication in book form as *The Roundabout Papers*. To fill the main fiction space, temporarily left vacant by Thackeray, Trollope was called on at short notice and supplied the immensely popular *Framley Parsonage*. Mrs Gaskell (who in due course contributed her finest novel, *Wives and Daughters*, to the magazine) was one of its earliest admirers: 'I wish Mr. Trollope would go on writing *Framley Parsonage* for ever,' she wrote to George Smith, after the third number had appeared.

To finish *The Virginians* in peace and give the girls a holiday, Thackeray took them to Folkestone in August 1859 – 'and very jolly it turned out to be', recorded Anny, 'except that when we got out of the train we found we were at Dover.' After six weeks they crossed over to Boulogne, on the first lap of a journey which took them through Tours – 'delightfully ghostly', it appeared to the night travellers on the train – to Milan, where they saw the French wounded from Magenta (fought on 4 June 1859) 'crawling in the sun . . . with the bullet marks still on the lamp posts and houses'.[2] From there they went to Como, where Anny began to be ill, and on to their journey's end at Chur in the Grisons, where she had to be put to bed. Chur proved to be so captivating a mountain village that Thackeray wrote a paper about it for the first number of the magazine, 'On a Lazy Idle Boy'. 'I have seldom seen a place more quaint, pretty, calm and pastoral, than this remote little Chur,' he wrote. He conjured up 'a sweet pretty river walk we used to take in the evening', and 'the mountains round glooming with a deeper purple'.[3] But with the master's touch, he converted what might have remained a mere travel piece into an evocation of youth – the Portrait of a Reading Boy – inspired by recollections of himself as a boy immobilized by a book. Drawing on his schoolboy memories, he goes through the likely and unlikely reading that rivets the truant on the rustic bridge spanning the mountain stream, and knows that it is not Livy or Euclid that holds him so but the King of Romancers, Alexandre Dumas.

It was also in Chur that Thackeray discovered the title for the

[2] Journal, Sept. 1859: *Ritchie Letters*, pp. 112–13.
[3] *Cornhill*, Jan. 1860.

new magazine which was still eluding George Smith, though time was pressing. Prowling about the musty old village church while poor Anny was confined to her bed, with Minny acting 'a famous nurse for her sister', he discovered the tomb of a certain St. Lucius, a very ancient British King, Saint, and Martyr who, 'de son vivant', founded the Church of St. Peter's Cornhill, that stood exactly opposite the premises of the firm Smith, Elder & Co. at 65 Cornhill. As one inspired, Thackeray wrote on 29 September to tell George Smith of his discovery, and the title *The Cornhill* was immediately adopted. Thackeray rightly said, 'It has a sound of jollity and abundance about it.'[4] A young South Kensington art student called Godfrey Sykes, one of Thackeray's protégés, was commissioned to design the cover and it was he who gave a character and a face to the magazine with his notable vision of the sower, ploughman, reaper, and thresher. With the New Year, the familiar golden emblem would be seen on every bookstall in the country.

Virtually every contemporary writer of any standing – poet, novelist, essayist, historian, art historian, critic – was invited in due course to contribute to the *Cornhill*. Thackeray's early months in the editorial chair were gruelling, persuading the famous to produce a paper on time, and fending off the unwanted contributors – a task he found excessively difficult. Among the contributions from the masters – from Tennyson, the Brownings, Carlyle, Monckton Milnes, Ruskin, Mrs Gaskell, Thomas Hood, William Allingham, Adelaide Procter, and many others – there crept in a short paper that Thackeray was unable to judge, and which he forwarded to George Smith with an accompanying note: 'And in the meantime comes a contribution called "Little Scholars", which I send you, and which moistened my parental spectacles. It is the article I talked of sending to Blackwood: but why should *Cornhill* lose such a sweet paper because it was my dear girl who wrote it? Papas, however, are bad judges – you decide whether we shall have it or not!'

'Little Scholars' was published in the May 1860 issue of the *Cornhill*, and thus Anne Thackeray made her first appearance in print. She was approaching her twenty-third birthday and had nearly sixty years of authorship ahead of her. The little tale's inception was revealed later.

4 Ray, iv. 156.

When George Smith asked her at what age she first began to write, she answered him: 'I had written several novels and a tragedy by the age of fifteen, but then my father forbade me to waste my time any more scribbling, and desired me to read *other* people's books.

'I never wrote any more except one short fairy tale until one day my father said he had got a very nice subject for me, and that he thought I might now begin to write again. That was *Little Scholars* which he christened for me and of which he corrected the stops and the spelling, and which you published to my still pride and rapture.'[5]

What strikes the reader of Anny's first 'paper' is its ease of tone, the absence of self-conscious portentousness, so often present in a beginner's writing. She wrote as she spoke, too absorbed in her subject to be anything but natural. She had just visited some 'ragged schools', and described with honesty and humour what she had seen. The piece was but ten pages long and was squeezed in between *Framley Parsonage* and an article on Hogarth; nevertheless, the 'sweet paper' holds its own very well.

'Yesterday morning, as I was walking up a street in Pimlico,' it opens, 'I came upon a crowd of little persons issuing from a narrow alley. Ever so many little people there were streaming through a wicket; running children, shouting children, loitering children, chattering children, and children spinning tops by the way, so that the whole street was awakened by the pleasant childish clatter.'

Anny had purposely arrived at the dinner hour when she could see the work of some charitable ladies who provided meals for the more destitute children – six children could be fed for a shilling. There were huge containers of mutton broth, and rice pudding. Spoons and little yellow bowls were distributed among them; the children sat on wooden benches at the same tables where they were taught. Anny wrote, 'the expectant company is growing rather impatient, and is battering the benches with its spoons, and tapping heads as well . . . the infants on the dolls' benches, at the other end, are the best fun. There they are – three, four, five years old – whispering and chattering, and tumbling over one another. Sometimes one infant falls suddenly forward, with its nose upon the table, and stops there quite contentedly; sometimes another disappears entirely under the legs, and is tugged up by its neighbours.'

[5] Fuller, pp. 87–8.

The warmth and sympathy that would always characterize her treatment of children were already apparent. She had in fact visited two or three such charitable institutions, and found in the East End a Jewish Charity School which greatly impressed her. While in France she had seen Catholic Charity Schools run by nuns, where the little Christians were taught to bob curtsies to their social 'superiors'. What pleased her most in the Jewish school was the way the children were taught independence and self-reliance. Anny preferred this absence of subservience among the Jewish children, who were friendly and well-mannered. It was not altogether a conventional point of view.

Contributions to the *Cornhill* were mostly anonymous, and it was particularly gratifying when an American reader, a Mrs Bigelow, picked unwittingly and certainly naïvely on 'Little Scholars' as her favourite piece in the May number, and told Thackeray so. 'Did you?' he shouted, jumping up and seizing her hands, 'My daughter wrote that!'[6] Thackeray was bursting with pride and could not conceal it. The anonymity of his daughter's little piece was rapidly dispelled: 'the article *Little Scholars* is by dear old fat Anny,' he wrote to his friend Davison within three days of its publication. A general and unusual euphoria possessed the household in Onslow Square in those early days of the magazine's success. Anny looked back on that time as conveying 'an impression of early youth, of constant sunshine mysteriously associated with the dawn of the golden covers, even though it was winter that they first appeared.'[7]

The new, and seemingly assured prosperity, decided Thackeray to launch out upon several more or less extravagant projects. The first of these was to please his daughters: he bought them a pair of ponies, which were named Theo and Hetty after the two delightful young women in the novel he had just finished. Then he set about the seemingly impossible task of persuading his mother and the Major to settle at last in London. He found them a charming little house quite near him in Brompton Crescent, where they arrived with the spring weather in 1860, and where they lived for the next two years in moderate contentment. The repeated emergency calls to Paris during the last two years had made such a move imperative as their health declined.

An enterprise of even greater moment and material risk was his

---

[6] Ray, *Thackeray, The Age of Wisdom*, p. 354.
[7] *From the Porch*, p. 227.

sudden decision to buy the Queen Anne house of his dreams. The period had always fascinated him, and reading Macaulay's history in 1848 he had dreamt of completing the history of the Stuarts with a comparable *History of the Reign of Queen Anne*. Whilst writing *Henry Esmond* and again *The Virginians* he had steeped himself in the atmosphere of the period, but for a historical work of this nature he knew that atmosphere was not enough: he also knew how inadequate were both his knowledge and the power of his imagination, immersed as he was in the life of his times, to create a living past. He convinced himself that by living in genuine Queen Anne surroundings, the work would take natural shape, and become a harmonious part of his own existence. He had never really liked the modern house in Onslow Square and had an increasing and deep-rooted prejudice against the damp climate of Brompton, as he conceived it. Now, coinciding with his new prosperity, he had the cash, the enthusiasm, and the opportunity to buy what appeared to be the ideal house in the perfect spot: a Queen Anne house facing Kensington Palace on Palace Green, where the gravel subsoil was allegedly healthy – and had, indeed, been the original cause of William III's removal there from fog-bound St. James's.

He was in such a hurry to get the house that he bought it before receiving the surveyor's full report. In the first flush of his delight he dashed off a note to George Smith, who knew of and encouraged the idea of the history: 'I have taken at last the house on Kensington Palace Green, in which I hope the history of Queen Anne will be written by yours always, W.M.T.' By the time he received the surveyor's report, the house had been found, in Anny's words, to be 'tumbling to pieces and not safe to knock about'.[8] So the 'restoration' that Thackeray had planned had to be abandoned, and a new house had to be built, though on strictly similar lines. He reckoned the work cost him £4,000: 'all built of Cornhill money,' he quipped, 'and I shall put two wheatsheaves on the door.' He expected to earn £10,000 in the next year, and was literally crowing. 'Cockadoodleoodloodle,' he wrote to Davison on 4 May 1860, after telling him of Anny's bit in the *Cornhill*. 'We've got two hosses in our carriage now. . . . We are going to spend £4,000 in building a new house on Palace Green, Kensington. We have our health. We have brought Granny and G.P. to live at Brompton Crescent, close by us, and we are my dear old Davus's/Faithful W.M. A.I. and

[8] Fuller, p. 89.

H.M.T.'[9] Hubris could go no further, but it was a schoolboy hubris that only his ill-wishers could resent.

Of all those boasted possessions that spring, the most precious and the most rare as far as he was concerned was his health. It was a long time since he could report anything but bouts of sickness. It was on account of his health, however, that he decided that summer (1860) to try a season at Tunbridge Wells, where he had located his favourite section of *The Virginians*, and where perhaps he felt most at home in the whole vast areas of territory of that unwieldy work.

He had, presumably, visited Tunbridge Wells while writing the book, but he left no record of it in his sometimes very detailed diary for the year 1858. Of the current visit on which the old people accompanied them, so that Mrs Carmichael-Smyth might take the waters with Thackeray, Anny recorded several circumstances. They lodged at Rock Villa, 'an old wooden house at the foot of Mount Ephraim', as she described it. 'The drawing-room windows looked across a garden towards the common.'[10] Relaxed and in good spirits, Thackeray wrote two pieces for the *Cornhill* – included ultimately among the *Roundabout Papers* – 'De Juventute' and 'Tunbridge Toys', which have a bearing on the place. In such holiday mood did he feel, in fact, that he allowed himself the luxury of reading a colleague's fiction – Wilkie Collins's *Woman in White*, which he swallowed with delight 'from dawn till sunset'. Anny later wrote of the two essays, 'I remember my father showing me the Manuscript at the time, and as I read it now everything comes back. The grandparents were living in the groundfloor sitting-room; we were established overhead, with a couple of puppies, whose antics were the chief events of those peaceful days. The puppies were called Gumbo and Sadie, after the nigger boys in *The Virginians*. Gumbo had a fine time of it, driving vast herds of sheep before him across Rustington Common. Sadie was of a meeker disposition.'[11] While the elders took the waters, the girls evidently were having an uneventful holiday. Soon after their return home Thackery took them away again for a week in Holland.

He was puzzled – while wholeheartedly thankful – that no one came to marry them, as he shortly told his American friends: 'I am surprised they don't. But I hardly know any men under fifty, and can't be on the lookout for eligible bachelors as good dear London

---

[9] Ray, iv. 185–6.
[10] Introduction, Biog. Ed., *The Virginians*.   [11] Ibid.

mamas can. I have not made their fortunes as yet, but am getting towards it.'[12] He may have been earning £10,000 on paper, but it was nearer £5,000 in fact, and his expenses were heavy: with his sick wife and now his parents to care for; with his admittedly 'free-handed' ways in helping 'poor literary folk'; and with a great new house under construction. The pattern of his life was changing. Now he was no longer the literary lion with no appendages as he had been for years, but the father of two daughters both 'out' in society, and now less attractive to the great hostesses. He registered the fact, which could hardly have surprised the author of *Vanity Fair*, but the surprise for him lay in his daughters' reactions. 'I have well nigh broken with the world the grand world,' he wrote to Mrs Baxter, 'and only go to the people who make my daughters welcome. The fine ladies won't; or is it that the girls are haughty, and very difficult to please? They won't submit to be patronised by the grandees at all, that's the fact; and I think I rather like them for being rebellious and independent – more so than their Papa, who is older and more worldly.'[13]

Whatever may have been wanting in their formal education there had never been much doubt about their independence of thought. That was the great quality bequeathed by their father, the lesson of life learnt from the daily contact with his mind. His judgements were never predictable; there was nothing rigid about his opinions; he might be wholly frivolous in a reaction, or deeply serious. Self-doubting he always was, and generally conscience-ridden, though reputed the great cynic of the age. The girls alone knew how vulnerable he could be in his affections, how completely ruled by them. The unchanging and constant butt of his sarcasm was pretension of every sort. From such a father they had never suffered tyranny of any kind and were probably unique in their time and circle – as girls – for the freedom they had enjoyed.

Only during his first absence in America, when subjected to the regimen of their grandmother, had they experienced mental coercion of any sort, and against this they had rebelled. It would not be out of character if, once again living in close proximity, there did not enter an element of perhaps unintentional coercion on her part and of resistance on theirs. They were now fully grown-up young women, their father's housekeepers and hostesses - however gauche and diffident at first – but naturally jealous of their privilege. Mrs

[12] Ray, iv. 213.   [13] Ray, iv. 235–6.

Carmichael-Smyth, despite ill health and old age, was still a memorable hostess and former beauty, whose standards of decorum would be impossible of attainment by her granddaughters, brought up on such totally different lines in their motherless home. As neither girl was domesticated and Anny was a positively bad housekeeper, it was fortunate for the comfort of the home that Amy Crowe was there; otherwise their grandmother would have interfered more than she did, and of necessity.

The account that Thackeray sent his American friends of the family Christmas of 1860 in Onslow Square would appear to be a fair summing-up of their lives after the first year of his editing the *Cornhill*, of the first stages of his new novel, *Philip*, and during the construction of the Queen Anne house. He wrote on Christmas morning itself: 'The autumn has passed away in which you were to have come to England and here is a bitter cold Christmas day and no news of you. I am unwell. I am hard at work trying to get the new story on a head. I have been quill-driving all the morning, but I must say a word of God bless you to my dear kind friends at Brown House Street. . . . [The situation in the States prevented their visit] . . . Is it this horrid Separation that has prevented your all coming to Europe. Or are you waiting till next year when my fine house will be built – at Palace Green, Kensington – opposite the old palace. . . . I wonder whom you have got at dinner today? Our house is all hollyfied from bottom to top. We have asked a poor widow from India with her *five* children, and two or 3 men friends, and we have got a delicate feast consisting of *Boiled Turkey/Roast Goose/Roast Beef/* and I am going to make a great bowl of punch in the grand silver bowl you know – the testimonial bowl. No one has come to marry either of my dear girls. I am surprised they don't. . . . Health very soso. Repeated attacks of illness. Great thankfulness to God Almighty for good means, for good children. And thats all. Hadn't I better go on with Philip?'[14]

The *Adventures of Philip* appeared in the *Cornhill Magazine* on 1 January 1861 and ran until the August number of 1862. Completing the monthly numbers on top of his hard editorial toil strained Thackeray's health beyond the limits of its powers. Anny's help was increasingly necessary to him both as scribe and as letter-writer; the personal letters were more and more left to her to answer. She sent a report to the Baxters in April 1861 that sets the

[14] Ray, iv. 212–14.

tone of her communications and gives a peculiarly vivid image of the Thackeray household. 'When are we going to see you all really?' she wrote. 'Only three days before your letter came Papa and I were saying we can put Mrs. Baxter into the big front room and Lucy into the back and the boys up above when the new house is finished. . . . Do you know what our household consists of? 1. a little dog with a curly tail. 2.3. Jack and Jill two puppies that squeak a good deal. 4. a little cat passionately attached to Papa, and she purrs and jumps on his knee and wont be turned off. 5. a certain kind gentleman whose picture I send you – tho' to me it is not him a bit. 6. Miss Anny 7 Miss Minny. Im nearly 24 and Minny nearly 21 and absurdly young for her age for she still likes playing with children and kittens and hates reading and is very shy tho' she does not show it and very clever tho' she does not do any thing in particular and always helps me out of scrapes which I am always getting into. Then there is Amy Crowe who has lived with us these 7 years and who is one of the best and gentlest and kindest of women and then there is a faithful but tearful but affected cook, a pretty little maid called Fanny who is literary and quotes the Cornhill Magazine; and a gawky housemaid; and also a faithful reckless youth who breaks the china and tumbles down stairs and is called the Butler. And now good night for tonight dear Mrs. Baxter here is a message from Minny to say I must go and dress as we are going to fetch Papa at the club and on to some tea-parties.'

With regard to the Baxters' anticipated visit, Anny spoke of her father's health: 'I don't think you will find him a bit changed when you do come and see us, he is always ill but rallies and cheers again in the wonderfullest way – When his attacks come we are as I need not tell you very wretched and anxious and when they go away we forget all about them as he does himself he is up in his room now at work and he will wonder at my coolness in writing you such a letter as this only as I know you are the Mrs. Baxter I'm sure you are I am not afraid that you will be angry.'[15]

The 'Palazzo', as it came to be called in the family, was finally ready for occupation in the spring of 1862, after total reconstruction and prolonged interior decoration.

The house-warming party took an original form: private theatricals running for two nights, in which the cast was composed of the girls and close friends like the Merivales. Anny recorded the scene in her Journal: 'The theatre was put up in the dining-room and the play came to life . . . Papa was amused and delighted – Everyone was in fun and good humour. A jolly sort of meal in the drawing-room, and then the 2 great nights and all the people pouring in. . . . I remember standing by Papa when all was over and saying good-bye . . . and remember such an odd feeling came over me. I suppose this is the *summit*. I shall never feel so jubilant so grand so wildly important and happy again – It was a sort of feeling like Fate knocking at the door.'[16]

The actual removal to Palace Green took place on 31 March and Thackeray loved the house from the beginning. A large man with a need for space, it suited his sense of scale. 'Upon my word, it is one of the nicest houses I have ever seen,' he wrote to his American friends on 9 May; 'there is an old green and an old palace and magnificent trees before the windows at which I write. I have the most delightful study, bedroom, and so forth. . . have a strong idea that in the next world I shan't be a bit better off.'[17] And he wrote to his mother, 'The actual increase of health and comfort since we got into the Palazzo is quite curious. I am certainly much better in body.'[18]

At right angles to the old palace and gardens, and facing the royal stables, it was a perfect replica of a Queen Anne house; two storeys high, six windows wide (three on each side of the portico) with mansarded roof, and built throughout of red brick, faced with stone. It was said to have set the fashion for the 'red rash' of buildings which were starting to spring up in the Kensington area.

On 3 July (1862) Thackeray finished *Philip* – 'at 6.15', as he liked precisely to note of so important an event, and reported spending the following day 'in great delectation and rest of mind after making a very bad drawing.' The relief of a burden lifted was always accompanied by devout thankfulness for a task accomplished and expressed as a sort of prayer; on this occasion he wrote to his mother of 'one person of the Congregation . . . very thankful for our preservation and all the blessings of this life which have fallen me'.[19] For him the dread of leaving a work unfinished, that every writer must know, was exacerbated by his bad health, and the end brought a special sense of triumph. He could now enjoy 'a little lull', though as he added to his mother, 'not yet quite. Mr. Smith

---

16 Journal, 1862.   17 Ray, iv. 264.
18 Ray, iv. 271.   19 Ray, iv. 270.

says, "Do, pray write a Roundabout paper." And that, you see, is
churning in my brain while I am writing off a scrap to my dear old
mother.' The Roundabout Paper in question – De Finibus –
published in the August Number of the Cornhill is of special
interest in the context of Thackeray's attitude towards his work; the
slave of his creation, haunted by his creatures, groaning to be rid of
them, broken-hearted when the time for parting comes, and calling
them back. It is one of the most tenderly expressed of all his
writings on the theme of his imaginary world; of the pains and
anguish, of the mere mechanics of writing, 'of the scratches and
corrections . . . those last corrections never to be finished', and the
sobering reflection as the end is in sight: 'Yet a few chapters more,
and then the last; after which, behold Finis itself come to an end,
and the Infinite begun.'[20]

On the day following his sober farewell to Philip, he took the
girls to Twickenham, 'like persons of quality in our pretty new
(paid for) carriage with our "gens" on the box', to attend the grand
Garden Fête given by the exiled Orleans duc d'Aumale and his
duchess, where there was such a crush that he 'could only get a crust
to eat and a scrap of galatine left in a lady's plate and a bottle of
excellent claret'.[21] To Anny, remembering the fête as a red-letter day
in later years, it provided a link between her Parisian childhood
when she thrilled to see the old Orleans King and his little
grandson, and the sound of the tolling bell of the Madeleine in Paris
in May 1897 when that very duc d'Aumale of Twickenham was
allowed 'home' for burial.[22]

Anny herself was now finishing a task repeatedly laid aside: her
first novel, The Story of Elizabeth. George Smith has told how, as
he was leaving Thackeray's house one-day, where he constantly
called in connection with editorial business, he was stopped by
Anny who was waiting for him and thrust a little parcel into his
hand whispering: 'Do you mind looking at that?' It was the
manuscript of her novel and Smith, when he came to look at it, was
delighted. He sent Thackeray, as general editor, the proofs, and
asked him at their next meeting if he had read them. 'No,'
Thackeray said, 'I could not. I read some of them and then broke
down so thoroughly I could not face the rest.' Though overjoyed at
George Smith's good opinion – 'Anny's style is admirable and
Smith and Elder are in raptures about it', he told his mother on the

[20] Cornhill, Aug. 1862.   [21] Ray, iv. 270.   [22] Fuller, p. 91.

book's acceptance – he never brought himself to read it. 'It would tear my guts out', he confided to Fanny Kemble at the time.[23]

The story ran serially in the *Cornhill* from September 1862 to January 1863. Despite its immediate success, it was neither well planned nor consistently realized. Its qualities, like those of the works to follow, lay in analysis of feelings, descriptive passages of scenes familiar to her, flashes of insight into character rather than in cumulative action. Her vision and her style were impressionist, presenting a mood, a moment, a passing feeling. It was the sketch of a story composed of its separate parts, not apprehended whole.

The Story of Elizabeth is a young person's book. Its main location in Paris suggests that it was begun shortly after the winter of 1852/3 when the author was living there with her grandparents, and its subject-matter, her conflict with the Calvinist circles frequented by her grandmother, was still painfully fresh in her mind. The dominant emotion is still the rebellious aftermath of that experience. Anny was probably no more than seventeen when she began it. The love interest is also patently immature, though it could relate to personal experience, if there were any foundation at all for Anny's reported attachment to Robert Creyke. Her lack of inventive power confines the action strictly to things seen and felt. In that sense, it is an autobiographical tale, situated in the very street where her grandparents lived in Paris: the rue d'Angoulême, in the 'section' of St. Philip du Roule, leading off the Champs Élysées. So far as she keeps to things known, like her own schoolgirl passions and the places she has seen, it rings true; beyond that, the structure does not hold. Elizabeth is a young and passionate girl, wholly untrained by a worthless and jealous mother, almost young enough to be her sister. Both are equally incapable of self-control, both equally bent on pleasure. The mother resents the daughter's budding love for John Dampier. A widow without objective in life, she falls under the powerful influence of the Protestant Pasteur Tourneur, and accepts him as a husband; from where begin Elizabeth's real troubles and her open rebellion against both mother and stepfather, and his even more disagreeable widowed sister Madame Jacob. Elizabeth's tribulations are further complicated by the calf-love of Tourneur's son, Anthony, who pursues her with his clumsy attentions. Her only happiness comes from the friendship of the Dampier family and her

[23] Ray, iv. 271–2.

own as yet unrequited love for John Dampier. Towards her his feelings are protective and amused, not those of a lover.

Scenes recording first-hand impressions, like Anny's own attendances at Pasteur Monod's Confirmation classes, are sharply focused. The dismal house belonging to the Tourneurs where Elizabeth and her mother go to live after the marriage is feelingly described. Staring out of the window of her new prison, Elizabeth thinks: '"Ah! how dull it is to be here! Ah! how I hate it, how I hate them all! . . . There is some music, all the Champs Élysées are crowded with people, the soldiers are marching along with glistening bayonets and flags flying. Not one of them thinks that in a dismal house not very far away there is anybody so unhappy as I am. This day year – it breaks my heart to think of it – I was nineteen; to-day I am twenty, and I feel a hundred. Oh, what a sin and shame it is to condemn me to this hateful life. Oh, what wicked people these good people are."

'With what distaste she set herself to live her new life I cannot attempt to tell you. It bored her, and wearied and displeased her, and she made no secret of her displeasure, you may be certain. But what annoyed her most of all, what seemed to her so inconceivable that she could never understand or credit it, was the extraordinary change which had come over her mother. Mme Tourneur was like Mrs. Gilmour[24] in many things, but so different in others that Elly could hardly believe her to be the same woman. The secret of it all was a love of power and admiration, purchased no matter at what sacrifice.'[25]

Elizabeth's clandestine relationship with John Dampier leads her into outright rebellion, and also predictably to disaster. Dampier plainly sees how vulnerable she is. 'You are such a sensitive, weak-minded little girl that you will go on breaking your heart a dozen times a day to the end of your life.' he tells her.[26] She accepts an invitation to the opera where a mutual acquaintance, recognizing them, calls round at their box, and Dampier, to extricate himself and Elly from an embarrassing situation, introduces her as his fiancée. No sooner has their visitor gone, than he apologizes: 'I ought never to have brought you, and I could think of no better way to get out of my scrape than to tell him that lie.'[27] She cannot believe that he does not mean what he said and that he is engaged to

---

[24] Her previous name.   [25] *Story of Elizabeth*, p. 56.
[26] Ibid., p. 139.   [27] Ibid., p. 146.

another girl. Her stepfather has, moreover, followed them to the theatre and come to take her home. The inevitable breakdown, nervous fever, follows. Dampier hears that she is dying, confides in an aunt of his who sympathizes with him, and obtains an interview with the sick girl. The aunt takes charge of the invalid, who is restored to health and allowed to accompany her back to England. With old Miss Dampier Elly is taken to the coast and regains a zest for living. 'It is late in the autumn. Tourists are flocking home; a little procession of battered ladies and gentlemen carrying all sorts of bundles, and bags, and parcels, disembarks every day. . . . Any moment you may chance to encounter some wan sea-sick friend staggering along. . . . The waves wash up and down, painted yellow by the sunset.'[28] Inevitably, among the travellers is a brother of Dampier's, Will Dampier, come to see his old aunt. He is a bright young man much prejudiced against Elly, judging her to have entangled his brother. But when he meets the 'imbroglio' in person, he cannot help liking her. 'She has a sweet pretty face, and her voice . . . pipes and thrills like a musical snuff-box. Aunt Jenny wants her for a niece, that is certain.'[29]

As the tale progresses, a greater flexibility in the writing, a less feverish pace, is achieved. Anny shows herself capable of greater objectivity, of less self-absorption, and she is in better control of her subject. Her impressionistic descriptions become more vivid; there is a reflection of Boudin in the following seascape: 'Everybody knows what twelve o'clock is like on a fine day at the sea-side. It means little children, nurses in clean cotton gowns, groups of young ladies scattered here and there; it means a great cheerfulness and tranquillity, a delightful glitter, and life, and light: happy folks splashing in the water, bathing-dresses drying in the sun.'[30]

After numerous and confusing delays the happy ending is duly reached, and the author's personal involvement in it is made patent in the postscript describing her return to the old Paris street where she had first imagined the story: 'The old house is done away with and exists no longer. It was pulled down by order of the Government, and a grand new boulevard runs right across the place where it stood.'

It is fairest to judge *Elizabeth* in the context of its own day. Its contemporary success is testified to by Rhoda Broughton, herself a very young girl at the time and astounded by a young contempor-

[28] Ibid., p. 186.   [29] Ibid., p. 196.   [30] Ibid., p. 243.

ary's achievement. 'Vividly comes back to me', she wrote, 'the memory of my astonished delight when *The Story of Elizabeth* burst in its wonderful novelty and spring-like quality on my consciousness, written, as I was told, by a girl hardly older than myself.'[31] *Elizabeth*, Anny recorded, 'continues to be a success. It's quite a little fortune and more that is coming to me. My good fortune, I don't know why, makes me feel ashamed.'[32] Thackeray wrote on 5 July 1862, before publication, 'She is very modest and I am mistrustful too. I am sure I shan't love her a bit better for being successful.'[33] And after publication and her immediate success, it was the same comment: 'she is very modest, thank God, whilst everybody is praising her.'

But curiously it was at this moment of initial success that Anny was reported to be so unwell as to need a change of air.[34] It was arranged that she would go to the Isle of Wight in November with the photographer Mrs Cameron, her father's old friend who was to become a close personal friend of Anny's too. It was with Mrs Cameron that she made her first visit to Freshwater, which proved such a rewarding experience. It not only restored her health, but greatly improved her spirits for she came into close contact for the first time with Tennyson. He chose her as his companion on his walks, and opened up a whole new world by his talk – or perhaps even more by his silences. He paid her the compliment of assuming she shared his feeling for the scenes about them.[35]

For Anny's ill health there were no doubt psychological causes. Ever since the arrival in London of the grandparents in 1860, and their establishment in Brompton Crescent, the intercourse between the two households had necessarily been close and constant, even to the extent of spending holidays together. In the summer of 1860 they all shared a house at Tunbridge Wells, and for 1861 the plan was for a joint holiday at Hythe. The very prospect cast gloom over Thackeray: 'I suppose she inherits from me rather a gloomy temper', he wrote to his American friends of his mother, 'and the prospect of a summer at Hythe does not add much to my cheerfulness.'[36] It could not have added much to the cheerfulness of the young girls either. Thackeray had suffered all his life from her possessive love, and for many years from the insoluble problem of

[31] *Ritchie Letters*, p. 118.   [32] Ibid., Journal, 9 Feb. 1862.
[33] Ray, iv. 272.   [34] Ray, iv. 236.
[35] *Tennyson, Ruskin and Browning*, pp. 41–2.   [36] Ray, iv. 233.

her Parisian connections. In London she became 'very rebellious' and wanted to go back. 'There's a little clique of old ladies there', Thackeray wrote in a letter of 24 May 1861, 'who are very fond of her and with whom she is a much more important personage than she is in this great city. If anything happens to the Major she will go to Paris and give us the slip and grumble when she is there and presently come back.'[37]

These proved to be strangely prophetic words. During a holiday in Scotland in the autumn of that year which the old couple took alone, the Major died quite suddenly, on 9 September, without any previous signs of illness. Thackeray had to hurry north to support his mother and arrange the funeral. The Major was buried in the Episcopal church at Ayr, where Thackeray had a mural monument placed to his memory. It was a terrible blow to Mrs Carmichael-Smyth. She had a habitually sibylline look, and her temperament, like her features, fell most naturally into tragic lines, even more so now. There was no recourse for Thackeray but to take her home with him and to give her what comfort he and his daughters could. But she would not be comforted. 'My poor old mother is wandering about happy no where,' Thackeray wrote in May 1862. 'I inherit from her this despondency I suppose – but have the pull over her of a strong sense of humour.'[38]

It was in these circumstances that Anny was trying to finish her book. While the whole circle of her father's friends gave her their heart-warming encouragement, it is not said that she received the same from her grandmother. The subject alone, the old dispute between them, could not please the old lady, and although Anny had maintained a respectful tone in portraying the Calvinist preacher it could but strike the dowager as presumptuous on the part of a young and ignorant girl to criticize the judgement of her elders and betters. This kind of friction may well have contributed to the spirit of 'independence and rebellion' lately noted by their Father in the girls' social attitudes, and have had something to do with Anny's recurrent lapses into ill health. One further explanation was touched on in a letter of Thackeray's at the time, when he wrote that both the girls were 'beginning to bewail their Virginity in the mountains and seem to be much excited because Ella Merivale who is only 17 has had 3 or 4 lovers already'.[39] One feels that if Anny's illness was the age-old affection of the heart, Thackeray, the

[37] Ray, iv. 237.   [38] Ray, iv. 264.   [39] Ray, iv. 272.

specialist in such matters, would have diagnosed it.

They were, inevitably, very much aware of the flirtations and marriages of their young contemporaries. The Merivales had long been close friends of the Thackerays, and were now near neighbours at Palace Green. Herman Merivale was Permanent Under-Secretary for India, and the children, Ella and Herman Charles, were of the same age as the Thackeray girls. It was of Ella that Thackeray had written long ago: 'Little maid with sparkling eye, / Will you have some mutton pie? / Little maid with tender heart / Will you have some apple tart?' Understandably Ella's conquests caused considerable excitement. Their close friends were marrying each other. Kate Dickens and Charles Collins, younger brother of Wilkie Collins, were married in 1860. To the great pleasure of the Thackeray girls, the young couple settled close by in a little house in Kensington High Street within sight of Palace Green. There was a deeper and closer involvement in the marriage of their own beloved Amy Crowe, who had lived with them for seven years to the satisfaction of all parties. She was carried off by their distinguished young cousin, Captain Edward Thackeray, who had recently been awarded the VC for capturing the Kashmir Gate at Delhi during the Indian Mutiny. Thackeray had acted *in loco parentis* to young Edward Thackeray throughout his school and naval college years, and to the Thackerays' home Edward came on leave from India in the summer of 1862. It did not take him long to fall in love with and get engaged to Amy Crowe, and the marriage took place in December. Once again, Thackeray gave the bride away. The young couple were shortly to leave for India, and the intensity of Thackeray's feelings on parting from 'Little Dorrit' were described by Millais's son, in his life of his father.[40] He records that Thackeray was 'so grieved at the thought of parting from Miss Crowe that on her wedding day he came for consolation to my father's studio at nearby Palace Gate and spent most of the afternoon in tears'.

They were none of them to see little Amy again. She died in India in June 1864, leaving two baby girls. Thackeray had given her a home when her mother died, and it seemed but natural to Anny and Minny, when the time came, to give Amy's orphans a permanent home too.

[40] Ray, iv. 404 n.. quoting from *Life and Letters of Sir John Everett Millais* by his Son.

DE FINIBUS

NUMBER 2 Palace Green was to be the ideal background, the inspirational period setting, for writing *The History of the Reign of Queen Anne*. To this end, and gradually to clear himself of the heavy commitments of recent years, Thackeray had resigned from the editorial chair of the *Cornhill*, while remaining on excellent terms with George Smith, even before the move to Palace Green. He had one full-length novel to complete for the magazine (*Denis Duval*) before becoming a free man, at liberty to write whatever he wished. A strong suspicion that he had written himself out as a novelist, and that every story with a love interest was but a repetition of the last, encouraged him in the ambition to attempt a task that, even in the first euphoria of its inception, he saw clearly to be gigantic, needing months of reading, research, travel, and above all reliable health. Such labour was still far enough away, as he wrote *Denis Duval*, to be seen in a rosy light, and this was a relatively happy period in his life.

A young witness to his happiness in his new surroundings was Blanche Ritchie, one of the daughters of his cousin William Ritchie who had died in Calcutta the previous year. Legal Member of the Council of India, William left a widow and eight children, of whom the oldest, Augusta and Blanche, had long since lived in Paris with their Ritchie aunts and become friends with Anny and Minny on their visits there. Thackeray had immediately assumed the role of protector of the widow and orphans, and invited to his home the older girls in 1862 and again in May 1863. Blanche, who later married the Vice-Provost of Eton, Frank Warre-Cornish, recorded her happy impressions of that visit. 'Out of my girlish remembrances of visits to Palace Green', she wrote, 'the impression made upon me by the creation of *Denis Duval* remains extraordinarily clear. It was in the summer of 1863, and I believe that Mr. Thackeray was just then very happy, finding himself once more.

. . . in the full vein of historical romance. But I knew nothing of this at the time, only that the atmosphere of *Denis Duval* permeated everything. The beautiful red house shaded by tall elms, on Palace Green; the pieces of plate, china, and furniture, collected by Mr. Thackeray, when it was easier than it is now to make genuine last-century purchases, "brand new and intensely old", as he would describe some Louis XVI clock or *gueridon* just brought home – all these old-world things seemed to be a part of the spell.'[1]

But the acquisition of the splendid house, conducive to the writing of history – even to the writing of historical fiction – had cost more than its proud owner had bargained for. Realist that he was, he did not forget a certain famous precedent for his case, and took warning from it. 'If I don't mistake there was a man who lived at Abbotsford', he wrote to Brown, 'who overhoused himself. I am not in debt, thank my stars, but instead of writing to you why am I not writing the history of Denis Duval Esq., Admiral of the White Squadron? Because I don't know anything about the sea and seamen; and get brought up by my ignorance every other page; above all, because I am lazy.'[2]

Because of the great comfort of the house, its roominess and cheerfulness, Thackeray appeared to the girls to be more regularly at home than before, and to confide more openly in them about the book. 'My father used to talk a great deal about it all to us,' Anny remembered. 'He was anxious about the novel. I can remember him saying that *Philip* had not enough story, and that this new book *must* be a success. . . . He used to carry the chapters about with him, and often pull them out from his coat pocket to consult.

'He said it was a superstition of his to write at least one line in every day whether he was ill or well. Only once to my recollection, did he try to dictate some pages of *Denis Duval*, but he very soon sent his secretary away, saying that he must write for himself.'[3] But the fact was that obstacles and allurements, all of a most pleasant nature, were constantly interrupting his work. To begin with there was exceptionally radiant weather that spring, and sitting in the garden at the back of the house listening to the cawing of the rooks in the trees seemed more agreeable than sitting down to write in his study.

Then, at Easter, came a most tempting invitation from Thackeray's old Cambridge friend Richard Monckton Milnes (shortly to

---

[1] Fuller, p. 93.   [2] Ray, iv. 291.   [3] Fuller. p. 92.

become Lord Houghton) to visit his Yorkshire home, Fryston Hall. There they spent ten days particularly memorable for Anny because of the presence of the young, and virtually unknown, Swinburne. Ever on the look-out for fresh talent, Monckton Milnes was eager to launch what he perceived was a poet of genius, and was anxious for Thackeray's opinion.

Edmund Gosse, Swinburne's eventual biographer, heard of the occasion from Anny herself, as her vivid impressions served her in old age. She happened to be the first to spot the poet's arrival, climbing up 'the sloping lawn swinging his hat in his hand, and letting the sunshine flood the bush of his red-gold hair. He looked like Apollo or a fairy prince . . . and immediately attracted the approval of Mr. Thackeray by the wit and wisdom of his conversation.' Anny told Gosse that she had never seen anybody so disconcerting or so charming, and dwelt on Swinburne's kind and cordial ways throughout the visit. She admitted to shedding tears when the time came for them to leave, while Swinburne remained at Fryston.[4] It was a friendship between them that, begun there, lasted until the poet's death. Not all Swinburne's friends were able to combine fidelity and admiration.

The Thackerays' visit to Fryston lasted from 6 to 13 April, and was combined with another Yorkshire journey to Hampsthwaite, near Harrogate, the birthplace of the Thackeray family in the seventeenth century. Thackeray had long had a reverential yearning to go there on a sort of pilgrimage.

It was May before he seriously set pen to paper, and resolved firmly to reject all other temptations. Refusing social engagements, he wrote to an eager hostess that he had been visiting '3 country houses in the last 2 months', and had got into 'awful arrears' with his work. He was even sending 'the Infantas' away to the Isle of Wight so as 'to be alone – alone, alone'. The Island, which was shortly to become their refuge in disaster, was already, after Anny's first visit the previous autumn, taking a hold on her and it seemed the natural place for a spring holiday with Minny. The Tennysons and Mrs Cameron were there to welcome them.

Mrs Carmichael-Smyth spent the best part of the year by choice in Paris, so that domestic calm and tranquillity were assured. Thackeray told the widow of his cousin William Ritchie that 'when I am in labour with a book I sit for hours before my paper, not

---

[4] Quoted in Fuller, p. 94.

doing my book, but incapable of doing anything else and thinking upon that subject always, eating with it, walking about with it, and going to bed with it.'[5] Even so he tore himself away for a very short summer holiday with the girls. It proved one of the most delightful they ever had together, in Anny's recollection. 'We had the happiest little Journey together – we did not see one other soul. We were with him all day long, and we thought we had never been so happy in our lives', she wrote to Mrs Baxter afterwards.[6] It was a very limited itinerary. They crossed to Calais on 17 August, went on to Brussels, to Dinan via Namur, and reached Paris on the 21st, where they stayed till the 27th, and were home on the 28th. It was all well-trodden country, with no new sights to divert her, but to Anny it seemed that a new level'of intimacy and harmony was achieved between them.

Thackeray, always on the look-out for signs of fatigue or nervous strain in Minny, feared that the holiday had been too short and that she needed a further change. She went on a month's visit to Edinburgh to stay with his old friend, Dr John Brown. Thackeray's letter of thanks reveals once again what a rare success he made of fatherhood by creating that special relationship between himself and his motherless daughters. It was twenty-three years by then since he had been left with a couple of infants on his hands. 'My dear J.B.,' he wrote on 23 September 1863, 'I am very glad you like my little Min. With her and her Sister I have led such a happy life, that I am afraid almost as I think of it, lest any accident should disturb it. She seems to be enjoying herself greatly; but when she has done with the Lows, I think she ought to come back to her Papa and sister. We three get on so comfortably together, that the house is not the house, when one is away. I know how kind you and your childrem would be to her. But Anny wants her companion, and a month will give her as much change of air as, please God, will be good for her. . . . Goodbye, my dear J.B. – My love to the children from your grateful old friend, WMT.'[7]

Though Thackeray himself reported feeling considerably better for the move to the gravel soil and fresher air of Kensington, he was never free for long from those recurrent attacks which had beset him for years and which he generally called 'spasms' – painful constrictions of the bladder, sickness, and diarrhoea – for which he relentlessly doctored himself with calomel, 'blue pills', and col-

[5] Ray, iv. 292 n.   [6] Ray, iv. 298.

ocynth. On his last visit to Paris the doctor had told him he had an incurable disease. His London doctor, however, denied it. At times of great pain, at the height of an attack, he frequently said he wished himself dead, were it not for his daughters; and recovering, as was usually the case, within two days, would joke away their anxiety. It is true that his diary of 1863 carries many fewer entries of such attacks. In July he noted 'a slight attack lasting only a day', and another on 21 September 'yielding to 9 gr. Colocynth in a few hours.'

Anny was the less prepared to find him brooding over the dining-room fire one day in very sombre mood. 'I have been thinking in fact', he said to her, 'that it will be a very dismal life for you when I am gone.' And he added, 'I have a great mind to put it in my will that you are not to live with Grannie.' Much distressed, Anny told him that he ought not to be thinking of a new will. He informed her that he had torn up the previous one, in which he had left Amy Crowe a legacy of £500, and he also explained to Anny the legal position with regard to her mother. If he died without making a will his estate would be divided into three to provide for her on the same basis as for his daughters. This he could not afford to do, as he must also provide for his own mother, and he anxiously wondered what would be right for them all. He was still haunted by the need to make more money in order to make sure that everybody would be well provided for. Not for the first time that year Anny, seeing him driving himself beyond his strength, urged him to give up work, retire to the country, and reduce the expenses of their style of living. It was a subject on which they came as near as they ever did to quarrelling. He would not hear of it; he would always brush the subject aside, and she remembered him 'passing his hand through his hair, laughing, pouring out his tea from his little silver tea-pot. I can see him looking in the glass and saying, "I am sure I look well enough, don't I?"' He hoped he had at least ten years' work in him. 'It is absurd to expect a man to give up his work at 50,' he said.[8]

For the sake of *Denis Duval* he made a special trip to Rye and Winchelsea to gather topographical data and background. 'He came back delighted from the old places,' recorded Anny. 'Winchelsea was everything he had hoped for . . . the great churches, and the old houses, all sailing inland from the sea.'[9] He assured George

[7] Ray, iv. 291.   [8] MS Reminiscences.
[9] Introduction, Biog. Ed., Vol. xii, *Denis Duval*, p. xxvi.

Smith that if there were no interruptions from illness he would get *Denis Duval* advanced enough in a month to begin serialization in the *Cornhill*. 'If I could get a month's ease,' he wrote on 17 December, 'I could finish the eight numbers handsomely with the marriage of Denis and Agnes. . . . "The Course of True Love" I thought of as a pretty name.'[10] He was so identifying himself with his new hero that in the course of planning the book he wrote several letters to George Smith under the name and in the character of Denis Duval. He did the same to his friend Albany Fonblanque, a critic on *The Examiner* , explaining that he was born in 1763 at Winchelsea, where his parents lived, having been expelled from France after the Revocation of the Edict of Nantes – 'which I suspect brought the Fonblanques to England too'. What was holding him up at the moment, he told his friend, was information 'about sailing, smuggling and so forth – how we went out at night, what we did, how we came back'.[11] No man, at the height of his powers, untroubled by illness, could be more immersed in his work than he was at the end of that year.

It never prevented him, however, from living his own life to the full. On Sunday 6 December, being invited to tea at the Temple rooms of young Herman Merivale (their friend Ella's brother), Thackeray suggested that the girls should join him just to attend the evening service at the Temple Church. They were late, as he so often had occasion to scold them for being, and could not sit together. But they found him after the service 'standing quite still with his back turned to us until we should come up to him', as Anny remembered, 'and as we came out into the open air he began to chaunt Rejoice and again I say unto you Rejoice. And then he said – How beautiful that evening hymn is. So simple and un-affected and so entirely to the purpose. It says just what is needful and no more.' He had been greatly moved by the service. They walked across to Herman's rooms. Anny recalled the scene. 'The sun was setting over the garden and the river . . . and everybody went away through the courts and archways but we went and walked along the terrace and down some steps into the garden. It was all golden and shining, when we came out of the lamp-lit church and the organ was booming and the people were passing out and the sky was very bright and warm and red, but in the garden by degrees the twilight came and the lights faded out of the sky and

[10] Ray, iv. 295.   [11] Ray, iv. 294.

river. We went up some twisting stairs into Young Herman's room where the tea was ready spread for us. And Papa laughed because we were so pleased and happy.'[12]

With the young Mr and Mrs Collins, their near neighbours now, the Thackerays were in constant touch, as Thackeray's diary of dinner-dates for that season shows. He had a great regard for Collins (a former 'Pre-Raphaelite Brother' turned writer), and never spoke of Kate otherwise than as 'pretty little Mrs. Collins'. Noted from childhood for her striking looks, her pallor and the coil of her auburn hair which, together with her fiery temper, had earned her the family nickname of 'lucifer-box', Kate was the perfect artist's model, very much to the taste of her husband's Pre-Raphaelite friends. Trained by Millais, she was herself a gifted water-colourist, and in later years exhibited regularly in the London galleries. When Thackeray's American friends, the Baxters, eventually made their visit to London, they were 'entranced' by Kate's beauty and deeply impressed by the taste shown in the decoration of her little Kensington home. The Collinses were never well off, but Kate resolutely refused to borrow from her father or to allow her delicate husband to overwork.[13] (He died prematurely in 1873.)

Thackeray often spoke to Kate deploring the false rivalry created between him and Dickens by their ill-judged 'partisans'. 'It is ridiculous', he exploded one day, 'that your father and I should be placed in a position of enmity towards one another.' He had always wholeheartedly admired – and not seldom envied – Dickens's extraordinary fecundity and his creative powers. They had been forced into a false position and into opposing camps by their followers far more than by any inimical sentiments of their own. Kate urged Thackeray to be the conciliating party and to make the first advance.

Thackeray had not, of course, approved of Dickens's treatment of his wife, for whom Thackeray and his daughters felt the deepest sympathy; and it is unlikely that he would ever have consented to anything resembling an official apology, as Kate proposed. But, as luck would have it, on the Monday before Christmas he ran into Dickens at the Athenaeum. Moved by spontaneous reflexes much more than by calculation, he could not stop himself swinging round

[12] MS Reminiscences.
[13] Fields Papers, 1869. Boston Historical Society Library. After Charles Collins's death, she married the sculptor Perugini, and lived at 2, St. Albans' Grove, Kensington. See below, p. 253.

as he saw Dickens on the stairs and warmly wringing his hand. Without a humiliating apology, the healing words were spoken in the cordial exchange that followed between the friends.

Thackeray's first engagement of the Christmas week was at the Garrick Club on the Tuesday, whose meetings always put him into high spirits, and he was noted that evening for being 'radiant and buoyant with glee'. He dined, however, not wisely but too well, and found himself quite prostrated next morning. 'It can't be helped darling,' he told Anny when she came into his bedroom, 'I did not take enough medicine last night. I shall be better presently.' The doctor said he would be all right again in twenty-four hours; and he felt well enough to sit out in the garden a while with a book in the afternoon. They were all so accustomed to his attacks, which had recently lasted so short a time, that they went to bed that night confident that he would be himself by morning and able to celebrate Christmas as usual. His servant had offered to sit up with him, but Thackeray would not hear of it. His mother, who had the room over his, heard him being sick in the night, and wished she were at hand to help, but assumed it to be but another of his bouts. Not until Anny was dressing in the morning did she hear from the cries of the servants that her father was dead. She sent for the doctor and for the Collinses.

Charles Collins and his wife were at breakfast on the morning of Christmas eve when a servant from Palace Green came running, begging them to come over at once. Charles Pearson had found Thackeray on going in in the morning, with his arms flung up above his head, as he had died, obviously several hours before.

Charles Collins later wrote to his brother Wilkie: 'I never shall forget the day which we passed at the house – we went there of course – or the horror of seeing him lying there so dreadfully changed. It was apoplexy after all, and I don't think that what he had suffered from so long had much, if anything to do with it.'[14] Mrs Carmichael-Smyth and Anny were reported utterly prostrated. Strangely enough, Minny, the most nervously delicate, was bearing up 'with some courage'. The Collinses were indeed their main support: they insisted on the bereaved women coming across to sleep at their house, until the funeral.

The fact that it was Christmas added, to a ghastly degree, to their affliction. They wanted only to hide themselves from the sounds of

[14] Ray, iv. 296 n.

cheer that surrounded them from the carol singers in the streets; and even more, from the flow of callers – and, it must be admitted, from the eyes of the curious – who beseiged their home. True friends thronged about them also, and though it was Christmas and meant travelling from the Isle of Wight, Tennyson and his wife had no sooner heard the news than they hurried to London to bring what consolation they could. It was a gesture that touched Anny to the core.

Legal friends, like Henry Cole, the father of their three girl friends, were there to help them through the agonizing formalities of the time. They knew, and firmly stuck to, Thackeray's wishes regarding his funeral: no Westminster Abbey for him. He had ordered them to bury him beside his little lost Jane, buried at Kensal Green all those years ago, and to avoid those trappings, black-plumed hearse, scarved hats, mourning bandannas in which the Mutes at Victorian funerals were arrayed and which had so profoundly disgusted him at young Hallam's funeral at Clevedon. It was in strict accordance with his wishes that his daughters ordered the arrangements of his funeral, on 30 December, the simplicity of which astonished the enormous attendance and the representatives of the Press.

The cortège left Palace Green shortly before 11 o'clock and arrived at the cemetery at noon, where Anny and Minny were already waiting, escorted by Henry Cole, and their only male relatives, their mother's brother Captain Arthur Shawe (whom their father had so constantly befriended) and Sir James Carmichael, on their grandfather's side of the family.

The chapel was far too small to hold the immense crowd of mourners, estimated between 1,500 and 2,000. The service was conducted by the chaplain, the Revd Charles Stuart. The *Express*, reporting the event, noted: 'One of the most touching sights that could be witnessed were his two young daughters, veiled in crepe, advancing from the crowd that pressed about the grave, taking a last look at the coffin and then suddenly turning away.'

Almost the whole of literary and artistic London was present: Dickens, Browning, Tennyson, Trollope, Carlyle, Millais, Cruikshank, George Richmond, the whole staff of *Punch* with Leech at its head, G. H. Lewes, and countless others. Squeezed in between Tennyson and Dickens (who came with Charles Collins) at the graveside was Brookfield, the old and lost friend who had nevertheless probably hurt Thackeray more than any man alive. Those prevented from coming because of distance or the 'festive Season' wrote their concern. Mrs Gaskell wrote from Manchester to George Smith, anxious 'for a word or two about the poor Miss Thackerays', realizing 'how desolate they must be'.

It was Dickens, the most qualified of all his contemporaries by his identical art and comparable genius, to judge of Thackeray's achievement, who wrote the obituary notice in the *Cornhill* for January – the first number of the year 1864. In his grandest vein Dickens wrote in tribute to the Artist and the Man; recalling their last meeting less than a week before Thackeray's death. He spoke of his unfinished work: 'The last words he corrected in print were: "And my heart throbbed with an exquisite bliss." God grant that on that Christmas Eve, when he laid his head on his pillow and threw up his arms as he had been wont to do when very weary, some consciousness of duty done and Christian hope throughout life humbly cherished, may have caused his heart so to throb, when he passed away to his Redeemer's rest!

'He was found lying peacefully, as above described, composed, undisturbed, to all appearances asleep, on the 24th December 1863. He was only in his 53rd year, so young a man that the mother who blessed him in his first sleep blessed him in his last.' Going on to speak of the girls and the exceptional relationship between them and their father ever since their infancy, he said: 'Those little girls had grown to be women . . . In those twenty years of companionship with him they had learned much from him; and one of them has a literary course before her worthy of her famous father.'

In that prophecy, as yet unread by Anny, would lie, in her desolation, the incentive to live, the signpost pointing to the direction she must take.

PART II

THE INHERITANCE OF GENIUS

CHAPTER 12

THE ISLAND

OFFERS of help came from all sides. There was only one that suited their needs: Mrs Cameron offered them her vacant cottage at Freshwater, where they could be alone, unmolested by the curious or by those well-wishers whose good intentions did more harm than good. They went there at once, arriving at dusk on the snow-covered island. 'After our Father's death, my sister and I came to Freshwater,' Anny wrote. 'It seemed to us that perhaps there, more than anywhere else, we might find some gleam of the light of our home, with the friend [Tennyson] who had known him and belonged to his life and whom we trusted.'

They were not deceived in their trust. 'We arrived late in the afternoon,' she went on. 'It was bitter weather, the snow lying upon the ground. Mrs. Cameron had lent us a cottage and the fires were already burning, and as we rested aimlessly in the twilight, we seemed aware of a tall figure standing in the window wrapped in a heavy cloak with a broad rimmed hat. This was Tennyson, who had walked down to see us in silent sympathy.'[1]

Since 1853 the Tennysons had sought refuge at Freshwater from the prying public that had made their first home at Twickenham untenable. For a time the shrubberies and plantations sheltering their house, Farringford, had effectively shielded this essentially shy man. He had not been best pleased when Mrs Cameron, a former Twickenham neighbour, had followed them to the Island in 1860; but time, and her own good nature, had gradually reconciled him to her presence.

Mrs Cameron's ivy-covered cottage, Dimbola, overlooking Freshwater Bay, and near the gates of Farringford, was in fact two separate cottages, which she had linked together by building a central 'tower' between. The west side she kept for herself, the east she kept for visitors. On her previous visits, Anny had enjoyed

[1] *Tennyson, Ruskin and Browning*, p. 39.

walking with Tennyson along High Down, 'treading the turf, listening to his talk', as she remembered, 'while the gulls came sideways, flashing their white breasts against the edge of the cliffs, and the poet's cloak flapped time to the gusts of the west wind'. She had thought of Farringford as a 'charmed palace', with 'a glow of crimson' everywhere within, and beyond 'the sounds of birds and of the distant sea'.[2]

Anny's vision, as her own books were to show, was of a sudden, flashing, glancing kind, and she saw with a poet's rather than a novelist's eye. This perhaps explains the sympathy that grew up between the ageing Laureate and the relatively inexperienced girl. At least he had always accepted her as a companion on his walks, using her keen eyes to compensate for his own short-sightedness. She found that his eyes saw further than those of most people, but he liked her to confirm his observations. She recalled how on one occasion he told her 'to look and tell him if the field-lark did not come down sideways upon its wing'.[3]

Their friends Herman Merivale, James Fitzjames Stephen, and George Smith tried to spare them the many business complications caused by their father's sudden death. He had not, in the end, had time to sign his latest will, making it necessary to establish a Trust for the maintenance of his wife. The 'grand new house' on Palace Green had to be sold, with most of its valuable contents, before the actual assets assured to the girls could be reckoned. The house was almost immediately advertised for sale. Meanwhile they had no home of their own and had to accept the hospitality of friends. On 15 January they were compelled to return to London to pack up their personal possessions, staying with Kate Collins. At the same time they began house-hunting, and Anny's comment on what they saw – and could afford – was 'horrid little houses'.[4] Another painful obligation was to sell their little carriage and the ponies. On 28 January they went to Henbury, near Wimborne, where their Ritchie relations from India, the widowed Mrs William Ritchie and her children, were settled, and where their grandmother joined them.

The reunion with Mrs Carmichael-Smyth proved every bit as trying as they had feared. Anny recorded 'Terrible religious discussions'[5] – the very thing their father had wanted to spare them. Mrs

2 Ibid., p. 42.   3 Ibid., p. 48.
4 Journal, 21 Jan. 1864.   5 Journal, Feb. 1864.

Carmichael-Smyth intensified not only her own very deep sorrow for the loss of a beloved son, but increased the girls' desolation by her forbidding creed, that cast doubt on the sinner's hope of salvation unless he had 'repented him of his ways'. She lacerated her own wounded feelings with doubts as to her son's salvation, and admonished her granddaughters to take warning in time. Such an unhappy creed was wholly contrary to their father's charitable nature and trusting faith. He himself had once confided to his old friend Mrs Procter, on the occasion of a bereavement, some of his own beliefs, always associated with the death of his infant daughter Jane. 'Little children step off this earth into the infinite and we tear our hearts out over their sweet cold hands and smiling faces, that drop indifferent when you cease holding them, and smile as the lid is closing over them. I don't think we deplore the old who have had enough of living – it seems time for them to go – . . . I go – to what I don't know – but to God's next world which is His and He made it. One paces up and down the shore yet awhile – and looks towards the unknown ocean, and thinks of the traveller whose boat sailed yesterday. Those we love can but walk down to the pier with us – the voyage we must make alone. Except for the young and very happy, I can't say I am sorry for anyone who dies.' Anny, who quoted these words in her Introduction to his last book, *Denis Duval*,[6] as fitting end to her account of his 'dear life', added that 'whenever my father wrote of death it was with peaceful encouragement and good-will'.

Their grandmother was greatly to be pitied, but for Anny the first consideration had always to be Minny, and she saw Minny visibly withering in the atmosphere created by these bitter arguments. 'Grannie's religious views', she wrote, 'were always very intense and she took our different habits of thought passionately to heart. It used to make us miserable to make her so unhappy. Minny would be downright ill and I used to get half distracted.'[7] At last Mrs Carmichael-Smyth returned to London looking, as Anny noted, very ill. 'I can see her still as she looked at Henbury,' she wrote, 'a noble and magnificent figure, like one of Michael Angelo's sybils.'[8] Her departure, like her presence, further lacerated the girls' feelings. Anny's journal for 22 February reads: 'Had a good cry under a

---

[6] Introduction, Biog. Ed., vol. xii, *Denis Duval*, p. xxxvi.
[7] Journal, Feb. – Mar. 1864.
[8] Ibid.

tree among the crows. For a walk with Minny along the road; all the trees looked like people we know. Birds circling over the fields.'

On 2 March they returned to Freshwater for a while, and then accepted an invitation to go to Mrs Sartoris's country house at Warnford – 'a great house in a great park', where 'a wide river ran across the meadows . . . bare ashtrees and willows everywhere'. The drawing-room was magnificently splendid, and so was Mrs Sartoris's singing, but nothing could assuage the girls' desolation. 'Everything was harmonious and bright', wrote Anny, 'except that my heart ached and ached. Minny sat leaning her head against the chimney. Grief amidst carving and splendours . . .' Seeing the advertisements of their old home for sale in the papers, they felt they could bear no more of this precious atmosphere, or even of Mrs Sartoris's kindness, and they made up their minds to go. They had nowhere of their own to go to, but when not at Freshwater the Camerons, whose tea-plantations were in Ceylon, lived at Putney Heath, and there Anny and Minny were persuaded to stay, in a little cottage on the Heath, till their affairs could be settled.

Meanwhile their grandmother went back to Paris. On 1 May Anny wrote for the first time since her father's death to his American friends, the Baxters. She knew how genuine had been the friendship between them. 'Dear Mrs. Baxter,' she wrote, 'I must write you one line tonight before I go to bed. I have not written before because I can only write about Papa and sometimes I *cant* – . . . I thought of you often and often when I was in his study burning and putting away papers in a sort of dream.' The Baxters were also in the throes of grief, having lost their daughter Sally shortly before Thackeray's death, and they exchanged letters of mutual sorrow. 'Forgive me for speaking of your daughter as I speak. To me the dead are dearer than the living and more alive at times. I think Papa knows perhaps I am writing to you now. Our home where you were once to have come is sold – We have only kept enough furniture for a small house where we are going to live with my Grandmother we believe – Friends are kindness itself there is money enough because Papa was always working for us, and our pain is far far less than it has been – It seems to us that sorrow at first is not sorrow but a terrible physical suffering. It seems to us that we could bear anything with only Papa to talk to about it, but to go on stumbling and falling without him is weary work. My little Minny is asleep now too sad to keep awake tonight – But she is much better thank God and the aching leaves off for a while now and then – Only she looks thin and so wan at times that I can't bear it. . . . Granny has gone to Paris for a little change – perhaps we should have gone with her – but we could not bear it, and there is so much for us to see to that it was decided we should stay. We are in a little cottage on Putney Heath all the gorse is coming out and the green trees; and the birds are singing and it is much better than London Lodgings.

' – *Next morning* Minny and the little dog are standing at the garden gate. Here come some children with flowers who tell us it is Mayday – . . .'[9]

They found their future home, if not yet a direction for their disorientated lives. 'We are going to live in some new houses near Onslow Square, 8, *Onslow Gardens, Brompton*, if ever you write to us, please write there. My sister and I have bought the house and my grandmother is to rent it of us and we are to live with her. We try not to look forward much and to get through each day as it comes. Granny is very kind, but very ill and feeble and every thing seems uncertain and dim. But we have had so much sunshine in our lives such a measure of love that we must not complain now if the light is hidden for a while. I know some day we shall all find our way to the Dearest and Brightest who love us still pray God.'[10]

The 'grand house' had been sold for £10,000 (£4,000 more than it had cost) and Thackeray's copyrights had been sold to George Smith for far more than they had expected. Financially they would be well off. They paid £1,800 for the new house on the advice of their friend Mr Cole.

To please their grandmother they took a French holiday in August, staying with her at Arromanches into September. It was no greater success than their previous meetings; the 'terrible religious discussions' continued unabated. Anny noted in her Journal for 20 August: 'Grannie looks very ill. Minnie says *she* herself is half mad. . . . We want to do our duty but seeing no one makes it so much worse.' Anny felt 'torn and crazed between the two dear ones . . . so miserable and so fearing for the future'. On 9 September she wrote: 'I am crying Minnie is crying, Granny is crying and thinking of G.P. How very miserable we are. What can we do?' They moved sadly into their new house at Michaelmas, in advance of their grandmother, who was to join them later. With their favourite

⁹ Ray, iv. 298–300.   ¹⁰ Ibid.

pieces of old furniture about them, it did not look all that unfamiliar, Anny told Mrs Baxter. London was empty and their best friends away but, she added, 'I don't think we should have liked it to be less sad.'[11]

There was one old friend who had stood by them that year and given them untold comfort. Anny wrote to Mrs Baxter: 'Did Papa ever talk to you about Mrs. Brookfield? She has taken us under her kind wing she is coming to live close by only to be near us. All this terrible year she has been so good to us all three that I do not know how we could have dragged through without her.'[12]

Mrs Carmichael-Smyth joined them at the beginning of November. Their tribulation was to be short-lived. Her strength was visibly waning. She was in fact far more gentle and conciliatory than she had been, almost serene. She had changed her mind, she told Anny, walking with her on 16 December, on many things, especially on religious subjects, and felt more at peace and in sympathy with her son's way of thinking. They were all dreading the approach of the anniversay of his death. She reminisced about her long life and especially of her youth in India and of the time when her first husband, Thackeray's father, came courting her on his white horse. She kissed them goodnight as usual on the evening of 18 December, left the room to go to bed, but before even reaching the stairs she died. Her maid, Fanny, who had come for her, opened the parlour door to tell them she was gone.

On the exact anniversary of her son's death, Christmas Eve, Mrs Carmichael-Smyth was buried beside him at Kensal Green cemetery.

The terrible year was over.

The repetition of the ghastly ordeal of attending Victorian funerals was almost too much for the girls. Kind friends rallied as before. Trollope, whom Thackeray had once called 'a Trojan of a man' for his great heart and benevolence, invited them to his home at Waltham Cross. With him and his wife they were in a wholly sympathetic environment. Trollope esteemed Thackeray, both as an artist and a man, above all their contemporaries. 'I do not hesitate', he wrote in his *Autobiography*, 'to name Thackeray the first. His knowledge of human nature was supreme, and his characters stand out as human beings, with a force and a truth which has not, I think, been within the reach of any other English novelist in any

---

[11] Ray, iv. 302.   [12] Ray, iv. 303–4.

period.' He had only known Thackeray for four years, but felt that he 'had grown into much intimacy with him and his family. I regard him as one of the most tender-hearted human beings I ever knew.[3]

The Trollopes had also invited the girls' young friends, the Merivales, to surround them with the warmth of affection they so intensely needed. Anny, hearing Trollope called each morning at 4.00 a.m. by his manservant to start his day's work, was astonished by his energy. He told her that 'he gave his man half a crown every time he (Mr Trollope) didn't get up! "The labourer is worthy of his hire"' said Mr. Trollope in his deep cheerful lispy voice.'[14] Thanks to Trollope, a note of cheerfulness was at last creeping into Anny's records of that time, something wholly absent for the past agonizing year.

By Easter, the healing process was advanced. The girls were once again staying at Freshwater, and this time able to absorb and enjoy the stimulating company they found there. The Island was working its enchantment again. Anny wrote three letters while there that have been preserved: to George Smith, to Walter Senior, and to Millais. In each, her return to normal is apparent in her sharp and humorous observations, in her ready enjoyment of the passing scene.

The eccentricity of her hostess, Mrs Cameron, and of her guests, the friendship of the Tennysons, and the colony of friends springing up around them in the neighbouring cottages, became of absorbing interest. 'It is the funniest place in the world,' Anny wrote to Walter Senior. 'Everybody is either a genius, or a poet, or a painter or peculiar in some way, poor Miss Stephen says is there *nobody* common-place?'[15]

The mention of 'Miss Stephen' marked the beginning of a new phase in their lives, the friendship of the Stephen family that was to affect them closely. Caroline Stephen was the sister of Fitzjames, barrister of the Inner Temple, a long-standing friend of Thackeray's, contributor to the *Cornhill*, and since Thackeray's death one of those who had looked after the girls' interests over probate, the sale of the house, and other business matters. He was a regular reviewer for the *Saturday Review*, had a prominent role on the *Pall*

[13] *Autobiography*, 159–60, 209.
[14] Journal, 12 Jan. 1865.
[15] *Ritchie Letters*, pp. 125–6.

Mall Gazette, and was altogether a brilliant man. Through him they shortly became acquainted with his brother Leslie.

Mrs Cameron (née Pattle) had been one of seven sisters, all of whom had made notable marriages. They gravitated around her at Freshwater at holiday times, and the Thackeray girls now found themselves caught up in their orbit. There was Mrs Prinsep (Sarah Pattle) staying at Dimbola next door, with her large family, who when in London were Kensington neighbours of the girls. Jowett (not yet Master of Balliol) was a regular visitor and was this Easter staying with Mrs Cameron, hard at work on his translation of Plato. He had brought with him four Oxford students, whose hilarious spirits acted as a tonic on the Thackeray girls. Mrs. Cameron had recently taken up what proved to be her life's great hobby and passion, photography, and all her guests – and passing strangers – were pressed into her service either as models (exposures took anything up to ten minutes), or as acolytes in 'fixing' and washing her plates. The fever of activity that this caused frequently lasted late into the night and there was little time to eat. Anny described the food as 'shocking; and having to be compensated for by eggs and bacon to make up for almost every meal'. But the place was intoxicating, reviving. 'I cannot tell you how much we enjoy it all,' she wrote to Walter Senior. 'Of a morning then sun comes blazing so cheerfully, and the sea sparkles, and there is a far-away hill all green, and a cottage which takes away one's breath it looks so pretty in the morning mists. Then comes eggs and bacon. Then we go to the down top. Then we lunch off eggs and bacon. Then we have tea and look out of the window, then we pay little visits, then we dine off eggs and bacon, and of an evening Minny and Emmy robed in picturesque Indian shawls, sit by the fire, and Miss Stephen and I stroll about in the moon-light.'[16]

There were evening visits to the Tennysons, when sometimes he would consent to read aloud. 'Last night', Anny wrote to Millais, '"King Alfred" read out *Maud*. It was like harmonious thunder and lightning.'[17] Walking on the downs and by the sea they almost expected to see 'poor Boadicea up on the cliff, with her passionate eyes', she told Millais, alluding to his picture 'The Romans leaving Britain'. The painter Watts who had painted her and Minny for Thackeray, was doing portraits of the two Tennyson boys, Hallam and Lionel, aged thirteen and ten respectively. As Anny told

[16] *Ritchie Letters*, p. 126.   [17] Ibid., p. 128.

George Smith, there 'are nothing but poets and painters everywhere and all gold and delicious over the hills'. She had undertaken to write two articles for *Cornhill*, and begged George Smith for a short reprieve. It was a good sign that she had accepted the commission, but she found it harder to concentrate in that distracting atmosphere than at home. 'It is very different', she explained, 'writing with a pencil on a down top, with the sea and a lark twiddling most beautifully overhead, to a two-pair front in London.' Even so, she confessed that she would like to stay on there in lodgings for the rest of her life. 'It is so heavenly lilac down here,' she told him.[18]

[18] Murray Archives.

CHAPTER 13

MINNY

NUMBER 8 Onslow Gardens was a small house, but it was more than they could really afford, and Anny said they would have to practise economy. For this she had no talent at all. Despite the sadness and misgivings with which they had moved in, they were beginning to settle down. The house had a square grey-walled drawing-room, 'with chintz and china', airy bedrooms, a bath, and importantly for Anny a study where she could work undisturbed.

They were still within easy reach of their closest friends: the Collinses, the Coles, the Merivales, and the Carlyles in Chelsea. Mrs Carlyle frequently took them out driving, and Thomas had become very dear to them since their father's death. Two incidents relating to him remained fixed in Anny's memory: Carlyle himself wrote about one of them which occurred some days before Thackeray's death: 'I was riding in the dusk, heavy of heart, along by the Serpentine and Hyde Park, when some human brother from a chariot, with a young lady in it, threw me a shower of salutations. I looked up – it was Thackeray with his daughter: the last time I was to see him in this world. He had many fine qualities, no guile or malice against any mortal; a big mass of a soul, but not strong in proportion; a beautiful vein of genius lay struggling about in him. Nobody in our day wrote, I should say, with such perfection of style.'[1]

Of the other incident Anny wrote: 'Minny is going out for a drive with Mrs. Carlyle this afternoon, – we met old Thomas the other day on his horse and he suddenly began to cry. I shall always love him in future, for I used to fancy he did not care about Papa.'[2] That was one account put right, and for the remainder of Carlyle's life Anny cherished him.

---

[1] Reid, *Life of Lord Houghton*, ii. 113, to Monckton Milnes, 29 Dec. 1863: quoted by Ray, iv. 304.
[2] Ray, ibid.

Another, and more painful rift was healed when, some eighteen months after their father's death, Kate Collins called one day and begged Anny and Minny to come with her to hear a Dickens Reading at the St. James's Hall. She knew it would be painful for them, but 'she was so affectionately insistent', Anny recalled, 'that we could not help agreeing'. After it was over – a reading of *Copperfield*, 'unforgettably grand' – Kate hurried them round behind the platform to meet Dickens, who held 'our hands with kindest grasps of greeting and comfort'.[3]

The sisters divided their household duties according to their inclinations and talents. Minny was an excellent housekeeper and caterer and Anny, who was a disaster in either capacity, was the hostess. This role left her free to work by day, and to welcome their friends in the evening with her spontaneous talk, her sympathy, her sincerity. As she became more assured, her talk took on a character of its own: unconventional to a degree, inconsequential, but sparkling with wit and fantasy. She was never dull and never malicious. As she came into her own, and was accepted as herself and not merely as Thackeray's daughter, she was greatly loved by a growing number of people. Mrs Cameron herself was so inordinately, extravagantly fond of her that she wanted Anny, and her cousin Blanche Ritchie, for daughters-in-law. She never wrote to her in more moderate terms than 'My own darling beloved Annie'. But then Mrs Cameron was inordinate in all her actions, feelings, and pronouncements.

Through Mrs Cameron there was a large increase in the circle of Anny and Minny's acquaintance. Living in Kensington, at Little Holland House, a rambling converted old farmhouse in what is now Melbury Road, were Mrs Cameron's sister Sarah and her husband Thoby Prinsep, an Indian Civil Servant. The Prinseps had three sons and one daughter, all highly gifted young people with whom Anny and Minny were soon on intimate terms. They shared the house with Watts and Ellen Terry. The friendship begun at Freshwater with Caroline Stephen also ripened quickly. Caroline lived with her mother and second brother Leslie in Porchester Square. It was there, at a luncheon to which Lady Stephen invited the Thackeray girls, that they first met Leslie.[4] They were already friends of his brother Fitzjames.

Leslie was in his early thirties at the time, a Fellow and Tutor of

[3] Fuller, pp. 107–8.   [4] Journal, 3 Mar. 1865.

Trinity Hall, Cambridge, anxious to make a career as a writer, but naturally shy and withdrawn. His great passion was for mountaineering. He considered himself a dry-as-dust old bachelor and was generally ill at ease with young women. He found himself, however, getting on surprisingly well with Anny Thackeray at this first meeting, talking about books. Without considering how his words might be received, on being asked which was his favourite novel he said *Vanity Fair*, and was immediately overcome at the thought that Anny might suppose him insincere. He was speaking the truth.

At that luncheon, as Stephen later recorded, he was given, and took the chance 'of falling in love with my darling Minny'.[5] Minny, as Watts painted her and as Caroline Stephen described her, must have been an enchanting creature. 'She had a singular and indescribable social charm – a humourous wayward and changeful grace, which captivated not only for the moment but for life. She was, beyond anyone I have known, quaintly picturesque, tender and true. She could never have been put into intellectual harness, but there was a rare sureness and delicacy in her critical intuitions, whether as to personal or literary qualities. Her own pen, though sparingly used, had a felicity worthy of her parentage, but what comes back most vividly in one's memory of her, is the half playful motherliness of her household ways, which was both amusing and pathetic in the youngest and most fragile of the little family party.'[6]

Minny's predominant traits, her tenderness and motherliness – one remembers her saving drowned flies and bedding them on roseleaves, and the saucers put out for stray Kensington cats – had evidently remained constant since childhood, as well as that fragility that had been of such concern to Thackeray. The combination of these childlike qualities with the maternal concern for others was only a part of Minny's embracing charm. Leslie Stephen was in love with her before he knew it. Thanks to George Smith, living at Hampstead at the time, Stephen had a second and speedy opportunity of meeting her. They sat together at table and he remembered long afterwards what he said, a sure mark of the importance of the occasion for him. Mrs Gaskell (another of Smith's authors) was a fellow guest. With four daughters of her own, she was something of

[5] Alan Bell (ed.), *Sir Leslie Stephen's Mausoleum Book*, p. 9.
[6] *Ritchie Letters*, p. 131.

a judge of young love; and she diagnosed, then and there (Stephen learnt later), that Minny would become his wife.[7]

Shy, uncertain of himself, without a recognized profession as yet, and cautious by nature, Leslie did not allow himself to be carried away by his feelings; he was afraid of committing himself in human relationships, though intrepid on a mountainside. He was content to meet Minny socially for the following months, accepted as a friend by the Thackeray girls, as were his sister Caroline and brother Fitzjames.

Into this happy and hopeful atmosphere there came a bolt from the blue on 24 August (1865) – 'the dreadful news from India', as Anny recorded it, of the death of Amy Crowe following the birth of her second baby, another little girl, called after Anny. The Thackeray girls were immediately caught up in the disaster and, on the return of their cousin Edward from India with his two infants, they went to Paris to meet him on 2 October and brought them all back to Onslow Gardens.

Anny wrote of his ordeal to George Smith: 'Poor fellow his gentleness and tenderness is quite affecting. I can remember so well Papa bringing us to Paris and how we cried all night – These little things only wail, they have never ceased for six weeks and are quite worn out but I hope please God quiet and care will set them up again. . . . Minny says "Now Anny don't you find our experience with puppies valuable." She is delightful with them and knows exactly what to do.'[8]

To care for two babies, one an infant of four months and another (called Margie) scarcely a year older, was no easy matter, as Anny and Minny soon found. Their first trials arose from unsatisfactory nurses, and there were repeated changes of nurse before satisfaction could be secured. From then on, the children became an integral part of Anny's life, and a major source of her happiness, as Edward in due course remarried and pursued his career. The children appeared upon the scene just as Minny's separate course was being mapped out, and Leslie's love for her declared.

On 9 June the following year (1866) Anny decided to celebrate her birthday, for the first time since her father's death, and in the style to which he had accustomed them. They were on holiday at Leith Hill at the time, and there was to be luncheon at the inn, 'tea

---

[7] *Mausoleum Book*, p. 9.   [8] Murray Archives.

under great trees, carts to the station, Mrs. Sartoris singing"[9] – as Anny recorded in her journal. Among the guests – the old circle of friends, the Merivales, Mrs Sartoris, the Prinseps, Mrs Cameron's niece Julia Jackson – Leslie Stephen figured for the first time. In his recollections of the occasion, Stephen explained that Anny and Minny were staying in lodgings at a farmhouse at Leith Hill and asked a party of their friends down for the day. He then noticed that Minny seemed pleased when, in the course of their rambles, they were thrown together. Slow as he was to believe in his good fortune, that day's events came 'as a sort of revelation' to him: he felt that they were drawing nearer.[10]

He planned as usual a summer trip to the Alps and wanted greatly to persuade the Thackeray girls to join him, but did not know how to achieve his end. By luck, the people who had bought their old home at Palace Green, a German couple called Huth, were going to Chamonix and invited Anny and Minny to join them. Stephen suggested a meeting at Zermatt. He arrived before them, in time to see the party arriving, riding on mules. It was the prelude to two or three of the happiest days of his life, he recorded, showing Minny his favourite beauty spots. He knew then that 'his fate was fixed', but being as he was, diffident and hesitant, perversely went on as planned to Vienna with a friend, and did not see Minny again till the autumn in London. Even then, he needed to be spurred on by reports that his peculiar conduct was being taken ill by Anny and Minny. He debated it all in his mind during a solitary meal at the Oxford and Cambridge Club, took his courage in both hands, and went round to Onslow Gardens. Fortunately he found Minny alone. He had prepared a long speech, none of which was needed. Her simple "Yes" dispersed all memory of the "reasons".'[11]

Anny had been away at Caen for background material for the book she was writing (she wanted particularly to visit a Normandy farm). She was busy in her study upstairs finishing *The Village on the Cliff* when Minny came up to tell her that Leslie had proposed. While she had always put Minny's happiness first, and was whole-hearted in sharing Minny's joy, she was so 'overwrought', as she admitted, by the news that she could not find the words with which to finish her book. When Tennyson happened to call two days later, she had to beg him to help her with the last paragraph.[12]

⁹ *Ritchie Letters*, p. 129.   ¹⁰ *Mausoleum Book*, p. 10.
¹¹ Ibid., p. 11.   ¹² *Ritchie Letters*, p. 129.

Leslie and Minny became engaged on 4 December, but were not married until 19 June 1867. There were several matters that needed settling first. From the moment of her engagement, Minny declared that she wished Anny to remain with them; she could not conceive of parting from her. 'I hope never to be separated from Anny', she wrote to a friend, 'except perhaps during my wedding tour. I am sure she will have no reason to regret this change in our lives.'[13] Financially the girls had separate settlements, but the house was jointly owned.

Fortunately Stephen had a deep and whole-hearted affection for Anny. She was not like some other unmarried sisters-in-law, a duty, even a burden upon a man's home. He valued Anny for her great resemblance to Minny; for the 'no small share she inherited from her father's genius'; but above all for her sympathetic nature. She was, he said, 'the most sympathetic person I ever knew. By "sympathetic" I mean able to sympathize quickly with the feelings of all manner of people, to throw herself into their interests and thoughts and even for a time adopt their opinions. I have never observed such readiness, such accessibility to appeals from others, in any human being.'[14] The house in Onslow Gardens became the joint home of all three.

The marriage took place at Onslow Square Church. Herman Merivale recorded that it was a very quiet wedding in the early, almost twilit, morning, in a restful grey church in the Kensington district so much associated with Thackeray. 'Very few of us were present, and it was almost dark. Mr Cole had volunteered to give the bride away, but he was in Paris, and my father, who had been much with the daughters since their father died, was ready to take his place. But when the words "Who giveth?" were spoken, a figure, until then unobserved, emerged from the shadow of a pillar and solemnly said: "I do". It was Henry Cole perfectly dressed for the occasion: how he had crossed the Channel was never known.'

The wedding tour, as was to be expected, was spent in the Alps. Anny told George Smith that she had 'such happy letters from my bride and bridegroom who are scrambling about, Minny on and Leslie walking beside the mule, which has to have steps cut out for it as if it were a member of the Alpine Club.'[15] Leslie had been voted

[13] Ibid., p. 131.   [14] *Mausoleum Book*, p. 12.
[15] Murray Archives, undated.

President of the Alpine Club, a post he held for three successive years.

Stephen wrote regularly for the *Pall Mall Gazette* and the *Saturday Review*. As a wedding present, the editor of the *Saturday Review* gave him a retaining fee of £50 a year. He wrote occasionally for *Fraser's Magazine* (of which Froude was editor), and in 1871 George Smith offered him the editorship of the *Cornhill*. This he accepted the more willingly, as he said, 'from its connection with Thackeray'. The regular salary, £500 a year, enabled him to give up some of his free-lance journalism and gave him the time to settle to writing the book he had long planned *The History of English Thought in the Eighteenth Century*. By the age of forty his reputation as a distinguished man of letters was established.

Happy in his work and ideally happy in his marriage, Leslie never ceased wondering at and observing the charming creature who was his wife: 'her nature was one of quiet love: of a sort of complacent indulgence of tender, cherishing, caressing emotions towards those dearest to her.' She had, he remarked, the most perfect manner towards children. 'She made no ostentation of special appreciation of children, but showed herself to children just as she was – tender, gentle, affectionate, capable of entering naturally into all their little amusements and pleasures.'[16]

After a first miscarriage, Minny gave birth successfully though prematurely to a daughter on 7 December 1870. She was named Laura Makepeace. Though delicate from birth, she appeared quite normal and brought her mother untold joy. 'O Anny,' Minny exclaimed one day when Laura was about two, 'how one does like one's own child!' Leslie was equally infatuated. The moment he came home, 'tired, dusty, overworked', Anny heard the 'clump, clump, of footsteps running upstairs to the nursery.'[17] They took the baby with them everywhere, even on their annual holidays to the Alps. Leslie recalled Minny's 'intense delight' playing with Laura upon sunny Alpine meadows.

Anny was determined never to be in the way in the joint establishment or to allow the others to think she felt so. As a precaution against such an eventuality, she bought herself a cottage on Rememham Hill, Henley, to which she could retire at times on the plea of work, or on the adopted babies' behalf to give them country air. At other times she visited relatives. She kept in closest

---

[16] *Mausoleum Book*, p. 16.   [17] *Ritchie Letters*, p. 147.

touch with the Ritchies, the companions of her Parisian childhood. Early in 1871, after the débâcle of Sedan and the victory of the Germans, Anny was so distraught with worry about her cousin Charlotte Ritchie, the only one of the family still in Paris then, that she hurred over on 14 March, taking the last remaining means of communication via Le Havre, in an attempt to persuade her to come to England. While the fruit-trees were in blossom the snow was still on the ground, and German helmets were to be seen everywhere as she passed through the countryside towards Paris. Her arrival coincided with the outbreak of the 'Commune'. She witnessed scenes that she could only compare with the French Revolution. She was caught in cross-fire in the rue St. Honoré, had to seek shelter in the church of St. Roch (familiar to her from childhood), saw the beginning of massacres in the Place Vendôme, and panic everywhere with the shopkeepers putting up their shutters and people shouting to her, as an Englishwoman, to go home while she could. Unable to persuade Charlotte, she saw it was useless to remain, and hurried back. She had felt deeply involved in the war from the outbreak and was shattered by the events in France. She could not shake off the impression of some of the scenes she had witnessed, and incorporated them in her novel *Mrs. Dymond*, which was not written till much later and published in 1885.[18]

As soon as normal conditions were restored in France, she was back there, joining her Ritchie cousins for holidays on the Normandy coast. Blanche Ritchie, now married to Frank Warre-Cornish, had little girls of an age with Anny's adopted children, Margie and Annie Thackeray, and they often spent their seaside holidays together. Wherever she was, Anny wrote almost daily to Minny. From the Calvados coast in August 1872 she wrote: 'What shall my letter be about to-day darling? . . . We have had a grand bathing this morning. It was such fun to see the children rushing across the sands screaming with laughter, in funny little trousers and jackets. Margaret, Margy, Dolcie and Anny. Then they went into the sea, and the waves rushed over them . . . and Blanche and Charlotte and I shrieked to the bathing men to get them out. But the children all declared it was delightful.'[19]

In March 1873 the Stephens and Anny moved to Southwell Gardens. Leslie's financial position was much improved since his marriage and they wanted a larger house. The new house was

[18] Journal, 14 Mar. 1871.   [19] MS Letters.

certainly more spacious, but for Anny the parting with the old one was sorrowful. 'Good-bye dear old house,' she noted in her Journal. 'You have sheltered warmed and comforted us. We were having a tea party I remember when the vans came to move us and our cups were carried right away out of the drawing room.'[20]

Minny and Leslie were always there to welcome her back after her wanderings. On her return from a journey to Venice later in 1873 with the Ritchies, she found Leslie awaiting her at the station with a hansom cab, 'and Minny and Leslie . . . so glad to see me,' as she remembered, 'and Laura gave such darling little capers'. After Italy, she commented, it would not be in human nature not to shudder at the contrast with foggy Southwell Gardens, but after such a welcome 'it would be inhuman nature', she wrote to Hallam Tennyson, 'to grumble really'.[21]

It was in Leslie Stephen's drawing-room, at his Sunday gatherings of promising young men, that Anny first came into contact with the rising generation of writers, some of whom were to be as famous in their time as her father's great contemporaries. Three of them in particular were to become trusted friends: Meredith, Henry James, and Hardy.

In 1874, when he first met Anny at Leslie's house, Hardy was a practising architect of thirty-four, new to letters, painfully shy, and provincial in his view of women. He was startled to meet emancipated ladies like Anny, who on top of her great name had already an established reputation of her own. After several meetings, he perceived that she had not only plenty of assurance, but plenty of practical advice to give a novice, and great natural kindness.[22] With time, he proved the value of both. Anny met George Eliot socially on select occasions – at dinners at Lord Houghton's and Tennyson's, both before and after she was married. She was taken to call upon her by Mrs Sartoris once and by Mrs Procter (on 18 January 1872 and 18 February 1873 respectively). Anny confided to her Journal and to Emily Ritchie that she found the atmosphere rather '"Too precious" at the "shrine", and the cult of the "divinity" too oppressive. . . . There is a want of reality in it . . . Each talking their best and neither listening to the other.'[23]

George Eliot was, however, one of Anny's admirers. To an

[20] Journal, 8 March, 1873.
[21] *Ritchie Letters*, p. 162.
[22] Robert Gittings, *The Young Thomas Hardy*, pp. 275–6, 278, 286.
[23] Journal, 18 Jan. 1872, 18 Feb. 1873.

acquaintance, she wrote, '"The Story of Elizabeth" is by Miss Thackeray. It is not so cheerful as Trollope, but is charmingly written. You can taste it and reject it if it is too melancholy.'[24] Answering Blackwood, who had asked her view on current fiction, she wrote much later: 'It is a long while since I read a story newer than Rasselas. . . . So I was a bad judge of comparative merits among popular writers. I am obliged to fast from fiction. . . . I ought to except Miss Thackeray's stories, which I cannot resist when they come near me.'[25] 'In general', she declared, 'it is my rule not to read contemporary fiction. . . . I know nothing of our contemporary English novelists with the exception of Miss Thackeray's and (a few of) Anthony Trollope's works.'[26]

The enthusiasm with which the young contemporaries of Anny had received her earliest novels, voiced by Rhoda Broughton as a girl (see p. 129), has been noted; but the commendation of George Eliot was another matter. One is not surprised to read Sir William Hunter writing after that: 'Thackeray's genius was the flowering of a century and a half of family culture; a culture of which the beautiful after-efflorescence still blooms in *Old Kensington*, the *Story of Elizabeth*, and the *Village on the Cliff*.'[27] George Eliot's praise laid a consecrating hand on Anny's work.

George Eliot never called on anyone (she only dined with intimates) but she liked the world to call on her, and she was never less than welcoming to Anny. A somewhat more relaxed encounter than the previous ones might have resulted from a call paid her by Minny (Mrs Leslie Stephen as she then was) and Anny taking the two-and-a-half-year-old Laura with them, in December 1873. George Eliot was notably susceptible to the charms of babies, but on that occasion she was out. 'I was much discontented', she wrote to Minny afterwards, 'to have missed you and Miss Thackeray when you were kind enough to call the other day. In case you should be inclined to the pretty action of coming to me again, I write to say that we have taken of late to the aged habit of driving more and walking less, so that we go farther and remain out a little later than we used to do. But after ½ past 4 we should not be out on any but a rarely exceptional occasion. . . . With best regards – reverentially including Miss Laura . . .'[28]

[24] Gordon S. Haight, *The George Eliot Letters*, iv. 209.
[25] Ibid. vi. 123.   [26] Ibid. vi. 418.
[27] *The Thackerays in India* (OUP, 1897).
[28] *The George Eliot Letters*, v. 478.

In the summer of 1875, Minny was pregnant again and was overjoyed when her doctor said it would do her good to go for some weeks to the Alps. She and Leslie went to Interlaken and Murren. Anny joined them there and they went on to Gründelwald and Rosenlaui. They stayed there till the autumn, travelling part of the time with Mrs Oliphant the authoress.

On the way back from Switzerland, Anny stopped off in Paris. Minny's pregnancy was not an easy one, but they all remembered how well she had been after Laura was born. At home again in November Anny went to spend the night at Windsor with her new friend, Mrs Oliphant. Leslie and Minny spent the evening as usual 'in perfect happiness and security'. Julia Duckworth, a niece of Mrs Cameron recently widowed, called, and found them so happy together that she felt an incongruous intruder in her desolate state and withdrew. The baby was not expected for some time yet, but on going to bed Minny felt unwell and, not wishing to disturb her husband, decided to sleep apart, with her maid. During the night, Leslie was roused by the maid who said Minny was taken ill. He found her in convulsions, already unconscious. He ran for the doctor but he could do nothing. She never regained consciousness and died the next day at noon. It was Stephen's forty-third birthday.

A telegram had been sent to Anny, not specifying the cause of the alarm. When she arrived at the station, Fitzjames was there to meet her. He told her that the child had been prematurely – and still-born. 'Yes, Yes, that I can bear', cried Anny, 'it's my Minny, tell me quick, my Minny?' She had to be told that Minny was dead. Writing some time later to Mrs Baxter, she said: 'I have no words, and I am still so unaccustomed to [her death] that I don't think very much, only that I have [lost] the tenderest, faithfullest, and most unspeakably loving sister that any one ever had. . . . One day I went away for the night, and she was dead when I came back the next day, with tender closed eyes and a face so radiant. . . . Poor Leslie has been so good, but is so wrung and strained. He goes up and down. He is down just now, all life seems to go out of him; he doesn't complain but seems to fade and fade, and then perhaps the tide turns and for a few days I get happy about him again.'[29]

Anny was left with a formidable charge. Not only had she lost what was dearest in life, but she was left with a heart-broken and

[29] Fuller, p. 142.

increasingly eccentric man who relied totally on her, and a little girl who, as she grew, was found to be mentally deficient. The terrible heritage feared by Thackeray for Minny – the child Isabella had borne just before going mad – had mercifully passed over one generation, to blight the next. Laura, like her ill-fated grandmother, was a charming creature, gentle and pretty, with a happy disposition. She lived to a good age, dying only in 1946.

Unhesitatingly, Anny took up the burden, but for her there seemed nothing further to look forward to in life.

CHAPTER 14

THE AUTHOR'S PATH

THE death of Minny deprived Anny not only of her lifelong and dearest companion, but of the main object of her life. Three years older than Minny, and always intellectually ahead of her, from the childish days in Young Street, Minny had been constant pet, care, and amusement in her father's lifetime; and after his death, the receptacle of all her love; and Minny had a touching belief in her 'genius'. Leslie Stephen tells the tale of Minny's indignation over Fitzjames Stephen's unappreciative review of Anny's *Village on the Cliff*. Leslie and Minny were in the train going to Anny's cottage at Henley which she lent them on their return from their wedding-trip to Switzerland, and Leslie passed Minny the review in *Fraser's Magazine*. She flared up; '"Fitzy"' she exclaimed, "does not see that Anny is a genius!"'[1]

While Minny's marriage had not separated them, it had inevitably turned Anny more decidedly than ever towards her writing as the main outlet for her immense energies. Since Minny was the perfect home-maker, the practical housekeeper, Anny could without compunction live the life of her imagination and pursue the author's path. Without false pretensions or exaggerated estimates of her abilities, she was optimistic and believed she could make a success of her chosen career. The encouraging reception given her first ventures by the press prepared her for the success that so easily came her way with *The Story of Elizabeth* and *The Village on the Cliff*. George Smith's faith in her abilities was of particular value, both in giving her confidence and in providing her with the platform from which to reach her public, by serializing her work in the *Cornhill Magazine*. Anny wished passionately to justify Smith's belief in her and to become a writer worthy of the name she bore. She was her own taskmaster and no indulgent one at that, driving herself for long hours daily, travelling when necessary in search of a

[1] *Mausoleum Book*, p. 15.

detail – as to the Normandy farm for *The Village on the Cliff*. Time, and her increasingly fastidious criteria in judging other writers and herself, would incline her to regard a sense of reality as a book's major requisite.

Her own novels were invariably based upon some personal experience. Thus *The Village on the Cliff* was obviously the result of the visit to Arromanches made with her grandmother in the summer of 1864. Its position relative to Caen and Bayeux, and its distinctive features – a little fishing port set among high cliffs and dominated by a picturesque village – make it sufficiently recognizable. In the novel she calls it Petitport. A short holiday could not on its own have given the author that insight into French peasant character, and that familiarity with 'small-town politics', that the book reveals. But there were the many years of experience of French country manners that she had accumulated with her grandparents during the summer holidays at their little 'hunting lodge' at Mennecy. In the course of writing the novel, she returned to Caen specifically to gather local colour. Familiarity with the French way of life exempted her from that condescension in writing of foreigners, so general at the time, even in Dickens and Wilkie Collins.

She was at her best in noting country scenes: a cartful of peasants returning from a day's holiday, a christening or family gathering of sorts, at the end of a hot summer's day. 'It was full of country people: a young man with a flower stuck into his cap was driving, an old man was sitting beside him. Inside the cart were three women and some children. One little fellow was leaning right over, blowing a big trumpet and holding a flag. The other children were waving branches and pulling at a garland of vine-leaves, of which one end was dragging, baskets were slung to the shafts below, two dogs were following and barking, while the people in the cart were chaunting a sort of chorus as they went jolting along the road.'[2]

The action of the novel is almost equally divided between 'Petitport' and London. Anny chose for her heroine a young, inexperienced, and singularly naïve little governess, Catherine George, employed by a large and demanding family – the Butlers – living at Eaton Square. The contrast between her own obscure existence and the gay and brilliant destinies awaiting her namesake, the Butlers' eldest daughter also being called Catherine, emphasizes

[2] *The Village on the Cliff*, p. 20.

the dreary lot of the governess, with no other relatives than two plain little stepsisters, whose schooling in Kensington Square she pays for out of her own salary. Anny was here plainly calling on her own girlhood memories of the dinginess of schoolroom years, and not without touches of humour. Writing of the 'Domestic Bastille' overlooking the mews at the rear of the house, she notes that all the 'ancient terrors and appliances are kept up: the solitary confinement, Question by Torture, the walls and the maps, and the drugget and the crumpled chintz; the worn-out table-cover, the blotted ink-stand; blots everywhere, on the children's fingers and elbows, even on Sarah's nose'. Every sharply observed item brings out forcibly the contrasts conditioning the lives of the fortunate and unfortunate girls. 'Miss George' inevitably falls in love with the Butlers' nephew, a Thackerian young man, lazy, kind, a sufficiently good painter to wish to make art his career. There has been no flirtation on his part, simply a kindly word from time to time, enough to kindle her highly inflammable feelings. It is his friend, Beamish of the Foreign Office, who is the impeccable fiancé of the fortunate Catherine. Miss George's insufficiently concealed feelings for young Butler lead to her dismissal from her post – a dismissal disguised however as being to her advantage because it secures her a post with a sister of Mrs Butler's, Mme de Tracy in Normandy, at 'Petitport', where Mme de Tracy's family are the landowners. Thus the little governess is brought into the Village on the Cliff, safely out of reach, so her late employers believe, of the seductive Richard Butler. It was not for nothing, however, that he was made an artist by his creator, with a fine eye for a landscape – and a handsome woman. While lazing at Petitport on his previous visit, Richard had been struck by Reine Chrétien, the beautiful, powerful, capable farmer's daughter and manager of his prosperous estate, and inevitably he returns to Petitport. Reine is a fully realized and successful creation; purposeful, never trivial, generous, but shrewd in business dealings, convincing in her femininity and attractiveness to men, but too self-sufficient and contemptuous of mediocre admirers to be touched by any of them. She is very French. Her characterization marks a considerable advance in Anny's power as a novelist, though nobody else in the book quite measures up to the same degree of credibility. There are lively sketches of the small provincial society surrounding Mme de Tracy at the château: her married son's family, his chic wife, their children, their regular circle for evening cards and a glass of 'Calvados' – the Curé and the Maire, M. Fontaine.

The Maire is a widower left with a small boy, Toto. Though M. Fontaine was one of Reine's rejected suitors, she was very fond of children, and gave Toto like the other village children little treats whenever a saint's day or public holiday gave her respite from her labour as manageress of her father's farm. Miss George, governess to the children at the château now, comes into contact with Reine, who holds her land from the de Tracys. Miss George's first sight of Reine sets the tone to their subsequent friendship: Miss George, so unsure of herself, Reine so wholly self-reliant. With her pupils Miss George had been sent to the farm: 'As the children and Miss George pushed open the heavy doors and came into the wide sunny court, a figure descended the stone steps leading from the strong tower where the apples are kept. It was Reine in her white coiffe, who advanced with deliberate footsteps, carrying an earthenware pan under her arm, and who stood waiting in the middle of the great deserted-looking place until they should come up to her.

'Catherine wondered whether all Normandy peasant-girls were like this one. It was a princess keeping the cows. There she stood, straight, slender, vigorous; dressed in the Sunday dress of the women of those parts.'[3]

It is not long before the Maire, repulsed by his first choice and ever on the look-out for a wife, begins to show an interest in the governess; she is pretty and he understands that Englishwomen are frugal and not frivolous regarding clothes. He could see that she was very kind to children. His nascent inclination is strongly encouraged by the de Tracys. There is no room for Catherine in their Paris flat, where they will be going at the summer's end, and Catherine must be safely settled before their departure. Marriage to the Maire would be the perfect solution they think, little concerned with Catherine's own feelings.

Complications arise when Dick Butler makes a return visit to Petitport, to finish the picture he had begun there on the previous visit, but in truth lured there by Reine whose image has haunted him ever since. It is for Reine, Catherine realizes, that Dick has come back. Wholly unaware of Catherine's feelings for him, he confides to her his love for Reine under the seal of secrecy. He proposes to Reine, who had previously rejected him – too sensitive

---

[3] *The Village on the Cliff*, p. 136.

of the social barriers dividing them – and is now accepted by her. This seals Catherine's own fate. Certain now of never winning Dick's love, she accepts the Maire's proposal. The marriage is hurried forward to suit the De Tracys, and celebrated at Caen. As the bridal party enters the church a funeral is still in progress, an ill omen that deeply impresses Catherine.

Despite his pomposity and self-importance, Fontaine is not a bad man, but genuinely anxious to make Catherine happy. She is to have her young stepsisters to stay in their holidays and her least wish is law to him. She cannot but be grateful for his kindness. Anne Thackeray knew enough about the clannishness of French provincial family life to realize the suspicion and contempt with which a 'second wife' – and a foreigner at that – would be received by Fontaine's all-licensed servant and by his in-laws.

Drama is not lacking in the development of the plot. Anne always made good use of the topography of her novels' settings. Here the sea is a constant presence in the action; its sound lulling the sleepless Catherine at night, its shimmer and sparkle affecting her spirits by day, the fishermen of the little port constantly in the foreground. It is the sea that becomes the catalyst to the human drama. Fontaine is drowned attempting to rescue a fisherman caught in a sudden storm. Catherine is widowed in time for Dick Butler to realize her long love for him. Reine, too proud to submit to his family's opposition, herself breaks off their engagement and dismisses him. The climax, however, provides yet further surprise: Dick does *not* console himself with Catherine, much as he likes her. She is well provided for by her husband's legacy and by a further legacy from an English aunt. She is able to make a home for her little sisters and Toto in England (in the Richmond that Anny knew so well) and, finally, to direct Dick's wavering purpose and urge him to return where he is really wanted, to Reine, who has never ceased to love him.

The first edition in book form was dedicated to 'Harriet Thackeray' and dated from 'Brighton, January 27th 1867'. The success was immediate and it ran into three editions the same year: in February, March, and July.

During the years of Minny's marriage, Anny produced her most successful novel, *Old Kensington*, and *Miss Angel*, the life story of Angelica Kauffmann, serialized in the *Cornhill* between January 1874 and January 1875. The death of Minny proved to be a turning-point not only in the author's life, but in the development of her career as a writer. In 1877, a momentous year for Anny in every way, she produced the novella *From the Island*, in which her development as both woman and writer is first triumphantly made apparent. Short as it is (a mere hundred pages), it marks the change that the last two years had effected in her. She is no longer a hesitant, inexperienced onlooker but a principal participant in life, and a writer in command of her medium. *Mrs. Dymond*, her last novel, was published after a ten-year interval. In the meantime she turned from fiction to critical and biographical essays, in the manner made fashionable by Macaulay. It was in this form, begun with her Introductions to the works of other writers, that she achieved her more lasting success: her critical introductions to the works of her predecessors – notably Maria Edgeworth, Susan Ferrier, Mrs Opie. These in turn led to the personal memorials of her great contemporaries – Tennyson, Ruskin, Browning, Mrs Gaskell – and then to her own *Chapters from some Memoirs*. The Biographical Introductions to her father's Complete Works in thirteen volumes can fairly be called her *magnum opus*.

Her literary output thus divides itself into three distinct periods and styles of writing: fiction; critical and biographical essays; personal memoirs and journals. Her fiction for the most part belongs to her youth. To write novels had appeared the most natural of ambitions. But the hard fact was that she had neither the experience, the invention, nor the sheer command of language (which lifted the equally inexperienced young Brontës immediately to the forefront of contemporary writers) to create the true microcosm from which every good novel springs.

Her artist's eye for detail, sensibility to impressions, honesty in self-judgement, exceptional sympathy – all these served her ten times better as a memorialist than as a writer of fiction. Her memory, often proven faulty over hard facts, was incomparably rich in supplying the atmosphere of a scene, the highlights of an encounter, the essence of an emotion. Experience and the society of her great contemporaries enabled her to write memorably, wisely, and charitably about the lives of others. She was a natural biographer.

Meanwhile, the immediate success of her first two novels stirred her to fresh endeavours. While Minny was happily married her time was her own and she had much she wanted to say. Now that those

Kensington years of her adolescence were behind her and the main actors gone beyond recall, she appeared to feel the need to re-live them. *Old Kensington* was serialized in the *Cornhill* from April 1872 to April 1873. A note to George Smith of March/April 1869 is significant in dating its inception; also in betraying the author's degree of involvement with her characters, which was both typical of her and harmful to her work. It also revealed her awareness of her true talent, as a memorialist. Thanking him for a too-generous payment for 'a stupid little sketch', she went on: 'I see it doesn't do to write about things one likes very much, for one has such a pleasant notion of them in one's mind that one proses on and on. I wish Miss Vanborough[4] would get on – I shall take her to Rome with me. It is odd and sad to go back to one's heroine of fifteen years ago. And after this I shall take to writing memoirs.'[5]

If her words are to be taken literally, this dates the beginning of *Old Kensington* in 1854, after the first visit to Rome with her father and the move from Young Street to Onslow Square – which might account for the nostalgia of its tone in referring to the old house and those youthful Kensington years. 'In those days', she writes, 'the hawthorn spread across the fields and market-gardens that lay between Kensington and the river. Lanes ran to Chelsea, to Fulham, to North End, where Richardson once lived and wrote in his garden-house . . . . close at hand, all round about the old house were country corners untouched – blossoms instead of bricks in spring-time. . . . There were strawberry-beds, green, white, and crimson in turn. . . . Sometimes in May mornings the children would gather hawthorn branches out of the lanes, and make what they liked to call garlands for themselves. . . . There was a Kensington world (I am writing of twenty years ago) somewhat apart from the big uneasy world surging beyond the turnpike – a world of neighbours bound together by the old winding streets and narrow corners in a community of venerable elm-trees and traditions that are almost levelled away.'[6]

While *Old Kensington* is by far the most ambitious and successful of the novels so far (it was mainly written in 1872), its weaknesses are the same as ever: want of structure, want of an independent existence. Anne had still not reached the point of seeing her story as

[4] The heroine of *Old Kensington*.
[5] Murray Archives: *Ritchie Letters*, p. 133.
[6] *Old Kensington*, pp. 14, 15, 17.

existing outside herself, as a separate creation. The personal experience on which it was based was all-pervading, leaving little or no licence for invention to lend it a life of its own. The story is built up of a succession of vividly realized, or rather remembered, episodes, feebly linked together. Lacking a unifying structure, *Old Kensington* still has charming and original qualities of its own, which can well account for its great success.

While the range of incidents and characters is much wider than in her previous stories, the plot, such as it is, remains basically autobiographical. There are the Anglo-Indian children, George and Dorothea Vanborough, sent home in childhood to a kind old aunt in Kensington, Lady Sarah Francis, who lives in 'Old Street' (Young Street) in just such a Queen Anne house as the one in which Anny grew up. There is the Kensington circle of young and old friends from which she conjures up the scheming little figure of Rhoda who bewitches George but flirts with any man, and ultimately despoils Dorothea of her lover and her fortune. There are the Paris scenes, drawn from the incidents she had witnessed both as a child and as a young woman, memories later recorded again in *Chapters from some Memoirs*. There are Cambridge students and Eton boys, whose talk and manners she had observed in her cousin Richmond Ritchie and his friends. Above all, there is a deeper analysis of the pains and tribulations of first love, described not in conventional terms as in *The Story of Elizabeth* and *The Village on the Cliff* but more directly with all the doubts and uncertainty of inexperience groping after truth. Dorothea has much charm; absolute honesty, generosity, kindness. But her vain, futile, frivolous mother (Mrs Palmer) is far more completely realized in a much briefer space.[7] Her total selfishness brings a fresh breath of humour into the story. Both she and the scheming little Rhoda (a Becky-ish creation this) are a great advance in character-building. The elderly gentlemen – military, legal, land-owning, hard-working clergymen – are good cameos; and the rough Crimean soldiers and the downright French *bonnes* enlarge the social canvas. Seen in the context of Anny's growing experience of life, the deepening of the emotional tone, the touches of melancholy, are explained; and the complex character of the hero, Frank Raban, accounted for by her growing intimacy with Richmond Ritchie. The self-righteous, rigidly conventional, masterful fiancé whom Dorothea is too young

[7] See Appendix, p. 282

to resist, Robert Henley, is not only a complete and convincing creation of a prig, but a symptom of Anny's growing rebellion against the accepted masculine domination of the time. *Old Kensington* is no longer a novice's book.

The subject of Angelica Kauffmann was suggested to her by a chance introduction to her work at a dinner in Stratford Place in Kensington in February 1873, when her host pointed out the ceiling of his dining-room painted by the artist and told Anny the dramatic story of her life (1741–1807). Her immediate reaction, noted in her Journal for the year was: 'thought of writing story.'[8]

She evidently read the account of Angelica's life written by John Rossi (1762–1839), the sculptor, whom she quotes in the course of her text, for her narrative, though written in fictional form, keeps closely to the facts of Angelica's career. She describes her early studies in Italy, the interest taken in her by Lady Wentworth, who brought her to England to launch her on London society; her flirtation with Reynolds; her unfortunate marriage to the fashionable portrait painter and allegorical decorative painter with commissions from the Court, the impostor Horn (who pretended to be the Swedish ambassador, Count de Horn); her eventual marriage to the Italian painter Antonio Zucchi. Her trials were succeeded by triumphs. She was one of the first Academicians at the founding of the Royal Academy in 1769. Anny's story concludes with this happy end to her heroine's tribulations, and does not follow her through the remainder of her successful career, mostly spent in Rome where she knew Goethe intimately (during his 'Italiensche Reise'), and where she was highly esteemed. Canova superintended her funeral and the Academicians of St. Luke acted as her pall-bearers[9]

The character as Anny describes her is a creature of impulse, of uncontrolled emotions, of generous responses, and ill-judgement. The aspect that evidently most attracted the author to the subject was some similarity to her own predicament at the moment of writing, as revealed by her Journals of 1873–5. For all her talent, Angelica lacks direction in life; she feels her essential loneliness despite her many friends and patrons; she feels intensely the need of guidance, of support. Though she received several proposals of marriage, even apparently one from Reynolds, she refused them all.

[8] Journal, 15 Mar. 1873: *Ritchie Letters*, p. 152.   [9] *D.N.B.*

She longed for love and did not find it and is shown as deluded by an impostor into a bigamous marriage, out of her intense need for support, for the love lacking at the centre of her life.

While Anny's own situation was in fact very different, there was all too evidently, after her father's death, an agonizing need for support and guidance, and also a want of direction, as expressed covertly if not overtly in her Journals. Inevitably, these feelings were greatly heightened when Minny became engaged and married. From the literary point of view, *Miss Angel* is an advance on Anny's previous novels (the narrative being supplied by the biographical data of her subject's life): it is more concentrated, the scenes develop more naturally out of each other, the incidents are more closely related. There are a few powerfully described episodes: the Queen's first sitting to Angelica at Windsor, which coincides with the discovery of the imposture played on her by Horn, while the snow-bound landscape reflects the cold gripping at Angelica's heart.

There are passages in the book, treating of Angelica's heartbreak and of the consolation she sought and found in her art alone, that make revealing reading when seen in the context of Anne Thackeray's own life at the time. The actual writing of the book was begun, as her Journal shows, in March 1874 during a visit to Venice taken with her Ritchie relations, including the youngest son Richmond who was then about to go up to Cambridge. In a very muted mood she wrote in the book of the compensation that art can bring for the deceptions and disappointments of life. 'The sympathies and consolations of light, of harmony, of work, are as effectual as many a form of words. They are *substitutions* of one particular manner of feeling and expression for another. To hungry, naked, and imprisoned souls, art ministers with a bountiful hand, shows them a way of escape (even though they carry their chains with them); leads silently, pointing into a still and tranquil world enclosed within our noise-bound life, where true and false exist, but harassing duty and conflicting consciences are not, nor remorse, nor its terrors, nor sorrowful disappointments. . . . Angelica was never more grateful to her pursuit than now when time was difficult on her hands.'[10]

'It may be our blessing as well as our punishment that the *now* is not all with us as we hold it, nor the moment all over that is past. It is never quite too late to remember, never quite too late to love;

[10] *Miss Angel*, p. 135.

although the heart no longer throbs that we might have warmed, the arms are laid low that would have opened to us. But who shall say that time and place are to be a limit to the intangible spirit of love and reconciliation, and that new-found trust and long-delayed gratitude may not mean more than we imagine in our lonely and silenced regret?'[11]

Sympathy for her subject was either moving her to unknown depths of perception, or life itself had broken its early promise to her. The sequel would show what motives were strongest at the time.

[11] Ibid., p. 170.

13. Minny Thackeray

14. Richmond Ritchie in 1877

CHAPTER 15

RICHMOND

EVEN before the death of Minny, even before Minny's marriage, Anny was subject to fits of depression. Understandable as these were after the loss of her father (the passing of time scarcely lessened the intensity of her grief expressed in recurrent nightmares about his funeral), there were other reasons that could not be accounted for by material worries, like the painful changes in her circumstances, and her chronic inability to deal with money matters.

Together with her father's mercurial temperament, soaring sky-high one moment and in the depths the next, she had inherited from her Irish mother a highly emotional nature easily affected by adverse surroundings, by the criticisms or approbation of her companions. Leslie Stephen, despite their mutual affection and respect, had a depressing effect on her; as Minny had laughingly described it, he acted like a 'cold-bath' on their enthusiasms. He and Anny were constitutionally ill-assorted. She was crushed by his pedantic intellect, and he was irritated by her 'ignorance'. 'Anny, for example,' he wrote to Julia Duckworth in 1877, 'is about the most uneducated person I ever knew. She has not two facts in her head and one of them is a mistake. But certainly I think her one of the best and most attractive people I ever met – and worth a dozen senior wranglers and the whole staff of professors at Girton and Newnham. What I said of her want of education is what I should say (I suppose) of a first-rate musical performer who had a bad violin. . . . Anny always reminds me of an admirable painter whose colours or brushes or something or other are so confused that all her outlines are muddled and indistinct. She would not lose her genius nor have more genius if she were as clever in her workmanship as Miss Austen.' Even Leslie had to admit that Anny had genius. He wrote again: 'But she has real genius and originality – more than almost anybody now working . . . if only it could be just a little combed out!'[1]

Anny's extravagance was a constant source of exasperation to Leslie. Despite the generous provision Thackeray had made for the girls and the financial success of her books, Anny was always short of money. Generous to a fault, as impulsive in her benefactions as she was ardent in her sympathies, the money was always gone by the quarter's end. This was the main reason for the exhausting arguments with Leslie, recorded by him in his *Mausoleum Book*. Repeatedly, he had to lend her money to pay her bills. She invariably repaid him but as invariably, at the next quarter's close, had to borrow from him again. There were times when her want of cash (sometimes she had only £35 in the bank) caused her to panic and seek ways and means of earning more, but the lesson was never learned. In fact she was suffering from an essential loneliness. For all her independence of conduct and strong personal opinions, she needed consolations which could not after all be found in her work. Whatever she might write to the contrary, she sought them in her impetuous trips abroad and in her eager involvement in the lives of others. But she needed passionately to commit herself, to devote herself, to lose herself in a love which, so far, she had not known.

Fortunately, at the time of her loss, Anny could find some comfort in her adopted little girls, Amy's children, and Laura. She loved to have children about her, though Laura was becoming more of a sorrow than a joy. For a time after his remarriage, in 1870, Edward Thackeray had wished to have his children back and Anny had had to part with them. As he was temporarily settled in Hampstead she was able to visit them as often as she liked. They were always her 'dear darling children'; and now, presumably on Edward's return to active service, the children were restored to Anny and, with Leslie's consent, lived permanently with her. It was Leslie who took them daily to school. Before Minny's death, Mrs Cameron had persuaded Anny to take one of her Freshwater cottages, The Porch. While she mostly let it to friends, it became a chosen retreat for her in times of stress; and her home in old age.

After 'a miserable and terrible winter in Southwell Gardens' following Minny's death, Anny and Leslie moved to Hyde Park Gardens. They sold the Southwell Gardens house for £4,100. Leslie

[1] *Mausoleum Book*, pp. xxiii–xxiv.

showed the generosity of his nature by buying for Anny a little house in Wimbledon (in Lingfield Road) for her mother, so that she would be nearer. Ever since Thackeray's death, Anny had made regular visits to her 'mama', as she always called her, at Southend where she had been settled for years in the care of the faithful Mrs Bakewell. These visits touched Anny deeply and brought delight to the always sprightly Isabella, who on occasions still sang sweetly for her. The care of Isabella devolved entirely on Anny now, and this together with the expenses of the children was one permanent reason for her shortage of cash. The move to Wimbledon was a great success, both Isabella and Mrs Bakewell delighting in their new comfortable quarters.

Wimbledon had become known to Anny through the move there of her Ritchie relations, with whom she remained in constant touch, and with whom she had stayed when they were living at Henbury, after her father's death. Subsequently Mrs Ritchie, her older daughters having married, had moved to Wimbledon with Emily to be near her two boys then at school, Gerald and Richmond. The youngest of the family, born in Calcutta in 1854, Richmond had always been precocious. He had won a King's Scholarship for Eton at the age of eight. He was indeed exceptionally intelligent and Anny had early enjoyed encouraging him by an exchange of letters. One of his surviving letters from Eton, describing the spring, showed how he responded to nature and had an observant eye. Anny sent him a tie from Rome (while staying with the Storys in 1869) and, thanking her for it and telling her that it was 'universally admired', he explained that, unfortunately, it 'must now obligatorily be put away' for him to resume the regulation white tie of the college. He wrote to her with complete ease, as to a contemporary, and signed himself 'Your affectionate cousin'.

Intelligent and maturing fast, he fitted unassumingly into the domestic pattern of Anny's organized children's holidays at Brighton or elsewhere. Staying at Brighton in 1873 with Minny and Laura, Anny wrote to Richmond's sister Emily (known as 'Pinkie' in the family), referring to 'Minnie with a thimble and dear little Laura in a sailor's costume.' She added, 'I enjoy having Richmond very much as I needn't tell you, and I insisted on going on rather crazy expeditions and showing him Brighton.'[2] He was by then nineteen. The word 'crazy' might suggest that Anny was allowing

[2] MS Letters: N-B collection.

herself already to be carried away upon an unpredictable tide of feeling.

The following year, in the autumn of 1874, Anny went to Venice with a large party of Ritchies, which included Gussie, then engaged to Douglas Freshfield,[3] Blanche (now Mrs Warre-Cornish), Emily, and Richmond. On the return journey the party split up, Richmond and Gussie going on to Rome, and Anny returning to Bologna with one of Blanche's children. Writing to Minny from Perugia, she said: 'We are very sorry to part. We have all been in a most absurd state of rapture, and next time, unless you come, I shall come alone and gush less, and write descriptions for a book.'[4] Richmond was in his last year at Eton and was to sit for a scholarship at Trinity, Cambridge (the 'Newcastle Prize') early the following year. From Trinity while up for his scholarship exam, he wrote to Anny '*late* at night'. On returning to his rooms in College, he had found a letter from her awaiting him: 'It makes all the difference to me,' he wrote, 'and I feel scholarships don't really matter in the least. Goodnight dearest. Yr. grateful Richmond Ritchie.' He was delighted with a new second-hand bureau in which he could stow away 'all your letters comfortably'. He would go to sleep thinking of her.

The progress of their intimacy had gone at lightning speed. His letters were now addressing her as 'Darling'. Fortunately, despite the distraction of his growing feelings, he won a £50 bursary to Trinity, and went up in the Michaelmas Term of 1875. He was expected to go for high academic honours. He was not only intellectually brilliant, but exceptionally good-looking. He was tall and dark, with plenty of self-assurance, a resolute character, and a sensitive and sympathetic nature. He had everything to captivate women, certainly everything to captivate Anny. Before she could analyse the change in her attitude to him, her growing dependence on his letters and on his thoughtful kindness told her that she was in love. She found that with Richmond she could talk about anything. He shared her keen response to beauty in all its forms. She could tell him about the concerts she went to – Joachim playing 'like a soul in bliss, like the end of that poem of Shelley's, a sort of ecstatic stream'. Typically vague, she could already rely on Richmond knowing the poem she referred to and knowing what she meant, without correcting her as Leslie always did. She could talk to him

---

[3] Freshfield was a solicitor and distinguished Alpinist.
[4] *Ritchie Letters*, p. 161.

about her father whom she missed as acutely as ever, needing to recall his words, his looks, his presence. 'Do you know', she wrote to Richmond on 15 February 1875, 'the last time I saw his dear face he sent me away. I just remember going back and standing by his bedside . . . looking at him, and you see after eleven years I find you my dear to talk to about him and to be yourself too.' [5] Richmond loved Anny with a kind of easy assurance. He saw no inequality in the match – neither her success, her famous name, nor her age appeared obstacles to him. He had total confidence in his ability to make her happy and to match her success with a successful career of his own. In all these assumptions he proved himself to be right. On 11 December he wrote protectively to Anny, giving her good advice: 'Darling – . . . it is rather funny . . . to find myself giving you good advice but I do feel quite capable now of taking care of you and putting a little finger to your burdens.'[6]

During Anny's last holiday with Minny and Leslie at Interlaken in the August of 1875, when Minny was expecting her baby in the winter, Anny wrote at length to Richmond, objectively, vividly, entertainingly, as she always did, reporting their doings and meetings with amusing people, and told him of 'a very nice gentle doctor' travelling with them with whom they pleasantly fraternized: 'The Dr. is talking gently about health to Leslie', she wrote. 'He says medicines are a mere accident, but that people certainly are medicinal, some are sedatives, some are tonics, some irritants. ("Ah!" says Leslie). Dearest Tonic, Good-bye. What pages and pages!'[7] In her diary following Minny's death in November, she wrote, 'Leslie and I spent a miserable and terrible winter in Southwell Gardens. Richmond used to come up and see me from Cambridge, like new life in the darkness and gloom.'[8]

According to Leslie Stephen's admittedly biased account, Richmond's family were beginning to remark 'ominous symptoms of a love affair' between him and Anny, and bitterly to complain of her 'goings on'. Minny, who was still alive when these reports were received, treated them 'as nonsense and as rather unpleasant nonsense, due to the gossipping propensities of the Ritchies, and was rather indignant and quite incredulous'.[9] Richmond's family, none too prosperous, had only one end in view, that he should do well at

[5] MS Letters: N-B Collection.   [6] Ibid.
[7] *Ritchie Letters*, p. 169.   [8] Ibid., p. 170.
[9] *Mausoleum Book*, p. 45.

Cambridge, and make a successful career for himself. Whatever their hopes and ambitions for him, Richmond was by then writing daily to Anny, enclosing his notes in tiny envelopes, written in the finest possible script, as though meant only for her eyes. They were unmistakably the letters of a lover. Anny replied as regularly as he wrote. She told him of the 'burning hopeless ache' of her sorrow for Minny, which she supposed must now be for ever. Understandably the presence of the shattered and utterly silent Leslie made the need for some relief to her feelings desperate. In the same December she wrote to Richmond: 'I feel as if my Min was alive and always would be after people have forgotten even her name , but somehow her dear little soft hands (with healing power) will have been laid on us and her dear unselfish tender spirit will be at work – and now it seems as if we must all do our business in our respective places and ages and accept – that is all I can see . . . except not to forget to say thank God.'[10] Richmond was, indeed, acting as a 'tonic'.

It was her fundamental belief in life, in happiness, and in the immortality of the soul, that caused the bitterest division between herself and Leslie that 'terrible winter' and the following year. He was vehement in his opposition to all religion. It seemed to him 'not only untrue but harmful', and he never hesitated to state 'in the plainest terms his rejection of the Christian dogma'.[11] Anny, like her father, hated all the trappings of woe, and confided to Richmond, in a letter of early 1876, that she had just torn off the black edging to the notepaper: 'If I had my way I should scarcely put on black . . . I didn't think so once. There was a great field full of lambs and hares yesterday and chestnut trees in bud which put me more in mind of Minnie than all the gloom that ever was . . . such sweet little lambs scampering and then hares darting right across and black birds wheeling across the blue sky and rows of nests balancing on the tree tops.' In a postscript she added: 'Darling! my post *has* come and the thought of you *is* a "blessing"'[12] – as though in answer to a query from him.

On his own avowal, Leslie had always shown a 'rather pedantic mania' for correcting Anny's 'flights of imagination and checking her exuberant impulses'. Both she and Minny said he was 'a cold bath' in 'drenching Anny's little schemes and fancies'.[13] If this was so in their happy times, how much more repressive must now have

[10] MS Letters: N-B Collection.   [11] Fuller, p. 143.
[12] MS Letters: N-B Collection.   [13] *Mausoleum Book*, p. 23.

been his deeply melancholy state of mind. Other matters, disconnected with their mutual grief, provoked discord between them. For one thing the German nurse who had been engaged to take care of Laura resented Anny's views on the right treatment for her, complaining of 'interference', and Leslie sided with the German. Then Anny's incurable recklessness with money irritated the cautious Leslie indescribably. Small wonder that he saw the 'ominous signs' of a growing love affair between Anny and Richmond as 'a disaster!' Leslie declared that the Ritchies 'hated' the idea of a marriage, and that he positively 'loathed it'.

Always inclined to doubts and despondencies, Leslie saw only the difficulties in the case, and grossly exaggerated the Ritchies' reactions to it. Far from the whole family 'hating' the marriage, Richmond's sisters, Anny's lifelong friends, warmly welcomed it. It was only Mrs Ritchie who opposed it, and even so her objection was based less on the disparity in their ages than on her fears that it might prejudice Richmond's career.

While Minny lived and utterly discredited the Ritchie family's suspicions, Leslie might discredit them too. But Richmond's frequent visits to the house after Minny's death could not be overlooked or dismissed as portending nothing, and when the evidence of his own eyes confirmed everyone's suspicions Leslie was in no state to control his outraged feelings. He admitted later to a great admixture of jealousy entering into his reactions to Richmond's courtship of Anny; and even more to Anny's acceptance of it. Coming into the drawing-room of the house in Hyde Park Gate one January afternoon in 1877, he found Richmond and Anny kissing. He was wholly unnerved by the sight and, venting his anger on Anny rather than on Richmond, He told her 'at once' – by his own admission – that she must 'make up her mind one way or other: for it was quite plain that as things were going, there could be only one result'.[14] He evidently assumed that his ultimatum would bring her to her senses then and there. He was quite unprepared for the result.

She came to him later that afternoon and told him that she and Richmond were engaged. Impulsive as Leslie knew her to be, he had not expected such a total disregard for his advice, for his wishes, and for what he regarded as her own reputation. She was thirty-nine and Richmond twenty-three. He was still at college and would not

[14] Ibid.,p. 45.

be getting his degree until the following year: he had nothing to marry on. While Leslie deceived himself into believing his main concern was for Anny, there entered a strong element not only of jealousy but of pique and alarm – alarm at the prospect of being abandoned. He was thrown into utter confusion by Anny's conduct, unable to understand her feelings at all, or the promptings of her highly emotional nature. With her vitality, her enthusiasm, and, as Leslie himself had said, with her exceptional powers of sympathy, she was young for her age, even by modern standards, doubly so by Victorian ones. Her mind – the mind of Thackeray's daughter – was far too flexible, too detached from the conventions of her class and time, to accept any set standards on any subject.

She had not been without proposals of marriage before; they had been advantageous ones from a worldly point of view – from Hastings Hughes[15] for one in 1875. But she had never considered them seriously for, like her father, she could not contemplate marrying without love. She was certain now that she loved Richmond. Her immediate acceptance of his proposal, however, did not mean that she was without qualms. These were all on Richmond's account, not on her own. Would such a marriage really injure his career as his mother claimed? While the engagement remained unofficial, to her closest friends she admitted to being tormented by fears for him. If it were anyone but Richmond, she said, she would have hesitated, but he was so sure of himself. Asked if she was certain of her own feelings, if she were unmistakably in love, she answered: 'Yes, but not well enough to refuse him.'[16]

Suspicious of Richmond for proposing without the means of supporting a wife, Leslie advised him – barely hiding his contempt – to enter for a clerkship in the India Office recently advertised in the press. Without demur, Richmond agreed to do so and lost no time in going to the India Office to find out the date when candidates were to present themselves and the qualifications required. Once again, the ground was cut from under Leslie's feet. Richmond continued to come and go between Cambridge and Hyde Park Gate. Finally, Richmond requested an interview with him to which Leslie brought Julia Duckworth, already his close confidante and adviser, and also as it happened one of Anny's strongest supporters. Julia, who now lived near them, had come in almost daily since Minny's death to bring healing sympathy to Anny at first, and

[15] A Freshwater Friend: Journal, Apr. 1875.   [16] Fuller, p. 150.

gradually to Leslie as well. Her influence over him was considerable, for he was already beginning to fall in love with her himself.
He was in short acting very much as Anny had done, whilst he had
so unreasonably condemned her. Thanks largely to the influence of
Julia, the interview with Richmond was successful and Leslie was at
least partially placated. Richmond agreed to enter for the India
Office post, and meanwhile, until sent for to sit the entrance exam,
returned composedly to Cambridge to pursue his studies.

It was in the course of these emotional months, both before and
after Richmond's proposal, that Anny wrote the novella *From the
Island*, as near to being a little masterpiece as anything she had yet
produced. The setting was Mrs Cameron's house at Freshwater,
Dimbola, and the characters, barely disguised under psuedonyms,
were the group of trusted friends Anny had made in her successive
visits to the Island. Tennyson is there, the Camerons, Lewis
Carroll, Anny's own cousins Blanche and Pinkie, and her little
adopted Margie, called 'Missy', as she was herself in childhood. The
action is contained within one week-end house party and concerns
three very different love affairs: the first happy love of a quite
young couple; the anguish experienced by a young wife whose
husband is on a mission in South America and incorrectly reported
killed; and a clandestine affair between a highly emancipated society
woman and an unsuitable lover. The quality of the story lies in its
analysis of feeling and, as usual, in the descriptions of the natural
surroundings which deeply affect the emotions and decisions of the
characters.

Anny was disturbed, so 'overdone' with worry, that she had in
fact as well as in fiction fled to Freshwater at the beginning of May
with her little girls, to avoid any more acrimonious arguments with
Leslie and to think out her own problems in peace. It was while she
was there that, on 11 May, she received the decisive telegram from
Richmond: 'Mother consents I am appointed to the India Office.'
She knew she could count on the understanding of the Tennysons,
and went straight round to Farringford to announce her news. She
found them as she expected, 'very, very kind'.[17] They never failed
her.

The engagement being now made public, she returned home and
found 'piles and piles of letters' awaiting her. Inevitably, the
proposed marriage shocked some of her acquaintances, and a few

[17] Journal, 11 May 1877.

friends. Millais shouted on hearing the news: 'Preposterous! It must not be! It shall not be!'[18] She received comfort and encouragement from many others. To Andrew Hitchens she wrote in reply to his congratulations: 'If it were not Richmond I should be afraid to take such a life's gift, but he knows his own mind so clearly that the blessing of affection seems to have lightened the darkness in which I am living . . . it has come like a sort of miracle.'

Thackeray had left as trustee for the girls' money his friend Charles Norman, partner in Martin's Bank, who lived at Bromley in Kent. It was necessary to consult him about her finances in view of the impending marriage. Her visit to Bromley with her fiancé was awaited with some apprehension by Mr Norman and his brother. They expected an 'elderly' young lady and a boyish bridegroom, and were wholly astounded to see enter a vivid rosy-cheeked girl and a very manly self-assured young man. Of the two, he appeared the older. The cautious hosts concluded that Miss Thackeray had 'been born young and Mr. Ritchie had been born old'. Howard Sturgis, one of her father's very old friends, dismissed the question of the disparity in their ages. Anny, he said, brought to the union 'the eternal youth of genius'.[19] Thackeray had once said he would rather she waited till forty than marry an ass in her teens. She appeared to be following his advice, and the fact that the man she loved happened to be the son of Thackeray's favourite relative could only have confirmed her in the wisdom of her choice.

The wedding took place from Hyde Park Gardens on 2 August 1877, early in the morning – they were 'one of the many bank holiday couples', as Anny remarked. Leslie Stephen had come back from the Lake District in order to attend it, whatever his inner misgivings. How wrong he had been about the Ritchies' attitude to the marriage can be seen from Emily Ritchie's account of the wedding sent to Lady Tennyson who had begged to be told all the details. Emily wrote: 'It was a dear little wedding, with just the amount of true friends that ought to have been there. Anny and Richmond seemed as utterly lost in each other and unconscious of anybody listening to them as if they had gone off by themselves, but then, the Service did barely last four minutes.

'Was it an omen that Anny, for the first time in her life, was before her time? It was hard on Mrs. Brookfield to find the Service just over. . . . Anny looked delightful and quite calm, I thought.

[18] Fuller, p. 151.   [19] Fuller, p. 154.

Her gown was very becoming, made all in one sweep and tight-fitting, but her bonnet of muslin and lace rather trying. Richmond looked to me a perfect bridegroom, strong and tender, and when they joined hands they seemed to enjoy a long romantic "shake hands!" One thing struck me, the contrast between Richmond's best man[20] at the right hand, and Anny's supporters on the left – poor Leslie, who looked very deplorable, and Julia Duckworth, who wore the thickest black velvet dress and heavy black veil, and gave the gloomiest, most tragic aspect to her side of the chancel.

'. . . I placed myself as Anny's bridesmaid at the side of the children, who were most pathetically upset at the emotional scene; dear Margie's teeth chattering, little Annie sucking lozenges to stifle her sobs, Stella Duckworth with her mother's tragic mask, and Margaret Cornish with tears streaming down her cheeks. However, they all became happy on being given champagne by Richmond.'[21]

The honeymoon was brief and simple, spent in the Guildford countryside. It lasted barely a week. By 7 August, Richmond was back at his desk at the India Office, where over the years he proved his worth, becoming Permanent Under-Secretary of State for India, and receiving a knighthood.

With no home of their own they spent the next months in furnished rooms, first at Bath Place, Kensington, and then at 153 Gloucester Road – 'a happy little house'. It was not until 1 December that they saw and decided on the house in Young Street where they spent the next seven years.

Anny recorded that they saw a great deal of their friends all that winter, and that she visited little Laura constantly. Their relations with Hyde Park Gate were perfectly restored by then, the more so that Leslie needed to confide in Anny his tribulations over Julia Duckworth's repeated rejections of his proposals. Also of a pessimistic disposition, Julia was even more doubtful than he of possible happiness together. She had greatly loved her first husband. In the end, however, Leslie was rewarded for his patience and consideration. They were married on 26 March 1878. He could say years after: 'Not a fibre in me but thrills at the thought of all the goodness lavished upon me since that day.'[22] No one rejoiced for them more sincerely than Anne Ritchie. To both of them she was a loyal and tried friend, and relations with Hyde Park Gate were never strained again. After her own marriage, Anny called to collect

[20] Lionel Tennyson.   [21] Fuller, pp. 151-3.   [22] *Mausoleum Book*, p. 57.

her belongings, and the dog Boxer which she and Leslie had kept rushed down the stairs and jumped straight into her arms, refusing to leave her. So Leslie agreed that she should take him with her, a humble pledge of their lasting amity.

One of Anny's warmest well-wishers in the event was George Eliot, who had been among her first, and remained one of her most constant admirers. She wrote on the very day of the marriage to Mme Bodichon in Paris: 'And Miss Thackeray's married to-day to young Ritchie. I saw him at Cambridge and felt that the nearly 20 years' difference between them was bridged hopefully by his solidarity and gravity. This is one of several instances that I have known of lately, showing that young men with even brilliant advantages will often choose as their life's companion a woman whose attractions are wholly of the spiritual order.'[23]

George Eliot's judgement on the marriage was prophetic, as she herself was in little more than two years to do as Anny had done and marry a man considerably her junior.

Ignorant as yet of her destiny she wrote to Anny on 29 August:

Dear Mrs. Ritchie,
  Your letter came on to me this morning. I am so glad to have it, for I have been long wishing that some sign of remembrance from you would fall to my share. No one has thought of your twofold self with more sympathy than 'meine Kleinigkeit', with more earnest desire that you may have the best sort of happiness.
  Do come and see me. By the beginning of November we shall be in town again. Either there or here we should heartily welcome a visit from you and Mr. Ritchie. At lunch time – half-past one – we are sure to be at home. . . .
  Ask Mr. Ritchie to remember me kindly.
      Always sincerely yours
        M.E. Lewes[24]

          [23] Haight, *George Eliot Letters*, vi. 398.   [24] Ibid. p. 402.

CHAPTER 16

MATERNITY

NUMBER 27 Young Street was exactly opposite the old home at No. 13, the bow-windowed Queen Anne house where her father had written *Pendennis*, *Esmond*, and the first part of *The Newcomes*. 'Our house', as Anny described it, 'was the prettiest old house, with a long garden at the back and an ancient medlar tree with a hole in it. There was also a lovely tall acacia tree. In those days, before Kensington Court, there were other gardens full of birds and trees beyond the walls and the tall spire of the church.'[1] Characteristically, she dwelt on the natural and environmental advantages of her new home, rather than on its internal amenities, or perhaps, as it was a Queen Anne house, on the want of them. It was an old street with old houses, and old customs still prevailed. On looking out of the window on her first May Day she saw a Jack-in-the-Green dancing by, with all his rout.[2]

Here, on 1 June 1848, at 4 o'clock in the morning her daughter was born, and her record of the event was typical again: 'All the birds were singing when Mrs. Brookfield brought her to my bedside in her arms and said: "she has beautiful brown eyes like Richmond."'[3]

On 28 June at Old Kensington Church, the baby was christened Hester Helen – after Thackeray's favourite heroine in *The Virginians*, Hetty Lambert, and her godmother Helen Fawcett (Lady Martin) who with her husband had been neighbours of the Thackerays in the Onslow Square days, and had remained close friends. The godfather was George Smith. He may well have thought, seeing Anny's joy in the beribboned bundle held over the font, that there was the end of an author.

Anny was forty-one the month Hester was born, but she was not one to rest on her laurels. In March 1880 she gave birth to a son, inevitably called after his grandfather, William Makepeace Denis,

---

[1] Journal, 1 May 1878.   [2] Ibid.   [3] Ibid., 1 June 1878.

but familiarly known all his life as Billy – a name that perfectly suited his genial temperament. Even Billy's birth was uncomplicated. In later years Anny told her expectant daughter-in-law that having a second baby was nothing - 'just a few rumblings of trains', as she put it. In those days there were no official Registrars of Births, Deaths and Marriages. Anny and Richmond registered Billy 'at a grocer's shop on Campden Hill on 31st March'.[4]

Anny delighted in her children as intensely as Thackeray had delighted in her and Minny. She was absorbed in everything they did. 'Baby Hester is so uproarious,' she reported to her sister-in-law Emily. 'The Bach Choir is nothing to her' – and Billy burst into song every time his mother 'strummed the piano'. Anny was resigned to the house 'never being in order quite', but the garden was 'doing its first duty and the jessamine is delicious, most of our clematis have taken a start. . . . What are perfectly delicious are the mulberries – I see tartfuls still up the tree and we have them for dinner every day since we came back besides jam and presents for the neighbours.' The old house in Young Street seemed to have solved the problem of how to live cheaply and contentedly on a moderate income. Anny was too happy to bother about bills and Leslie was not there to reproach her. If she and Richmond went out together (their chief outings were to concerts), she did not have to think of the expense but rejoiced in his company; and on their return 'it was so sweet to find those two beloved little beings to welcome us with raptures. O what a darling little pair they are.'[5]

Anny's spirits had never been so high, her energies so kindled. She had to share her joy. She took the babies to show old friends, like Kate Perry who no longer went out. She took Billy, when not a year old, to visit the remaining occupants of the house in Cheyne Walk where she had gone so often as a child herself. Carlyle had recently died and his brother Alexander and his wife lived there now. To show them Billy, and at the same time as an act of piety towards the past, she went on 7 March 1881 and described the curious scene to Emily, who was in India at the time. 'Think of my taking Billy yesterday to see little Tom Carlyle. The little Carlyle baby is very much like his Great-Uncle. He gave a grunt like him and Billy opened his eyes and laughed and looked like his Grandfather for a moment. It was the oddest, most affecting moment to me. There were the two babies in the dear old room, and old me

⁴ Ibid., 31 Mar. 1880.   ⁵ MS Letters: N-B Collection.

looking on at the new, like a shadow in the past. It was strange indeed.'[6]

The death of Carlyle had affected Anny for more reasons than one. There had been his long connection with her father, her childhood memories of Jane, and the kindness of both Jane and himself on Thackeray's death. She remembered the bleak years of Carlyle's loneliness which she herself had tried, by a small gesture of affection, to alleviate. It was she who had initiated the presentation to him of a testimonial clock, writing to all his women friends to raise the money for it. The presentation had been made on the occasion of his seventy-sixth birthday, 27 February 1871, in Lady Stanley's drawing-room in Dover Street. The gift had carried a message: 'To Mr. Carlyle from his affectionate friends', together with the date, and the signatures of all his old admirers, some of the most illustrious women of the day. Anny had been so much affected that she could not speak, and feared greatly that she had blundered in initiating the plan. Carlyle himself had been silent, saying only after a painful silence: 'Oh, what have I to do with Time any more?' But in fact he had been moved by the tribute of his old friends, and Minny on meeting him shortly afterwards said, 'he still talks about his clock and the paper of signatures'.[7]

Margie and Annie completed the family circle. Towards them, as they always said, she had never been less than a true mother. They were young teenagers when Anny's children were born, and as they got older their father, whose career took him constantly back and forth to India, occasionally took one or other of them with him. It was with grief that Anny said goodby to her 'dear child Margie' when Edward Thackeray and his wife took her back to India in October 1881, leaving the younger sister with her. Anny was waiting on Charing Cross Station, two years later, to welcome Margie's return. With her new sisters-in-law – Blanche, Gussie, and especially Emily – Anny remained very close. Holidays, as before her marriage, were occasions for great family gatherings.

Billy's christening at Old Kensington Church on 7 June 1880 was the occasion for another family party, with the Tennysons as godparents (Anny had already stood sponsor for Lionel Tennyson's second son Charlie at Westminster Abbey the previous year) and many old friends who came for 'a strawberry dinner' with the children. The service, Anny recorded, 'was alright', but Hester,

[6] *Ritchie Letters*, p. 183.   [7] Ibid., p. 142 n.

much like herself at the same age, ran away, and in the dim old church was nowhere to be found till her mother penetrated into a side-chapel where another service was going on, and found her 'right up on the Altar steps'. Anny saw a great deal of the Tennysons that winter (1882) in London, going for long walks with Alfred; her children and Tennyson's small grandsons, Charlie and Alfred, who were of an age, played together. She reported the four of them 'all gone out together hand in hand to see a Black Bishop who is to preach'. Billy, aged two, walking out with her alone, was 'very sweet and talkative'.

The Tennysons invited her to bring the children when she went to stay with them at Aldworth, the Sussex home that became their refuge after the poet's renown had made Farringford a place of pilgrimage. This was in the spring of 1882, and she was much touched by the welcome they received. 'The dear dear old fellow took us in his arms as an old father might have done,' Anny wrote. 'He is indeed the last of my Father's old friends and long may he continue to last.' The affection was reciprocal. Hallam told her that it was a long time since his father had been moved to talk so well or at such length as by her visit.

It was as though her new life, for all its richness, made her cling ever more closely to the landmarks of the past. In the spring of the same year (1882) the Darwins invited her and the children to visit them at Down. Characteristically, she mistook the date and disarmingly reported on her blunder, with a frankness which accounts perhaps for the great affection in which she was held by so many people. 'I was so anxious to go', she confessed to her Journal, 'that I mistook the day and went just a week before they asked us!' When admitted by the butler and realizing her mistake she was tempted to flee, but he assured her that Mr Darwin would be upset if she did so. On his being told of her arrival, Darwin came out laughing till the tears ran down his cheeks. 'You're as welcome as can be,' he said, stretching out his arms, 'but you must forgive me for laughing.' Her friends were long since inured to her unpunctuality, but she had never before miscalculated by a whole week. 'There never was such a charming little visit,' she happily remembered afterwards. Darwin told the children all about his travels, about the strange birds he had seen, the tortoises and other wonders. As it happened, her mistake appears to have been strangely prescient. On the very day she should have made her visit, Darwin was taken with his fatal illness. He died on 19 April 1882. 'Those 2 happy days were the last bright flash of that glorious life,' Anny noted in her Journal.[8]

Anthony Trollope, another old friend of her girlhood with whom she had stupidly 'quarrelled' (presumably over *Cornhill* matters), came to see the children, and stood by the fireplace, as she noted, 'very big and kind and made it up. He said Billy was like his grandfather. I said I'm so sorry I quarrelled with you. He said so am I my dear. I never saw dear Mr. Trollope again.'[9] Trollope died on 6 December 1882.

Yet another close friend of her father's, Edward FitzGerald, died early in 1883. On 26 June Anny heard that he had left her a legacy of £500, 'for love of her Father'. She was touched and went to visit Tennyson, staying overnight and listening to him read aloud his poem to FitzGerald, written for a former birthday. His soothing influence worked as usual. Waking next day, she found the morning was 'divine' – the view 'glorious and wide' – and she came away 'feeling as I used to do as a girl', intoxicated with greatness.[10]

The old friends were indeed falling thick and fast about her. Marriage had not lessened her need of them; they were a part of her father's world, his legacy to her and Minny when he died. This did not mean that she found Richmond immature by comparison. On the contrary, he was far more settled in his mind and ways than Anny herself, but her artist's temperament naturally found a close affinity with these artist friends of her father's past, and though much senior to her they seemed intellectual contemporaries. The curious thing in her relations with Richmond, considering their difference in age and her strongly maternal nature, was that there appeared nothing protective in her attitude towards him. Richmond was so self-reliant, to some extent so self-sufficient, that she never regarded him as in need of her support; she relied on his as a matter of course. Howard Sturgis said of the marriage that 'Richmond's nature supplied the prop on which hers could spread itself most happily in the sun.'

He was a highly cultivated man – a passionate lover of music and to a lesser degree of art – and he responded to the same stimuli as Anny when they travelled together, or attended a concert by Joachim, whom they so much esteemed. But his was not an artistic temperament. He was essentially what his desinty had made him, an

[8] Journal, 1882, no date.   [9] Ibid., 11 Feb. 1882.   [10] Ibid., June 1883.

admirable administrator. Howard Sturgis, who vividly recalled the high expectations raised at Cambridge of Richmond's prospective career, was one of those who had 'never been able to get over a certain sense of waste at the harnessing of such a Pegasus' to the 'juggernaut' of Colonial Administration. But once 'harnessed', Richmond was not one to chafe.[11]

If sacrifice there were in the nature of the career he adopted to be able to marry Anny, he denied it. As financial burdens began to press upon the growing household and he recognized how far beyond their means they lived, there were times when he was despondent; as in the summer of 1880 after Billy's birth and on return from holiday at Coniston, when their bank statement was 'awful', in Anny's words. Richmond then admitted that he had been imprudent to marry – 'but was very glad he had been imprudent!'[12] Where money was concerned, Anny recorded how 'nobly' he behaved.

Inevitably, the regularity of his work and hours, and the sporadic nature of much of hers, made for divergence in their pursuits and movements. The record of their early married years reads like a fever chart of Anny's movements – visits to old friends, changes of air for the benefit of the children, pursuit of places in connection with her work. Richmond's, by contrast, is a steady upward curve, illustrating tenacity of purpose and progress in his profession.

In 1883 he was appointed private secretary to the Under-Secretary of State for India, Mr Kynaston-Cross, MP, which was a considerable step upwards. As a result, and because they needed a larger house, they decided to let, or sell, the Young Street home and build themselves one to their own specifications in Rosary Gardens, Hereford Square, a charming backwater off Gloucester Road. This could not be achieved at once or without more money than either had laid by. The want of it acted on Anny merely as an incentive to work harder, not to save. And always her calculations had to take into account the needs of others, the wider claims on her love outside the close circle of her home.

In 1882, barely a year after Billy' birth, there came an additional call on her maternal feelings. Laura's abnormal condition could no longer be overlooked. She was eleven by then, and for years her father and Anny had lulled themselves with the hope that she was merely backward and would, with time, outlive the trauma of her

[11] Obituary, *Cornhill*, Nov. 1919.   [12] Journal, 1880.

mother's death, and catch up with the Duckworth children – her stepbrothers and sister, George, Stella, and Gerald. On her father's remarriage in March 1878, these children were respectively ten, nine, and eight years old. They were all three exceptionally intelligent and with less compassion perhaps than the grown-ups, they very soon spotted poor Laura's deficiency and loudly proclaimed her wanting. Her poor father had to admit that she had never yet learnt to read, though he had taken her in hand himself; and now by comparison with his clever stepchildren, he could not overlook the fact that she was increasingly confused and inarticulate. The pitiful admission came as a heavy blow to Anny, for whom Laura was all that was left to her of Minny; and as the children of Leslie's second marriage followed fast in succession – Vanessa in 1879, Thoby in 1880, Virginia in 1882, and Adrian in 1883, it became all too apparent that it was unwise to keep Laura at home. In a sad little note in her Journal in July 1881 Anny wrote, 'Beginning to be very anxious about Laura'.

No less painful for Anny was her lifelong relationship with her touchingly childlike mother. While the whole of life had passed Isabella by, there was a kind of wisdom in the very quality of her isolation that impressed her daughter as compensating for her loss. To her friend Mrs Oliphant Anny wrote, after reading her notable biography of Laurence Oliphant whose life was all action, 'thank God, life doesn't depend on sanity or success or fulfillment, it is living *towards* the best one can which is the secret of it all. I've so often felt *that*, talking to my mother. There is her loving humble generous life quite clear – through all its incompleteness. Suppose she was a strong-minded woman, or a leader of fashion or anything else, what more would she be in the kingdom of heaven?'[13] Isabella's sister, the 'Aunt Jane' of Anny's childhood, was also by fits and starts mentally deranged, and a financial burden on Anny.

It was against the background of these tribulations, as much as through the redeeming joys of marriage and motherhood, that Anny produced her major work over the next twenty years. George Smith need not have feared that she would be lost to literature on marriage. As a writer, her best years were yet to come; the years that ensured her reputation.

[13] *Ritchie Letters*, p. 217.

CHAPTER 17

THE PRODUCTIVE YEARS

THE friendship with Mrs Oliphant might be said to mark a turning-point in Anny's career. Mrs Oliphant was ten years older and already had an established reputation when Anny began to write. 'It was Mrs. Oliphant', Anny recorded, 'who bestowed on me my first review when I was twenty-three. It was summer time and I opened *Blackwood*, and my father beamed with satisfaction.' The contact established then lasted until Mrs Oliphant's death, when Anny summed up her feelings for her lost friend in a letter of condolence to the son: 'I have lost a life-long friend, and the world too in that wise, tender and humourous woman whom all delighted to love and appreciate. She was to me one of those people who *make* life – so many un-make it'.[1]

Mrs Oliphant had followed the routine career of lady writers in the mid-nineteenth century with a succession of novels (1863–76), the most successful of which was *Miss Marjoribanks*, in which her delicate sense of humour had free play. What distinguished her from other women writers of the time was the fact that for many years she held a professional position on the staff of Blackwood's. Early widowed and left with two sons, she further burdened her very meagre resources by adopting her widower brother's children, educating and supporting them. Her brave struggles to do so were described in her *Autobiography* (1899). It was a gesture of which Anne Thackeray would have been equally capable and one that brought the two women into even closer sympathy and affection. Mrs Oliphant and her boys joined Anny and the Stephens on their last Swiss holiday. It was with Mrs Oliphant, who lived at Eton, that Anny was staying on the fatal night Minny miscarried and died in November 1875. Mrs Oliphant's understanding and comforting support for Anny over this tragedy deepened their friendship. Answering her letter of condolence, Anny wrote to her: 'I have not

[1] *Ritchie Letters*, pp. 242–3.

yet finished, for as I was crying my heart's bitterness away over your dear dear beautiful words, Leslie came in and I gave him your letter to read. How sweet of you to bring home back again round about us, and give it all back for a little bit – to take a day out of old days that were truly at peace. . . . It seems so strange only to have signs of all our happy past, and yours has been a real sign, and God bless you and thank you.'[2]

Mrs Oliphant's name naturally figured on the list of Carlyle's women friends assembled by Anny to present him with the clock; and despite the little distance to Eton, she and Anny saw a great deal of each other in the following years. 'She was always more effusive than myself,' Mrs Oliphant wrote, 'delightfully flattering, appreciating. I used to say that if you wanted the moon very much, she would eagerly, and for a moment quite seriously, think how she could help to get it for you, scorning the bounds of the possible.'[3]

An important outcome of their friendship, from Anny's point of view, was the invitation from Mrs Oliphant some time in 1879 to contribute to the projected Series on the Foreign Classics for Blackwood by writing the life of Mme de Sévigné. Mrs Oliphant, herself, contributed the monographs on Dante and Cervantes. It was self-evident that the subject of Mme de Sévigné would be immensely suited to Anne Thackeray, with her background of French life and deep-seated love of the culture and landscape of France. Moreover, the new experience of motherhood (her daughter was born in June 1878 and her son would be born in March 1880) brought her even closer to the dominant trait in her prospective subject: the intensely maternal quality that turned the 'brightly beautiful' Marquise, as Anne called her, into an incomparable writer. Had it not been for her daughter's marriage and removal from Paris to Provence, which separated her for long periods from her adoring mother, the immortal correspondence would never have been written.

Sympathy for her subject was, therefore, a foregone assumption when Anny accepted her assignment – and sympathy was the essential component in all her writings. What was new in her life of de Sévigné was the sense of history it revealed; the well-researched detail; the authenticated portraits of the brilliant circle surrounding the central figure; the familiarity with the writings, both profane

[2] Ibid., p. 171.
[3] Margaret Oliphant, *The Autobiography and Letters*, p. 144. Blackwood, 1899.

and devout, of the richest period in all French literature – in drama, poetry, philosophy, and religious eloquence. It was the period of La Fontaine, La Rochefoucauld, of Pascal, and of the great preachers, Fénelon, Massillon, Bourdaloue: of everything that was wittiest and also of everything that was most profound. Without pedantry, Anny Thackeray wrote of her subject as living in daily contact with the giants of this prodigious society; quoting their works, feeding on their maxims, influenced always whatever the heady distractions of the moment by the noble teachings of Port-Royal. It is an enthralling and convincing evocation of a period whose king set the pattern for the 'grand manner' of all subsequent courts and which was inhuman in its brutalities as it was 'polite' in its social conventions.

Anne Thackeray was not blinded by the glitter of the scene, or by the sweetness and charm of her heroine, to the want of pity for the poor, whose miserable condition was easily tolerated if not actually imposed upon them by those in power – like the son-in-law, the husband of the beloved daughter who could do no wrong in her mother's eyes. 'It is impossible not to be struck . . .', writes Anne, 'by the acquiescence of people at their ease in the misery and suffering around them. Madame de Sévigné, with all her loving heart, was not faultless and sometimes her sentences are witty where we should have still more loved her if she had been unsophisticated.'[4] Her total acceptance of the ruthless repression of two peasants' revolts in her own province of Brittany by the Governor, in 1675, shocked her biographer. She reports with sorrow that the Marquise turned away from the truth 'and from painful realities, and avoided any strong emotion that did not seem to her to be part of her own life. . . . In Madame de Sévigné, some such things . . . jar upon one's genuine admiration and enthusiasm . . . one grudges the inadvertent evidences of want of courage to face the truth – want of honest, righteous indignation where wrong was done, which she should have resented.'[5]

Astounding too in this highly civilized, warm-hearted woman was whatever vulgar emotion it was that prompted her to witness the prolonged and horrible public execution of the famous poisoner, Madame de la Brinvilliers.[6] The admission of her faults is

---

[4] *Mme de Sévigné*, Ch. xii, p. 82.
[5] Ibid., Ch. XVI, pp. 106–7.
[6] Ibid., Ch. XXII, p. 141.

sadly made by her biographer, and darkens the picture of this sunny-tempered, delightful, and generous woman, who could be the most faithful of friends – especially of those in misfortune, like Fouquet, hounded to his ruin by a revengeful king, which lost her no small share of royal favour.

In this book Anne Thackeray writes, perhaps for the first time, with style. It is sustainedly light, bright, and diverting, as suits its subject. She has, as always, some delightful flashes of impressionist vision, as in describing M. de Voiture arriving in a crowded room 'dandling on his silken legs'.[7] Her assessment of Mme de Sévigné's own achievement as an unconscious artist is well equal to that art: 'There is something almost of a great composer's art in the endless variations and modulations of this lady's fancy. She laments, she rejoices, she alters her note, her key; she modulates from tears to laughter, from laughter to wit. She looks round for sympathy, tells the stories of the people all about her, repeats their words, describes their hopes, their preoccupations. Then she remembers her own once more, and repeats again and again, in new words from fresh aspects, the fancies and feelings which fill her heart. No wonder Madame de Grignan valued such letters, and prized them, and kept them safe.'[8] Can one fault that description? It is as fresh as a de Sévigné letter itself.

There is a deepening also in the tone and colour of Anny's perception of her theme, the result not so much of reading as of experience and reflection. Considering the history of the time she is evoking, she writes: 'There is much truth in a remark of Michelet, who points out how curiously the pleasant, sprightly mind of one country lady, writing down second-hand gossip, influences our impression of an age, of a Court, of which she knew comparatively little; whereas the real actors . . . who have told their own stories in far less vivid language, are comparatively forgotten and ignored.'[9]

Though writing at the very height of her powers, at the zenith of her personal happiness, just after the birth of her cherished children, Anne Thackeray shows in this book what might be called a new philosophy of age, a ripening sense of values that was not only to enrich her subsequent writings, but support her through the coming tests of life. 'The end of a life', she writes, 'would be only sad to write and sad to read of, if it were not for certain redeeming things which in some degree perhaps make good the loss of the

[7] *Mme de Sévigné*, p. 22.   [8] Ibid., pp. 116–17.   [9] Ibid., p. 77.

brightest and best treasures of existence . . . and old age, to those who have lived in some sympathy with the people and the things around them, should be the good and pregnant seed-time – width of understanding, tranquillity of soul, charity and fearlessness, and the knowledge of human weakness and its pathetic possibilities and impossibilities, all these are good seeds bearing priceless fruit.'[10]

Following the success of her *Mme de Sévigné* Anny became a much sought-after contributor to American as well as English literary periodicals, for monographs, biographical notices of famous contemporaries, critical commentaries. The list of her subjects published over the next ten years shows the range of her output. In 1883 it was *A Book of Sibyls* containing her four previously published articles from the *Cornhill* on Mrs Barbauld, Mrs Opie, Maria Edgeworth, and Jane Austen. How she came by the title of this collection of monographs is typical of her spontaneous and generally undisciplined approach to her work. She had no idea what to call the book, right up to publication date, when its title suddenly came to her by merest chance. She was on holiday at Lynton with the children in the summer of 1883 when she wrote to George Smith on 1 September: 'Since I saw you, as I was crossing Lynton moor in a storm, with the children tucked up on my knees, and the wind whirling, I thought of Macbeth's Three Witches, and then it suddenly occurred to me, that my new book ought to be called:

A BOOK OF SIBYLS
by
Mrs. Richmond Ritchie.

It would also give a certain point to my volume, for the Sibyls were certainly authoresses.'[11]

In 1885 she was asked to contribute the article on Mrs Browning for the *Dictionary of National Biography*. This was accorded grudging praise by Leslie Stephen, the General Editor. 'I think you have done Mrs. B. very well,' he wrote to her in May 1885. 'I have read it and put in some savage criticisms, marking however, what I really think should be omitted in a dictionary. Too much sentimental reflection looks terribly out of place in our dismal work. . . . Substantially, in spite of my criticisms, I really think it very well done indeed.'[12]

There was one great woman writer, George Eliot, on whose

---

[10] Ibid., p. 169.   [11] Murray Archives.   [12] Fuller, p. 157.

work and life Anny did not feel competent to write. Her sudden death at the Christmas of 1880 had stunned the literary world, and obituary notices and appreciations had been pouring in over the following weeks. Anny was asked by Scribner's to contribute a memoir of her. Anny's answer was that she 'didn't feel up to it'.[13] Anny's attitude towards George Eliot had always been ambivalent. She confessed to feeling 'a wretch' at refusing to worship at the shrine, because of the kindness and 'serenity' always extended towards her personally. She admired George Eliot's works but wished that she liked them more, and the same applied to the author. But, as she had said after their first meeting, there was a 'want of reality' (or of simplicity) in the atmosphere surrounding her. When asked after the consecutive deaths of George Eliot and Carlyle in the Christmas and New Year of 1880/1, whom she thought the greater, she did not hesitate to say, 'Of course to my generation Carlyle is a far more powerful influence. George Eliot seems more to me like an expression and interpretation than an actual influence.'[14]

The sadness of George Eliot's death had been immeasurably heightened for those who loved her by the fact that only nine months before she had, at the age of sixty, married a man twenty years her junior, John Cross. Lewes had died barely eighteen months before, leaving George Eliot distraught. Her acceptance of Cross had shaken the London coteries and shocked her devotees. Intensely sensitive to criticism, George Eliot's fear of losing her 'influence' weighed most with her in hesitating to accept Cross. Yet she knew his great value, and her own terrible need of a prop in life. He was devoted to her, and, when all was said and done, he was the only man in her life to propose marriage. She could not refuse him. The marriage was celebrated with some pomp at St. George's Hanover Square, on 6 May 1880.

In an unusually flippant mood, Henry James commented on the event in a letter to his mother: 'Old women are marrying young men, by the way, all over the place. If you hear next that Mrs. Kemble, or Mrs. Procter or Mrs. Duncan Stewart is to marry *me*, you may know we have simply conformed to the fashion. But I will ask your consent first.'[15] The double allusion may have been

[13] *Ritchie Letters*, p. 182.
[14] Ibid.
[15] Leon Edel, *The Letters of Henry James*, ii. 352.

prompted by the fact that George Eliot was known to have been
influenced by the comparable case of Anne Thackeray. Anne herself
is unlikely to have admitted the similarity. There had been no
Lewes in her life and, despite the difference in age between herself
and Richmond, her marriage had given her children; and at forty
the children had only served to rejuvenate her.

The marriage of George Eliot nonplussed her, but for other
reasons, as she wrote to Richmond on 24 May 1880. Charles Lewes
had called, to 'tell her all about the wedding' and had left Anny 'still
thrrrrrilling' over the conversation. Lionel Tennyson was present
and declared 'his hair stood on end as he listened'. Anny asked
Charles if he had been consulted (he was the one remaining stepson
brought up by George Eliot). He said 'no, not consulted, but she
had told him a few weeks ago. She confided in Paget who approved
and told her it wouldn't make any difference in her influence. Here
I couldn't stand it, and said of course it would, but it was better to
be genuine than to have influence, and that I didn't suppose she
imagined herself inspired, though her clique did. It rather shocked
him, and he mumbled a good deal. Young Lewes is generous about
the marriage. He says he owes everything to her, his Gertrude [his
wife] included, and that his father had no grain of jealousy in him,
and only would have wished her happy, and that she was of such a
delicate fastidious nature that she couldn't be satisfied with anything but an ideal tête-à-tête. George Eliot said to him if she hadn't
been human with feelings and failings like other people, how could
she have written her books? . . . altogether it was the strangest page
of life I ever skimmed over. She is an honest woman, and goes in
with all her might for what she is about. She did not confide in
Herbert Spencer. They have taken a beautiful house in Cheyne
Walk.'[16]

The admission to the 'feelings and failings', the 'honesty' that
Anny recognized in the enigma of the great woman's conduct,
counted patently more with Anny than all the moral 'influence' so
highly prized by the great woman herself. When so soon after the
marriage George Eliot died of a septic throat, Anny wrote to Emily
Ritchie: 'It is absurd, but I do feel George Eliot's death very much.
There is nothing to be sorry for – all is at peace for her, poor soul,
but it haunts one somehow. She was buried in a great storm of wind
and rain or I think I should have gone to the funeral.'[17]

[16] *Ritchie Letters*, pp. 180–1.   [17] *Ritchie Letters*, p. 182.

Mme de Sévigné was, as we have seen, a commissioned work which Anny took very seriously; but before she had undertaken it she had begun a new full–length novel – the eventual *Mrs. Dymond* – soon after the birth of Hester, in June 1878. By the spring of 1879 she was finding it 'tedious work', so absorbed was she in her daughter's engaging ways. 'I don't believe Goethe himself could have written while Wolfgang was a baby', she wrote to her cousin Emily in India.[18] This nice excuse strengthened by the arrival of Billy in March 1880, and the commission to write *de Sévigné*, effectively stopped work on *Mrs. Dymond* till the *Sibyls* were off her hands in the autumn of 1883. She did not resume regular work on it till early 1884. Then it was suddenly due for serialization in the *Cornhill* for March, and the very thought of the commitment threw her into a panic. 'I am more Jellyby than ever now,' she wrote to Emily again, 'for *Mrs. Dymond* is coming out in March or April, and I had a regular stage fright last week.'[19] The book had suffered yet another interruption in the winter of 1883–4 by the decision to move from Young Street to a little house of their own construction in Rosary Gardens, Hereford Square, which necessarily demanded all Anny's attention. The move actually took place in August 1884 (bringing Anny into close contact with Mrs Kemble, a neighbour in Hereford Square). A protracted bout of sciatica through the early months of 1885 still further delayed the completion of *Mrs. Dymond*. It seemed an ill-fated book.

It is, however, for all its vicissitudes, undoubtedly the best-written of Anny's novels, the least dispersed, the most concentrated in interest. Once again the sense of place is all important, the feeling for landscape not being used for decoration but as an essential part of the structure. Here the setting is twofold: Coniston in the Lake District; and Paris, the old Paris Anny knew so well.

Anny first went to Coniston in the summer of 1876, when she accompanied the recently widowed Leslie Stephen on a visit to his friend Victor Marshall, during which in Leslie's somewhat spiteful comment, 'Anny, of course, made a conquest of Ruskin'.[20] Undeniably she was conquered by the beauty of the landscape which she evokes most eloquently in *Mrs. Dymond*. 'Terndale Water', she writes, 'is not the least beautiful of the Cumberland lakes, although

[18] MS Letters: N-B Collection.
[19] *Ritchie Letters*, p. 190.
[20] *Mausoleum Book*, p. 44. See below, pp. 220.

it is comparatively little known. The swallows have found it out, and dart hither and thither along the banks; tourists come there from time to time, not in shoals, but sparingly and by chance . . . The whole place is athrill. . . . Everything is awake and astir and alive with that indescribable life of the field and the waters: the cows are cropping the long grass down by the water-side; the dew is shining on the delicate leaves, one single drop is brimming in each emerald trefoil cup, the white and lilac weeds are sparkling in the sunlight; the banks cast long shadows into the water; the queen-of-the-meadows is scenting the air with her fragrant white blossom, a great honeysuckle head rises above the hedge.'[21]

Into this morning mood of Nature at her freshest and newest, Anny introduced her young characters, a motherless brother and sister, Jo and Tempy (Temperance) Dymond, dependent, as are so many of her young people, on tyrannical elderly relatives. The clashes between age and youth are one of the salient themes of the book. Tempy in particular is in revolt against the old aunts and the cranky uncle with whom they live. Their retired father, Colonel Dymond, spends most of his time abroad, living in a Paris boarding-house. There, Susannah, a young friend of the Dymonds who has just lost her grandfather with whom she lived, goes to join her mother, remarried to an Irish wastrel, who lives for economy's sake in the same Paris *pension de famille* – a setting so well known to Anny, and admirably and humorously evoked in the chapters that follow. The description of the shabby-genteel Parisian 'pensions de famille', and indeed the Paris scenes generally are among the most vivid in the book. The *Villa du Parc*, set in the old Paris environ of Neuilly, has a mainly English 'connection', as its owner proudly boasts – Susannah's mother, husband, and two boys among them. It is run by an admirably efficient and masterful old lady, Mme du Parc, who has all the keen business sense and kind heart that Anny knew to be typical of hard-working French women. She is unashamedly boastful of her flourishing business, of her son Max, and proves a match even for the drunken stepfather at his most violent. To escape this loathsome man and help her mother, Susannah makes an unequal marriage with the Colonel, old enough to be her father, and becomes the 'Mrs. Dymond' of the title. Her predicament (which shows, incidentally, that Anny was already considering the effects of marriage between partners of

[21] *Mrs. Dymond*, pp. 7, 8.

widely divergent ages, though strangely enough it is she who always sees the young person's point of view) is treated delicately and subtly as one for which there is no easy issue: it is a matter involving deep sentiment and mutual respect. The Colonel is not a Casaubon or a Grandcourt, but a man of heart and honour, shown as tenderly though not passionately attached to his young wife; while she is shown as content because unaware of other feelings, too young to know deeper longings than a wish for wings to take her away from the stifling atmosphere of the Colonel's old home back in Coniston and the domineering relations. They alone threaten her happiness, she thinks. 'When these ladies contradicted or utterly ignored her, she would smile good-humouredly; and yet in her heart she now and then had experienced a strange feeling that she scarcely realised, something tired, desperate, sudden, unreasonable, almost wicked – the feeling she thought must go, and she would forget it for a time, and then suddenly there it was again.'[22] It is only gradually that Susy realizes the 'mental suicide' of her acquiescence in the narrow regime of her home.

The birth of a baby girl, though bringing her joy, does not remove the sense of oppression permeating her husband's home. She is constantly tormented by fears for her mother's welfare and making flying visits to Paris. Madame du Parc's son, Max, is an engraver and prospective artist (Anny's knowledge of the processes of making wood-blocks, acquired while helping her father, served her well here in describing the work of Max and his circle of artist friends). In his spare time he is also something of a political agitator, with hirsute journalist friends whom his mother describes as a 'good-for-nothing set', to whom she orders her *bonne* to 'shut the door on their noses'. Max, so new a type to the conventionally reared Susannah, inevitably interests her; he becomes the main-spring in the action, and Susannah's ultimate destiny. The connection between the well-ordered old Cumberland home and the artistic and revolutionary circles in Paris is thus quite naturally established through the links between Susannah and her mother, and allows the plot in its development to include the Siege of Paris and the outbreak of the Commune in the spring of 1871, which Anny had herself witnessed. The scenes described in *Mrs. Dymond* echo the descriptions Anny wrote at the time. 'When Susy stepped out of the train and looked around, she was struck by the change in

[22] Ibid., p. 230.

the people standing all about the station. They had strange, grave, scared faces . . . every woman was in mourning . . . . A cold east wind was blowing up the silent street and across the open place in front of the railway. A man came to offer to carry her bag; when she told him she wanted a carriage to take her to Neuilly, he shrugged his shoulders – "A carriage" said he; "where am I to find a carriage? the Prussians have made cutlets of our horses."'

The reader of these breathless pages is struck not only by Anny's remembered sadness at the destruction of places she had long loved (like the lovely Château of St. Cloud), but by her sense of the justice of much of the fury of a people betrayed by a rotten regime. 'One of the very first sights which met Susy along the road was a dispirited, straggling regiment marching into Paris from the frontier, torn, shabby, weary, the mud-stained officers marching with the men. These men were boys, for the most part half grown, half clothed, dragging on with a dull and piteous look of hunger and fatigue, while the piercing wind came whistling up the street. "They are disarmed, that is why they look so cold," said the porter . . . "There is one who can keep up no longer;" as he spoke one of the poor fellows fell out of the ranks . . . a halt was called, and many of them sank down on the pavement just where they stopped.'[23] When at last Susy reaches the villa, 'It seemed like a miracle to see the old green gates actually standing, and the villa unaltered in the shaded garden. The gates were splintered and half broken down, the garden trampled over, but the house was little changed and stood in the cold spring sunshine, with no sign of the terrible wave of war which had passed over the village.'[24]

Elsewhere, searching for missing persons, her mother's disreputable husband among them, Susannah gets as far as St. Cloud accompanied by old Madame du Parc. 'So they started along the desolate road. Madame's grunts, groans and exclamations seemed the most lively and cheerful sounds by the way.

'"Oh! Oh! Oh! Only look at the ruined houses! That is poor Mademoiselle Fayard's apartment up there, right up there."

Mademoiselle Fayard's late apartment was now nothing but a sort of hanging grotto in the air, and consisted of three sides of a blackened room, of which the floor was gone, the ceiling was gone, although by some strange freak of chance and war the gilt looking-glass still hung upon its nail in which Mademoiselle Fayard had

[23] Ibid., pp. 408–9.   [24] Ibid., pp. 411–12.

been used to crimp her curls. All the rest of the tidy little home had crumbled and fallen away.'[25]

The village of St. Cloud looked like a pile of children's bricks overthrown by a wayward hand. . . . only the shells of the tall houses were standing still, with strips of paper fluttering from the ruined walls. . . . High up against the sky she could see the gutted *château*, still standing on its terrace, while the sky showed pink through the walls . . . . Although the whole place was thus ravaged and destroyed . . . the spire of the church and its bells remained untouched.'[26]

The philosophy of the new Republic, sprung from the ashes of a military defeat and a government's betrayal, finds its mouthpiece in the friend of Max, the old printer Caron. Putting the needs of their country before personal safety, they both reject the easy way of flight, like the majority of Parisians, before the advance of the 'Communards', and hope to use their influence with the extremists to prevent the worst violence. Reproving Susy for speaking of the advancing mobs, armed, Phrygian-capped, and maniacal in expression, as 'those horrible people', he says: 'Ah! my dear young lady, do not call them horrible people. . . . They want good things, which pleasant and well-mannered people withhold from them and their children. They are only asking for justice, for happiness. They ask rudely, in loud voices, because when they ask politely they are not listened to.'[27]

Caron had long been trying to apply the principles of socialism to his paper-mills, with the workmen as equal shareholders, and reinvesting the profits made in the company at the end of the year. He had the vision to see beyond the miserable present; but, inevitably, in the violence that ensues it is the idealist Caron who is killed. Conveniently, the worthy Colonel has died a natural death some while before, and Susy and Max, whom the shared dangers of the Commune had brought close to each other, can eventually marry.

Writing *Mrs. Dymond* throughout 1884 and 1885 was a crushing burden on Anny. She was supervising the building of the new home in Rosary Gardens, she was teaching the children (Billy's comment on the events of English History, as expounded by his mother, was that there were 'so many Kings and Uncles and Wat Tylers and Piers Gavestons – and the more the Kings die the more History

[25] Ibid., p. 433.   [26] Ibid., pp. 435–6.   [27] Ibid., p. 463.

there is', seems both just and perspicacious for a five-year old[28]), and then choosing their first kindergarten. She also acted 'mother' at the wedding of her adopted daughter, Margie Thackeray to Gerald Ritchie, Richmond's elder brother, on 24 January 1885, and prepared for their immediate departure for India. At the same time she was writing her article on Mrs Browning for the *Dictionary of National Biography* and had several more commitments lined up. It was all too much, even for her enormous energy. She recorded a first crippling attack of sciatica in the April of 1885; with Richmond nursing her, making tea for her, playing patience at her bedside, and 'comforting my soul'. The affected leg was 'in hell at night'. The breakdown of her health was not the only effect of the heavy demands made on her resources by her whole way of life. She could no more stand up to them financially than she could physically.

The building, decorating, and furnishing of the 'beautiful new house' seems to have been carried out very much in her father's manner, when he would get carried away in the pursuit of perfection. Richmond's rising position at the India Office was sufficient excuse, it was argued, for the extravagance; a move from 'dear Young Street' was, in any case, a necessity. Billy, as his views on English history already showed, was uncommonly observant. Being next door to an old pub, the Greyhound, had its disadvantages. Billy had an all too retentive memory of the language currently used by its customers; it was time, alas, to put a distance between him and them. The move was made in August 1884.

However enchanting the house in Rosary Gardens, within little more than a year the 'awful banker's book' was making it irrefutably plain that it was too expensive to keep up. The proofs of *Mrs. Dymond* were scarcely gone to the printers in September 1885 when the desperate decision had to be made to sublet it, and a search for temporary accommodation was begun. This might prove but a small economy as the house was eventually let for £200 p.a.

Happily, help was forthcoming from two sources. Firstly Leslie Stephen and his wife were 'touchingly kind', as Anny gratefully recorded, in offering them part of their large and only semi-occupied house at Hyde Park Gate. Then Richmond's mother and sister Emily bore down on them and urged them to join them in their recently acquired home at Southmead in Wimbledon. Not without heartbreak, this is what they did in the spring of 1886.

[28] MS Letters: N-B Collection: ATR to Richmond, May 1885.

15. The garden of 27 Young Street

27, YOUNG STREET,
KENSINGTON SQUARE. W.

16. Anny's children.
Facsimile of letter with
sketches, c. 1881

PART III

LADY RITCHIE

CHAPTER 18

THE PRICE OF FAME

HOWEVER warm the welcome awaiting them from Richmond's mother and sister, and however pleasant the new surroundings in a spacious house close to the Common, a home had been lost and for that there could be no consolation. What more would be lost would only gradually be discovered, when their very marriage was at stake. One thing seemed certain to them both at the time, however: what had been lost could never be found again.

Throughout this period Anny was in almost constant ill health. She was frequently ordered away to thermal stations, at Aix-les-Bains, Malvern, or other baths, for the strenuous treatment; or just to Brighton or Cromer for the good air. The inability to work consistently, the almost constant pain, above all the separation from Richmond and the children for long periods at a time, were her worst deprivations. Though whenever possible, in their school holidays and during Richmond's scant leaves of absence, they joined her wherever she was, she lost what was best to her in life, their daily presence, their endearing comments on each day's discoveries, all of which she recorded with so much humour when she was with them.

For Richmond, even more than Anny, the move to Wimbledon called for sacrifices. For one thing, it entailed a longer journey each day to the India Office and back. Whatever his inmost feelings, he never showed them; he had an exceptional power of restraint, of self-control; this Anny knew so well that she often feared other people would not realize the depth of his feelings and misjudge him as lacking them. 'He never complains of the distance', she now wrote, 'and this is my one trouble.' When his mother died, Anny wrote of his being 'deeply affected but not articulate. In his deep heart he is so tender and so afraid of showing it or shamming that it makes him seem stern and cold when he is not, one bit.'[1] It was

[1] Journal, Nov. 1888.

decided now to send the children to school, to the South London College at Putney, as Anny was too often 'laid up' to teach them regularly; and she reported to Mrs Kemble (her constant correspondent at the time), 'Richmond going devotedly nearly an hour earlier to the office every morning in order to drop them in his fly at the station.'[2] The children were soon 'firmly established' at their school and very happy there; and Richmond bore the extra burdens with perfect equanimity.

With the thoughtful kindness that marked everything in her reception of her son's family, Mrs Ritchie had placed neighbouring ground-floor rooms at the couple's disposal, so that Richmond's study led out of Anny's room, allowing them, as Anny reported, 'plenty of tête-à-têtes' on his return from the office before the somewhat formal family dinner. Emily was a genuinely gifted pianist (she was sometimes invited to accompany Joachim, who became a friend of the family), and her playing was a regular feature of the evenings. At week-ends Richmond took the children for long walks on the Common, followed by the dogs. During their first winter there Anny reported that, after reading aloud 'The Peasant and the Prince' to the children, they went out and soon returned, 'bursting in with red, red cheeks, and saying there was such *good* news, the pond was frozen!' On none of these outings could she accompany them, being immured in the house, and in too much pain to write more than scribbled notes to her friends. As she herself said, 'My health was so broken all the time.'[3]

When she considered their financial position, which had brought about the loss of their home, it must have been impossible for her *not* to lay some of the blame on herself, incapable as she had always been of grappling with money matters. But no doubt it also seemed a little unjust that, despite all the hard work, her considerable earnings would not supply the deficit caused by the extravagance of her generosity. On a former occasion when Anny's finances had got them into trouble, Richmond had showed himself 'noble'. On him, one cannot help feeling, the crisis bore heaviest again; and was most hurtful to his pride. A man in his position should have been able to keep a wife and two children, but Anny was no ordinary wife. She lived on a heightened plane of being, and her sense of reality did not always coincide with that of more ordinary creatures. She was very much her father's daughter. Like him, she hated 'twaddling' second-rate things. The had lived in altogether too grand a style; at one time one hears of three maidservants and a lady's-maid. One wonders just what she spent, in this year of financial crisis, on Margie's trousseau and wedding-day alone. Humbly, clear-sight-edly (in the confessional of her Journal), Anny saw the folly of her ways, and vowed amendment. It might have been better for both it, like Lelsie Stephen, Richmond had sometimes remonstrated; but Leslie did not love her as Richmond did. So, without recrimination, he bore with the loss of privacy, of independence, of standing in his own eyes, so peculiarly dear to a man of his reserved character.

Happily for all, the friction almost inevitable when two families share the same home seems miraculously to have been avoided, thanks largely to the character of Mrs Ritchie senior, to whose exceptional sweetness and understanding Anny paid tribute after her death. When all was over and the time come for leaving Southmead, she wrote to Mrs Oliphant: 'O how I do rejoice that we came and how sweet and loyal and unfailing she has been. The dearest of friends. Was there ever a sweeter mother-in-law – I can only feel love and gratitude and thankfulness that we all fitted and learnt to know each other. I sometimes long that she should have known how deeply Richmond has felt her loss, how silently he stood by, making no sign or fuss, but never leaving her, not when all the saddest part of such partings was happening and I had run away to my room. His heart is as true as hers tho' he says so little and the others all so very much.'[4] It is evident that Anny's gratitude to her mother-in-law was not merely due to her providing the family with a refuge in time of financial trouble; for nursing her when ill; for surrounding the children with love; but for her support in a yet greater emergency: for helping to avert the wreck of a marriage that was in danger of foundering.

In Anny's Journal for April 1886 appeared an item of news that had affected her deeply and that had wholly unpredictable consequences. She wrote: 'heard dear Lionel Tennyson was dangerously ill in India – Then came the news that he had died at sea. . . . He died when they reached Aden and was buried at sea.' This was on 20 April 1886.

Sympathy for the parents, for the old Laureate who wrote so touchingly of his loss, would first afflict Anny. Then her personal memories of the charming boy, the Tennysons' second son, whom

4 Letter to Mrs Oliphant, 28 Nov. 1888.

she had known since her first visit to Farringford when he was eight and dressed like a page of King Arthur's court. A close personal friendship had developed over the years, with a regular exchange of letters throughout his Eton and university days. His marriage, to Eleanor Locker, followed closely on her own in 1878. Anny was godmother to his second son, Charlie, soon to be a playmate for Hester and Billy. Overpoweringly, she felt pity for the young widow, Eleanor, on her solitary return.

Had Anny not been incapacitated by illness, she would have been among the first to bring comfort to the bereaved friend. Eleanor had devoted parents living at Cromer, however, and the deeply afflicted parents-in-law ready to give her their consoling love. But as the weeks passed and the difficulties of her widowed situation were borne in on her, she found that what she lacked most was a friend capable of dealing with her business affairs, of helping her through the intricacies of Probate. As Lionel's post had been at the India Office, Anny proposed that Richmond should step in to help. Eleanor was an old friend they had known long before her marriage.

During her own enforced absences at Aix or elsewhere to take the treatment that summer and autumn, Richmond was in less of a hurry to reach home and the more willing to stay late at the Office and give up his evenings to helping Eleanor. Anny got used to receiving his letters 'dated by his midnight office lamp'.

Richmond, as his photographs show, was an exceptionally handsome man, commandingly tall, even of regal appearance, and certainly very attractive to women. At that particular time the disruption of his life, the sickness of his wife, and the uncertainty of his own affairs all conspired to make him peculiarly vulnerable to an emotional appeal. He himself stood in need of moral support. As for Eleanor, suddenly deprived of everything at one stroke, she was in the depths and seemingly incapable of raising herself by her own volition. They fell mutually in love.

To a man of Richmond's strict code of conduct, this was not a joy, but a catastrophe. Self-possessed in the fullest sense of the term all his life, it was like an invasion of his private soul, the exposure of an open nerve to agony. He had no intention of deceiving Anny; she must be told.

Ill as she was and loving him as she did, she rose magnificently to the occasion. Putting Richmond's happiness first, she said the decision must rest with him. He could choose Eleanor if he needed her more than his wife. She would abide by his decision.

The shock of the discovery that their love – Richmond's and hers – was not unassailable, but as vulnerable as her body was to pain, was another crippling blow to her physical state, and a thousand times more wounding to her soul. She had never been smug about their happiness. She had never taken it for granted, but thanked heaven every year of their marriage for the continuance of the joy. Every shared happiness – planning their homes, going to a Brahms concert, a walk in a wood, a book, above all the children – had seemed so much evidence of the indestructible nature of their union. The reliability, the unassailability of Richmond, had seemed as secure as the rocks beneath. Like many another woman, given such guarantees, she might be forgiven for thinking so. That she had been wrong was *her* fault, not his. He was only human after all, open to temptation.

It was even more bitter to reflect that it had been she who asked Richmond to help Eleanor in her difficulties. And knowing him as she did, she could measure his suffering now, as equal to her own. She asked him to go away by himself and think it over. Whatever he decided she would accept. He did not prolong her torment. Fleeing to Brighton to face the issue squarely on his own, he sent her a laconic card within two days, addressed: 'Dearest wife', and saying he would be home in a couple of days.

There remains no written trace of the ordeal through which they passed. Only indications, here and there, emerge of the highlights of a joy recovered in the following year. The 'white world of snow' with which 1887 began; the family party when Anny could note in her Journal 'Richmond was happy, children happy, I happy'; 'A lovely walk in a wood with Richmond, the children and 2 dogs' in June 1887; the crossing to Boulogne in May all together, with the 'delicious walk along the old ramparts of my childhood and the children radiant'[5], such jottings proclaim the fullness of a mutual life recovered.

The ordeal had taken its toll on Richmond's nerves, however, and on his hitherto unassailable constitution. When his mother died shortly after in November (1888) he very nearly suffered a breakdown, and had to take a prolonged leave of absence from the office. Wounding, or reassuring to Richmond, the news soon came of

[5] MS Letters: N-B Collection.

Eleanor's marriage to Augustine Birrell. That nightmare was over. But like many nightmares, it left the sleeper a haunted man, one who had come face to face with his own 'familiar' – not so strong a man morally or physically as he had thought himself.

The responsibility for the 'tidying and packing up' of Mrs Ritchie's house in December 1888 fell upon Anny. At the same time they were expecting the return of Richmond's brother Gerald on leave from India with his wife, Margie, and their baby girl, bearing the good Thackerean name of Theo. They urgently needed a house to hold them all, and were fortunate to find one in Lexham Gardens – such 'a charming little commonplace birdcage of a house hung up mid air', as Anny described it to Mrs Oliphant. They took it for six weeks. Both she and Richmond were in need of a change after the 'sad sad time of his mother's illness and death', and they wanted the children to have a 'sort of Christmas' and make 'a happy welcome for the travellers'. They remained till the end of January 1889.

They were then once again in search of a home and rented a house at Wimbledon – Kingsley Lodge in Lingfield Road – so as not to interrupt the children's schooling and in order to stay in a place to which they had become attached. But once again Anny was ordered away, to Aix and to Malvern – where Richmond and the children could join her in the summer. Malvern delighted them, and as Anny wrote to Emily, 'somehow Richmond's mere presence set things right again'.[6]

Richmond was now recommended by his doctors to take up golf, and from then on they regularly paid visits to St. Andrews. After a first visit there in 1889, Anny could report him 'more like himself than for two months and more – Now he is very jolly, very happy, surrounded by happy people.'[7] She herself was 'walking like a free woman', after a treatment of 'strychnine and arsenic' which she extolled as having come 'just at the right moment'.

Soon after Richmond's return to the Office he was appointed Private Secretary to Mr Curzon (as he then was) and put up for election in the Athenaeum. With Anny fully caught up in her writing again, it looked as though they might be reaching calm waters once more, when in 1893 Richmond was found to be ill with 'Meniers' Disease (correctly Menière's from the doctor who first diagnosed the symptoms). It was a form of severe vertigo that frequently affected people under stress, as a result of overwork or

6 Ibid.   7 Ibid.

anxiety, as Richmond had been for the past few years. Though a 'serious illness', as the doctor told Anny, he was hopeful. The patient was liable to attacks at unpredictable times, and there was a risk that he might fall and injure himself. Anny was much alarmed. 'One never felt safe,' she wrote at the time. Richmond's nerves were chiefly affected. And they were worried about houses again. It was time for a decision to be taken on where Billy should go to school. He would be thirteen in March. Anny reported herself as 'floored with worry and nerves', and recorded a visit to her mother when she threw herself down on the sofa there 'while she played her sweet hymn tunes and I felt like a child again and all unlocked and cried and cried and cried'. Poor Isabella's undemanding patience often soothed Anny and put her own cares into a different perspective.

In September 1893 it was decided to send Billy to Sedbergh, which proved to be a happy solution all round. Billy was one of those fortunate characters who create their own happiness and radiate cheerfulness about them. Apart from mumps and measles, his parents never had a day's worry over him. The school holidays became the highlights of the family's year. Hester was sent to Putney High School and became, in her own quiet way, an invaluable companion to both parents.

On 26 July 1893, Anny could note in her Journal that Richmond had said, 'speaking of our perturbations: Thro' it all I have felt that the only mistake I *didn't* make was in marrying.' How fully the travail of that year was exorcised by those words can be felt in Anny's added exclamation: 'Ah! thank God in heaven for that!'

CHAPTER 19

'THIS WAS MY FRIEND'

MORE than once in periods of intense overwork and financial crisis, Anny had debated with herself the question: 'Whether to write or to live – to earn or to save?' Sometimes she could see clearly enough the incompatability of her two roles, as wife and mother on the one hand and as writer on the other. But in practice she was unable to divide herself, to suppress one half of her nature for the benefit of the other. At no time during the period of illness and family crises had she wholly abandoned her work. Indeed, if she had given up creative writing at the height of her ill health it is doubtful whether she would have physically recovered. She needed to exercise that gift in order to sustain the will to live. Certainly if she had given up, her name would be remembered today for no more than a couple of novels. At the age of fifty, in 1887, when she had written her last novel, *Mrs. Dymond*, she began the long series of biographical memoirs of her great contemporaries with the article on Ruskin, and she was only just entering on the period of her most characteristic work – the personal reminiscences which came so spontaneously and naturally from her. She was now being constantly commissioned by the periodical press.

In the thirty-odd pages or so that the flourishing periodicals of the time made available to their contributors there was no obligation to cover the full careers of her subjects in detail after the style of Macaulay. The art that Anny evolved was essentially different, something intimately personal and subjective. It called for other methods, for she was almost always dealing with people she had known well, and not, like Macaulay, with great figures of the past.

Anny's method was to conjure up an impression of the man or woman she was describing – by look, word, and gesture, by the very tone of voice. She was not repeating what others knew of them or how they were generally assessed. It was how they struck her that mattered. She wrote for instance to Browning's sister after his death, sending her the article she had written on him for *Harper's*, expressing how she felt in dealing with such tributes. 'It is only a very slight thing, but a record of a great deal of happy remembrance . . . I had to tear up all I tried to write that wasn't personal, for I thought it so dull: and my article became only personal reminiscences at last. . . . Goodbye dear, I'll never write about anyone I knew and *really* cared for again, for it is so complicated; and yet at the same time it is a very *proud* and grateful feeling to say to oneself, "and *this* was my Friend". I can only say thank God, for having known such dear and noble people.'[1] In spite of her misgivings, this was the very method most suited to her temperament.

She also saw her subjects as figures in a landscape, certainly not as studio portraits. In her article on Ruskin, written early in 1887, she records her first recollection of him, as deeply sad when he visited her father as a young man, and recalls meeting him again years later in a totally different environment, at his home at Brantwood on Coniston Water: 'Ruskin seems to me less picturesque as a young man than now in his latter days. . . . Meeting us after fifteen years I was struck by the change for the better in him; by the bright, radiant, sylvan look which a man gains by living among woods and hills and pure breezes.'

She found in the great men and women she had known not only their inherent and individual qualities but a capacity to enhance the stature of others. As she wrote in her essay on Ruskin, there is one element to be found in all – 'a certain directness, simplicity, and vivid reality; a gift for reaching their hearers at once, going straight from themselves, and not in reflections from other minds; sunshine, in short, not moonshine. . . . I have never met a really great man without it . . . he shows us the best of that which concerns him, and the best of ourselves too in that which concerns *us* in his work or his teaching.'[2]

The value of her approach lay in its essentially personal quality, but it is not that she seeks to put herself in the picture, rather that without her presence the picture would not exist. It grows through the intensity of her absorption in particular moments and scenes which set her memory alight and her imagination afire. She kindles to a subject. 'Who', she asks with perfect honesty, 'can ever recall a good talk that is over? You can remember the room in which it was held, the look of the chairs, but the actual talk takes wings and flies

[1] *Ritchie Letters*, p. 219.   [2] *Tennyson, Ruskin and Browning*, p. 74.

away. A dull talk has no wings, and is remembered more easily; so are those tiresome conversations which consist of sentences which we all repeat by rote. . . . But a real talk leaps into life; it is there almost before we are conscious of its existence. What system of notation can mark it down as it flows, modulating from its opening chords to those delightful exhilarating strains which are gone again almost before we have realised them?'[3]

Anny met Ruskin on three specific occasions before becoming his friend and regular correspondent: as a girl in her father's house, when Ruskin was very sad; in the summer of 1876 after Minny's death when she and Stephen and little Laura first stayed at Coniston; and again after she was married in 1881–2 when she found there the ideal setting for *Mrs. Dymond.*

On the second occasion, she described Ruskin's talk as they sat by the lakeside in his lovely garden. 'I should do him ill justice if I tried to transcribe his sermon,' she writes. 'The text was that "strawberries should be eaten ripe and sweet" and that that standard of perfection should be applied to everything'.[4]

It was the Ruskin of these encounters that she evoked. Though not ignoring the decisive events of his life altogether – she quoted from his autobiography, *Praeterita*, to describe the child his parents had made of him, and the importance of art and nature in restoring his sanity – it could be said in criticism that Anny avoided all unpleasant themes connected with her subject. No word of his miserable marriage with Effie Gray appears in the article. For one thing, both Ruskin and Effie were still alive, and Effie as Millais's wife was a part of that charmed household full of children beloved by Anny. Equally, she was not a malicious writer seeking to turn up mud, and what she sympathetically avoided more than anything was the wreck and ruin people cause each other.

But even without the Effies and the other destructive elements, Anny could build the edifice of a man's life entire, picking out its highlights, and those qualities by which great men make other people live. This is her recurrent theme. To her, Ruskin is still going ahead in the tunnel and crying out to his followers 'sesame' and 'sesame', and teaching them to see. 'He sees the glorious world', she wrote, 'as we have never known it, or have perhaps forgotten to look upon it. He takes the first example to hand – the stones, which he makes into bread; the dust and scraps and dry sticks and moss

---

[3] Ibid., p. 72.   [4] Ibid.

which are lying to his hand: he is so penetrated with the glory and beauty of it all, of the harmony into which we are set, that it signifies little to him upon what subject he preaches. . . . there is a blessing upon his words, and surely the fragments which remain are worthy of the twelve baskets of the Apostles.'[5]

There were for Anny two distinct categories of people: those few, as she was to write of Mrs Oliphant, who '*make* life', and the many who 'un-make it'. It was by their creative influence that she recognized the great men and women she had known. What strikes the reader of today in her accounts of them is her total ease in their company. She is never otherwise than natural in their presence. And this want of affectation of any kind, no matter the degree of her admiration and reverence, was probably one of the reasons why they, in their turn, were themselves with her, all too accustomed as they were to the fulsome deference of so many of those who pursued them.

Leslie Stephen frequently reproved Anny; for her unpunctuality, for her extravagance, for the howlers she made over facts and figures – as when she declared at a dinner party, 'There are forty millions of unmarried women in London alone'. But he never accused her of insincerity or affectation. What made her especially loved, he said, was her 'openness'. Her gifts were of a kind that no education could bestow. Her mind appeared 'oddly unmethodical' to a trained academic like him, but he had to own that she 'showed more perception and humour, more delicate and tender and beautiful emotion, than would have made the fortune of a dozen novelists. . . . Her . . . quick sympathies and her bright perceptions made her one of the most delightful of persons in all social intercourse.'[6]

Such qualities, testified to by so many, account for the indulgent affection in which she was held, despite the inconveniences to which her lapses of memory and her unpunctuality sometimes exposed her friends. Ruskin's cousin and housekeeper, Mrs Severn, remembered such an incident on a later visit to Coniston. 'After her marriage and with the children almost babies, she came back to the old quarters [at Coniston]. O what funny things happened then from her delightful absent-mindedness. Once on a Saturday after the butcher had been I called and found dear "Mrs. Thackeray" much perplexed at having asked a good many people to lunch and

[5] Ibid., pp. 151–2.   [6] *Mausoleum Book*, pp. 13–15.

the landlady with nothing extra got in, and no means of getting more! and the little dining-room not capable of holding more than 6 and that with the seat close to a wall – so I suggested that, Ruskin and I, should send on the Brantwood lunch, and come and eat it there with her guests, knowing that she particularly wished us to be there, so we and our cold pigeon pie and roast leg of lamb arrived with plenty of strawberries (cream at farm for them) tart, etc. etc. and tables were joined together on a pretty bit of lawn under 3 old walnut trees (alas! two blown down since then) the weather was divine and the party "a very great *sooccess!*" the talk brilliant – an American, Mr. Field, with friend came and much amusement created over the impromptu banquet.'[7]

Absent-minded though she might be, no false note ever entered into her memories of people and events and the authenticity of her recollections of her famous friends need not be doubted The truth of these is at times further confirmed by letters written much earlier. Thus, after that first meeting with Ruskin at Coniston in 1876, she wrote to George Smith: 'I wish you could see our lovely lake . . . Laura is with her little rake in the hayfield, and there is a Jane Eyre kitchen out of the parlour, with a dear old woman . . . cooking our mutton. . . . Ruskin has beautiful old bibles, and missals and above all such strawberries at his house. He says if you can draw a strawberry you can draw anything.'[8] This evidently refers to the talk 'on perfection' recorded in the article on Ruskin ten years later. She was writing it for Macmillans in 1887, and it was later published in *Harper's Magazine*, for a fee of £100, in March 1890.

It was Tennyson himself who had asked Anny to accept the commission from Harper's to write the article on him in 1882. She had been seeing a lot of him at the time, as her Journal records, during his annual London visit to his quarters in Eaton Square. They would go walking on Hampstead Heath where, on this particular occasion, urging her to write the article, he said, 'I could tell you things.' Such confidence between an old man, whose image was already becoming fossilized in the public mind, and a younger woman whose fresh response and unconventional approach to most subjects were well known to him, indicates a degree of trust not only in her truthfulness but in her understanding. What he had to tell would not be sensational, but revealing of his inward self. It was

[7] Fuller, p. 148.   [8] *Ritchie Letters*, p. 176.

twenty years now that they had known each other, twenty years since her first visit to Farringford before her father's death, when she and the poet had walked over the Downs together. Since then, there had never been a year, as her letters and journals record, during which they did not meet.

The valuable thing about Anny's article on Tennyson is precisely that the admissions and the feelings revealed were derived directly from him, and from these she was able to create an original and moving likeness. She records, what he admitted to her at the time and what at that stage of his fame must have been known to only a few, his early poverty, his self-doubt, his loneliness, and the chorus of contempt with which the critics 'demolished' his early poetry – the volumes of 1842 and 1847. She already knew about this through his visits to her father and from other members of the Cambridge circle. One thing she did learn, however, gave an added Byronic lustre to her memory of the poet as she had first seen him through clouds of smoke sitting in her father's study: his Pyrenean adventure, undertaken as a Cambridge student with Arthur Hallam, to carry money to the Spanish insurgents.[9]

The essay is marked by the modesty of its tone, the moderation of its assumptions. 'One must be English born, I think, to know how English is the spell which this great enchanter casts over one.' She evokes the places of his chief inspiration – Lincolnshire, the Isle of Wight, the Sussex Downs. And she quotes those contemporaries who first recognized the secret power in him: her own father, FitzGerald, Carlyle, William Howitt. It was their faith in him that helped to restore faith in himself at a time when he had been deeply afflicted, a man, as Carlyle saw him, 'solitary and sad'.

'The very names of the people who had stood upon the lawn at Farringford', she writes, 'would be an interesting study for some future biographer – Longfellow, Maurice, Kingsley, the Duke of Argyll, Locker, Dean Stanley, the Prince Consort. Good Garibaldi once planted a tree there, off which some too ardent republican broke a branch before twenty-four hours had passed. Here came Clough in the last year of his life. Here Mrs. Cameron fixed her lens, marking the well-known faces as they passed – Darwin, Browning, and Henry Taylor, Watts and Aubrey de Vere, Lecky and Jowett, and a score of others.'[10]

The group of Eminent Victorians here seen at home at Farring-

---

[9] *Tennyson, Ruskin and Browning*, p. 23.   [10] Ibid., p. 43.

1

ford were not only Tennyson's friends, but Anne Ritchie's as well. From such a diversity of deep friendships with some, easy contacts with others, she acquired that independence of judgement, that freshness of outlook that singled her out. Seeking to convey the range of Tennyson's reputation, she chose the following example. 'Perhaps the best compliment that Tennyson ever received was one day walking in Covent Garden, when he was suddenly stopped by a rough-looking man, who held out his hand, and said: "You're Mr. Tennyson. Look here, sir, here am I. I've been drunk for six days out of the seven, but if you will shake me by the hand, I'm d——d if I ever get drunk again."'[11]

When she had written the article she sent the manuscript to Aldworth at Christmas 1882 for Tennyson to read. He returned it almost at once, unchanged, so that on 11 January she could send it to Harpers. She owned to being disappointed at receiving from them a fee of £50 and rather courageously returned the cheque, asking for the £100 which she thought the article merited. This was promptly sent. After Tennyson's death in October 1892 when Macmillans asked her for permission to reprint the article in book form, it appeared together with her Ruskin and Browning articles, both previously published, in *Records of Tennyson, Ruskin and Robert and Elizabeth Browning*, 1892.

It was Leslie Stephen who had commissioned the article on Mrs Browning for the *Dictionary of National Biography* in 1885. Anny incorporated the text of much of this in her subsequent article on Browning, written after his death in 1891 for *Macmillan's Magazine* and the American journal, *Atalanta*. Then as usual, her approach was personal, introducing the Brownings by the impact they had first made on her, as a child in Paris, when rooms had to be found for them, and her grandmother busied herself looking for something suitable. Anny was told that Mr and Mrs Browning 'were very gifted and celebrated people', that Mrs Browning was an invalid 'who could not possibly live without light and warmth'. They were coming from Italy and therefore every care must be taken for their comfort. 'So that by the time the travellers had really arrived, and were installed, we were all greatly excited and interested in their whereabouts.' Then came Mrs Carmichael-Smyth's first call. 'Mr. Browning was not there, but Mrs. Browning received us in a low room with Napoleonic chairs and tables, and a wood-fire burning on the hearth.'

[11] Ibid., p. 51.

Anny, maybe a girl of thirteen at the time, vividly remembered the occasion forty years later. 'I do not think any girl who had once experienced it could fail to respond to Mrs. Browning's motherly advance,' she wrote. 'There was something more than kindness in it; there was an implied interest, equality, and understanding which is very difficult to describe and impossible to forget. This generous humility of nature was also to the last one special attribute of Robert Browning himself, translated by him into cheerful and vigorous good-will and utter absence of affectation.'[12]

'But, again and again one is struck by that form of greatness which consists in reaching the reality in all things, instead of keeping to the formalities and the affectations of life. The free-and-easiness of the small is a very different thing from this. It may be as false in its way as formality itself, if it is founded on conditions which do not and can never exist.'[13]

Mrs Browning died in 1861, and Anny regretted that the times spent with her had not been 'so very many'; but they were 'all the more vivid' to her in recollection. 'Whether at Florence, at Rome, at Paris, or in London,' she wrote, 'she seemed to carry her own atmosphere always, something serious, motherly, absolutely artless, and yet impassioned, noble, and sincere.'[14] It was clearly this 'motherly' quality in Mrs Browning that attracted Anny most. She wrote again, 'Mrs. Browning was a great writer; but I think she was even more a wife and a mother than a writer, and any account of her would be incomplete which did not put these facts first and foremost in her history.'[15]

Anny grew to know Browning more intimately as an old man than during his wife's lifetime. Thackeray was still alive when he returned to England after her death, and Anny records their first meeting. 'I can remember walking with my father under the trees in Kensington Gardens, when we met Mr. Browning just after his return to England. He was coming towards us along the broad walk in his blackness through the sunshine. We were then living in Palace Green, close by, and he came to see us very soon after. But he was in a jarred and troubled state, and not himself as yet, although I remember his speaking of the house he had just taken for himself and his boy.'[16] It was during Browning's London years, when his sister made a home for him, that Anny's friendship ripened; and

[12] Ibid., pp. 159–61. [13] Ibid., p. 161.
[14] Ibid., p. 162. [15] Ibid., p. 209.
[16] Ibid., p. 211.

especially after her marriage, when they frequently spent holidays on the same Normandy coast at Luc-sur-Mer, which inspired his 'Red Cotton Nightcap Country' sequence.

Over the next few years she met him at the dinner-tables of friends and on occasion heard him read aloud his latest poem. Her circle of friends was both wide-flung and closely-knit, so that encounters could be regularly expected. If it was not at the homes of George Smith, the Procters, the Wattses, the Holman Hunts, the Burne-Joneses, it was at the Tennysons or at Pen Browning's studio. Browning had an incisive way of speaking that she found particularly memorable. At a dinner early in 1880 she recorded him as saying that: 'the great charm of music lay in its surprises and that once you knew every note you lost that pleasure. He said Paganini could play any 2 notes so as to raise the soul out of the body.'[17]

For her 'birthday treat' on 9 June in 1888 she took the children to see Browning in De Vere Gardens, and noted how he kissed them and 'was most charming'.[18] She told him that it was a family festival and that she had brought the children to ask for his blessing. 'Is that all?' he said, laughing, with a kind look, not without relief. He was besieged by American tuft-hunters in one room and a deputation of the Browning Society in another, and told her she had 'no conception what it was like'. As for his fanmail, he was quite worn out with answering letters by the time he began his day's work. After a lifetime of public neglect and incomprehension, he was recognized at last. Anny was deeply moved when, after his death in Venice on 12 December 1889, he was brought home and given what amounted to a national funeral. She watched the great procession passing along the London streets to follow him to 'his honoured grave' in the Abbey.

Dreading the Abbey and the great public emotion, as she put it, she went round early to the house in De Vere Gardens to make her own last farewell, and found 'Poor Miss Browning was ill in bed', as she told Margie in India. 'There was a light in the drawing-room window, and in the ground floor room was the dear old friend's coffin, with its purple pall and the great Italian wreaths spread at its foot.'[19]

'I can only thank God', she wrote subsequently to Miss Browning, 'for having counted him among those who live in my soul's life. . . . And to think of him who is with us all, though gone, is like

---

[17] Journal, 1880.   [18] Ibid., 1888.   [19] *Ritchie Letters*, p. 210.

thinking of the sunshine which survives and warms . . . the only help to one's sorrow is to feel the priceless treasure of those who made one's life what it was, and who *still* make it.' Looking across the open grave in Poet's Corner at the faces of the friends that loved him, was to see all the writers and the painters 'of their time come to pay their last tribute to this great and generous poet'.[20]

Shortly after her article appeared in *Macmillan's Magazine* in 1891 she was asked by the publisher to write on Mrs Gaskell, a commission which took her to Manchester and Knutsford in the November of that year. This was one of those happy assignments where everything – subject, setting, hospitality – were in total harmony. Few writers were more attuned to the spirit of Mrs Gaskell's work, the gaiety and warmth and freshness, than was Anne Ritchie. How like the subject of her memoir does she herself sound, writing to Richmond while staying with Meta and Julia Gaskell:

'O what kind ladies!

O what a delicious dinner!

O what a nice room!

O how extraordinarily rejuvenated and cheered I feel!

'I only wish you were here too. . . . I am writing to catch the early worm! . . . The sun is shining, the air is delicious. I like the climate of Manchester!!! I arrived far less tired than when I started. I do wonder how you and the children are getting on.'[21] She delighted in the perfect 'Cranford' appearance of Knutsford, where Meta and Julia took her.

The article was published as an introduction to a reprint of *Cranford* issued by Macmillans. She noted on the book's appearance that the Gaskells, being in London, 'rushed in to say how pleased they were with the Preface'.[22] This and the appearance in book form of her *Tennyson, Ruskin and Robert and Elizabeth Browning* in 1892 brought her a greatly enhanced reputation. It prompted George Smith seriously to consider the plan first discussed with Anny early in 1891 for launching a complete, revised, annotated edition of Thackeray's Works, with introductions – biographical introductions – by Anny herself. It was one way round the embargo imposed by Thackeray on any biography of him being

[20] *Tennyson, Ruskin and Browning*, p. 245.
[21] *Ritchie Letters*, p. 215.
[22] Journal, 30 Nov. 1891.

written. This would deal with the inception and settings of the books chronologically as they were written and thus present not an official 'life' but at least a biographical commentary on the works.

It would also, Anny hoped, help to put a stop to the numerous uninformed articles constantly appearing in the periodical press, by providing an authoritative account of her father's way of working and his attitude to his work which she alone could supply. At the same time it would not positively flout his declared prohibition. In one respect it might fulfil her heart's desire to make him better and more enduringly known; on the other hand she was terrified of failure. For once, it was not a matter she could decide impulsively in her usual way.

It occupied her thoughts for a considerable time. In a light-hearted letter written at Easter 1891 to Emily Ritchie, with Billy home for the holidays engaged in gymnastic capers in the next room by the open window in his shirt-sleeves, she observed that there was 'something very ludicrous in discussing whether my father's memoirs should or shouldn't be written, while his grandson is catching influenza in the next room. Not that he is. He is very jolly and in the seventh heaven with Arthur.'[23]

There were various influences at work which would in time persuade her to accept George Smith's proposal. One by one the great figures of her girlhood were disappearing and the need to preserve what she could from the wreck of time was becoming a personal imperative. Throughout 1892 her mother's health was visibly failing. Anny visited her even more often than she generally did, with a great tenderness of longing to keep her. Then on 6 October the news came from Aldworth that Tennyson had died. She had to hurry out of doors to walk off the shock, 'thinking of Him and of them', as she noted in her Journal. She attended the funeral in the Abbey, on 16 October, sitting between Mrs Oliphant and Ellen Terry. To the former she wrote, 'I have been wondering about you, ever since we parted at the Abbey door, and I fear . . . that you are very tired and worn out. . . . I am only now shaking off the feeling of almost despair which came over me, as I looked at all that should have been of comfort and help. . . . It seemed to me like my whole generation passing away.' A strange thing for a woman of fifty-five to say of a man of eighty – her father's contemporary. But Thackeray's friends were always to seem like

[23] *Ritchie Letters*, p. 214. Arthur Ritchie, a nephew.

contemporaries to her, for by the circumstances of her childhood
that generation had provided her earliest friends and companions. 'I
will go to no more funerals', she said, 'unless I can cry comfortably
by myself. . . . I was really touched by Ellen Terry's genuine grief,
tho' I think, if I had only been alone with you, I should have felt in
better harmony with that, to me, most *wrenching* scene.'[24] She had
written a few years earlier to Tennyson, on receiving his presentation copy of *Locksley Hall*, 'When I think of the past (I always
think of old days on Freshwater Downs as the nearest thing to
heaven I ever could imagine), you will still walk ahead and point to
the sea and to the sky, and touch things and make them shine for us
and flash into our hearts, as you have ever done.' Tennyson had
been one of the great inspirations of her life. Her feeling for him
was special: filial, pious, almost religious, yet familiar; a father-
figure and trusted friend in whom she could always confide and
who confided in her.

After the death of her father's old banker friend, Russell Sturgis,
his son Julian published a memoir of him – *Books and Papers of
Russell Sturgis* – and sent Anny a copy. It struck so vibrant a chord
that perhaps more than any other single influence it prompted her
to collect her own memories and write of her own past, to produce
what became *Chapters from some Memoirs* which was published in
1894 and from which developed quite naturally the records of her
father for which George Smith had importuned her for so long. In
writing of old friends and the eminent figures of the age, reliving in
memory scenes and experiences that had filled her early life, she
found much satisfaction. 'What a delightful cheering fillip to warm
my old and failing steps,' she wrote to Julian Sturgis acknowledging
his book. 'I *love* my recollections, and now I understand why
everybody writes them. One begins to dance again, and lark, and
frisk, and thrill, and do all the things one can hardly believe one
ever did. I'm sure some of our happiest joys and carols were under
your kind kindest home, and I think of Mount Felix as Mount
Happy indeed. . . . I am very grateful and glad to have this little bit
of my own past safely written down and printed by you.'[25]

It was unusual for her to confess to feeling her age, but the feeling
had been exacerbated by the death of her mother at the beginning of
that year. She wrote in her Journal: 'What a difference these last five
years have made in my life and my way of life. My mother's death

[24] Ibid., p. 221.   [25] *Ritchie Letters*, pp. 225–6.

has made me feel like an old woman. Till then I felt ill but not old.'

Sent for by telegram early on 10 January 1894, Anny hurried to Leigh-on-Sea, where her mother had now lived for years, and found her already unconscious. She held her hand in hers throughout the day and the following night, and just as the doctor arrived in the morning she died. Anny described how 'her dear face lighted into serene and unspeakable wisdom and knowledge. It seemed to me that the room was full of light'. On her return home later in the day, she found Richmond waiting for her at the station and was strangely affected by seeing on the evening-paper placards: 'Death of Mrs. Thackeray'. Poor Isabella, after her long deprived life, was once more of the world.

Isabella had always shown a keen interest in the children. She had in fact been speaking of Billy when she fainted, and they cried 'bitterly' on hearing of her death. The whole family attended her funeral at Leigh Church on 13 January. The little choirboy sang 'O Rest in the Lord', one of Isabella's favourite hymns. Later, Anny had an Irish cross placed over her grave. Yet, as Anny wrote to a friend afterwards, it was 'more of thankfulness than sorrow . . . those who saw her die, now know her, and what she was within the tranquil person of her life. Dear Mama, so silent, so undemanding, so loving, so contented. As she lay there, she looked wise and strong and full of peace, and one couldn't feel sorrow, and yet I shall miss her day after day. . . . Her death was something far beyond peace. It seemed to me like a reality of Life and Knowledge, and her dear face looked translated, supreme. I have no words to tell you how great she seemed to me. Richmond and the children, and Julia [Stephen] and Edward Thackeray came and laid her in her grave – my kind, sweet, patient mother.'[26]

It was in the year following her mother's death that she wrote those memories of childhood that she came to call, for their incompleteness, *Chapters from some Memoirs*, eagerly published by Smith, Elder in December. They were immediately and enthusiastically reviewed in the *Pall Mall Gazette*.[27]

The book was divided into eight chapters covering her Parisian childhood, the years in Young Street living with her father, and some accounts of her first travels abroad with him – from which large sections have been quoted earlier in this account of her life. Once again, in the *Chapters*, Anny drew the portraits of her father's

[26] Ibid., p. 223.   [27] Journal, Dec. 1894.

famous friends, as they had first appeared to her in childhood –
FitzGerald, Tennyson, the Carlyles, Dickens, Mrs Kemble, Mrs
Sartoris, the Brownings – bringing to their evocation such freshness
of feeling, vision, enthusiasm, and hero-worship, that she might in
fact have been writing of them in her childhood. It is one of the
curiosities of the book that the ecstasies of a girl of ten are so
faithfully recorded, in the memories of a woman in her fifties,
almost trembling with the excitement of those long-past gatherings
– Thackeray's lectures in Willis's Assembly Rooms, the evening
Currer Bell dined in Young Street. Her sense of the importance of
each occasion – be it a drive to Richmond or a supper at Greenwich
– is not only that of a little girl enjoying a rare treat, however, but as
a portion of that total experience that makes up a life. It was typical
of Anny's whole approach to the business of living, as an adventure
of boundless variety and interest to be shared and enjoyed. Central
to it all is her father himself, the tall, stooping, burly figure whose
presence was the source of all happiness. George Smith could be
well satisfied by the success of the first sketch of the man whose
complete portrait he hoped to secure from this writer's pen. Within
a month of the publication of *Chapters*, he had prevailed on her to
agree to begin work on the Biographical Introductions. Anny noted
in her Journal for December 1894, 'beginning work on *Vanity Fair*
and *Pendennis*' – the first novels to appear under her father's own
name, and the first titles to appear in the new edition.

It was a daunting task she was undertaking, as she soon began to
realize. She knew her manner of working well enough to recognize
the difference between what was required now and her usual erratic
course. Neither punctuality nor precision was her strength. Here a
sustained effort would be required, a regular programme of work.
The very regularity such a commitment imposed was alien to her
temperament, and would have been frankly uncongenial had she
not passionately cared for the end in sight. It would take her three
and a half years of hard work. But George Smith, in his wisdom,
knew that it would prove to be not only a labour of love for
Thackeray's daughter, but her own surest guarantee of fame.

CHAPTER 20

THE *MAGNUM OPUS*

THE Edition was advertised by its publishers as comprising 'Additional Material and Hitherto Unpublished Letters, Sketches, and Drawings derived from the Author's Original Manuscripts and Note-Books. And each volume will include a Memoir, in the form of an Introduction, by Mrs. Richmond Ritchie. A Volume will be published Monthly until the completion of the Edition.'

In the press it was made plain that 'Mrs. Ritchie, his daughter, will contribute to each volume . . . her memories of the circumstances under which her father produced it. Such memoirs, when complete, cannot fall far short of being an actual biography.'[1]

It would have been a formidable undertaking even for a more methodical worker than Anny. The search for unpublished material among the remaining mass of Thackeray's manuscripts, his letters to friends in which he wrote of his books, itself demanded a regularity and order that were essentially alien to her way of working. The whole enterprise laid a strain on her mercurial temperament that constantly affected her health. But she stuck to it, though her methods were far removed from the more conventional and scholarly approach to the task of editing.

In her General Introduction to the Edition, published in Volume I in 1898 (*Vanity Fair*), she wrote: 'My father never wished for any Biography of himself to be written, and for this reason I have never attempted to write one. It is only after a quarter of a century that I have determined to publish memories which chiefly concern his books. Certain selections from his letters are also included, which tell of the places where his work was done, and of the times when he wrote. So much has been forgotten, so much that is ephemeral has been recorded, that it is my desire to mark down some of the truer chords to which his life was habitually set. For this reason I have

---

[1] Publication would be in thirteen monthly volumes, Large Crown 8vo, Gilt top, 6s each. (Smith, Elder's Advertisement.)

included one letter to my Mother among the rest: it will show that he knew how to value the priceless gifts of home and of happiness while they lasted, as well as to bear trouble and loneliness when they fell upon him.'

From the start the keynote to her approach was its freshness and frankness. There were no traces of conventional 'piety', and in her appreciation of the importance of her father's achievement there was no pomposity. She did not attempt to falsify the image of her father to meet the conventions of the day, or to conform to preconceived notions of his character. She portrayed him very simply as he appeared to her.

In the Introduction to *Vanity Fair*, which was written between 1845 and 1848, she dates its inception many years before she was born, in 1817 in fact, when her father was sent to school at Dr Turner's Academy on Chiswick Mall as a child of six freshly arrived from India. The first chapter of the book was derived from that experience. Quoting his statement that he never consciously *copied* a character from life, she related an incident that affords a glimpse of his 'grass-widower' existence before he made a home for the girls at Young Street, and began writing *Vanity Fair*. Rumours about the original of Becky had always been rife. 'I may as well state here', she writes, 'that one morning a hansom drove up to the door, and out of it emerged a most charming, dazzling little lady dressed in black, who greeted my father with great affection and brilliancy, and who, departing presently, gave him a large bunch of fresh violets. This was the only time I ever saw the fascinating little person who was by many supposed to be the original of Becky; my father only laughed when people asked him, but he never quite owned to it. . . . It was, of course, impossible that suggestions should not come to him.'[2]

Two valuable pieces of information about *Vanity Fair* which she revealed were the number of publishers who had initially refused the book, and the poor sales of the early numbers, published in monthly parts. For months after its first appearance on 1 January 1847, it was a complete failure with the public. It brought the unknown author recognition among a small élite (the *Edinburgh*

[2] Introduction, Biog. Ed. i. xxx. Ray, i. clvii–cix, identifies the 'little lady' as Theresa Reviss, the illegitimate daughter of WMT's friend Charles Buller. WMT mentions Mrs Buller's goodness in adopting the girl and 'Little Tizzy's' obstinacy in rejecting an offer of marriage worth £5,000 a year. Ray, ii. 383. I owe this detail to Professor Colby.

Review in particular), and personal friendships among a growing circle; it did everything, as Thackeray himself said, 'but sell'.

The book's painful start in life is revealed, Anny suggests, by the state of the manuscript, which is scored over with erasures and alterations. She compares the toil and trouble that the book evidently gave him to *Esmond* (his third book), the manuscript of which is notably clean.

Early poverty and initial ill luck with the book on which he counted to 'make his fortune' were not, in Anny's recollection, a misfortune for her father. She saw in them, what he himself ultimately recognized in adversity, a wholesome lesson. Had life been too easy, who knows if he would have appreciated it as he did? 'For years and years,' wrote Anny, 'he had to face the great question of daily bread: life was no playtime either to him or to many of his contemporaries . . . Carlyle, Tennyson, Dickens, John Leech, a dozen honoured names come to one's mind.' The benefits to them all of 'a little Adversity' (as the fairy Blackstick wished the infant heroine of *The Rose and the Ring*) were, in Anny's estimate, to give each of them a happiness in their work, a progress, a fulfilment, rather than a task; a spiritual satisfaction, if not a material one. Paradoxically, it gave their work its individual stamp. 'They worked on for the work's sake', wrote Anny, 'as much as for what it brought to them, and understood what was best worth having; learning the things that people often don't learn who have only bought their places in the world, or inherited them from others.' In the success that came with the book's finishing numbers, Anny noted that her father did not forget his early tribulations. He dedicated it 'affectionately' to his friend Procter ('Barry Cornwall') who, she writes, 'had been so good to my father when he was in great trouble'.[3]

The *Pendennis* introduction (Vol. II of the Edition) is a rather erratic assembly of valuable insights and memories, and of excerpts from Thackeray's letters from school and college, taken out of context and insufficiently integrated into Anny's own text. While seeking to evoke his 'Pendennis' years, she makes clear the distinction between the creator of Pen and the fictional Pen that only she could discern. Speaking of her father's early friendship with Fitz-Gerald as in some ways resembling that of Pen and Warrington in the novel, she comments, 'and yet my father was not Pendennis any

[3] Ibid. xxxviii.

more than the other was Warrington: they were both much more fastidious, critical, and imaginative persons.'⁴

The early readers of the novel (including Charlotte Brontë) were in no doubt about the original of Helen Pendennis, Thackeray's own mother, but not many readers knew which young creature had inspired the image of Laura. Her situation at Fairoaks as Mrs Pendennis's orphan niece was clearly enough modelled on the real-life situation of Thackeray's young orphan cousin, Mary Graham (later the wife of the Major's brother Colonel Charles Carmichael-Smyth) but Anny knew that the vision that enchanted Thackeray and gave rise to the fictional Laura was of 'a little girl living in Brighton, a charming little girl with dark eyes and curly brown hair'; she was Horace Smith's youngest daughter, whom Thackeray first saw as 'she came running into the room and said her name was Laura'.⁵

The vicissitudes attending all Thackeray's major works – ill health, sudden failures of inspiration and subsequent depression – afflicted *Pendennis* like the rest. But, as Anny said, 'he was not one of those people who give up what they have once undertaken to do, and he stuck to his book for better for worse.' Tennyson delighted in it from the start: 'it seemed to him so mature', FitzGerald reported, and for Anny herself 'and to many of my own generation it has always seemed as if there was a special music in "Pendennis" and the best wisdom of a strong heart beating under its yellow waistcoat.'⁶

From Thackeray's daughter alone could have come the following reminiscence: 'I can remember the morning Helen [Pendennis] died. My father was in his study in Young Street, sitting at the table at which he wrote. It stood in the middle of the room, and he used to sit facing the door. I was going into the room, but he motioned me away. An hour afterwards he came in to our schoolroom, half-laughing and half-ashamed, and said to us: "I do not know what James can have thought of me when he came in with the tax-gatherer just after you left, and found me blubbering over Helen Pendennis's death".' Minny said, '"Oh, papa, do make her well again; she can have a regular doctor, and be almost dead, and then will come a homeopathic doctor, who will make her well, you know. . . ."'⁷ – a comment from the nine-year-old Minny which

⁴ Ibid. ii. xxx.   ⁵ Ibid. xxxii.
⁶ Ibid. xxxv.   ⁷ Ibid. xxxix–xl.

showed how that the precepts of her homœopathic grandmother were not lost on her.

Thackeray dedicated the book to the doctor who saved his life after the almost fatal attack of cholera he suffered in the summer of 1849, which held up the book for three months. Anny quotes it in full:

To Dr. John Elliotson.
My dear Doctor,
Thirteen months ago, when it seemed likely that this story had come to a close, a kind friend brought you to my bedside, whence, in all probability, I never should have risen but for your constant watchfulness and skill. I like to recall your great goodness and kindness (as well as many acts of others, showing quite a surprising friendship and sympathy) at that time, when kindness and friendship were most needed and welcome.

And as you would take no other fee but thanks, let me record them here in behalf of me and mine, and subscribe myself, etc. etc. . . .[8]

Anny had set to work on the Biographical Introductions in December 1894, immediately following the publication of *Chapters*, and worked almost non-stop on the first two volumes till the following March. She had previously received an invitation (through Mrs Oliphant) from Macmillans to write Introductions to the Edgeworth novels that they were planning to reissue. She entered into the project with zest, although it meant working on a double bill, and stretching herself, as always, to the limit. Taking the sixteen-year-old Hester with her, she sailed to Dublin on 20 May – noting characteristically in her Journal: 'Lovely crossing – gulls following the ship – hills rising from the water – Dublin something between Paris and Battersea', and went on to Edgeworthstown, where she was warmly welcomed by the Edgeworth descendants, and worked hard on notes for her articles. She was back at Holyhead on the 31st and, being in the north, did not miss the chance of visiting Billy at Sedbergh next day. By mid-June she was dictating her Edgeworth notes to Hester. The three introductions, to *Castle Rackrent*, *Belinda*, and *Helen*, were finished by 27 September, and published in March 1895. This was how she liked to work, at high speed, in the heat of the freshly kindled enthusiasm, before the flame had time to die down. She spoke of the whole undertaking as 'my little series of Introductions' (as compared with

[8] Ibid. xiv.

the *magnum opus*, the Introductions to her father's works) but they contain some of her most sparkling writing.

The Introduction to *Castle Rackrent* (some 33 pages) is the most complete, and could serve for the whole series as a sufficient evocation of the Edgeworths' way of life, and the natural surroundings of their home which played so essential a part in Maria's fiction. To Anne Thackeray both the period and the place struck a deeply sympathetic chord: received by the present owners of the house, Lord and Lady Edgeworth (Maria's nephew and his wife), and taken into the lovely old rooms still furnished and appointed as when Maria lived and worked there, Anny responded immediately: 'What a strange fellow-feeling with the past it gave one to stand staring at the old books, with their paper backs and old-fashioned covers, at the gray boards, which were the liveries of literature in those days; at the first editions, with their inscriptions in the author's handwriting, or in Maria's pretty calligraphy. . . . Storied urn and monumental bust do not bring back the past as do the books which belong to it. Storied urns are in churches and stone niches, far removed from the lives of which they speak; books seem a part of our daily life, and are like the sound of a voice just outside the door. Here they were, as they had been read by her, stored away by her hands . . . bringing back the past with, as it were, a cheerful encouraging greeting to the present.'[9]

As for the countryside, Anny responded even more enthusiastically. She is at her observant best in writing of such scenes. Taken for a 'delightful flight on a jaunting car' by her host, she was bewitched by what she saw. 'The lights came and went; as the mist lifted we could see the exquisite colours, the green, the dazzling sweet lights on the meadows, playing upon the meadow-sweet and elder bushes; at last we came to the lovely glades of Carriglass. . . . It seemed to me that we had reached an enchanted forest amid this sweet tangle of ivy, of flowering summer trees, of immemorial oaks and sycamores. A squirrel was darting up the branches of a beautiful spreading beech-tree, a whole army of rabbits were flashing with silver tails into the brushwood; swallows, blackbirds, peacock butterflies, dragonflies on the wing, a mighty sylvan life was roaming in this lovely orderly wilderness'.[10]

The foreignness of the scene recalled her Continental childhood. 'English', she writes, 'does not seem exactly the language in which

---

[9] Introduction, *Castle Rackrent*, pp. ix–x. [10] Ibid., pp. x–xi.

to write of Ireland, with its sylvan wonders of natural beauty.
Madame de Sévigné's descriptions of her woods came to my mind.
. . . Ireland seems to me to contain some unique and most
impersonal charm, which is quite unwritable.'[11]

Of Maria Edgeworth's work she wrote concisely and with
justice: 'There is a curious matter-of-fact element in all she wrote,
combined with extraordinary quickness and cleverness; and, it must
be remembered, in trying to measure her place in literature, that in
her day the whole great school of English philosophical romance
was in its cradle; George Eliot was not in existence; my father was
born in the year in which *The Absentee* was published. Sir Walter
Scott has told us that it was Miss Edgeworth's writing which first
suggested to him the idea of writing about Scotland and its national
life. Turgenieff in the same way . . . began to write of his own
country and Russian peasants.'[12]

Noting the fundamental differences between nineteenth-century
fiction and Edgeworth's work, Anny wrote: 'I don't think she
troubled herself much about complication of feeling; she liked
people to make repartees, or to invent machines, to pay their bills,
and to do their duty in a commonplace and cheerfully stoical
fashion. . . . Perhaps we in our time scarcely do justice to Miss
Edgeworth's extraordinary cleverness and brightness of apprehension. There is more fun than humour in her work, and those were
the days of good rollicking jokes and laughter.'[13]

Of *Belinda*, no favourite with the author herself, Anny found
both plot and characters rather 'confused and disappointing; the
beginning much better than the end.' *Helen*, published in 1832 and
written after a ten-year interval to console the ageing Maria for the
death of a beloved brother, Anny thought contained more 'life and
spirit than any other of her works, with the exception of *Castle
Rackrent*', and she reminded her readers that Mrs Gaskell thought it
'one of the best of all English novels'.[14]

Anny's main task remained the Biographical Introductions to her
father's works, but family obligations always came first. The
children's lives absorbed her, especially Billy's happiness at Sedbergh. She always contrived to visit him each term, and meantime
wrote him gay, inconsequent, loving letters. Hester was increas-

[11] Ibid., p. xi.   [12] Ibid., pp. xxv–xxvi.
[13] Ibid., p. xxvii.   [14] Introduction, *Helen*, p. vii.

ingly with her, beginning to help her keep some order in her work. Laura she visited regularly at Earlswood. She kept up long, lively, and fond correspondence with her adopted daughters Margie and Annie, and her sister-in-law Emily Ritchie, during their frequent absences in India, and with Blanche Warre-Cornish and her growing family at Eton. As Rhoda Broughton said of her: 'Love was the keynote of her life.'[15]

In May 1895, Julia Stephen, Leslie's second wife, died suddenly of influenza. Julia left four young children by her marriage with Leslie – her three children by Duckworth being adult by then – ranging in age from 15 to 11. Anny reacted with characteristic feeling. It was for them, even more than for Leslie, that she grieved. On the day of the funeral, 8 May, she stayed with the younger children, as she noted in her Journal, in the garden at Hyde Park Gate, while Richmond and Hester attended the funeral. Their comfort, and that of the shattered Leslie, came before all other obligations that spring.

Long before Julia had married Herbert Duckworth, she had been Anny's friend. It was Anny, as Julia recorded, who had helped her more than anyone to recover from the shock of her husband's sudden death. 'What Anny has been to me', she said, 'I should find it difficult to describe. When I was very much alone, the children quite small, and every day seemed a fresh burden, she used to come . . . and . . . somehow took me into her life; and by making me take a sort of indirect interest in things she did and people she saw, helped me . . . and made things more real to me again.'[16] Julia, in her turn, had helped Anny with copying and arranging 'her disorderly manuscripts' (as Leslie recorded) and the friendship had taken deep and holding root. Julia's death, therefore, greatly affected Anny, and she quite naturally resumed the old burden of supporting Leslie. Hester recalls how, after Julia's death, he used to come 'with clock-like regularity' to see Anny once a week.[17] Their former affectionate, if frequently argumentative, relationship was restored, and she was 'never repelled "by the jeremiads and invectives he poured into her sympathetic ear".' As his health declined and he became a chronically sick man, Anny stood by him valiantly. In his juster moments, he recognized his debt to her. He

[15] *Cornhill*, Nov. 1919.
[16] *Mausoleum Book*, p. 42.   [17] Fuller, p. 156.

wrote to Charles Eliot Norton: 'My greatest help has been and is Mrs. Richmond Ritchie – the most sympathetic and social of beings that ever lived.'

Leslie was totally lacking in the sense of humour that was Anny's strongest asset and to forestall the lamentations that were his regular greeting on her visits, her daughter relates how she took the initiative on one occasion, came in brightly and sat down beside his bed, and before he could speak, said: 'Well Leslie – Damn – Damn – Damn!' – to which even he found no other answer than to burst out laughing.[18]

His reliance on Anny after Julia's death can be seen from a letter written in August 1895 – from her cottage The Porch, which she had lent to the bereaved family – in which he says among other things: 'I feel, as you suggest, that love of my children may in time make the grief endurable; but at present it brings almost as much pain as happiness. Some day if I live I shall look back at this period, I suspect, as a time of such misery that even this place will be hateful to me. . . . There, I have unburdened myself a bit. Don't trouble to answer. It is only a moan which relieves me for a few minutes. Your affectionate, L.S.'[19]

When away from home he always wrote regularly to his 'souffre douleur'. Her letters, he tells her, were always welcome. From Stroud, where the family were staying some time later, he wrote, 'I feel dreadfully solitary in myself, but the absence of neighbours is refreshing . . . I don't think I shall ever be better. I have written you a sad letter I fear. . . . I am, as I told you, depressed to-night, and it will come out in talking to my sister, but I think I have written a little of it off, and feel rather more cheeful.' Then, with a sudden flash of insight into their relative positions, he added: 'If anybody compared our letters they would say that it was a dove talking to a gorilla.'[20] The patience of the 'dove' was often sorely tried, but she continued to bring 'healing on her wings'.

A deeply loving and most tender father, the lack of joy in his nature must have been crushing for the children. Their almost constant ill health may have had something to do with his depressing influence. For the two years following Julia's death, Stella, aged twenty-six, looked after him – until, to his further dismay, she married on 10 April 1897. Then the burden of running the

[18] Ibid, *Mausoleum Book*, p. xxv.
[19] Ibid., p. 158.   [20] Ibid., p. 159.

17. Anny with Hester and Billy in the garden of Kingsley Lodge, Wimbledon

18. Anne Thackeray Ritchie

household and keeping the accounts (entailing a terrifying weekly
'auditing' from her father) fell on Vanessa, barely sixteen at the
time. Virginia was nearly always ill.

Anny's pity was chiefly for these bereft girls. It was from this
period of almost daily contacts, in all probability, that Virginia's
absorption in her aunt derived. Anny's status in the family as a
'famous author' was of special interest to the little girl who had
already chosen to be a writer, and who would leave such an
enduring likeness of her aunt in the character of 'Mrs. Hilbery' in
her novel *Night and Day*, which shows all the marks of close and
prolonged observation.

Physically, Virginia Woolf's portrait of 'Mrs. Hilbery', authoress
daughter of a great Victorian writer engaged on his biography, is
confirmed by Anny's photographs. 'She was a remarkable-looking
woman, well advanced in the sixties, but owing to the lightness of
her frame and the brighness of her eyes she seemed to have been
wafted over the surface of the years without taking much harm in
the passage. Her face was shrunken and aquiline, but any hint of
sharpness was dispelled by the large blue eyes, at once sagacious and
innocent, which seemed to regard the world with an enormous
desire that it should behave itself nobly, and an entire confidence
that it could do so. . . . Certain lines on the broad forehead and
about the lips might be taken to suggest that she had known
moments of some difficulty and perplexity in the course of her
career, but these had not destroyed her trustfulness. . . . She wore a
great resemblance to her father.'[21]

Watching her aunt at work, as Virginia must frequently have
done at this time, she noted not only her wholly inspirational and
erratic method of composition but the happy expression that
appeared on her face when once settled down to writing. 'She had
no difficulty in writing', Virginia said of Mrs. Hilbery, 'and covered
a page every morning as instinctively as a thrush sings.' But the
outpouring, like the thrush's, was intermittent. 'She liked to
perambulate the room with a duster in her hand, with which she
stopped to polish the backs of already lustrous books . . . Suddenly
the right phrase or the penetrating point of view would suggest
itself, and she would drop her duster and write ecstatically for a few
breathless moments; and then the mood would pass away. . . .
These spells of inspiration never burnt steadily . . . And yet they

[21] *Night and Day*, (Penguin Modern Classics, 1969), p. 18.

were so brilliant, these paragraphs, so nobly phrased, so lightning-
like in their illumination, that the dead seemed to crowd the very
room.'[22] Once settled at her desk, and returned in imagination to
those scenes of the past she loved, a state of euphoria possessed her,
as Virginia noted: 'Peace and happiness had relaxed every muscle in
her face; her lips were parted very slightly, and her breath came in
smooth, controlled inspirations, like those of a child who is
surrounding itself with a building of bricks, and increasing in
ecstasy as each brick is placed in position. So Mrs. Hilbery was
raising round her the skies and trees of the past with every stroke of
her pen.'[23]

At a dreary social gathering, Virginia describes Mrs Hilbery as
having recourse 'to an infallible remedy – she looked out of the
window'. On the occasion in question she exclaimed: '"Do look
out at that lovely little blue bird!" . . . and her eye looked with
extreme pleasure at the soft sky, at the trees, at the green fields
visible behind those trees, and at the leafless branches which
surrounded the body of the small blue tit. Her sympathy with
nature was exquisite.'[24]

There was clearly a bond between these two – the ageing but
eternally youthful author, and the prematurely disillusioned,
doubting, watchful child. Opposite in temperament, they had in
common the poet's vision, the capacity to see. It was Virginia's
recognition of this hidden power in her aunt that made her perhaps
take stock so closely of her every variation of mood. And Anny was
unwittingly setting her an example as the eminent writer she herself
intended to be.

The portrait of Mrs Hilbery, a woman of quick intuition,
unconventional and impulsive, incurably optimistic in the face of
adversity, corresponds to the image of Anny which she herself left
us in her writings. 'Who knows . . . where we are bound for, or
why, or who has sent us, or what we shall find – who knows
anything, except that love is our faith – love – . . .'[25] It is Mrs
Hilbery speaking, but it could just as characteristically have been
Anne Thackeray. We have Virginia Woolf's own unequivocal
testimony that 'Mrs. Hilbery' was a likeness of her aunt. She wrote
to her sister, Vanessa Bell, at Easter 1917 while engaged on the
novel: 'I am the principal character in it . . . I think the most

[22] Ibid., p. 36.   [23] Ibid., p. 103.
[24] Ibid., p. 198.   [25] Ibid., p. 449.

interesting character is evidently my mother who is made exactly like Lady Ritchie down to every detail apparently. Everyone will know who it is of course.'[26]

The zest Anny's Introductions to the Biographical Edition received from the revival of memories of her life with her father was noticeably lacking in the third volume – which contained *The Yellowplush Correspondence* and *The History of Samuel Titmarsh and the Great Hoggarty Diamond*. They belonged to a period in her father's youth about which she had no personal recollections, no visual images. Her Introduction covered the time of his law studies, his months at Taprell's office at No. 1 Hare Court, Temple; his abandonment of law for journalism which he combined with his attempts to make a living as an artist. His marriage is very briefly touched on. These were the days when his total income derived from his contributions to the periodical press. *Yellowplush* appeared in *Fraser's Magazine* in the year of Anny's birth (1837). There is little information in this Introduction not derived from Thackeray's own letters.

For Volume IV, *Barry Lyndon*, Anny could again write from personal recollections of her parents and of their home in Great Coram Street, although she had been only two at the time. 'I liked the world extremely at that age,' she wrote. 'One does not remember enough in after life the extraordinary variety of experiences comprised within the first two or three years of one's existence – those dawning hours, when the whole world is illuminated and enchanting, when animals can speak and inanimate things are alive, and when we were as gods.' It was the time when Thackeray himself could write to his mother: 'We are all wondrous well in health and my dear little Missy is as gay as a lark.'[27]

This was before her mother had to leave them, when barrel-organs played in the street and Anny could run away to dance with other children to their captivating tunes. Reviewing her life, years later, Virginia Woolf saw in this escape from even the loosest confinement an epitome of Anny's whole attitude to the realities of existence; she was always 'escaping from the Victorian gloom and dancing to the strains of her own enchanted organ'.[28]

[26] Quentin Bell, *Virginia Woolf*, ii. 42.
[27] Introduction, Biog. Ed. iv. xxiii.
[28] *Collected Essays*, Vol. iv, 'The Enchanted Organ', p. 73.

In her comments on *Barry Lyndon* itself, written in 1843–4, Anny recalls her father telling her as a girl that she need not read it, as she would not like it. The story, for all its incredible incidents, was based upon facts 'as quoted from the papers of the time, that were told to Thackeray by a friend in Paris, a Mr. Bowes'.[29] *Barry Lyndon*, which cost its author great pains and travail, was finished in Malta on 3 November 1844 during the course of his stimulating journey recorded in 'From Cornhill to Grand Cairo'.

Anny's Journal records progress on her work, but now and then there are items of family news. In July 1895 Richmond was promoted to the post of Private Secretary to Lord George Hamilton, the Secretary of State for India. Anny visited the India Office to see him in all the glory of his new surroundings – 'in grand new rooms!'[30] A cheering bank statement, showing £100 to the good, is reported, and the erection of an arbour in their garden at the End House; there was a visit to the Opera – in celebration of Richmond's promotion – to hear *Fidelio*, that drew from Anny the cry 'O.O.O. how beautiful it is! What ravishing music.'[31] Attending Billy's Confirmation service at Sedburgh she was struck after a term's absence by how 'he looked like Papa [Thackeray] with high shoulders and well set up.'[32]

Taking a short Continental holiday with Richmond and Hester – to Holland for pictures and Dresden for music – she was moved by paintings she had seen years before with her father and sister: 'I could almost hear his voice again explaining', she wrote, and was unable to assimilate her existing surroundings *'for thinking* of the old days and Papa and Minnie'.[33] So deep had been those impressions and so constantly were they being revived by her present work, that she found herself more often lost in the past than living in the present, seeing herself as a girl again in relation to her father. She took herself severely to task on the subject. She entered in her Journal: 'a lecture to myself to feel a certain elderly dignity and self-reliance to help me through the *variations of feeling* which are such a plague'.[34]

With age (she would be sixty-one when the Edition was finished in 1898) she was developing ever more strongly a sense not so much of living in the past as of the past overtaking the present, possessing

[29] Intro., Biog. Ed., iv. xiii.
[30] Journal, 2 July 1895.
[31] Ibid., 5 July.
[32] Ibid., 14 July.
[33] Ibid., 18 Nov.
[34] Ibid., 27 Oct.

it, coexisting with it. The feeling was at times so confusing that, as she confided to her Journal, it could be 'a plague'. She refers to it in much of her later work. In the Introduction to the fifth volume of the Biographical Edition (*The Sketch-Books*), she said: 'Time flies, but the great wings come beating backwards again as one looks over the records of the days that were, and which indeed are also now, and not in the past only.'

The years 1896 and 1897, when she was most taken up by the work on the Biographical Edition, were also the years of the deaths of some of her closest friends from the past: Millais, Lady Tennyson, Mrs Brookfield, Mrs Oliphant. Their last illnesses and deaths drew from her the cry, entered in her Journal, 'How I hate old age and my friends growing old! I wish I could finish my notes to the Edition, I am always afraid of dying before they are done,'

It was always with infinite thankfulness that she finished each section and sent it off to the publisher. From time to time she had to stop work, to recharge her batteries; then she would go to Brighton which she always found 'the most blessed spot'. From there she wrote triumphantly after checking proofs, 'Think of our getting *Esmond* done yesterday, sorted, corrected in one day! I am rather exhausted but jubilant and feeling a load of relief.' Her jubilation was always apparent in her refreshed vision of the world about her. 'Our Brighton has been a triumph rather than a success. I don't think in all my life I ever saw anything more lovely and vast than yesterday morning. Proud, capering, beautiful waves dashing against the beach, a divine light in the horizon, and exquisite lights on shore and on the clouds overhead, and all the tribes, Christians and Jews alike, dancing before the Ark.'[35]

In February 1897 she allowed herself a month's holiday abroad, with Hester, starting with some days at 'dear delightful rapturous Paris',[36] where she made a point of going to tea with wonderful Félicie, her Aunt Ritchie's former devoted maid, and sat up late 'looking at the stars'. 'Happy Happy day', she noted in her Journal, 'yet a wave of utter despair came over me as I remember still the hopelessness of certainty and the aloneness of life.'[37] She returned home to attend the wedding of Stella Duckworth on 10 April at Kensington Church to John Hills, a rising young politician. Stella's sudden death, from peritonitis, on her return from honeymoon,

[35] *Ritchie Letters*, p. 236.
[36] Journal, 20 Feb. 1897.   [37] Ibid.

could only further convince Anny of the 'hopelessness of certainty'. Once again, Leslie had need of all her support. She visited him frequently, noting in her Journal how 'the dear little girls [Vanessa and Virginia] ran into my arms'. Stella had been most dear to her for her kindness to Laura; as she noted once after they had visited Laura at Earlswood together, 'Stella has all along been so wise and sweet about her.'

The summer of 1897 was very hot, the Diamond Jubilee year of Queen Victoria's accession. While the country was celebrating the event, with bonfires on Wimbledon Common among other things, Anny's heart was wrung by the death of Mrs Oliphant. She had hurried to Eton, and sat by her old friend on the last day, held her hand and listened to her talk. 'I could not have believed it was so easy to die', Mrs Oliphant had said[38]. And in the midst of the national rejoicing, on 26 June, Anny noted in her Journal: 'Dear Mrs. Oliphant at rest at last.' She attended the funeral, a 'most touching service at Eton on a beautiful day'.

Outside her own family, Mrs Oliphant was perhaps the person Anny loved and admired most. Writing to Billy on 'Pre-Jubilee Sunday' about her friend's death, she said: 'It was Mrs. Oliphant who bestowed on me my first review when I was twenty-three. It was summer time and I opened *Blackwood*, and my father beamed with satisfaction. It is so curious how all one's life remains – things don't go, we fade not they. It is all there.'[39] With each succeeding loss she evolved ever more compellingly her philosophy of the permanence of experience. 'I, who am near the end,' she wrote to Mrs Oliphant's son Denis, 'can only tell you who have a busy life . . . before you, that death is *no* parting . . . our dead love is not gone but lives again in the present.'[40]

Gradually her work advanced and she saw the end in sight. An authentic and indeed unique portrait of her father was emerging. 'I can't tell you how I do feel more and more', she wrote to her son Billy, 'what a courageous tender-hearted father I had, and how proud I am of him.'[41]

The words seem to reflect her own satisfaction in her work, the confidence that she was doing justice to him. Her account may have been biased, but on the other hand had he not been the warm-hearted generous man she described she would not have idolized

[38] Ibid., 26 June 1897.   [39] *Ritchie Letters*, p. 242.
[40] Ibid., p. 243.   [41] Ibid., p. 244.

him as she did. To her great credit, moreover, she hid no aspects of his character that might offend the prejudices of the day, like his heterodoxy, his love of pleasure, his self-indulgence. It is all there, as he with his hatred of humbug would have wished. It is also a tribute to his influence on Anny, who was so little of a bigot herself. With all the emotional ups and downs that inevitably accompanied such a prolonged effort, Anny was sustained throughout by Richmond's encouragement. A man of few words at any time, and sincere at all times, his praise lifted her as alittle else could do.

In July 1897 as the over-all merit of her work, now well advanced, could be judged by her publishers, the question of her fee was broached for the first time. George Smith offered her £4,000 for the finished work. The 'splendid offer', as she called it, utterly astounded her. Overwhelmed by its generosity, she was yet all too aware of what remained to be done and of its toll on her health. 'When I have done six more introductions,' she wrote to Billy in October, 'I shall go to Brighton and bask for a week, and when you first come back I mean to do no work at all until the end of January. I love doing it and it makes me very happy, but it certainly disagrees with your excitable Mama.'[42]

It is not often in the Introductions that she judges her father's works, or strays from a strictly biographical approach, but in the Introduction to his *Paris Sketch-Book* (Volume V) she casts a fresh appraising glance upon his method of work. 'Mr. Titmarsh was for ever observing and recording what he saw. He wrote it down, and he drew the pictures and sketches – specially the sketches – abroad, where shadows are crisper than with us, and houses are quainter, and the people and the scenes more pleasantly varied. Our curates are curates, but they do not wear the romantic pastoral robes of the Catholic curés, nor such religious hats with curly brims.'[43]

Of *Cornhill to Cairo*, written in 1844, Anny writes that it 'was always a chief favourite with my Grandmother; nor do I wonder at it, it is full of the most beautiful thoughts and conviction nobly expressed. Life and enjoyment were returning to him after the sad experience of the last few years. Duty spoke to him, hope called to him; a charity full of good humour, not blind, but droll and observant and merry, was his travelling companion.' Anny recorded her father's dilemma in writing of the holy places visited in the course of his travels, and quotes from his notebook some

[42] Ibid.   [43] Intro., Biog. Ed. v. xx.

thoughts scribbled down in Jerusalem: 'The feelings of almost terror with which, riding through the night, we approached this awful place, the centre of the world's past and future history, have no need to be noted down here. The recollection of those sensations must remain with a man as long as his memory lasts; and he should think of them as often, as he should talk of them little.'[44] Anny recalled hearing from Mrs Carlyle about her father's problems in writing on this delicate and awesome subject. On his return to London, being without a home, he put up at a Chelsea pub, Don Saltero's, and worked up his notes. Not wishing to offend his readers with his heterodoxy, he studied countless church histories and commentaries. Finding himself without a Bible, he sent across to Cheyne Row to borrow one from the Carlyles.

In accordance with some modern reappraisals of Thackeray's work, Anny considered that 'much of my father's best work will be associated with the name of that friendly and supernatural being, Mr. Punch, for whom he was now writing'. In her Introduction to Volume VI, which contained the contributions to *Punch*, Anny recognized that the satirical writings, which became so natural a form of self-expression, at the same time earned for him the reputation for cynicism. Whereas, as he had written to his old Scots friend, Dr John Brown, 'under the mask satirical there walks about a sentimental gentleman, who means not unkindly to any mortal person'.[45]

So informal was Anny's manner that she sometimes assumed a conversational style that further emphasized the purely personal character of the Introduction. In her opening words to Volume IX (*The Christmas Books*, etc.) she wrote, 'I have been wondering whereabouts in my father's life the FitzGerald chapter should come in.'

Thackeray's friendship with FitzGerald, which lasted from 1829 to 1863, was not only the longest but, despite silences and separations, also the closest to his heart. At the end of his life, when Anny asked him 'one day on some impulse' which of his old friends he cared for most, he answered 'Old Fitz'. She recalled the exact scene with her usual visual precision: 'He was standing near the window in the dining-room at Palace Green. He paused a moment then he said in a gentle sort of way "Old Fitz".'

FitzGerald survived his friend by twenty years, but he had been

[44] Ibid. xl.　　　　[45] Intro., Biog. Ed. vi. xxxvii.

dead some time before Anny wrote her tribute to him in this volume. *The FitzGerald Letters* had been published by Aldis Wright shortly before, and revived all her girlhood memories, when 'Mr. FitzGerald's name was always an integral part of our home life'. The evocation of these memories prompted her to reflect on human relations. 'It was a friendship', as she writes, 'carried on sometimes with words and signs, sometimes in silence, but it did not ever break off, though at times it passed through the phases to which all that is alive must be subject: it is only the dead friendships which do not vary any more.'[46]

Her intuitive feeling for the quality of people appears in her description of Richard Doyle, who illustrated so many of Thackeray's books. 'Besides people's being and appearance,' she writes, 'there is also the difference of impression which they create. Some come into a room with a rustling and a sound of footsteps, of opening doors . . . their entrance is an event more or less agreeable. There are others who seem to *be* there, or *to have been* there always, and whose coming is a rest rather than excitement, and I think these are perhaps among the best loved companions of life. Richard Doyle, whose very name is a greeting . . . was among these tranquil presences, loved by children no less than by elders.'[47] The Introductions, besides gradually building up the full-length portrait of her father, are rich in giving the likenesses of his friends in little cameos such as these.

With *Esmond* (Volume VII) were bound up the lectures, *The English Humourists* and *The Four Georges*, and of this felicitous coming-together of Thackeray's eighteenth-century works, Anny wrote: 'One feels how much my father was at ease with all these people, whom he loved and admired. He trod in the actual footsteps of Johnson and Goldsmith, Addison and Steele. He saw the things they had seen, heard the echoes to which they listened, he walked up the very streets where they had walked. He was one of them. . . . As my father says in one of his letters – the eighteenth century occupies him to the exclusion almost of the nineteenth . . .'[48]

Of *Esmond* she writes that it did not seem so much a part of their lives as *Pendennis* had been. During a great part of its writing (1852) she and Minny were living with their grandparents in Paris. Thackeray was so imbued with the sense of Esmond's 'melancholy' that he refused to serialize it. To his friend Lady Stanley he wrote: 'I

[46] Ibid., ix. xliv.   [47] Ibid. liii.   [48] Ibid. vii.

am writing a book of cut-throat melancholy suitable to my state, and have no news of myself . . . to give you that shouldn't be written on black-edged paper, and sealed with a hatchment.'[49] On the cause of his melancholy, Mrs Brookfield's defection, Anny is silent. We learn that he often fled to an inn near Tunbridge Wells for week-ends of undisturbed work. Towards the end, feeling the book's incompleteness, he wished he had six months more to work on it; he considered it had cost him as much labour to write as Macaulay's History had cost *him*. *Esmond* was the only one of his books 'first published in all the dignity of three volumes', and Anny well recalled the arrival of the parcel containing the books in Paris after his departure for America in October 1852.

Of particular biographical interest to Anny was the fact that her father had pointed out to her the house in Kensington Square – No 7 – which was where, he said, 'Lady Castlewood lived', 'and I think he added something about the back windows looking across the lanes to Chelsea'. 'We know how Colonel Esmond from Chelsea spent one night at the "Greyhound" "over against" Lady Castlewood's house in Kensington Square, the house to which the portrait of Frank Esmond by Rigaud was sent.' Anny included for the first time here several of her father's letters written during his lecture-tour of America.

In her Introductions to both *The Newcomes* (Volume VIII) and *The Adventures of Philip* (Volume XI) Anny related many details concerning her father's childhood and young manhood that bore on the incidents in the books, events occurring long before her birth but which, because they concerned people and relatives she was later to know, had their effect on herself. Thus, in the *Newcomes* Introduction, she describes her grandmother's early home and the old aunts who had tyrannized over *her* childhood, as they were in turn to oppress Thackeray's. One at least, Miss Becher of Fareham in Hants, served as the model for Miss Honeyman in *The Newcomes*. The lasting imprint of this upbringing on Mrs Carmichael-Smyth was in time to affect Anny herself. *The Newcomes* was very much bound up with Thackeray's family. The Colonel himself is based on the model of his beloved stepfather, and the appalling 'Mrs. Mackenzie' portrays with terrifying conviction Thackeray's mother-in-law, Mrs Shawe. These aspects of the *Newcomes* have already been dealt with in their place in the present work. In the

[49] Ray, ii. 807.

highly autobiographical *Adventures of Philip*, Thackeray relived his early struggles in Paris; his poverty, his ardent courtship, and marriage. Anny wrote: 'I can remember hearing him say how much of his own early life was written down in its pages.' In her view, *Philip* contained 'some of the wisest and most beautiful things my father ever wrote'. (See Chapter 1 of the present work.)

Writing the Introduction to *Denis Duval* (Volume XII), Thackeray's last, and unfinished novel, was peculiarly painful for Anny, since it brought back acutely the incidents of his last months. She recalled the zest with which he entered upon the work, and his delight with old Winchelsea, where he placed much of the action and which he visited to make sketches.

For Volume XIII, the last of the Edition, and published later than the main body of the works (in 1899), there remained only the scraps and snippets of Thackeray's occasional pieces – Ballads, Critical Essays, Speeches, Translations, Sketches. The volume is distinguished from the others by including the *DNB* life of Thackeray by Leslie Stephen. To this was prefaced the following note by Anny: 'To Leslie Stephen, my brother-in-law, I owe a brother's help and advice. In his biography of my father, reprinted from the *Dictionary of National Biography*, the whole framework of the life is given; the story he purposely left for me to tell.'[50]

When Leslie's article appeared in the *DNB* (January 1898), it made Anny feel 'rather choky at first'.[51] Though not openly expressed, there is in Stephen's 'framework' to Thackeray's life, especially in the early passages of the article, an undercurrent of censoriousness that could not be pleasing to Thackeray's daughter. There was admittedly too little of the academical in Thackeray's early life, too much of the 'Bohemian', for him to be fully appreciated by Stephen; though later in the article he does justice to Thackeray's domestic qualities, his generosity, and to his literary genius. 'The loss of his fortune and the ruin of his domestic happiness stimulated him to sustained and vigorous efforts. . . . He worked, as he was bound to work, for money. . . . He slowly forced his way to the front, helping his comrades liberally whenever occasion offered . . . he was the tenderest and most devoted of fathers. His "social success" never distracted him from his home duties, and he found his chief happiness in his domestic affections.'

Anny resembled her father too closely not to be oppressed at

---

[50] Intro., Biog. Ed. xiii. 688.   [51] Journal, 27 Jan. 1898.

times by the sheer drudgery required of the editor of so large-scale a
work. Leslie, in his *DNB* article, noted that Thackeray was
'unmethodical and given to procrastination' as Editor of the *Cornhill*; and that 'his health found the labour trying'. Anny's health
could not stand up to it either, and the whole wearisome labour of
proof-reading found her almost constantly established at Brighton
in the late autumn of 1897. Between 2 October and 3 December, she
was working virtually non-stop and had to admit to ending the year
'very unwell' as the family assembled there for Christmas. But she
was well enough to be able to enjoy the satisfaction of the finished
task, when at last the work was off her hands, and she wrote to her
adopted daughter and sister-in-law (Margie Ritchie), 'The last of the
MSS is despatched and the notes go off to-day, and this great and,
to me, very real event is a cause of most genuine thankfulness and
gratitude. I love to think of my father's unconscious protest against
the coldness and flippancy and silliness of the present fashion, and I
think it may add something good and simple, as he was himself, to
the thoughts of those who are yet to read and to love him. It is a
finer standard than this hateful low standard of to-day.'[52] When one
recalls that Henry James, young Hardy and Meredith, Kipling and
Stevenson – to name but a few – were then writing, this judgement
on current writers cannot be classed among Anny's most discern-
ing. But she was preoccupied with the task of freshly presenting her
father's works to a new generation, to whom she now committed
the treasury of his humanity and truth. The world will be the richer,
she predicts, for knowing him.

The Edition 'was born', as Anny put it, on 15 April 1898, when
Volume I appeared, and was reviewed in 'six leaders in six morning
papers' the following day. Anny named the reviews in *The Times*,
the *Standard*, *Daily News*, *Daily Chronicle*, and *Daily Telegraph*
where there were 'columns about it'.[53] The whole Edition appeared,
a volume at a time, monthly, throughout 1898, in a handsome red-
cloth binding with gilt-topped pages, profusely illustrated throughout, not only with the original illustrations but with scores of
drawings from Thackeray's letters and his satirical sketches.

[52] *Ritchie Letters*, pp. 244–5.   [53] MS Letters: N-B Collection.

CHAPTER 21

GRAND OLD LADY

THE year 1898 was altogether a signal year for the Ritchie family. Billy went up to Trinity College, Oxford, in the Michaelmas Term. Richmond received the CB in May. Though delighted that Richmond's toil at the India Office was recognized, Anny was highly diverted by the terms of his summons to Windsor in July to receive his insignia, or, as Anny put it, 'to be bathed by the Queen', for which 'on no account would his travelling expenses be refunded',[1] and his demeanour was clearly spelt out: three obeisances were commanded, one on entering the Presence, one half-way up the room, a third on reaching the Queen. It was the Duke of Connaught who pinned on the insignia.

After twelve years at Wimbledon, they felt the need to live in London again, partly on Richmond's account, partly on Anny's, who anticipated a busy year. They let the End House and rented a flat in Kensington, at 12 Kensington Court Gardens. It had great charms for her, reviving all her girlhood memories. She noted in her journal for successive Sundays in April and May 'delicious mornings in Kensington Gardens' walking with Richmond there. The proximity to her old friends was a great stimulus to her. She could visit Kate Perugini (née Dickens) and enjoy 'an enchanting talk with her';[2] she could be in direct contact with her publishers again, and instead of communing by letter could have 'dear George Smith' to tea. The success of the Edition was a shared satisfaction, and his society she always enjoyed. But he was ageing and gradually withdrawing from the business of the firm. This was carried on by his son-in-law and successor, Reginald Smith, who had married his daughter, Isabel.

Unfortunately, the rest from work, the relaxation from the efforts of the last years, did not improve Anny's health. On the contrary, it brought to a head a glandular condition which she had

<hr />

[1] MS Letters: N-B Collection.   [2] Journal, 17 Apr. 1898.

been fighting for some time with treatment at Woodhall Spa, and which necessitated at length an operation under gas – the 'slitting' of the swelling in the neck. Though temporarily successful, it was not conclusive, and left her subject to recurrent attacks during the next two years. It was not until 1900 that she was sufficiently restored and able to sign a letter to her sister-in-law, Emily Ritchie, her most constant helper and correspondent, 'your loving Rejuvenata'.

The word 'thyroid' was never used in speaking of her glandular illness, but the symptoms would suggest it. The immense bursts of energy, followed by nervous exhaustion, seem characteristic. She had inherited from her father a great restlessness which drove her, like him, to want constant change of scene. Happily, the handsome fee paid her for the Edition left her for the first time in years free from money worries. It allowed her, in February 1900, to have a Continental holiday with Hester. They went to Florence and stayed 'at a wonderful boarding-house'. No one ever responded more keenly to fresh surroundings, or was more grateful for them. From Lucerne, on their return journey in March, she wrote: 'Lovely day – to church – one doesn't deserve such heavenly beauty – the hills and the mountains were like the word of God on earth.'[3]

The necessary changes of scene did not have to take Anny abroad or even to new places. Brighton worked its familiar magic whenever she returned there. 'Brighton balm always enters one's soul', she wrote, echoing her father's sentiments on 'Dr. Brighton'. A moonlit night, as she sat with Richmond on their garden bench at the End House (where, between sub-lets, they spent summer weeks), was inspiration enough to set her writing to Billy, in France during holidays: 'The English moon has been most glorious, quite as lovely as your French moon, and the End House has been flooded with silver. I shall certainly be very glad to see the End House again by moonlight, or sunlight or even paraffin! God bless you my darling beloved boy, and "He will"! as the old apple-woman used to say to my father.'[4]

The allusion to seeing the End House once again by moonlight was in connection with the family's growing intention to move finally to London and sell the End House. The chief reason for this was to spare Richmond the daily journey to town; and the family's improved financial situation made it possible to face the additional expenses of life in the centre (with the CB Richmond had received

[3] Journal, 20 Mar. 1900.   [4] *Ritchie Letters*, p. 248.

promotion). Anny's improved health and regained leisure made her long to live once more at the heart of those things that had for so long been the background to her life: concerts, art exhibitions, social functions. The reasons for her flight to Wimbledon fourteen years before, crippled with sciatica and overburdened with work, harassed by money troubles and her very marriage threatened, mercifully no longer existed. She had outlived or transcended her troubles, but not without damage. At times she confessed to feeling like 'an old broken butterfly', and though not yet seventy looked very frail and talked increasingly about her age. One of her reasons for wanting the move to town was to be nearer her friends, but as she remarked, 'Tho' I am not such a very old woman, except the Sterlings and the Gaskells I have hardly got any one single friend left of my own age.'[5]

The move to London took place in stages in 1901, to a roomy house near the river, at 109 St. George's Square. They were there when Queen Victoria died. 'Saw History in the streets,' Anny noted in her Journal for 23 January, 'crowds in black, *all* black, waiting for King. Blinds down everywhere, and cabmen with bits of crepe. . . . Leslie came, who remembers mourning for William IV.' Anny had never been one of the old Queen's devotees. Hester, in her records of her mother's life, reporting on her obligation as Richmond's wife to attend the Abbey service, comments: 'Could the old Queen have seen Thackeray's daughter present at the Abbey she might well have been displeased; for she never forgave the author of *The Four Georges* his frankness when dealing with her ancestors.'[6]

A far closer loss for Anny was the death of George Smith on 6 April 1901, whose gradual sinking she recorded daily in her Journal. Theirs had been, from their first meeting long ago at her father's house, a personal friendship even more than a business contact. Leslie Stephen wrote of his death: 'He was a fine generous fellow and always very friendly to me. He had his rows with some authors but was, I believe, as liberal and honest as a publisher can be. Mrs. Smith has been a model wife for near fifty years – I met Minny at their house . . . and feel grateful for their kindness to her and to Anny.'[7]

The first years at St. George's Square, despite the renewed

[5] MS Letters: N-B Collection, Sept. 1899.
[6] Fuller, p. 170.   [7] *Mausoleum Book*, p. 109.

interest they brought Anny, were overshadowed by their losses too. Leslie himself was failing throughout 1903, and visits to him were almost a daily feature of her life. 'I go and look almost every day at my dear Leslie,' she noted in her Journal. 'he is in bed with 2 nurses . . . He is quite cheerful – and his eyes look so young. The dear children flit round – and are so good . . . Leslie said it is nice to think of the young people following us.'

Neither Anny nor Leslie were the sort of people to humbug one another. They knew quite well what was coming and faced it with philosophy on his side and unbroken spirit on hers. '"I don't think the world will be nearly so nice without us,' she said, sitting at his bedside. Leslie said: "It will go on. You have others. Life will go on." I said "Dear Leslie I love you. I don't know what else to say." He said: "I know it dear Annie . . . They say it cannot last beyond Christmas."'[8] In the event Leslie lived until 22 February 1904.

The passing of the world she had known lent an elegiac tone to many of her reflections on her renewed contacts with London life at the beginning of the new century. She visited Leighton House 'after my long years of illness'. The portrait of Mrs Sartoris by Leighton, the evocation of the illustrious group of friends in the Watts's portraits, was a saddening experience. 'There were all my old friends lighted up by brilliant electric light – the least changed of all the people present was Leighton himself; but it was like a walk in a crypt to me. . . . It is horrid, being old and remembering all these vanished visions as Ruskin says, some I like to dwell upon, others I try to forget.'[9]

She was resolved, however, to give the new era a fair trial. The artists who had been her friends and who had formed her tastes were gone, but she had too great a zest for living not to be open to fresh experiences. She set out to visit the current Exhibition of Impressionist painters, 'to see if we are quite too old to appreciate them. I am sure I am!' Music, which was a necessity both for her and for Richmond, had a permanence which modern painting lacked for her. Anny was at Victoria Station 'with a staggering white bouquet' to join the crowd of well-wishers who saw Joachim off for the last time, receiving his embraces and carrying his love back for the whole family – for Emily Ritchie, particularly, who had often been his partner. Now Fanny Davies was the rising

[8] Journal, Oct. 1903.   [9] *Ritchie Letters*, p. 267.

concert star and none of her recitals must be missed; even when so far out of town as the Crystal Palace, they had to go.

Desmond MacCarthy's wife, who was a niece of Anny's, née Mary Warre-Cornish, recalled visits she made to her aunt at this time. 'I can see her at this moment, beautifully fresh in her lace cap, coming down the staircase of her London house in the morning after breakfast, with a few pages of MS. fluttering in her hand. She would tell me to read it over aloud to her by the dining-room fire, then she would dictate a few alterations, put the charming impressionist writing into an envelope, and rapidly address it to Messrs. Smith and Elder.'[10]

In what a condition the manuscript was dispatched (one notes Mary's adverbial 'rapidly') George Smith recorded in his 'Recollections', years later. 'Her "copy" for her books was a medley of pieces of paper of all shapes and sizes, written here and there and fastened together with a needle and thread: an expressive symbol of her somewhat vagrant genius.' Furthermore, the manuscript, though committed to the post, was liable to arrive a day late for, as George Smith explained: 'if you happen to live at 40 Park Lane and have business at 15 Waterloo Place: and if your letters are constantly addressed "40 Park Lane *and* 15 Waterloo Place: this has all the relish of a jest; and, thanks to our excellent postal arrangements, your letters reach you only one post late.' George Smith did not hesitate to sum her up as 'a woman of genius – with many of the characteristics – and some of the limitations, of a woman of genius'.[11]

Her movements were dictated by much the same impulses as her writing. After the dispatch of her days's work to Smith, Elder, there were, as Mary MacCarthy remembered, 'plans for the day to be made, and then came the unmaking of plans too impulsively undertaken. A letter is swiftly written to a millionairess to say that, alas! after all she had been rash in saying she could join her in a yachting cruise; she did not feel equal to it; and she would laugh at herself as she sat by the fire for having thought that she ever could impulsively have accepted anything so unsuitable to herself as going on a yachting cruise and undergoing all the fatigues it would involve, such as conversation in the wind on deck. Then she must

[10] Mary MacCarthy, *A Nineteenth-Century Childhood*, p. 85.
[11] George Smith, 'Recollections'.

give up a sitting for her portrait next day. Her order has been given
to an artist whose talent is almost nil, but who must be helped. "He
hasn't allowed me to look at my picture yet, but I see him squeezing
piles of vermilion on to his palette, and I quite dread it;" and she
posts a cheque to the painter.

'Very soon after we are whirling away in a little victoria in the
morning sunshine. An old lady who has lost her husband must be
visited; and all in a moment Aunt Anny has alighted in Queen's
Gate, and is sitting in a heavy, early Victorian dining-room, under
an East India Company member's portrait, among the massive
mahogany chairs, encouraging and improving the old lady's spirits.
The canary begins to sing. A gaunt, depressed daughter, with red
hands in mittens, arranges in specimen glasses the roses the visitor
has brought, and shows signs of cheering up. Whether the pair
subside into dankness after Aunt Anny's departure I do not know,
but her kindness has been like sun flooding into their gloomy room
for the moment.

'We whirl on and leave a hobbyhorse and some dolls with the
coachman's children who have had the measles. We converse with
their mother at the top of a stair in a mews. Other children playing
about the mews stop in their play, arrested by her charming voice as
she comes down the stairs to greet them.'[12]

'Her wit', Mary went on, 'was so lightly lambent that often
people missed her points. Samuel Butler went to call upon her one
day soon after his *Authoress of the Odyssey* (which insists that the
book was written by a woman) had been published. He told her he
was at work on a book on Shakespeare's sonnets. He was, however,
only bewildered at her saying, "Oh, Mr. Butler, do you know my
theory about the sonnets? They were written by Anne Hatha-
way?!" It was not she who repeated this story, but the author of
"Erewhon". He never saw that she was laughing at him, and used to
tell it, shaking his head sadly and saying, "Poor lady, that was a silly
thing to say."'[13]

Samuel Butler was not the only one to be bewildered by some of
Anny's startling statements. George Smith was also often non-
plussed by the extraordinary tales she would tell, with the 'gravest
face and the most perfect good faith'. She was not actually telling
lies, he well knew, but her reports were remote from the known

[12] Mary MacCarthy, op. cit, pp. 86–7.
[13] Mary MacCarthy, op. cit., p. 88–9.

facts, 'all bred in the chambers of her dreamy imagination', as he put it.

He was infinitely tolerant. He had known her since her imaginative, highly emotional, sensitive girlhood (he remembered seeing her cry because her father was unable to find his glasses) and could allow for her vagaries. Famous authoress as she was, she had the same inability to keep pace with her social engagements as she had with her accounts. Here again, George Smith could witness to her aberrations. Like Darwin, he experienced her arriving on the wrong day to dinner; and making up for the mistake by coming on the right date as well – a lapse of memory that 'gave you the pleasure of her company twice', as he charitably recorded.[14] He would have endorsed Leslie Stephen's judgement of her as 'at once the most sympathetic and the most sociable of beings'.

Only where Anny's affections were engaged could regularity or consistency be found. Then, as in her visits to the dying Leslie, she could be depended on not to fail. So it was with her care for Laura, who was giving her great concern. For some years now Laura had been removed from Earlswood and placed with a couple, very much as Isabella had been. Her condition varied. To give her a change, Anny would take her to stay with her for a few days in some quiet country place – Godalming, Hampstead, or at her own cottage The Porch. Then she might be rewarded by seeing a flash of her former self, and sometimes even Laura 'looked radiant' when she appeared and Anny could 'see Minnie in her merry peeping face and even tried to talk a little – and then this cruel nightmare again'.[15]

Virginia Stephen was also beginning to alarm her. After Leslie's death, and a Continental trip, the young Stephens sold the great house in Hyde Park Gate, and set themselves up in Gordon Square. The emotional upheaval, first of her father's death and then of the removal, was too much for Virginia. She had another breakdown, as after her mother's death, and was sent to stay with her Aunt Caroline, Leslie's sister, at Anny's cottage. Anny visited Vanessa and Thoby in their 'new charming home, bright, with French windows', and urged them to get someone especially nice whom she knew to look after Virginia.

Anny had probably never been more socially active than during her temporary rest from writing, and her days were sometimes murderously overcharged with morning visits to the National

[14] Smith, 'Recollections'.   [15] MS Letters: N-B, Collection.

Portrait Gallery with Desmond MacCarthy, literary luncheons, receptions, dinners for Richmond's colleagues from the India Office, at which she had the gift of at once enlivening and illuminating what might easily have been for her rather dull occasions. All agreed she was an excellent hostess, though she had little time for small talk. 'In any society', her old friend Howard Sturgis said of her, 'we may be sure she brought at least as good as she got; and through all contacts she remains a highly individual figure, her character and temperament not less her own than her gifts.'[16]

She was meeting the new generation of writers. While she found the writing of Henry James at times 'like a mountain . . . quite beyond my level', she delighted in his letters and his talk. His letters she found even 'more head over heels than his writing, but O so kind and all-present'.[17] They met frequently at dinners, and he was a regular guest at her house. After one such occasion, she reported to her son: 'I asked him if he had read Sarah Grand's books, he said, "It may be Pride, it may be Prejudice, but I have not", so I said, "Perhaps it may be Sense or Sensibility," and Henry burst out laughing and said: "I only need Persuasion!"'[18]

She met the young Kipling, then settled at Rottingdean, on her frequent visits to Brighton. The first time he called, with his wife, Anny found him 'a Fascinator – merry, talkative, kind beyond compare . . . He talked enchantingly all about wild things and animals and places none of which I had ever heard of.'[19] The young Robert Louis Stevenson, whom she had first met at Leslie's and whom she liked for his youth, his ardour, and the unmanageable toss of his hair, was one of her most enthusiastic admirers. After reading her *Book of Sibyls* he wrote the following verses to her:

> The faces and the forms of yore
> Again recall, again recast;
> Let your fine fingers raise once more
> The curtains of the quiet past;
>
> And then, beside the English fires
> That sing and sparkled long ago,

[16] *Cornhill*, Nov. 1919.
[17] MS Letters: N-B Collection.
[18] *Ritchie Letters*, pp. 247–8. See Appendix B, p.000.
[19] MS Letters: N-B Collection.

The sires of our departed sires
The mothers of our mothers show.

(Quoted *Cornhill*, November 1919.)

Hardy, Meredith, Syndey Lee, Arnold Bennett, she knew them all – though none of them, with the possible exception of Henry James, came near to taking the place of her father's friends who had created her world for her. 'Just now', she wrote in 1903, after reading a 'very fine' article by Henry James, 'I feel as if only the people one loved mattered – books, poetry, pictures, nowhere – even bodies nowhere – but the dear souls remain untouched by age and unveiled by death.'[20]

The bust of her father in Poets' Corner in Westminster Abbey had never pleased Anny. It had been done by his Italian friend, and sometime neighbour at Onslow Square, Marochetti, and she had found fault with it from the start, though she did not wish to hurt the sculptor's feelings. The whiskers were too long and too profuse. Thackeray had never worn them like that and they spoiled the likeness for her on each occasion she entered the Abbey. She decided at last to approach the Abbey authorities and ask for alterations to be made.

It was not usual to tamper with Abbey memorials. However, the Dean, Dr G. G. Bradley, gave his authorization, admitting that the bust of Thackeray had always seemed to him to have too much whisker and to be one of the least satisfactory in the Abbey. He gave instructions for it to be removed from its corner overnight by the Clerk of the Works and kept in his office in Dean's Yard, and there Anny in the company of Mary MacCarthy and in some trepidation was received. She was taken down to the crypt where the deed was to be executed. Mary reported the Dean looking grave and the sculptor, Onslow Ford, whom Anny had begged to do the work, looking 'very cross'. He did not like undoing another sculptor's work, Mary recorded, and if the daughter of Thackeray had not happened to be such a charming old lady, it is probable she would not have had her way. It was his assistant who chipped away at the offending whiskers, looking from time to time towards Anny for a nod of approval. Anny talked to the sculptor without paying any attention to his crossness, and made him smile at last. 'Finally',

[20] Ibid.

as Mary recorded, 'the bust is flicked over with a cloth, as after a
shave, and it is carried up into the nave and back into its own niche
. . . We all survey it in silence, and then disperse. Aunt Anny is a
little emotional as she gets into the victoria, smiling in her tears . . .
she is triumphant, for it has been a great relief to her mind.'²¹ Anny
wrote in her Journal: 'Happy day – drove to London – saw my
Father's bust altered and replaced – delighted and thankful.'²²

Anny's 'holiday' following the completion of the Biographical
Edition with the publication of the last volume in 1900, could never
be anything but a temporary respite from work, as her publishers
and she herself were well aware. The very success of the Edition
presumed a successor to it. It was only a matter of how soon. The
warmth of its reception was extraordinary. Of all the words written
in praise of her labours, perhaps those of Swinburne touched her
most, because of the context in which they figured. In an article on
Dickens written for the *Quarterly*, which appeared in the July
number of 1902, he concluded with a comparison of Dickens and
Thackeray which in her eyes gave the final accolade to her work. 'It
is curious to compare', he wrote, 'the posthumous fortune of two
such compeers in fame as Dickens and Thackeray. Rivals they were
not and could not be: comparison or preference of their respective
work is a subject fit only to be debated by the energetic idleness of
boyhood. In life Dickens was the more prosperous: Thackeray has
had the better fortune after death. To the exquisite genius, the
tender devotion, the faultless taste and the unfailing tact of his
daughter, we owe the most perfect memorial ever raised to the fame
and to the character of any great writer on record by any editor or
commentator or writer of prefaces or preludes to his work. A
daughter of Dickens has left us a very charming volume of
reminiscences in which we enjoy the pleasure and honour of
admission to his private presence: we yet await an edition of his
works which may be worthy to stand beside the biographical
edition of Thackeray's. So much we ought to have: we can demand
and we can desire no more.'²³

Swinburne, the flame-headed young poet whom she had first met
at Monckton Milnes's house in the last year of her father's life, had
become a close friend and, since his virtual sequestration at the
Pines under the care of Watts-Dunton, a constant correspondent.

²¹ Mary MacCarthy, op. cit., p. 88.
²² Journal, 19 July 1900.   ²³ *Quarterly*, July 1902, p. 39.

On reading his article she wrote immediately to him: 'Dear Old Friend – I have just seen your kind words, which made me very happy and grateful to you. My daughter found the *Quarterly* and came and read it to me!

'As Tennyson once wrote to my father, "It is because you are the old friend that you are, and also because you are the great man that you are, that I feel all the fullness of your praise". . . . These were not quite the words, but it was the sense, and I who am grateful to think that I am the daughter of a great man and the friend of great men, send you my love and my thanks for this bit of new life and pride and happiness for mine and me, and I am yours – decorated by you – Affectionately Anne Ritchie'[24]

The degree of their friendship and intimacy can be even better judged from the charming letter Swinburne wrote Anny on the birth of her first grandchild. After leaving Oxford, Billy had been articled to a firm of solicitors, Johnsons, Long, & Co., in 1901, and married in 1906 Margaret Booth, the daughter of Charles Booth, the philanthropist. A son, James, was born in 1908. 'I do congratulate you cordially on being a grandmother,' Swinburne wrote. 'To have a baby at hand or within reach is to belong to the "Kingdom of heaven" yourself. I met this cold morning on my daily walk, a fair friend not yet "well stricken in" months, who beamed and chuckled inarticulately . . . at sight of me, from the depths of her pushwain-ling (I hope you never use the barbaric word "perambulator"?) . . . Sir Theodore Watts-Dunton belongs to the same order of creation as Mrs. Harris. But Mr. T. W.-D. is none the less grateful for your so kindly misplaced congratulations. Ever sincerely and cordially yours, A. C. Swinburne.'[25]

In the summer of 1905 Reginald Smith approached Anny with a project for another edition of Thackeray's works, and asked her to revise and extend the former Introductions. The Edition was planned in twenty-six volumes, twice the number of the preceding one, which meant dividing the previous Introductions up to fit the new division of the works – and 'hence all this chopping and changing', as Anny put it. As before, Hester and Emily Ritchie were her efficient aides. 'I think you and Hester ought to set up as Editors altogether some day,' she told Emily.[26]

In the event, the Standard Edition, as it was to be called, fell

[24] *Ritchie Letters*, p. 244.
[25] *Ritchie Letters*, pp. 277–8.   [26] MS Letters: N-B Collection.

through, owing to the defection in 1907 of the third contracting party, Messrs. Harper's of New York. Their unexplained withdrawal when the work of editing was already quite advanced deprived Anny of a considerable amount of money. By the terms of the contract, dated 4 July 1905, and signed by Smith, Elder, Harper's, and herself, Anny was to receive £500 on account of the royalty on the forthcoming edition, agreed at 10 per cent.[27] For the first time ever in her long connection with the firm, with whose late head she and her father had had such close and friendly relations, Anny was in disagreement with her publisher. Reginald Smith was not inclined to take Harper's to court as she would have wished; nor, when the extent of her loss in the matter was spelt out to him, could he agree to paying her a fee in compensation. In a subsequent very moderate but formal letter, he pointed out to her that she had already benefited considerably – to the extent of £8,000, he alleged – from the Biographical Edition. Her own solicitors, Billy's firm of Johnsons, Long, & Co., advised her not to go to court, assuring her that Smith, Elder were in no way to blame, and that the breach of contract was solely Harper's.[28] The temporary disagreement with her publishers – and the financial loss to Anny – were with the passage of time made good, when Reginald Smith entered into a final partnership with Anny for the Centenary Edition in 1911. (The royalties from this edition topped the £8,000 earned by Anny, and provide an interesting commentary on the profits available to women at the time, through the career of letters.)

Fleeting visits abroad still seemed a condition of Anny's wellbeing, as they had been for her father. The very act of escaping from the routine of home, however dear to her, was revitalizing. On her return from Paris on one occasion, and finding Richmond 'cheerful', she wrote to Emily, 'I can only be hourly thankful for the general lightening of the overcharged atmosphere of my beloved home. What good going away does one!'[29] Richmond's ill health, which had been a source of anxiety for some time, was the inevitable result of overwork. Chained more than ever to his post at the India Office as his responsibilities grew, he suffered at times from a form of depression that kept him silent for days. When he recovered his spirits it was an occasion for family rejoicing. When, in 1907, his signal services were recognized by a knighthood, it was received by all – himself included – as a source of 'great fun'. Anny

[27] Ibid.   [28] Ibid.   [29] Ibid.

at the time was keeping an engagement to visit her old girlhood friends, the Coleses, now settled in Norway, and just setting off from Hull with Hester on the RMS *Tasso* for Bergen. As she herself put it, she 'went on board as Mrs. Richmond Ritchie and stepped ashore as Lady Ritchie'. She was, of course, delighted, and thanking him for his first letter giving her the news she wrote, 'It was knightly of you to write in time for the post.' One of the recommended hobbies for his health, together with golf, was fishing, and she longed for him to be there, salmon-fishing with Hester. 'You must bring her some year. Your holiday would be twice as long, for one goes to bed quite fresh at midnight, and gets up again quite brisk and the perpetual daylight instead of bothering as I expected, becomes a sort of alabaster lamp-light, most healing and soothing.' Norway, like all fresh experiences, impressed her sharply: 'I send my love to you from this wonderful new world,' she wrote to him, cruising up the fiords; 'it is like being *Eternal* for one instant, as you come into the heart of the great mountains and look and look. It is so solemn one can hardly admire, and one finds oneself building an altar in spirit – and then by degrees kind every day comes in.'[30]

In October 1909, Richmond's long dedication to his service received its final accolade by his appointment as Permanent Under-Secretary of State for India. Lord Morley wrote to Anny to tell her that, after consulting five colleagues, they had unanimously said: 'appoint Ritchie'. Richmond himself commented: 'the KCB was all fun – this is real responsibility.' There is no doubt that Richmond had made a success of his career, but one cannot avoid the question – how happy was he? Had marriage to a famous authoress brought him the home life he needed? He never wrote to Anny otherwise than as 'Sweetheart' (she in turn always addressed him as 'My Heart') and they were certainly tenderly attached. Temperamentally, they were probably not well suited; he was an introvert, she an ebullient extrovert. She needed to express herself in more ways than one, in restless movement; his was a self-contained nature, silent and still. They shared many tastes, but his were the more limited, more concentrated, hers of course ranging far and wide. Anny said of him, 'an afternoon of James [his grandson] and an evening of Mozart to follow, were his idea of Heaven.' Tied to his desk as he too constantly was, he could not often indulge his

[30] Ibid., July 1907.

favourite pursuits. Between his daughter Hester and himself a close and loving connection existed. Billy's marriage brought him great happiness; he adored his daughter-in-law, Meg. With the coming of Billy's children, James and Belinda at first, he found a quite new delight in practising 'l'Art d'être Grand'père'. 'His happiness with his grandchildren can hardly be described,' Anny wrote later.[31]

With the added responsibilities that his promotion brought, and growing fatigue, Anny decided towards the end of 1909 to make her cottage at Freshwater – The Porch – regularly habitable as a holiday home for the family in general, and Richmond in particular. She had acquired it all those years ago, in 1874, when Mrs Cameron decided to return to Ceylon. At the time and for years after, she had chiefly regarded the house as a holiday refuge for the members of her far-flung family, Margie and Gerald, the Cornishes and Freshfields and their children; for Laura on occasions; for the young Stephens; seldom as a home for her own family. Now, in January 1910, she went there with Hester, and with the help of a local girl and an odd-job man, converted it into a delightful home: 'as nice as mortal dream can attain to'. They ate their meals in the kitchen, and decided on calling the two sitting-rooms 'the reading room' and 'the writing room'. It was sparsely furnished, so they went to Yarmouth (their port) to buy, among other things, a round table. The whole house, considering the icy weather, was very warm and cosy inside.

From then on The Porch gave them a permanent haven on the Island that had for so long fascinated Anny. At Whitsun the whole family assembled there, Billy, his wife, and children joining them; and Anny was rewarded for her pains by Richmond's being 'perfectly delighted with it'. But even then he could not entirely shake off the burden of office. Edward VII had died on 7 May and Richmond had to return for the funeral.

For Anny also the intervals of respite were measured. After the failure of the projected Standard Edition, Reginald Smith's new proposal was for a twenty-six-volume edition, making use of Anny's amended Introductions, to coincide with the centenary of Thackeray's birth in 1911. It was to be called The Centenary Edition. Once again, Anny had to start 'chopping and changing' to meet the new requirements. The volumes were to come out two at a time, beginning in November 1910.

The edition was to be completed and enlarged on the previous

<hr>

[31] Ibid., Oct. 1912.

one by including Thackeray's hitherto unidentified contributions to *Punch*, a task only made possible by M. H. Spielman's reference to Bradbury and Evans's Account Books in 1899; by the personal recollections of a youthful friend of Thackeray's since become Canon Elwin, which concerned his days in Cambridge, Weimar, and Paris as an art student and his short legal apprenticeship in the Temple. Some early fragments and sketches antedating the *Irish Sketch-Book* were already, in Anny's opinion, written 'in his best style.'

To Anny's gratification Thackeray's centenary was to be celebrated in style. Her own part in sustaining his reputation and in contributing, by her own works, to the literature of her country, was also to be marked: the Academic Committee of the Royal Society of Literature (founded by George IV in 1825) voted unanimously to make her a Fellow, an honour that pleased Richmond as much as it did herself.

At the appropriate date, the Thackeray Celebrations opened with a Memorial Dinner in Middle Temple Hall. This was followed on Sunday 16 July by a Thanksgiving Service at his old school, Charterhouse. A sermon was preached in praise of his work. Anny, who of course was present, noted that the speaker 'abused Dobbin and Amelia roundly. He said V.F. was a book of books and he would feel the Rose and the Ring next to it.'[32] For an old lady of seventy-four it was emotional stuff. Richmond, 'who had to help the King [George V] with more medals yesterday (the Kg very friendly) couldn't come; but so many old friends, Kate Perugini among them, were there.' It was the beginning of a heady week, and the next day she was writing, 'I am in bed recovering my wits.'[33]

The actual day of the centenary of Thackeray's birth, Tuesday 18 July 1911, was radiantly fine, and Reginald Smith had organized a Garden Party on the lawns of the Middle Temple (Thackeray and Pen's old haunts as idling law students) to launch the new edition. Lady Ritchie played hostess to two thousand guests. Her daughter described the scene afterwards: 'The day was divine and the green and beautiful lawns stretching down to the river were crowded with guests. Austin Dobson, G. W. E. Russell, Sir Sidney Colvin, Mrs. Humphry Ward, Mrs. Perugini, Dickens' daughter, among hundreds of others, crowded round the central figure – Anny Ritchie, stood with her husband beside her – her children and grandchildren

[32] MS Letters: N-B Collection.   [33] Ibid.

about her.'[34] There was music on the lawns and the choristers of the Temple Church sang settings to three of Thackeray's poems. The actor Cyril Maude read aloud passages relating to Colonel New-come.[35]

The occasion marked something more for Anny than the centenary of her father's birth. It celebrated the completion of her labours to honour his name and make him known to a new generation of readers. Pre-eminent as his works appeared to her, they were not incontrovertibly attuned to the tastes of the emergent twentieth century. (By 1931, only twenty years later, Desmond MacCarthy was asking *why* people no longer read Thackeray?[36]) It had been Anny's task not only to present the works but also to portray the man, whose character had been so misrepresented. The word 'love' may be allowed to take on a special meaning in this relationship between father and daughter. Anne Thackeray's love for her father was of the essence of her life. She was more his child by inheritance of mind and spirit than most children are to their parents. He was central to her being, and he continued to inhabit her life like a living presence, a genial ghost whose company she wooed.

This is in no way to overlook the role of Richmond. Anny lived so intensely in the past that the swift adjustments to the dimensions of daily life were sometimes beyond her – and caused those lapses in presence of mind and punctuality for which she was noted. Richmond anchored her to reality. She needed him for support, as a ship needs to fasten its cables to the shore to be secured against the tide, for Anny was all too easily swept out to sea. She relied on Richmond to be always there, to call her back.

She had always assumed, from the difference in their ages, that she would predecease Richmond. She had told Howard Sturgis, years before at the time of her marriage, that if she was being unfair to Richmond in accepting his love, he would yet have time to remarry when she was gone. Her own chronic ill health made her, perhaps, take too much for granted. In the elation following her completed work, she felt, for the first time in years, the right to 'live' (as her father would have understood it), emancipated from

[34] Fuller, p. 173.

[35] Details supplied by R. A. Colby. From his introduction to the reprint of the Centenary Edition, 1979.

[36] *Sunday Times*, 13 Sept. 1931.

the need to earn money. Richmond's position, her own considerable income from royalties, the euphoria induced by Billy's happy
marriage and the grandparents' delight in the children, the possession of the 'dear Porch', all looked like being the guarantees for a
happy old age. The prospect seemed so pleasing to her that, even
when the warning signals went up, she was blind to them.

In the event, Richmond, who was seventeen years her junior, had
far less staying power than she. The illness, whose first symptoms
had shown themselves in 1889 (diagnosed as Ménière's disease'),
had never been cured. He had been subject to the attacks of vertigo
that characterized it, and as responsibility on responsibility was
piled upon him the severe symptoms returned.

In the spring of 1912 he was ordered to Malvern for treatment,
Hester going with him. Total rest and a 'starvation' diet were
prescribed. Laura, in care at Wimbledon, was taken ill at the same
time, which prevented Anny from joining them. August reunited
them all at Freshwater, and they planned a trip to the Lakes in
September to complete his cure. Though visibly a sick man, he was
bent on resuming his normal life and his work at the earliest
opportunity. It was not to be. After a month's relapse, he died on
12 October 1912 of pneumonia.

Without exception, his colleagues at the India Office wrote to
Anny expressing a quite unusual sense of loss. The Secretary of
State for India, Lord Crewe, wrote to Anny the next day. 'These
last weeks I have been fighting against dread of the calamity which
has come upon you, feeling convinced that the danger must be very
grave. And now that it is over, you will forgive me if I say nothing
of your and your daughter's loss, because I have no right to, and
dare not. But I can speak freely of the void in our Office, where he
can in no way be replaced, or anything approaching it. . . . I hope
in spite of his wonderful modesty he may have realized how much I
leant on his knowledge and even more on his judgement. . . . I keep
thinking of his perpetual consideration and of his determination to
relieve me of every possible burden, and it is grievous to know I can
never thank him.'

For once the voice of officialdom was tinged with genuine tones
of feeling. Lord Minto wrote, 'You know how my heart is with
you. Words are vain, for death is death. I wish you fortitude and
composure, and solace of kind memories.' Lord Kilbracken: 'You
know what my opinion of him was: he was certainly one of the

ablest men that I have known'; Sir Arthur Hirtzel: 'Certainly he has left us younger men a wonderful example of personal friendship and devotion to duty – illuminated by that characteristic humour which so often showed one in a flash the truth one had been vainly pursuing.'[37] Over and over again, in the tributes to Richmond that poured in, his kindness, his generous humanity, his high intelligence, his dry humour, received recognition.

By his own wish Richmond was buried in Hampstead Cemetery, near his admired friend George du Maurier, the funeral service taking place at Old Hampstead Church on 15 October. It was more than a month before Anny could write of Billy as having been 'a rock of loving help, and my Hester beginning to rally a little'.[38] The silence that follows on Richmond's death in the family records tells of Anny's broken spirit. One is put in mind of her own description of herself some years back as a 'broken butterfly'.

The 'huge' house in St. George's Square, as Hester called it, was of course too big now for the two women, and in order to remain near Billy, who lived at 3 Durham Place, Chelsea, they took a small house round the corner from him at 9 St. Leonard's Terrace, early in 1913. After the move, Billy saw that his mother and sister got away to Freshwater, where they could await the spring in the shelter of The Porch. As so often before, the healing power of the Island began to work and once again their kindest neighbour was a Tennyson. Hallam, whom Anny could not without pain address as 'Lord' Tennyson, came constantly to their help.

Anny could not fail to respond to natural beauty, and she never stayed on the Island without speaking of the birds' voices, the shimmering light on the Solent, the fields of barley and wheat in the golden haze. It was equally impossible for her to live without putting pen to paper. The need to communicate, whether by letters or by writing down her memories, was paramount. So, gradually, in the course of 1913, she collected material for what was to be her last published volume, to which she gave the title *From the Porch*. It appeared in October 1913.

She had written the opening article – A Discourse on Modern Sibyls' – the previous year to serve as the Inaugural Address to be delivered at the Annual General Meeting of the English Association on 10 January 1913. Under the circumstances it had to be read on her behalf by Professor Ernest von Glehn. In it she wrote of her

[37] MS Letters: N-B Collection, Oct. 1912.   [38] Ibid., 26 Nov.

female predecessors in the world of letters: Mrs Oliphant, George Eliot, Currer Bell, Mrs Gaskell. When the text was published in the *Cornhill*, Edmund Gosse wrote to her to tell her how beautiful he had found it. 'But you know that,' he said. 'You are yourself the one authentic Sibyl left, with your delicate wavering style that is like shot silk . . . George Eliot is satin, Mrs. Gaskell is velvet, but you are the dove's neck.'[39]

The articles, which ranged from 'Charles Dickens as I remember him' to 'Ste Jeanne Françoise de Chantal' – some thirteen in number – form a mixed posy of memories and meetings, in which the dual influences of her French and English cultures are harmoniously fused. Compiling the book did her good. 'I liked putting the scraps together', she told a friend, 're-writing some of them and thinking of the beloved past. It seems so great a boon to live back again.' The pace of life was slackening, but she could tell the same friend, a year after Richmond's death, 'I am very well on the whole, and except for sadness I am happy in a way.'[40]

She stayed increasingly at The Porch, where her grandchildren could be with her. In them she found delight, and noted their every quaint reflection. They became the repositories of her own long memories and to them she handed on not only the stories that had made her own childhood exciting, but the traditions of an older and perhaps merrier England. For May Day 1914, 'in a glorious spell of weather', she had a maypole erected in the garden of The Porch, and paper garlands cut out for the children to carry as they danced around it. There were three small Ritchies now, and James and Belinda's amazed reportings on the sounds and gestures issuing from the object in the pram, the baby Catherine, afforded Anny much entertainment. Henry James teased her for being an 'infatuated grandmother', but added truthfully that he felt '*that* would have been my real vocation'.

In June 1914, before the rumblings of the coming storm reached English ears, a group of her friends formed the project of having her portrait painted by Sargent, for which of course her consent was needed. No existing photograph of her, from the day of Mrs Cameron onwards, had done justice to the mercurial quality of her character. She was not photogenic. There was something fleeting and elusive that the camera could not catch, and they hoped that the eye of an artist might better capture her subtle spirit. The sight

[39] Ibid., 3 Mar. 1913.   [40] *Ritchie Letters*, p. 281.

of the frail figure reminded them too that time was running out. Henry James, who had himself been painted by Sargent at the instigation of his friends, seconded the proposal, and wrote to Anny on 30 June 1914:

'Dearest Anne, admirable old Friend and illustrious Confrère! – It is altogether delightful to think that this happy thought of your likeness being "took" by our all-responsive and all-ready Sargent is on the way to be effectively arranged, for such a Public Treasure shall the work appear destined to become, if all goes well with it.

'The happy thought sprang up in the breasts of the Protheros – to them alone I more than suspect belongs the grace of having first thrown it off.'[41]

James advised that her sittings for the portrait should be deferred until the autumn, to give the wide circle of her friends time to be contacted, and thus avoid disappointing those who would wish to be included among the subscribers. Fortunately it suited Sargent to go ahead at once with the portrait, a charcoal drawing. Otherwise, like so many other happy plans for that fateful summer, it would have been cancelled by the events of 4 August.

Anny returned expressly from Freshwater for the first sitting on 7 July. 'Naturally,' she wrote to the promoter, Mrs Prothero, 'my first thought was how pleased Richmond would have been – and my father – and my sister – as for my dear family it is radiant.'[42] She was delighted with the result. 'I have just come away from Sargent's studio,' she told Mrs Prothero on 9 July. 'It is the most lovely, *fine* picture, – I can't tell you how I have loved the gift, the givers and the devisers, or how I have enjoyed the sittings. I could only tell Mr. Sargent that I thought that when I came away, the picture itself would – could thank him for me.'[43]

She returned from Freshwater for a final sitting on 29 July and wrote to her friend and colleague, Rhoda Broughton, 'It really is an enchanting picture. I am more touched and interested and grateful than ever. I went for another sitting yesterday and he said I like your bonnet so much, may I add it? and so my poke bonnet is there supreme.'

Only when it was finished and she confronted her likeness did a

[41] Ibid., p. 282: George Prothero was Chairman of the Royal Society of Literature.
[42] *Ritchie Letters*, p. 284.   [43] Ibid.

19. Sir Richmond Ritchie, K.C.B.

20. Lady Ritchie

spark of self-consciousness enter her feelings towards it. 'I feel quite shy before my portrait it is *so human*, and I feel so like it, yet more *grim* alas!'[44]

The list of the subscribing friends, eventually sent her, totalled 139 names, mostly illustrous; many like the Tennysons, Darwins, Stracheys, Trevelyans, Stephens, and Murray-Smiths representing already a second generation of friends. Sadly absent from the list was Meredith's name, the friend of years, who had died in 1909. Meredith had had the pleasing habit of sending her boxes of violets from his garden at Box Hill. He spoke of the 'modest bouquets' as 'visitors' on his behalf, to express to her the feeling that dispatched them.

The war years that, at her age, Anny might excusably have spent in secure retirement found her mostly in London, organizing relief for French refugees, frequently 'bombed out of her sleep and befogged' by the proximity of the Thames. Her sympathy for those friends whose sons were at the war was acute, and she was intensely thankful that Billy had not been passed for Overseas Service, only for Home Service. He had in fact acquired a farm at Ware in Hertfordshire before the war, and was literally 'digging for Victory' on the land. She sometimes stayed with him, and indeed could have stayed there for the duration of the war had she not felt that she could help better in London. One of Henry James's last letters to her, in 1915, wishes he might be her messenger with the mugs of coffee she sent to the men on watch duty on the tower of Enfield Church. In November 1916 she organized, together with her old friend Kate Perugini, a 'Sale or Rare Books, 1st editions, Autographed editions, Modern MSS, in Aid of the Belgravia War Supply Depot', for which she wrote the Appeal. She and Kate ran the bookstall with Rhoda Broughton's help at Hyde Park House, Albert Gate on 22 November 1916. The Appeal read:

W. M. Thackeray   *Charles Dickens*

Great Public! You who love to read our fathers,
With memory of whom our work to-day is done;

Be generous as they; and for our Heroes
Give – as these writers gave their tears and fun.

[44] Ibid., p. 285. Sargent signed the drawing on 4 Aug. 1914.

She felt all the frustrations of age. In 1917, turned eighty, she wrote, 'I wish, how I wish, I could cut up into four active young women of twenty to come and go. I should like wings to fly with, and intelligence to know what might be of use.'

Her fate was decided for her by a German bomb that fell on Chelsea College, early in 1918, killing Major Ludlow, his wife, and two children, and shattering all the windows of Anny's house, 9 St. Leonard's Terrace, opposite. Her only grumble was the piercing cold. Typically she wrote, 'One was more angry than frightened.' There had been bombs before, but this one left her and Hester no choice but to evacuate. The previous November, writing to her small grandson for his birthday, she had told him, 'I remember that all the squibs and crackers were sounding and going off on Guy Fawkes Day when you were born, ten years ago. . . . We had squibs and crackers and banging and thundering on Wednesday night. Hester and I came down to the drawing-room and Hester fetched a rug and we poked up the fire. It was a lovely moonlight night.'[45]

Virginia Woolf was amused by Mrs. Hilbery's habit of 'giving thanks for unknown blessings'.[46] One might say that her appreciation of the 'lovely moonlight' pouring down from the bomber's sky was typical of Anny's way of accepting reality. At eighty she found the world still supremely beautiful and, like her father, believed love to be 'the crown and completion of all earthly good'. In 1916 Henry James, 'Jacques' to her, had died. Paying tribute to her understanding of love and loss in one of his last letters, he wrote, 'but no one knows better than *you*, dear éprouvée and generous and exquisite friend. I have seen you far too little for far too long and yet you have always let me feel that no thread of our particular hold silver cord of friendship was the least bit loosened.' He signed himself 'Your-tenderly-constant though much-distanced old friend'.

Anny remained responsive to the new literature and could recognize the work of a 'Master' when she saw one. 'I have just finished *The Dynasts*', she wrote to Hardy from The Porch in 1917, 'with *awe* and with absolute admiration. It is a relief for my excitement to write to you and I feel as if I were one of your spirits speaking. I have almost forgotten the war for a day or two, in wonder at your inspired history of *now*, written in 1907.

[45] *Ritchie Letters*, p. 297.   [46] *Night and Day*, p. 434.

'Are our poor, poor grandchildren to go through it all again? Let them read *The Dynasts* and have chained copies fixed up in every home.

'How Leslie, how my sister would have admired, as does yours sincerely and sadly and gladly too for many things – Anne Ritchie.'[47]

Hardy wrote in reply, 'It makes me cheerful to get your feeling about *The Dynasts*, though I fear the effect may owe as much to your imagination as to my writing . . .'[48]

Virginia Woolf discerned how ill at ease the ageing Anny really felt in the company of the brilliant younger generation. Though Virginia noted in her diary that she 'sincerely admired' her aunt, and put herself through her works 'on a liberal scale', she recognized the need in Anny to retreat within herself in her presence. 'Unlike most old ladies she showed very little anxiety to see one; felt, I sometimes think, a little painfully at the sight of us, as if we'd gone far off and recalled unhappiness, which she never liked to dwell on. Also, unlike most old Aunts, she had the wits to feel how sharply we differed on current questions; and this, perhaps, gave her a sense, hardly existing with her usual circle, of age, obsoleteness, extinction.'[49] Virginia remembered a visit to Anny some two years before her death, when Virginia asked about her own father as a young man. Anny had said: 'how those young men laughed in a "loud melancholy way" and how their generation was a very happy one, but selfish; and how ours seemed to her fine but very terrible; but we hadn't any writers such as they had.'[50]

After the move to Freshwater early in 1918, to visit old friends, even to cross the water again was no longer possible. But she was granted her one remaining desire: to live to see the war end, and the assuaging of the world's sufferings. She lived into the beginning of 1919. Her last weeks were not marked by any grievous illness, only a gentle and gradual decline, watched over by her beloved Hester at The Porch, in a quite exceptional tranquillity of mind. Hallam visited them every day. The promise of spring was in the air when after only a brief illness she died quite suddenly, in Hester's arms, on 26 February 1919.

So unexpected was the end that Billy could not reach her in time.

[47] *Ritchie Letters*, p. 296.   [48] *Ritchie Letters*, p. 296.
[49] Virginia Woolf, *A Writers Diary*, Ed. Leonard Woolf, 1953 (5 March 1919), p. 8.
[50] Ibid., p. 9.

On Hester so deep an impression was left of the transfiguring joy marking Anny's death, that her letters brought as much consolation as grief to those to whom she had to announce the news. Emily Ritchie, Anny's closest friend and confidante over the years, wrote to Hester and her letter was typical of the vast number pouring in from Anny's family, friends and numberless admirers: 'My dear darling – I have no words to say what your letter is to me. I can only bless and bless you for writing it and giving me this most wonderfully beautiful vision of what surely is a sunrise for her – She has been the sunshine of all our lives and this radiance is like her whole life and can reach us all through you. It was just right you and she should have been like that absolutely together at the end. . . . No one had more lovely apprehensions and revelations of it all at times and at the end she left this divine message of what she had found. . . . Hallam has sent me a few lines with the true words: Her wonderful life of triumphant loving kindness . . .'[51]

Hallam's last tribute to his old and cherished friend she would herself have considered the most signal honour: he sent the embroidered pall that had covered his father's coffin to cover Anny's on her last crossing from the island. She had wished to be buried with Richmond at Hampstead. The cortège left by the night boat on 3 March after an island service at St. Agnes Church, Freshwater, where a commemorative tablet was later placed,

> Her writing reveals the inheritance of Genius,
> Her life the inspiration of loving kindness.

The announcement of her death received the fullest coverage in the national and literary press. The mourning letters of her friends and the tributes of her readers had only one refrain: how greatly she had been loved. J. M. Strachey on reading *The Times* for 28 February wrote: 'I feel quite overwhelmed at the thought that I shall never more see the dearest, kindest, most sympathetic of friends – the wittiest, most brilliant, most intellectually gifted of companions . . .'[52]

The official obituary, written by Virginia Woolf, appeared in *The Times Literary Supplement* on 6 March.[53] Coming from one of the pioneers of the new writing, the tribute to Anny as a 'writer of genius', 'un-equalled since the death of George Eliot', was all the more authoritative and compelling. Leonard Woolf wrote the

[51] MS Letters: N-B Collection.   [52] Ibid.   [53] See Appendix A.

tribute in *The Times*. Howard Sturgis, who had known her since the days of the Mount Felix Christmas parties, when he was three, wrote the obituary in the *Cornhill* for November 1919. 'I am thankful to say,' he wrote, 'it would take more than one pair of hands to number the hours my old friend and I have spent together since the day when her great father's spectacles grew dim as he watched me capering round a Christmas tree; yet now . . . it comes home to me with a sigh for the lost opportunites, how few the times have been when I have held her kind hand, looked into her face, and listened to her beautiful low voice, compared with the impression that remains of a singularly faithful friendship, the feeling of a presence tranquil and benign that has shone through my whole life. Many people must be thinking with me of what we have lost – of what we cannot lose – for wherever she has passed she left this sense of benediction behind her.'

APPENDICES

A. LADY RITCHIE

Times Literary Supplement, *Thursday, 6 March, 1919*
(Obituary by Virginia Woolf)

The death of Lady Ritchie will lead many people to ask themselves what she has written, or at least which of her books they have read; for she was never, or perhaps only as Miss Thackeray for a few years in the 'sixties and 'seventies of the last century, a popular writer. And, unless we are mistaken, they will find themselves, on taking down 'The Story of Elizabeth' or 'Old Kensington', faced with one of those curious problems which are more fruitful and more interesting than the questions which admit of only one answer. The first impression of such a reader will be one of surprise, and then, as he reads on, one of growing perplexity. How is it possible, he will ask, that a writer capable of such wit, such fantasy, marked by such a distinct and delightful personality, is not at least as famous as Mrs. Gaskell, or as popular as Anthony Trollope? How has she escaped notice all these years? And by what incredible oversight have we allowed passages which can only be matched in the classics of English fiction to be so hidden beneath the modern flood that the sight of them surprises like the flash of a jewel in a dust heap? What are the faults that have neutralized – if they have neutralized – this astonishing bounty of nature?

Some of the reasons at any rate for this neglect are not far to seek, and are to be ascribed more to the fault of the public than to the fault of the writer. Lady Ritchie was incapable of much that appears necessary to ensure popularity. She wrote neither for the busy man who wants to be diverted, nor for the earnest who wishes to be instructed; she offered neither sensation nor impropriety, and her beauty and distinction of manner were as unfailing as they were natural. Such characteristics are not those that appeal to a large public; and, indeed her gifts and her failings were so curiously and so provokingly combined that, while none of her novels can be called a masterpiece, each one is indisputably the work of a writer of genius. But the test of the masterpiece is not, after all, the only test. We can also ask ourselves whether a novelist has created a world which, with all its limitations, is still a habitable place, and a place which but for him would never have come into existence. Now Lady Ritchie's novels and recollections, although it is only honest to admit that they have their lapses, their unbridged abysses and their tracts of obscurity, offer us a world unlike any other when we are setting out upon one of our voyages of the imagination.

We doubt whether since the death of George Eliot in 1880 the same can be said of the work of any other Englishwoman. It is not only still possible to read with enjoyment 'The Story of Elizabeth', 'The Village on the Cliff', and 'Old Kensington', but as we read them we have the sense that there is nothing quite like them in existence. When we remember that they were published in 1866, 1865, and 1873 respectively, we may feel certain that they owe their survival to some real, and to some extremely rare, magic of their own.

We should ascribe it largely to their absolute individuality. Some writers, like Charlotte Brontë, triumph by means of one overwhelming gift; others, like George Borrow, are so queerly adjusted to the world that their vision reveals a new aspect of things; but Lady Ritchie's genius belonged to neither of these classes. It would be difficult to quote any scene in her books as one of surpassing power, or to claim that the reading of her writing has influenced our view of life one way or the other. On the other hand she possessed indisputably what seems to be as rare a gift as any – the gift of an entirely personal vision of life, of which her books are the more or less complete embodiment. She had her own sense of character, of conduct, of what amused her, of what delighted her eye, of trees and flowers and the beauty of the seasons. She was completely and transparently faithful to her vision. In other words she was a true artist; and when once we have said that of any writer we have to draw back a little and look at his work as a whole, with the understanding that whether great art or lesser art it is a thing unique of its kind.

With every excuse for taking shelter behind the great shield of tradition inherited from her father, nothing impresses one more in Lady Ritchie's work than the certainty that every stroke proceeded directly from her own hand; a more natural gift than hers never existed. It came to her directly, and owed nothing to discipline or to the painstaking study of other writers. Not many novelists can have assumed as early as she did complete command not only of their own method, but of their own language. 'The Story of Elizabeth', written in early youth, is as fluent, easy and composed in style as the work of one who has been framing sentences and casting scenes for a lifetime. This early maturity was the result of a great natural gift growing up with all the most polished tools at command in an atmosphere forbidding any but the most sensitive right use of them. Thus endowed, and thus wisely cherished, she rested we will not say indolently, but frankly and simply in her gift. She trusted to her instinct and her instinct served her well. Young writers might do worse than go to Lady Ritchie's pages for an example of the power of an apparently simple and yet inevitably right sense of the use of language. There is no premeditation, no effort at profundity; her prose appears to swim and float through the air rather than to march firmly with its feet set upon the ground. But every sentence is formed; they cohere together; and invariably at the end of a chapter or paragraph there is a sense that the melody has found its way through one variation and another to its natural close. The impression, it may be of the slightest, has been conveyed to us; the scene, it may be of the most transient, lives with the breath of life. She has, in fact, done exquisitely and exactly what she set out to do.

However this was achieved, and her instinct after all was a highly cultivated instinct, no one can read 'Old Kensington' or 'The Story of Elizabeth' without being aware of a certain spaciousness and composure of manner which are oddly unlike the style of the present time. The style, of course, corresponds to something in the point of view. Her heroes and heroines live in a world of their own, which is not quite our world, but a rather simpler and more dignified place. They do not analyse themselves very much, nor do they complicate their lot by taking upon them the burden of public right and wrong. They are blissfully unconscious even of themselves. Much that a modern writer would dissect into detail is presented to us in the mass. One might suppose that the process of building up such a character as Dolly Vanborough in 'Old Kensington' was a simple one calling only for a few strokes of the brush in comparison with the process by which some of our complex young women are now constructed. And yet Dolly Vanborough lives, and the others for the most part merely serve to tell the time of day like efficient little clocks whose machinery will soon be out of order. Like all true creations, Dolly Vanborough and Elly Gilmour, while they pay homage to the conventions of their time have within them capacities for feelings which are never called forth by the story.

We could fancy ourselves at ease to-day with one of these honest, arch, rather reserved young ladies in spite of the fact that she wears a crinoline and has no sort of desire for a vote. Against all probability, indeed, the thing we should feel strange in them is not their sentimentality or their extravagance of feeling, but rather their slight hardness of heart, their determination to keep always well within the bounds of common sense.

Here, indeed, lay one of the paradoxes and fascinations of Lady Ritchie's art. With all her power of creating an atmosphere of tremulous shadows and opal tinted lights, with all her delight in the idyllic and the rapturous, the shapes of things are quite hard underneath and have, indeed, some surprisingly sharp edges. It would be as superficial to sum her up as a sentimentalist as it was to call her father a cynic. In her case the sentiment is more hopefully and openly expressed, but her sight is singularly clear; the shrewd, witty judgement of a woman of the world smiles constantly upon her own rosy prospects. It is notable that she had neither heroes nor heroines in the accepted sense of those terms; her hero is generally a clumsy, ineffective young man who spends too much and fails to pass his examinations; and the heroine, even the first born of all, has a thousand follies of a natural human kind. Who, after all, had a greater delight than Lady Ritchie in the delineation of a fool – a delight naturally without a trace of cruelty? We need only recall the inimitable Mrs. Palmer, whose mother had been an Alderville, 'and the Aldervilles are all young and beautiful, helpless, stout, and elegantly dressed.' As an example of her vein of humour, here is a little scene from 'Old Kensington':-

'Hulloh!' shouted Sir Thomas, as he drove out of the park-gates. 'Look there, Anley! he is draining Medmere, and there is a new window to the schools. By jove!'

'Foolish young man!' said Mr. Anley, 'wasting his substance, draining cottages, and lighting school rooms!' and he looked out with some interest.

'Then, Uncle Jonah, you are foolish yourself,' said Bell.

'Are you turned philanthropist, Uncle Jonah?' said Mrs. Boswarrick. 'I wish someone would take me and Alfred up. What have you been doing?'

'I make it a rule never to do anything at the time that can be put off till the morrow,' said Mr. Anley apologetically. 'My cottages were tumbling down, my dear, so I was obliged to prop them up.'

'He bought them from papa' said Bell. 'I can't think why'.

'It is all very well for bachelors like you and Raban to amuse yourselves with rebuilding,' said Sir Thomas, joining in from his box in an aggravated tone; 'if you were a married man, Anley, with a wife and daughters and milliners' bills, you would see how much was left at the end of the year for improvements.'

'To hear the talk, one oughtn't to exist at all,' says Mrs. Boswarrick, with a laugh.

Or if we want to confute a charge of undue sentimentality, we can point to characters like Robert Henley and Rhoda, into whose shallow depths and twisted motives Lady Ritchie's art strikes like a beam of the sun.

But many fine talents have come to grief over the novel, which demands precisely those qualities of concentration and logical construction in which Lady Ritchie was most naturally or wilfully deficient. We could guess, if we had not good authority for knowing, that in composing her novels 'she wrote fragments as thoughts struck her and pinned them (with literal not metaphorical pins) at parts of her manuscript till it became a chaotic jumble maddening to the printers'. As Leslie Stephen, one of her warmest admirers, wrote of her:-

She showed more perception and humour, more delicate and tender and beautiful emotion, than would have made the fortune of a dozen novelists, had she had her faculties more in hand. Had she, for example, had any share of Miss Austen's gift for clearness, proportion, and neatness, her books would have been much better, as incomparably more successful.

It is true the string does not always unite the pearls; but the pearls are there, in tantalizing abundance — descriptions, sketches of character, wise and profound sayings, beyond the reach of any but a few modern writers, and well able to stand the ordeal of printing together in some book of selections.

But the qualities which militated against her success as a novelist did not stand in her way in another branch of literature in which she excelled. The lack of ambition, the childlike candour of mind which had so much rather praise and exult than weigh and ponder made her singularly happy in her task, or pleasure, of recording the great and small figures of her own past. Here the whimsical and capricious genius has its scope unfettered and exquisitely inspired. We should be inclined to put her at the head of all modern artists in this manner and to claim for her indeed, that she invented an art of her own. For her method is quite unlike the ordinary method. There is no analysis, no criticism, and few good stories — or the stories only become good in the telling. But her skill in suggesting the mood, the spirit, the look of places and people defies any attempt to explain it. How, we ask, from such apparently slight materials are such vivid impressions created? Here is Charlotte Brontë:-

My father, who had been walking up and down the room, goes out into the hall to meet his guests; then, after a moment's delay, the door opens wide, and the two gentlemen come in leading a tiny, delicate, serious, little lady, pale, with fair straight hair and steady eyes. She may be a little over thirty; she is dressed in a little *barège* dress with a pattern of faint green moss. She enters in mittens, in silence, in seriousness; our hearts are beating with wild excitement.

Trelawny:-

Not very long afterwards came a different visitor, still belonging to that same company of people. I had thrown open the dining-room door and come in looking for something, and then I stopped short, for the room was not empty. A striking and some what alarming-looking person stood alone by the fireplace with folded arms; a dark impressive looking man, not tall but broad and brown and weather beaten, gazing with a sort of scowl at his own reflecion in the glass. As I entered he turned slowly and looked at me over his shoulder. This was Trelawny, who had come to see my father. He frowned, walked deliberately and slowly from the room, and I saw him no more.

George Sand:-

She was a stout middle-aged woman, dressed in a stiff watered-silk dress, with a huge cameo, such as people then wore, at her throat. Her black shiny hair shone like polished ebony, she had a heavy red face, marked brows, great dark eyes; there was something — how shall I say it? — rather fierce, defiant, and set in her appearance, powerful, sulky; she frightened one a little. 'That is George Sand,' said Mrs. Sartoris, bending her head and making a friendly sign to the lady with her eye-glasses. The figure also bent its head, but I don't remember any smile or change of that fixed expression.

We feel that we have been in the same room with the people she describes. Very likely the great man has said nothing memorable, perhaps he has not even spoken; occasionally her memory is not of seeing him but of missing him; never mind — there was an ink-pot, perhaps a chair, he stood in this way, he held his hat just so, and miraculously and indubitably three he is before our eyes. Again and again it has happened to us to trace down our conception of one of the great figures of the past not to the stout official biography consecrated to him, but to some little hint or fact or fancy dropped lightly by Lady Ritchie in passing, as a bird alights on a branch, picks off the fruit and leaves the husk for another.

Something of the kind will perhaps be her destiny in the future. She will be the un-acknowledged source of much that remains in men's minds about the Victorian age. She will be the transparent medium through which we behold the dead. We shall see them lit up by her tender and radiant glow. Above all and for ever she will be the companion and interpreter of her father, whose spirit she has made to walk among us not only because she wrote of him but because even more wonderfully she lived in him. It would have pleased her well to claim no separate lot for herself, but to be merged in the greater light of his memory. Praise of her own work would have seemed to her unnecessary. It would have surprised her, but it would have pleased her, to realise with what a benediction many are to-day turning to the thought of her, thanking her not only for her work, but thanking her more profoundly for the bountiful and magnanimous nature, in which all tender and enchanting things seemed to grow — a garden, one might call it, where the airs blew sweetly and freely and the bird of the soul raised an unpremeditated song of thanksgiving for the life that it had found so good.

Henry James and Anne Thackeray Ritchie

Henry James first settled in London for any length of time in the winter of 1876–7, when he was thirty-three. He came after prolonged visits to Rome and Paris, the inspirational settings for his first long novels, *Roderick Hudson* and *The American* (both published in America). In Paris he had also made the fruitful friendship of Turgenev. He came to London, however, virtually a stranger and spent his first months exploring the bewildering city, mostly at night, as he later described in *The Princess Casamassima*. It was mainly due to Leslie Stephen, his only previous contact, that he first penetrated the literary circles of the capital; and this being so, it was inevitable that he soon met Anne Ritchie. It was in the year following her marriage, 1878, when she was already in an advanced state of pregnancy, that they met at a dinner party. James, who handed her in to dinner, was not only disconcerted by the fact, as he wrote to Grace Norton (Charles Eliot's sister), but non-plussed by the very qualities that were later to make them such fast friends. She was 'further advanced towards her confinement', he wrote, 'than I have ever seen a lady at a dinner party.' He found her 'lovable, and even touching in her extreme good nature and erratic spontaneity.' She combined, he judged, 'the minimum of good sense with the maximum of good feeling'.[1]

From then on, their meetings in the close-knit circles both frequented, were numerous. After James's final adoption of England as his home, they were seldom out of touch, growing in sympathy and mutual admiration towards that affectionate intimacy that their remaining correspondence reveals. The letters' many references to mutual friends show how closely their social lives intersected.

The following excerpts from James's letters, preserved at the Houghton Library, Harvard, are quoted by the kind permission of that body, and of James's literary executor, Mr. Alexander R. James.

Letter dated 30 June, 1897, from Bath Hotel, Bournemouth
(On the death of Mrs Oliphant and the Diamond Jubilee)

My dear Anne Ritchie,
It seems (at the pass things are come to) as if I *never* saw you – or almost never – which is all the more reason, however, for my making the best of *this* poor way of letting you know that Mrs. Oliphant's death gives me a

---

[1] Edel, *Henry James, The Conquest of London*. p.332.

fresh impulse to think of you – and with fresh consideration and sympathy and conscious as I am of your long attachment to her and of the difference now made for you, by her extinction as a neighbouring presence. That admirable niece wrote me the kindest of notes on the event – but it found me (and on the very day – yesterday – of the offices) and far away down here; so that I could only stand with you in thought where you laid the poor brave and wonderful Lady to the deepest and most contenting *rest* I should imagine, that any weary heroine ever earned. She was so remarkable in her large manner, that she ought to be fitly commemorated; and I hope that you, who knew her so well, will take it in hand.

She was a rare and extraordinary organization. That you know better than I. I saw too little of her and especially in these last times and when I didn't know that she was so directly failing. I am very sorry for it now. You too I have most intolerably missed and been deprived of – for months and months. Your rush abroad in the winter's middle – snatched you out of reach; and then at the time of your return (it must have been) I quitted London as I always do by the time the plot thickens. (*Mine* can only do so while the London plot is thin.) I have been for some time down here and I remain probably all July. I find myself on the edge of a sea that is often blue and *out* of various elements that make *me* so. I shunned altogether the Victorian Saturnalia; and was Saturnine here, the livelong day, on my own back. But I hope you were all *in* it, and the happier for it – and with none of your early Victorian headaches re-vamped to do it honour. When I shall see you seems, alas, a complex problem. When you leave Wimbledon at these times you go, alas, to the bleak North – and your ways are devious and dark. But I possess my soul in patience; and if it is the shadow of advancing life that the months which round with a velocity, so at least let it be that they *may* whirl an opportunity with them; I shall snatch at the first that comes. I greet with every amiability your husband and children – I hope R. R. bears up under the weight of empire. It is a comfort to feel him there.

Was Mrs. Oliphant able – and *had* she been (one has, alas, a doubt) to "provide" for her niece? I have a kind of fear that she may have only been able to see her self through. Let us sit close!

Yours, my dear Anne Ritchie, more constantly, I beg you to believe, than visibly.

Henry James

Letter dated New Year's Eve, 1902, from Lamb House, Rye, Sussex

Dearest Anne Ritchie,

I can't let the New Year grow a minute older – it is but a minute old since I took the sheet of paper and wrote the above – without sending you my benediction on it and expressing my great sorrow at my absence from your house to-morrow afternoon, inevitable as it has to be. I am tied fast here for

10 days more and then I come up to town for a series of weeks and shall promptly put myself into devoted relation with you. I shall even venture to ask for a private view (unless the thing lives in publicity in the middle of the room) of the great commemoration offering. I don't believe you realize *yet* the quantity of Sentiment that was offered with it. But let that sink in even as the Sentiment will continue to flow – certainly from yours, dear Anne Ritchie, (and invoking blessings on Richmond's head and those of the filial Pair) always and ever constantly.

Henry James

Letter dated 19 November, 1903 from Lamb House, Rye, Sussex
(On visit to Leslie Stephen during last illness: trouble with biography of W. W. Story)

Dearest Anne Ritchie,

All sorts of things have happened since I got a beautiful letter from you several days ago – one of which is that I have been up to town for 3 or 4 nights; that I there on Sunday last in particular, strove hard, and hoped exceedingly, to get to St. George's Square,[2] but was beaten by combinations and had to come home again baffled and rueful. I *did* on the Sunday p.m. make my pilgrimage to Hyde Park Gate[3] and as the time consumed therein and in being afterwards carried off elsewhere by Sidney Lee, whom I found there, was one of the reasons. The great reason, however, was all adequate, for I paid the dear man Leslie a *long* visit, almost by his insistence – and found him (and left him I think) brighter and firmer than I had ventured to hope. He is as infinitely touching and backward-reaching as you say, and particularly beautiful in his humorous kindly patience with his long ordeal. He is so gentle and friendly to me that he almost makes me cry – *does* make me indeed, so that I have to wink very hard to carry it off and not get forbidden the house – as a source of demoralisation. And when all's said and done, its a very handsome, noble, gentle end, full of all the achievement behind it and surrounded with such beauty in present and past beautiful ghosts, beautiful living images (how beautiful Vanessa!) beautiful inspired and communicated benevolence and consideration on the part of every one. He lay there always *reading* and I blessed, for him and to him, his invulnerable eyesight, and was able to tell him of two or three French books of some newness. He spoke with visible emotion of your assiduous tenderness to him and felt it clearly, so that to speak of it, and of your and his long links and your long fidelity almost made him break down.

How can I thank you enough for taking our poor W. W. S.[4] so kindly and *feelingly?* You know the difficult job it was with my so meagre material and how I *had* to invent an attitude (of general evocation and discursiveness) to fill out the form of a book at all. And now I feel that in *this* you

---

[2] ATR's home.   [3] Leslie Stephen's home.
[4] William Wetmore Story, sculptor.

might have helped me more than I have let you – when I did ask you what you remembered. The lady Mrs Proctor quarrelled with Kinglake about was Mene Blaze or Bury (no great figure of romance) and how I want to talk to you! But *pazienza*. I come up to town in January for 3 or 4 months and then will make it up. Yours meanwhile always and ever.

Henry James

Letter dated 15 August, 1904, from Lamb House, Rye, Sussex
Written on a typewriter

Oh yes, dear Anne Ritchie, I have often received postcards but the question is whether you· have ever received a letter produced with this deadly distinctness and this general grim machinery of expedition and convenience. Forgive me, out of your magnanimity, if, under pressure of many things, I make use of it to thank you for your generous remembrance of me, by which I am infinitely touched, and to shake hands before I start on my little pilgrimage. This last isn't much of an affair, after all, and I shan't add much to the dreary opportunities of missing you that I already feel the burden of only here at 60 miles from town. One of the many compensations of our rich maturity (don't you find?) is that the weeks, months, years, pass across our stage by leaps and bounds – so that I shall be knocking at your door in the spring to such a tune as to make you say: "What, my poor Jaques, *already* back? Dear me!" I shall try to have treasures at that time to tell you, and I wish you, all of you, all peace and plenty, all plain straightforward prosperity, meanwhile. I greatly hope this radiant summer has cooked you through, if you will allow me the image, so that even when cold, in the months to come, you may complacently feel *prepared*, thoroughly and completely, like the well-roasted joint on the sideboard. But these are the similitudes of scrambling haste, and I break off, to lock my last portmanteau and catch my puffing steamer, before I risk another. I insist on the tenderness of our parting and am yours all, but *yours* most.

Henry James

Letter dated 21 December, 1906, from Reform Club, Pall Mall S.W.

Dearest Anne Ritchie!

I am here in town – till tomorrow because I came up for dear old Hamilton's[5] Memorial Service (which I thought quite beautifully touching) and here your so characteristically charming and tender note reaches me. I looked for you helplessly yesterday, in that concourse of many and highly heterogeneous faces, but the confusion was great, at the issue, and I missed many more old friends than I found, or at least could speak to! I think I was struck, though, with there being (considering the immensity of H.A's social circle) rather less of an affluence than I had expected; till, at least, I

<hr/>

[5] Hamilton Aidé.

remembered how he had outlived, dear man, so much and so many, and that many who weren't there weren't there because, simply, they were dead. And it was of these many, I was more thinking, as I sat there – it made Aidé's charming kindly friendship go back very, very far even for myself as well as made me feel how he had been the soul of amiability and pleasantness and gentleness and even the soul of (what shall one call it?) *mondanities* in a way to make mondanity the most benignant and blessed of attributes. I am so glad we were there together (at Ascot) last summer, in that genial and graceful way; when under the slightly hard strain of a certain lady (not you!) he had such a mellowness of patience and good manners.

But I shall miss him, oddly (*we* shall miss him) beyond the use, as it were, that we had for him; he *was* such a pleasant part of our past going on into one's present and vouching still for the reality of vanished things. *Requiscat!* and he *will* rest, if ever a man may have needed to from "society"! – I like scarcely less the reminders you make me of that delightful verandah-day at Howard S's[6] to whom I came up 3 weeks ago and spent another Sunday (in view of his starting to take poor sweet tattered Mildred Seymour abroad.)

They are gone, poor Howard himself rather tattered and tending to fall to pieces (rather more than one wants to see) as a simple effect of having never consented all his life, to feel that he needn't be the sentimental factotum and consolating convenience and man-of-all-work of quite such a numerous circle. His reward may be in some better and kinder world, but I am afraid he will go on here knowing nothing but his penalties, till they at last overwhelm him.

And now of all melancholy matters it seems I can only write you this dusky Xmastide I haven't really heart to *think* of the bereavement of those brave and handsome young Stephen things (and Thoby's unnatural destruction itself) and I have to take refuge in throwing myself hard on the comparative cheer of Vanessa's engagement, quite as if it were an escape, a happy thought, I myself had invented.

So I cling to it, and make greatly much of it and your sympathetic words contribute.

Maitland's[7] book is really, I think, a thing of Beauty – ever so handsomely and feelingly done and giving Leslie all the light he needed to be seen in to be loved as one ended by loving him. One loves M. himself. I shall as soon as possible to tell him so. With so much affection in the air let me personally deliver the expression of some of it to you and yours, my dear old friend. May you be steeped these days, in all the peace and good will – some of it will serve – that you so endlessly merit! Yours ever so constantly.

Henry James

---

[6] Howard Sturgis.
[7] F. W. Maitland, author of *The Life and Letters of Leslie Stephen* (1906).

Letter dated 3 December, 1908, from Lamb House, Rye, Sussex

Dearest old Friend! A brave and delightful postscript to our too-brief meeting your little grey card superscribed with mystic and intricate characters! I take it as a token and symbol of your beautiful fidelity and undying grace and should like to wear it round my neck like some mystic figured amulet or consecrated charm. I make out on its kind, gentle vivid words, and rather than not, the fact that you were amused and beguiled (by the aid of your unquenchable fancy and humour) at Lady Pollock's afternoon sing-song. There also flushes through the crushed strawberry glow of Vanessa's beauty and credulity, and the promise of Virginia's pointed wit and the felicity of Hester's return. These things I note as items of your always enviable sense of the things about you – of which I wish it were often given me to partake. It must be so sweet and savoury to be, perceptively and spiritually, you – so when I am with you I get all the fragrance and all the distinction. Therefore I *must* be with you again soon, as soon as the dire complications of our massive maturity (that is of *mind*) show the 1st sign of intermitting a little. I am scribbling this in my little old celibatarean oak-parlour before being called to dinner – and oh so wish I were going to hand you in – to cold beef and pickles! for which you will say Thank-you! Here comes the mild announcement and I proceed to munch and mumble along – such a contrast to that bloated last Monday. However, you saved that, and now there is *nobody* to save your fondly-clinging old friend.

Henry James

Letter dated 25 March, 1913, from 21, Carlyle Mansions, Cheyne Walk, S.W.
(Re ATR'S proposed visit to America)

Dearest old Friend!

I am deeply interested and touched by your letter from the Island! so much so that I shall indeed rush to you this (day-after-tomorrow) Thursday at 5.15. Your idea is (as regards your sainted Self!) of the bravest and most ingenious, but needing no end of things to be said about it and I think I shall be able to say them All! The furore you would excite there, the glory in which you would swim (or sink!) would be of an ineffable resonance and effulgence, but I fear it would simply be a *fatal* Apotheosis and prostrating exaltation. The devil of the thing (for yourself) would be that that terrific country is in every pulse of its being and on every inch of its surface a roaring repudiation and negation of anything like Privacy, and of the blinding and deafening Publicity you might come near to perish. *But* we will jaw about it – there is so much to say – and for Hester it would be another matter: *she* could ride the whirlwind and enjoy, in a manner, the storm. Besides, *she* isn't the Princess Royal but only a *remove* of the Blood!

Again, however, Nous en causerons – on Thursday. I shall so hug the chance. I will then tell you about dear Howard [Sturgis] – I *believe* he is to be all right. Mrs Perugini told me yesterday that 109[8] is disposed of – whereat I wept for joy. But you will tell me more. I am impatient for it and am yours and the Child's all so faithfully.

Henry James

Letter dated 16 December, 1913, from 21 Carlyle Mansions, Cheyne Walk, S.W.
(Re his portrait by Sargent)

Dearest old Friend,

I have this evening written to Lord Haldane about poor Mrs Brookfield – adducing every argument that I could muster. *You* were the great one, I fear – I mean the fact that you plead for the poor little bounty – little, I fear, at best. But it's such a joy to do anything you ask. I talked of you to-day with William's[9] brave and charming young *sposa* and we made out together that you are more admirable and loveable (sic) and more supported by the felicities, than even at any previous time. It was at Sargent's studio (33 Tite St.) that I met her – having gone there brazenly to juxtapose my battered old original of H. J. with Sargent's magnificent translation of it. No one will read the original now – and it will be like Fitzgerald's "Omar Kayham" (sic) – no one will believe there ever *was* an original of so fine and free a work. *You* please insist however that you have a line or two of it by heart. I wonder if there is any possibility of your turning up there either tomorrow or next day. I shall immodestly return *both* tomorrow and Thursday: at 12, and again at 3. I *am* so obliged! Yours and Hester's in very fond fidelity.

Henry James

Letter dated 30 May, 1915, from 21, Carlyle Mansions, Cheyne Walk, S.W.
(Re the War)

My dear, dear Anne!

How beautiful and brave of you to have been so moved to write to me – though not more moved than I have been by the generous act itself. You are the kindest of old friends and the vividest of old correspondents, and the much-to-be trusted fellow-partaker in all the pangs and prides of this terrible time. I like to think of you as out of the strain and stress of London – little as we can shake ourselves free, even should we ignobly try to, anywhere, and I think I must have passed not far from you this very afternoon, when a kind and much-shaken American friend, a 'ladyfriend' of these later years, who was saved from the horrors of the Lusitania, after

[8] 109, St George's Square, ATR's home, sold after her husband's death in 1912.
[9] Billy's wife, Meg.

long life-battled hours in the sea, motored me out to St. Albans to see the Abbey and I have an idea that we rolled through John Gilpin's and Fairy Blackstick's Ware – toward your relation with which at any rate we would have deflected even from the massive pile to have a word with you had we but known your whereabouts. My poor friend needs much soothing and solid seated things (the sight and sense of them, like Norman Abbeys and spreading Hertfordshire trees) appeal to her as a correction of the obsession of that appalling welter (of which she has given me such details!) But soldiers, soldiers to-day everywhere – thank God, all things considered; and I think we must have seen among them the heroes of your and your children's – bless the ministering little angels! – home-bone and cleaned platters. How I feel with Billy[10] over that mowing-down of his friends and I ache with him in deepest participation and could close and cover over my poor old eyes from the vision forever. It doesn't bear thinking of, but every hour seems to rush us in to a greater soreness and sorrow. I am glad you write to poor dear lonely Rhoda [Broughton?], and I can't tell you how I applaud and honour every way your splendid possession of your soul and giving out of your genius. Deeply do I feel for that excellent Pullen. My own little servant (of 16 years of service) who enlisted in September came back to England to-day wounded. But good-night and all renewed thanks from your faithfully fond old

Jacques

Letter dated 11 August, 1915, from 21, Carlyle Mansions, Cheyne Walk, S.W.
[The original is typed]

Dearest old Friend,

Think of my having to set this machinery in motion at you! But I *have*, alas, in order to deal with my present situation at all. I am literally buried under letters, and being in no very active or triumphant state of health, I grasp any crutch that I can brandish to help me to hobble through the labyrinth. I have an idea that that is what they call a mixture of metaphors, but am afraid I really don't care *what* it is so long as you understand in what more than ever attached and brotherly fashion I greet and thank you, and how much I am with you, on your little green mountain, in imagination and fidelity. I am not much at climbing mountains nowadays, even when they are very little and very green, but you somehow lend me wings and I fancy myself fluttering, with a good heavy plump, down between or beside you. To do what I did the other day had become an absolute matter of course – not to do it would have been anguish pure and simple, and I now

---

[10] Billy was invalided out of the army, and suffered much at the holocaust among his relatives and friends.

know, after the fact, by the relief of soul given me, how indispensable it was. I wish I could go with Hester to Enfield, even if I don't quite know what she does there, and I could have almost climbed the tower of the perched soldier with her cup of coffee in my hand to save him his slide down. I am really not better, much, for towers than for mountains, but, as I say, I hang about you fondly in all your generous movements, and am your more than ever intimately associated old friend.

Henry James

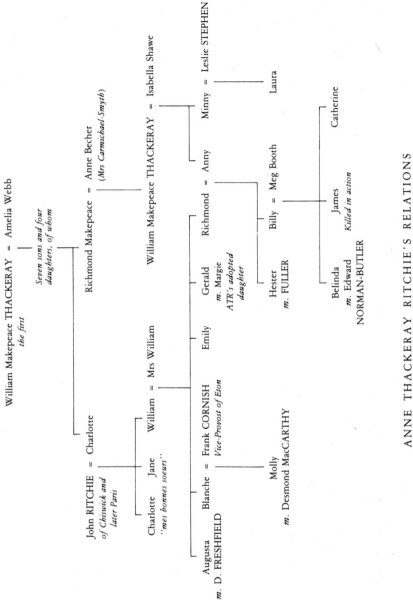

ANNE THACKERAY RITCHIE'S RELATIONS

BIBLIOGRAPHY

I. *Unpublished Material*

The Journals of Anne Thackeray Ritchie, MS, 4 vols.
  Vol. 1, 1859–1863; Vol. 2, 1864–1877; Vol. 3, 1877–1894; vol. 4, 1894–
  (incomplete). The property of Professor G. Ray and Mrs B. Norman-
  Butler.

Reminiscences of Anne Thackeray Ritchie, MS, 1864–5, *idem.*

Memoir for Laura, MS, 1877, *idem.*

Letters of Anne Thackeray Ritchie to relatives and friends, MS, 1863–1919,
  idem.

Letters of Anne Thackeray Ritchie to George Smith, MS. John Murray
  Archives.

Letters of Henry James to Anne Thackeray Ritchie, MS. Houghton
  Library, Harvard.

II. *Major Published Works by Anne Ritchie*

A. FICTION

The Story of Elizabeth, 1863.
The Village on the Cliff, 1867.
Old Kensington, 1873
Bluebeard's Keys and Other Stories, 1874
Miss Angel, 1875
Miss Williamson's Divagations, 1881.
Mrs Dymond, 1885.

B. OTHER WRITINGS

Toilers and Spinsters and Other Essays, 1874
Madame de Sévigné, 1881
A Book of Sibyls: Mrs Barbauld, Mrs Opie, Miss Edgeworth, Miss Austen,
  1883
Records of Tennyson, Ruskin and Robert and Elizabeth Browning, 1892.
Chapters from some Memoirs, 1894.
Blackstick Papers, 1908
From the Porch, 1913.
From Friend to Friend, edited by Emily Ritchie, 1919.
Biographical Introductions to the Works of William Makepeace Thackeray,
  13 vols., 1894–8.

Introductions to the Centenary Edition of the Complete Works of William Makepeace Thackeray, 26 vols., 1911.

Lady Ritchie also contributed introductions and prefaces to works by Mary Russell Mitford, Mrs Gaskell, and Miss Edgeworth.

III. *Some Biographical and Critical Works*

ADRIAN, ARTHUR A., *Georgina Hogarth and the Dickens Circle*, 1958.

BELL, ALAN, ed., *Sir Leslie Stephen's Mausoleum Book*, 1977.

BELL, QUENTIN, *Virginia Woolf: A Biography*, 2 vols., 1972–76

BLISS, T. ed., *Jane Welsh Carlyle: A New Selection of her letters*, 2 vols., 1950

BROOKFIELD, CHARLES & FRANCES, *Mrs Brookfield and her Circle*, 2 vols., 1905

CAREY, JOHN, *Thackeray: Prodigal Genius*, 1977.

CAMERON, JULIA MARGARET, *See* Gernsheim

COLBY, ROBERT A. & VINETA, *The Equivocal Virtue: Mrs Oliphant and the Victorian Literary Market*, 1966.

CROWE, EYRE EVANS, *Thackeray's Haunts and Houses*, 1897

DEXTER, WALTER, ed., *The Letters of Charles Dickens*, 3 vols., 1938.

EDEL, LEON, *Henry James: A Biography*. vol 2: *The Conquest of London*, 1962–.

—— *The Middle Years*, 1963.

—— *The Master*, 1972.

ELIOT, GEORGE, *See* Haight

ELWIN, MALCOLM, *Thackeray: A Personality* 1932.

FORSTER, JOHN, *The Life of Charles Dickens*. 2 vols., 1876.

FROUDE, J. A., ed., *The Letters of Jane Welsh Carlyle*, 3 vols., 1883.

FULLER, HESTER & HAMMERSLEY, V., *Thackeray's daughter*, 1951.

GAUNT, WILLIAM, *The Pre-Raphaelite Tragedy*, 1942.

GÉRIN, W., *Charlotte Brontë: The Evolution of Genius*, 1967.

GERNSHEIM, HELMUT, *Julia Margaret Cameron: Her Life and Photographic Work*, 1948.

GITTINGS, ROBERT, *The Young Thomas Hardy*, 1975.

—— *The Older Hardy*, 1978.

HAIGHT, GORDON S., ed., *George Eliot Letters*, 9 vols., 1954-77.

—— *George Eliot: A Biography*, 1968.

HEWLETT, DOROTHY, *Elizabeth Barrett Browning*, 1953.

HUXLEY, LEONARD, *The House of Smith, Elder* 1923.

JAMES, HENRY, *William Wetmore Story and His Friends*, 2 vols., 1903.

—— *See* Edel.

JOHNSON, EDGAR, *Charles Dickens: His Tragedy and Triumph*, 2 vols., 1953.

LEWIS, NAOMI, 'Thackeray's Daughter' (Essay in *A Visit to Mrs Wilcox*) 1957.

LUBBOCK, PERCY, ed., *The Collected Letters of Henry James*, 1928.

MACCARTHY, MARY, *A Nineteenth-Century Childhood*, 1924.

MARTIN, ROBERT BERNARD, *Tennyson: The Unquiet Heart*, 1980.

MARTINEAU, HARRIET, *Autobiography*, 3 vols., 1877.

MEREDITH, GEORGE, *Collected Letters* 2 vols., ed. C. L. Cline 1970.

MONTSARRAT, ANN, *Thackeray: The Uneasy Victorian*, 1980.

NICOLSON, NIGEL, *The Letters of Virginia Woolf*, vols. I–IV, 1975–9.

NORMAN-BUTLER, BELINDA, *Victorian Aspirations*, 1972.

OLIPHANT, MARGARET, *Autobiography*, ed Mrs Harry Coghill, 1899.

OLIPHANT, MARGARET, *Annals of a Publishing House* (Blackwoods), 2 vols., 1897.

RAY, GORDON N., *The Letters and Private Papers of W. M. Thackeray*, 4 vols., 1945.
—— *Thackeray: The Uses of Adversity*, 1955.
—— *Thackeray: The Age of Wisdom*, 1958.
—— *The Buried Life: A Study of the Relation between Thackeray's Fiction and His Personal Life*, 1945–6.

RITCHIE, HESTER, *Ritchie Letters*, 1924.

SADLEIR, MICHAEL, *Edward and Rosina* (A Life of Bulwer-Lytton), 1931.

SHORTER, CLEMENT K., *The Brontës and Their Circle*, 1914.

SMITH, GEORGE, 'A Memoir' by his Wife in The Cornhill 1902.

STURGIS, JULIAN, *Books and Papers of Russell Sturgis*, 1894.

TENNYSON, CHARLES, *Alfred Tennyson, his Family and Friends*, 1949.

THACKERAY, W. M., *The Complete Works*, 17 vols., ed. George Saintsbury, 1908.

TILLOTSON, GEOFFREY, *Thackeray: The Novelist*, 1954.

TROLLOPE, ANTHONY, *An Autobiography*, 1887.

TROLLOPE, ANTHONY, 'Thackeray', Obituary in *The Cornhill*, Jan–June, 1864.

WISE & SYMINGTON, ed., *The Brontës: Their Lives, Friendships and Correspondence*, 4 vols., 1932.
—— re-issued in *2 vols.*, *1980*.

WRIGHT, ALDIS, ED., *Letters and Literary Remains of Edward Fitz-Gerald*, 7 vols., 1902–3.

WOOLF, VIRGINIA. *Night and Day*, 1919.
—— *A Writer's Diary*, 1953.
—— *The Enchanted Organ* (Essays, iv), 1967.

INDEX